THE SLAVEHOLDING CRISIS

CONFLICTING WORLDS

New Dimensions of the American Civil War

T. Michael Parrish, Series Editor

THE SLAVEHOLDING CRISIS

FEAR OF INSURRECTION AND THE COMING OF THE CIVIL WAR

CARL LAWRENCE PAULUS

Louisiana State University Press
Baton Rouge

Published with the assistance of the V. Ray Cardozier Fund

Published by Louisiana State University Press

Manufactured in the United States of America
First printing

Designer: Michelle A. Neustrom
Typeface: Sentinel
Printer and binder: McNaughton & Gunn, Inc.

Library of Congress Cataloging-in-Publication Data

Names: Paulus, Carl Lawrence, 1983– author.
Title: The slaveholding crisis : fear of insurrection and the coming of the Civil War / Carl Lawrence Paulus.
Description: Baton Rouge : Louisiana State University Press, [2017] | Series: Conflicting worlds, new dimensions of the American Civil War | Includes bibliographical references and index.
Identifiers: LCCN 2016012830| ISBN 978-0-8071-6435-8 (cloth : alk. paper) | ISBN 978-0-8071-6436-5 (pdf) | ISBN 978-0-8071-6437-2 (epub) | ISBN 978-0-8071-6438-9 (mobi)
Subjects: LCSH: United States—Politics and government—1857–1861. | Slavery—United States—History—19th century. | Slave insurrections—History—19th century. | Antislavery movements—History—19th century. | Exceptionalism—United States.
Classification: LCC E440.5 .P35 2017 | DDC 326/.80973—dc23
LC record available at https://lccn.loc.gov/2016012830

The paper in this book meets the guidelines for permanence and durability of the Committee on Production Guidelines for Book Longevity of the Council on Library Resources. ♾

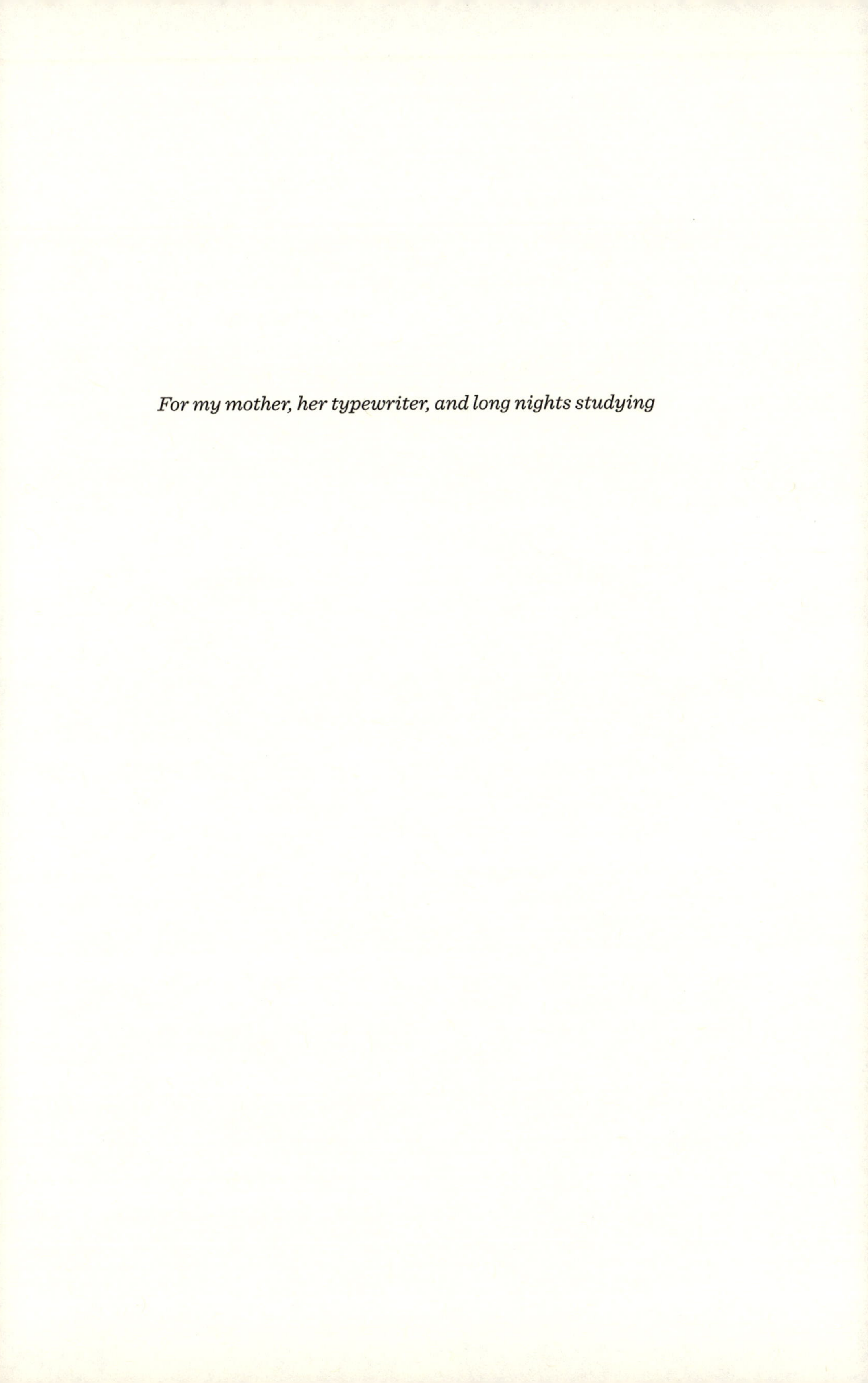

For my mother, her typewriter, and long nights studying

CONTENTS

ACKNOWLEDGMENTS

The first person I want to thank is my mother. Being a single parent with a small child is uneasy. Being a single parent and going to night school is doubly tough. Long evenings watching her pound away on the typewriter demonstrated to me the value of getting a degree, and I have no doubt that she is the reason I became a historian. My stepfather, a writer himself, and sister also encouraged me when I needed it and put up with me when I did not. The love and support of my family was invaluable.

I am also grateful for the incredible support of Rice University. Carl Caldwell and Edward Cox served as very generous, patient, and understanding directors of graduate studies. I learned much from Carl Caldwell, Ira Gruber, Kerry Ward, Lora Wildenthal, Stephanie Camp, Doug Brinkley, and Kathryn de Luna. Rebecca Goetz taught me how I should write and research. Edward Cox shaped this work considerably. Without our discussions about slavery in the West Indies, this book would not exist.

Kent Weier shared his love of history and inspired me to become a historian. Peter Knupfer introduced me to antebellum history as an undergraduate. Handing me a copy of David Potter's *The Impending Crisis* for summer reading changed my life. John Rubadeau tried his best to teach me how to write coherently, *quid pro quo,* my friend. Victor Lieberman, Megan Raphoon, and Catherine Cangany encouraged me to go to graduate school while at the University of Michigan. Finally, I never would have become a historian without the guidance of J. Mills Thornton III. As an undergraduate advisor he talked to me about the Wilmot Proviso and put this book on its path.

A number of historians helped me create this book. Eric H. Walther stood by me during every step of the process. His advice, especially on the fire-eaters and their expectations for the Republican Party, played an important role in the crafting of my argument. W. Caleb McDaniel influenced the scope of this book. His guidance, despite needing to settle into Houston and finish his own book, made me a better historian. Jason K. Phillips talked with me about the role of anticipation of the future in the study of history. Randall Hall, Bethany Johnson, and Pat Burgess provided a great academic atmosphere for my summer job at *the Journal of Southern History.* Rachel A. Shelden continues to act as a great sparring partner and even better friend. Christopher Childers always helped me stay positive while offering great insight. Despite her busy schedule, Caroline Levander graciously read an early version of this book. Finally, T. Michael Parrish offered great ideas, and he acted as a fantastic editor. My thanks also go out to Rand Dotson and Jo Ann Kiser, who helped me complete this project.

My primary academic debt is to John Boles. He has always known what to say and when to say it, telling me when to pump the brakes or plow ahead. His enthusiasm for my work made me glad to be doing what I was doing. His keen attention to my writing helped me pay closer attention to the craft. He helped bring me to Rice University and made me happy for that decision every day. I look forward to seeking his advice and wisdom in the future.

The graduate community at Rice as a whole, and my cohort in particular, served as an important pillar in my academic career. Jim and Rebecca Wainwright became like family. Drew Bledsoe let me know he was on my side and explained the Civil War. Andy Lang always let me bounce ideas off of him and showed that a Texan could like hockey. I could not have asked for a better role model in my studies than Luke Harlow. His continued mentorship is a blessing. I have valued Allison Madar's friendship since day one, even if she roots for the Buckeyes. Joe Locke and Ben Wright are great debate partners. Shani Roper always answered questions I had about the Caribbean. Zach Dresser needs no description. Robin Sager and Wes Phelps were great grad reps. Andrew Canady, Blake Ellis, Andrew Baker, John Marks, and Sam Abramson provided great camaraderie.

I also want to thank my friends and family outside of Texas. Andrew Mackenzie, Robert Greer, Nick Doherty, Brent Habitz, Steve Richert, Adam Long, John deVries, Erin Beck, Aaron Gadowski, John Keeton, Justin Combs, Donny Murdock, and Greg Moser boosted my decision to become a historian. My thanks also go to Brian Cook of Ann Arbor, Michigan, who kept his sanity during uncertain times and, with humor and excellent writing, helped me do the same. Thomas Lifson and Robert Gonzalez demonstrated to me what I can do with a history degree and gave me the leeway to do it. Lianne Russell and Heidi Theiss gave me a chance. Rep. Kerry Bentivolio, Tim Witt, Rob Wasinger, Mark McIntosh, Scoop Chisolm, Joe Kildea, Elise Jordan, and Eleanor May all encouraged me to complete this while working in politics. Tommy Behnke graciously gave this one last read. Ron and Kris Sawyer helped sustain my studies during a pivotal point in my career. Every aunt, uncle, and cousin supported me, especially Ryan Sawyer. Bob, Deb, Karsten, Hannah, and Mary Bischoff welcomed me with open arms when I joined their family in 2011.

The greatest debt I incurred during this entire process is to a brilliant writer and scholar, my wife, Sarah Bischoff Paulus. She read and helped edit every single word of this manuscript while also pursuing her own academic career. She told me to follow my dream of working in politics and being a scholar at the same time. She never let me quit on days when the task seemed insurmountable, and she made this book—like everything else in my life—infinitely better.

THE SLAVEHOLDING CRISIS

INTRODUCTION

EXPECTATIONS AND EXCEPTIONALISM

For the generality of men are naturally apt to be swayed by fear rather than by reverence.

—Aristotle, ***Nicomachean Ethics***

The perfect condition of slavery . . . is nothing else, but the state of war continued, between a lawful conqueror and a captive.

—John Locke, ***The Second Treatise of Civil Government***

On February 29, 1860, an exasperated Edmund Ruffin, white hair at shoulder length, focused on a piece of paper lying on his desk. It was blank. Pen in hand, he sat down to write a jeremiad about the future of the United States of America. A wealthy planter and stalwart member of the proslavery movement, the Virginian saw an abolitionist tempest taking shape in the free states. For decades, he and other southern intellectuals had been forecasting its formation. Their ideological weather vanes pointed to the winds of change finally arriving.

The success of *Uncle Tom's Cabin* conveyed to Ruffin the power that a novelist could wield. Appealing to a popular audience could change America's culture. A protest narrative with empathic characters might bolster once-controversial notions to the forefront of the nation's conscience. He hoped a story of his own would penetrate the minds of his countrymen—white southerners. Ruffin desperately pleaded for his fellow slave-state citizens to picture what life might be like if a Republican managed to win the upcoming election for the White House. He considered his *Anticipations of the Future to Serve as Lessons for the Present Time* to be a warning to the slaveholding South, ringing an alarm that danger approached.[1]

A "history of the future" crafted in epistolary form, *Anticipations of the Future* depicted the observations of a fictional Englishman visiting the United States in the aftermath of the 1864 re-election of William Seward, the anticipated presidential nominee for the antislavery Republicans in 1860. Although he wanted to issue an augury to the South, Ruffin claimed not "to possess any gift of prophecy, or extraordinary political foresight."[2] He shied away from theorizing about disunion explicitly, knowing a radical approach might prove self-defeating. Many southerners, after all, still viewed their nation's founding documents as having created an exceptional government—a Union that guarded liberty and prosperity for future generations. Not seeking to be a doomsayer, he merely submitted a worst-case scenario for the southern states if an antislavery Republican won the presidency. The planter wanted the slaveholding elite to actively think about their futures under such a circumstance.

Nevertheless, Ruffin predicted a grim scenario for the South if a Republican administration controlled the federal government. "Opposition to [slavery] in the North," he wrote, had "run into blind fanaticism." He told readers to expect an antislavery executive to exercise every tool at his disposal to promulgate the message of abolitionism in the slave states. His leading character explained the dire situation for the proslavery movement: "The chaplains in all their stations, are operating more or less as preaching missionaries of abolition. They have it very much in their power, and many use the facilities directly, and still more indirectly, to indoctrinate slaves as to their rights and interests (according to the abolition creed,) and to poison their minds, and make them discontented and insubordinate." Every port, every lighthouse, every national installation would become a haven for a style of abolitionism that invited "servile conspiracy and insurrection."[3] The slaveholder envisioned a Republican administration that eventually would drive the southern states to declaring independence, fracturing the Union and disavowing the compromise struck by the founding generation of Washington, Jefferson, and Adams.

The fear of a revolt—or revolution—being mounted by the enslaved became a defining characteristic of the slaveholding South, and during the first half of the nineteenth century, Ruffin and other planter intellectuals connected territorial expansion of slavery to the prevention of an enslaved uprising. *Anticipations of the Future* demonstrated what much of the proslavery movement imagined would happen in a war between the states. He expected Republicans to try to "[seduce] the slaves to desert their masters and seek freedom in the camp or country of the invaders—if not also to make extended insurrection, under such encouragement and aid, and to convert the whole slaveholding country to another St. Domingo."[4] The Virginian prophesied at great length that an antislavery federal government would attempt to incite countless "servile insurrections." Yankees would work to turn the slave states into a North American version of Haiti—a successful slave revolt and an area controlled by a black, formerly enslaved population. For many of the planter elite, those who opposed slavery had always plotted conspiracies to overthrow the American government and the Union, using violence and racial warfare to achieve their aim. A sympathetic president might promote their success through inaction, refusing to send federal military forces southward while black rebels burned plantations and toppled the racial hierarchy. Under such a situation, Ruffin contended that the unique nation created at the Constitutional Convention—which operated as a mutual protection pact between the states—would be destroyed. The United States would become indistinguishable from the British Empire their forefathers had defied in 1776.

Edmund Ruffin's prediction exemplified the tendency of human beings to categorize into groups those whom they wish to exploit.[5] To dehumanize African Americans as a way to justify their enslavement, the American slaveholding class essentialized black Americans and moralized the allies who helped perpetuate the system of bondage. Southern planters defined the enslaved as simultaneously barbarous and childlike. Stripping black Americans of adulthood enabled the self-styled master class to tell themselves, and white nonslaveholders, that slavery had a moral aspect: it was necessary to perpetuate progress, democracy, and civilization. In characterizing African Americans as naturally violent and incapable of self-control, planters gave reason for other whites to turn a blind eye to the millions held in thralldom. Supporters of slavery had an answer to the ideals expressed in the Declaration of Independence: the southern system of enslavement protected social order and secured white equality. The South stayed within the mainstream of American ideals by tying slavery to the destiny of the United States, the Union, and defining the country's exceptionalism through a proslavery lens.

Slaveholders, however, also expected that the dehumanizing institution of black enslavement would compel those held in chains to attempt acts of bloody revenge. Advocates for the enslavement of black Americans understood that subjugation of another person required two essential ingredients: a culture willing to sanction oppression and a government that commanded a monopoly on the legal distribution of violence and was capable of enforcing it. The planter elite labored to ensure that the Union fostered those components by maneuvering slavery into a position to be protected both by the Constitution, which established the federal government, and the Bill of Rights, which imparted federalism and local control as a national ideal. The proslavery interpretation of both the federal compact and American exceptionalism allowed southerners to claim support for Jefferson's desire for the United States to be an empire for liberty while also expanding an institution that enslaved millions of its residents. They knew that their dominance depended on the commitment of nonslaveholders to the perpetuation of slavery and employed stereotypes, prejudices, and anxieties regarding black people—a persistent theme throughout American history—as a way to direct the authority of the state toward promoting their interests, sculpting a society that matched their worldview.[6]

Historian James M. McPherson best articulates prevailing scholarly notions of the antebellum South's long-standing relationship with the federal government. In *Battle Cry of Freedom: The Civil War Era,* he writes, "On all issues but one, antebellum southerners stood for state's rights and a weak federal government. The exception was the fugitive slave law of 1850, which gave the national government more power than any other law yet passed by Congress." This belief, labeled by David Potter as "the perennial southern political doctrines of states rights," and complemented by Eva Sheppard Wolf, as "particularly southern," ignores the periods of American history in which enslavers—along with their successors during the era of Jim Crow—used federal authority to sustain racial oppression. For decades, the proponents of universal freedom relied on the Bill of Rights as the final defense against the encroachments of proslavery politicians who attempted to wield the power of Washington to silence them.[7]

As times changed, and abolitionism gained traction in the North, proslavery forces—in the name of American exceptionalism—labored to forge the power of the federal government into a hammer to smash the antislavery movement. Influential southerners often tried to employ Washington's authority to guide American culture away from supporting universal freedom. By the 1830s, the planter intellectual elite crafted a defense of slavery that claimed the mantle of federal politics. Advocating the creation of a strong national government that used its power to protect slavery extensively while also discharging the direct regulation of the South's peculiar institution to local enforcement, proslavery leaders defined American exceptionalism as the ability to employ either a congressional or states' rights approach to defend and perpetuate the institution of slavery. Planter politicians understood that most Americans distinguished the Union as vital to their nation's exceptional nature, and they used the American belief in the uniqueness of their system to undermine those who attempted to subvert slaveholding in the United States. Rather than define the nation's purpose to be based on the Declaration of Independence, however, the planter elite came to connect American exceptionalism to the perpetuation of black enslavement. Under those circumstances, the Constitution offered the slaveholders an extraordinary and flexible source of strength across the Atlantic world's slaveholding landscape, making plantation owners comfortably committed to the Union.

To have a fuller portrait of the coming of the Civil War, we must study the fears held by slaveholders and their expectations for future events if they lost power to expand their system of human servitude. Furthermore, the passionate belief of Americans that their nation, and their form of government, was truly exceptional in the history of the world must serve as a basis for understanding American politics in the nineteenth century. Northerners risked their lives in a war to defend the Union, which they saw as the fountainhead for American liberty and the prime example that President Abraham Lincoln uttered in his most famous address—that a government of the people, by the people, for the people could govern itself and prosper.[8] Southern secessionists held a similar outlook.

The belief in the United States that the success of the American Revolution created an exceptional nation inherently relied on a comparison between the United States and the rest of the world. After the ratification of the Constitution, Americans celebrated their break from Europe by declaring, in the words of John Adams, that their country had become the "freest and most enlightened" on Earth. In *Empire of Liberty: A History of the Early American Republic 1789–1815,* Gordon Wood explains that "just as Americans lacked the corrupting luxury of Europe, so too, they constantly told themselves, were they without Europe's great social distinctions of the wealthy few and poverty-stricken many. Compared to Great Britain, America had a truncated society."[9] The United States found itself without the ingredients for extreme radicalism, many in the founding generation declared. Americans reveled in the proclamations of their own distinction and anticipated their nation carrying the Enlightenment to the rest of mankind. Although the Founders envisioned the United States government as a fulfillment of European heritage that embraced the cosmopolitan ideal, the American people made it their duty to protect their exceptional nation from outside influence. This belief helped keep the Union together during the first half of the nineteenth century. However, what allowed the nation to remain in place during the turbulent decades after the Revolution also led to its eventual breaking apart.

Faith in American exceptionalism affected the behavior of the American public before the Civil War and shaped how they perceived the world and their future.[10] Questions about who might share the blessings of the exceptional nature of the country became the battleground on which Americans fought, first with words, then with guns. This book examines how, due to the fear of black insurrection, southerners developed their own version of American exceptionalism—one that placed the perpetuation of slavery at the forefront of the nation's purpose. As the planter elite lost power in the 1840s, they came to think that the Constitution and the Union they participated in no longer formed an exceptional government. They determined that being surrounded by free soil offered a riskier proposition than fighting a civil war.

In the rancorous political climate during the decades before the Civil War, both northerners who supported free labor ideology and southerners who promoted a proslavery agenda called their opponents un-American in the hope of winning an edge in national politics.[11] Although some historians have argued that "profound differences between the North and the South" made the United States like two different countries locked together, and thus the Civil War was "almost inevitable," both sections argued that they stood for specifically American ideals that came from the American Revolution.[12] Northerners and southerners eventually concluded that only their outlook could continue America's exemplification of the practice of liberty for other nations to follow.

By the late 1850s, Republican leaders routinely talked about American exceptionalism, declaring slavery as a source of degradation that prevented the United States, and its form of government, from reaching its natural place as the exemplar of democracy to the world.[13] In response to those critiques, and deriving from the fear of slave insurrection, southerners cultivated their own version of American exceptionalism that prioritized slaveholding, allowing them to claim that abolitionism corrupted America's unique constitutional government. Throughout the antebellum period slaveholders came to believe—and convince nonslaveholding southerners—that dire consequences would follow northerners veering away from the proslavery definition of national exceptionalism.[14]

Starting in the 1830s, northerners and southerners began to redefine why their country was distinct in comparison to the rest of the world. As the Atlantic world began to shun the institution of slavery, intellectuals in the North and South came to view differently the purpose of the Union and the role of the United States in the world. What so many historians have declared as the root cause of the Civil War is actually the stem. Within the Union, which both sides of the sectional divide considered the engine that propelled the nation into the future, the belief of American exceptionalism incubated both the free labor and proslavery ideologies. Eventually, both northerners and southerners embraced the notion that "this government cannot endure, permanently half slave and half free" and declared their ideological opponents to be un-American. This book examines how and why southerners came to define the idea of American exceptionalism with a proslavery varnish, revealing the expected results that slaveholders anticipated if their northern, antislavery counterparts refused to abide completely by their vision.

On December 20, 1860, in the wake of Republican electoral victory, South Carolinians voted to abandon the Union their forefathers had designed. Encouraged by Edmund Ruffin and other southern intellectuals, the proslavery movement deemed Abraham Lincoln's place at the head of the federal government as a real and present danger to the security of whites in the slave states. Many in the South became convinced that the government that succeeded the Revolution of 1776 had failed. Rather than staying within the United States and waiting to see how the new president might conduct himself, secessionists contended they were launching an audacious undertaking to change the providence of their heirs, labeling a continued attachment to the free states as a dance with future oblivion.

Although many planters practiced a form of proslavery capitalism and often found themselves motivated by profit—treating their landholding as agricultural versions of factories—much of the slaveholding class came to judge territorial expansion as a crucial, primary element for staving off massive slave uprisings like the one that occurred during the Haitian Revolution.[15] As a result, white southerners, slaveholders and nonslaveholders alike, willingly risked civil war instead of remaining loyal to the new president and the Constitution he swore to "preserve, protect and defend." The planter elite found it impossible to maintain a relationship with a president who won his election by promoting a free soil version of national exceptionalism. Unlike their counterparts in the Caribbean during the Age of Revolution or British emancipation of the West Indies, proslavery southerners deemed warfare and rebellion against their government to be a more secure venture for the continuation of their racial hierarchy than staying in the Union. No amount of money offered through a possible gradual emancipation plan sufficed. The southern planter class could never be convinced that their society—or their families—would safely survive emancipation in any form.[16]

By acting on anticipations about their future under a Republican president, slaveholders wagered on the possibility of a more propitious fate outside the Union. The dread of slave revolt, influenced by the Haitian Revolution and buoyed by the belief that only expansion prevented insurrection, shaped planter expectations. Secession functioned as the culmination of expectations that had developed within the minds of proslavery southerners for nearly a century.[17] When an antislavery candidate fairly won the Electoral College, the planter elite chose to abandon the nation of their birth and the constitutional contract they inherited from their ancestors. They mounted a revolution and created the Confederacy—a modern national government entirely devoted to the promotion and protection of slavery. The proslavery movement contended their actions preserved America's exceptional founding.

The fire-eaters did not have to wait for the new president to take action against slavery before they promoted secession. Nor did they act because, in the words of one historian, "if Northerners also gained a decisive majority in the Senate through the admission of additional free states, they might someday attempt to pass a constitutional amendment abolishing slavery."[18] Moreover, the bulk of their motivation did not originate from elevated concerns that if Arizona or New Mexico banned slavery the marketplace and price of slaveholding would decline. Slaveholders feared for their lives and the lives of their future descendants more than they valued their wealth. Yeomen families accepted calls for disunion because white southerners, both rich and poor, considered abolitionism to be the main ingredient for societal upheaval. Few in the slave states submitted to the possibility that the transition to universal freedom, rather gradual or immediate, could be peaceful.

Along with white nonslaveholders, the proslavery movement convinced itself that the South could not chance the fate of an American version of Toussaint rising in America while a Republican president held the reins of the military. In the aftermath of John Brown's raid at Harpers Ferry, planters came to think that northern politicians had become infected with "fanaticism."[19] They predicted that other radical abolitionists would inspire a North American version of the Haitian Revolution. For Confederates, their presumptions about how President Lincoln would behave as commander in chief during such an event served as a sufficient justification for secession. Slaveholders hoped to fashion a national government in which the protection of black enslavement and white supremacy reigned paramount.

Like Lincoln at Gettysburg, white southerners insisted that they were defending the extraordinary nature of America's founding against a world that, at best, wanted to turn the United States into just another nation among nations and, at worst, wanted the American experiment in governance to end in the extremism of racial warfare and political radicalism. Acting as a mirror image to Republicans in the North who warned the nation about a continuously growing and undemocratic Slave Power conspiracy, the proslavery movement in the South believed that the enslavement of black Americans allowed for a more perfect representative government into the future. With the firing of Fort Sumter, the northern and southern visions for American exceptionalism came into combat, initiating the bloodiest war in the history of North America.

1

THE HAITIAN REVOLUTION AND SLAVEHOLDING ANXIETY

To adopt any policy by which slavery would be hemmed in, within its present limits, does appear to me, when we look at the growing disparity of numbers between the races, the perpetual stimulus to dissatisfaction which will be held out to the negro, and his enlarging capacity and increasing facilities for mischief, to be providing for a renewal upon our own soil of the scenes of St. Domingo, and the destruction of the race or the relation, amid national and social convulsion.

—John Holcombe's Secessionist Speech,
Virginia, March 20, 1861

Sailing on the clear Caribbean waters, the color of turquoise surrounded him as he peered at a speck in the distance.[1] The salty ocean breeze blew through his brown hair. Waves roared around him, rocking the boat up and down as the sound of splashing muffled the creaking of the wooden deck. Far off, the dark spot on the horizon came slowly into view. Louis Moreau Gottschalk's piano had played for happy audiences across Cuba—from Matanzas to Santiago. Slaveholders showered him with both flowers and their applause, enjoying his concerts and welcoming him to the West Indies. On June 6, 1857, his ship headed toward St. Kitts.

Illuminated by the moon, seaside mountains "whose angular peaks seemed as if they wished to pierce the clouds" grew larger as he neared an island. The littoral palm trees, alone near the deserted beach, appeared to him sad in their isolation. As Haiti's coast became clearer, Gottschalk thought of his grandmother. As he passed the shoreline, two soft words mumbled across his breath: "Santo Domingo."[2] That place no longer existed. Born in New Orleans nearly four decades after the Haitian Revolution, Gottschalk had no personal memory of the Caribbean, but he still sensed an attachment to it, like an ancient ancestor in his family tree. The evening stars blurred from approaching rainclouds.

The first virtuoso pianist of the United States, Gottschalk decided to keep a diary while he performed throughout the West Indies in 1857. During his stay in Cuba, Spanish plantation owners assured him that the people enslaved on the island felt content with their lives. Less familiar with slavery, a few fellow travelers marveled that "they had not heard a single blow of the whip."[3] The visitors seemed untroubled by their encounter with human bondage. The southerner knew better. He was aware of the facade that covered the ghastly reality. The misery of the oppressed always lingered in the background, out of view for polite company. In his notes, Gottschalk mocked his naïve traveling companions: "Happy tourists! Suppose that, instead of looking upon those joyous faces that smile in the presence of their master, you had the curiosity to take off their clothes [and] examine their shoulders. You would have learned more . . . by the sight of certain scars badly healed, than all your observations, founded upon your suppositions, had taught you."[4] The piano player from Louisiana understood that violence and fear maintained the power of the plantation owners. At any moment the enslaved population might rise up to resist those who held them in chains.

Hardly a proslavery champion—he sided with the Union during the Civil War—Gottschalk sailed past the only black-controlled country of the Western Hemisphere and it sparked memories from his childhood. He never tired of the tales about his great-grandfather fighting insurgents at Gros Morne or his grandmother "half naked and dying of hunger" saving herself by "wandering many days in the woods" before happening upon an English ship. "It is," he explained, the "history of all the colonists of Santo Domingo toward the close of last century."[5] Stories from the Haitian Revolution passed from generation to generation, not just to the black community and abolitionists who celebrated the victory of the enslaved over slaveholders, but also to white planters started anew in the United States. The violence had been etched to their collective memory, never to be forgotten.

The American planter elite always held a strong association with their counterparts in the West Indies. Southern slaveholders often consumed news from the Caribbean and identified with the French and British colonies. The black uprising that turned Saint-Domingue into Haiti remained in the thoughts of southern plantation owners throughout the antebellum period because continental plantation owners recognized an association with their Caribbean counterparts. Slavery transcended differences in nationality and language because those who held other people in captivity shared similar concerns and underwent comparable experiences. As the South's own black populace grew and its slave society expanded, the events of that French colony in the Caribbean frightened American slaveholders, reminding them to be vigilant in the defense of their region's peculiar institution. The slave states, they thought, should take lessons from the mistakes made by the powerful slaveholders who once ruled in "Santo Domingo."[6]

Saint-Domingue was ripe for revolution in the early 1790s. White slaveholders of France's most valuable colony saw an explosion of the black population on its side of the Island of Hispaniola during the eighteenth century. Dubbed "the Pearl of the Antilles" because of its productivity in supplying sugar to the rest of the world, the colony welcomed a steady import of new slaves. In the years prior to the Haitian Revolution, the number of the enslaved residing on the massive plantations reached more than ten times that of the white residents in charge of perpetuating the deployment of human oppression. This contrasted sharply with the United States. Only South Carolina and Virginia's enslaved populace came close to being the majority at the turn of the century. That substantial difference, however, did little to quell southern anxiety as dispatches about a large slave uprising in the West Indies trickled into the United States in 1791.[7]

News of a large revolt that saw the brutal deaths of planters caused dread in white America. Although some mainstream antislavery advocates pointed to the violent rebellion as an example of the evils or dangers of slavery, most shied away from endorsing the ferocious method of self-emancipation employed by the Haitians. In the first session of the United States Congress, an antislavery organization from Pennsylvania, with the help of Benjamin Franklin, had already caused a passionate uproar in the House of Representatives when they petitioned Congress to end the international slave trade. During the debate, proslavery advocates compared the religious group to the British who had used emancipation and insurrection as a military weapon during the Revolutionary War. Understanding their group was viewed with suspicion, the extreme violence in the Caribbean especially dismayed Quakers who served as the vanguard of the antislavery movement in the United States. Many who opposed slavery decided that the Haitian Revolution might cause a backlash against their movement and stayed away.[8]

Indicting the antislavery movement for the Haitian Revolution became common among the planter elite, especially in light of the *Historical Survey of the Colony of St. Domingo* by Bryan Edwards. A powerful British politician and outspoken antagonist to the famous abolitionist William Wilberforce, Edwards explicitly condemned the opponents of slavery for undermining the security of whites in the French colony. He claimed that their meddling had directly caused the violent end of white control of the wealthiest West Indian colony. Using graphic imagery to frighten readers into rejecting emancipation plans, his book gained high circulation in the United States. The success of the Haitians became a symbol to be scorned by proslavery whites living on the continent during the Age of Revolutions and caused mainstream members of the American antislavery movement to distance themselves from the violence in the West Indies.[9]

Although the Haitian leadership employed the sentiments professed in the Declaration of Independence to justify their actions, the black revolutionaries in the Caribbean received miniscule support from citizens in the fledgling republic of the United States. In Philadelphia—the capital during the nation's infancy—President George Washington referred to the slave rebellion as "lamentable!" and, stunned with the news, wondered, "Where it will stop, is difficult to say."[10] At the turn of the century, the American determination to propagate their ideals stopped at a color line. Slaveholders feared an insurrectionary spirit from Haiti influencing the enslaved population on their own plantations.

As the situation became increasingly dire for the Caribbean planters and the French Directory issued a proclamation of emancipation in Saint-Domingue, Jeffersonian Republicans distanced themselves from both the French Revolution they once embraced and the universal language of equality they formerly espoused. One northern Republican fumed that the "leveling principles" in France might ruin "the finest colony on earth." A South Carolinian maintained that acceding to French ideas penetrating the South would be "fatal." White racial communion trumped American ideological conflict between the Federalists and the Jeffersonian Republicans and the leadership of the first two political parties in the United States shared a similar reaction to the black revolution in the West Indies. Those in charge of American foreign policy deemed the Haitian Revolution a threat to national security and planned to conduct themselves accordingly.[11]

American leadership worried that French ideas threatened to unravel their newly independent republic. In the mid-1790s, South Carolina's Ralph Izard, one of the earliest presidents pro tempore in the Senate, argued against joint war exercises with their ally from the Revolution. Although it kept with the treaty obligations signed during the Revolutionary War, he feared that such cooperation might lead to lower-ranking French military officials fraternizing "with our Democratical Clubs, [and] introduce the same horrid tragedies among our negroes, which have been so fatally exhibited in the French islands." South Carolinians agreed with their senator. A friend wrote to Izard's daughter, "The account of the intended designs of the French negroes have given us a great deal of concern—we dread the future, and are fearful that our feelings for the unfortunate inhabitants of the wretched island of St. Domingo may be our own destruction."[12]

Although trade between northern merchants and the black military forces in the colony continued during the conflict, the official stance of the United States towards the revolution in the Caribbean concentrated on undermining the revolt and restoring control of Saint-Domingue to planters. Sympathetic to the West Indian slaveholders, President Washington granted France $726,000—drawn from the United States debt incurred from the American Revolution—

in the form of weapons and ammunition taken from the arsenal at West Point. Meanwhile, American agents supplied food to the white forces fighting to crush the rebellion. As the French planter class on the western third of Hispaniola became overrun, United States aid waned. American officials refused to risk supplies ending up in the hands of the now battle-tested army of the formerly enslaved.[13]

Despite receiving desperate requests from the Caribbean, Charles Pinckney, the author of the Fugitive Slave Clause in the American Constitution and then serving as South Carolina's governor during the Haitian Revolution, declined to send troops. He did, however, agree that the insurrection in Saint-Domingue imperiled his state and forwarded the request for help to President Washington. Along with the French letter, Pinckney noted his fear in correspondence of his own, telling the commander in chief that if the slave revolt went unchecked the "flame which will extend to all neighboring islands, may prove not a very pleasing or agreeable example to the Southern states."[14] A slave uprising in the South, he argued, could vanquish the new republic on the continent. He requested quick action from the president.

Like the rest of the slaveholding territories throughout the Atlantic, the white South had been placed on high alert. Slaveholders took every precaution to prevent the Haitian Revolution from coming to America. South Carolina's legislature, at Pinckney's request, strengthened the state's militia. The governor insisted that the state's armed forces needed to be able to "act with promptness and effect," quickly putting down any American slave who might dream of following the model of Toussaint Louverture in the West Indies. Although South Carolina refused to offer soldiers, it did send money to aid the crumbling plantation class of the French West Indies. Slaveholders in the United States could not abandon their Caribbean counterparts entirely.[15]

Help from America did not turn the tide of war, and the black population took control of the colony in 1793. With the fall of white power in Saint-Domingue, the United States found itself neighbors with the only black-led nation in the Western Hemisphere. The wealthiest colony in the New World now belonged to those who had been brought there in shackles. The vulnerability of slavery as an institution had been exposed. American slaveholders detected their greatest horrors turning into reality merely a few hundred miles away. They feared that the ideology of the Haitian Revolution might spread to the continent, that the fires of insurrection might consume the South next.

If white southerners expressed a high degree of paranoia during the early days of the Haitian rebellion, their fears became even greater with the news that the French had lost the colony altogether. The *Charleston City Gazette and Daily Advertiser* reported that stories from the Caribbean filled Americans "with horror" as descriptions of "burning estates, and putting all prisoners to death, fill up the measure of every day's calamity." Secretary of State Thomas Jefferson shared his concerns about the Haitian Revolution in a letter to James Monroe, then serving as a senator from Virginia. He envisioned a day when plantation owners in the United States suffered the same fate as the French planters, writing, "I become daily more and more convinced that all the West India islands will remain in the hands of the people of color, and a total expulsion of the whites sooner or later take place. It is high time we should foresee the bloody scenes which our children certainly, and possibly ourselves (south of the Patowmac [*sic*]) have to wade through, and try avert them."[16] In the wake of the successful revolution in Haiti, southern planters imagined a grim future that ended in the brutality of racial warfare.

As the situation in Saint-Domingue became exceedingly chaotic, refugees—like Louis Moreau Gottschalk's family—poured into the United States. In a number of instances, American slaveholders eagerly helped their peers from the West Indies. In the same letter to Monroe, Jefferson explained, "The situation of the St. Domingo fugitives (aristocrats as they are) calls aloud for pity and charity. Never was so deep a tragedy presented to the feelings of man I deny the power of the general government to apply money to such a purpose but I deny it with a bleeding heart. It belongs to the state governments. Pray urge ours to be liberal."[17] The author of the Declaration of Independence seemed to practice a slaveholding version of the Golden Rule: Americans in the South should help French planters because southerners might find themselves in need of assistance someday.

Federal officials throughout the country received entreaties for help from West Indian planters who flooded American port cities. The most powerful leaders in the United States treated the Haitian Revolution as a kind of natural disaster, like an earthquake or hurricane. Some refugees from Saint-Domingue contacted President Washington asking for his assistance. The president often wrote back, offering his sympathies and some advice. The Father of the United States, for example, responded to a pair of refugees by sending twenty dollars. The president clarified that he could not give more individual aid, but informed the petitioners that in "almost every city and large town in the United States" committees had been formed to help the refugees. He also asked the secretary of the treasury to send two thousand dollars to the "Committee at Baltimore, appointed to superintend" the French planters who had arrived into Maryland's largest city. Throughout the 1790s, roughly 90 percent of the white population in Saint-Domingue left the French colony. Nearly one-quarter of them ended up in cities across the eastern seaboard. Most immigrants retained their cultural identity as Frenchmen while they adapted to their new residences. Very few expected to ever go back to the colony they once called home.[18]

Many people besides white slaveholders came to the northern United States in the aftermath of the Haitian Revolution, as well, particularly the enslaved and the *gens de couleur,* the French name given to free blacks. Their arrival added to a black population that expanded dramatically during the 1790s. Despite being more impoverished, and receiving almost no help from the private and public organizations formed to aid West Indian refugees, black immigrants found a welcoming African American community when they arrived to the continent. Although free blacks in the North showed hospitality to the new arrivals, whites worried that they had brought a rebellious spirit with them. The fear of insurrection transcended any divide between the free and slave states, and authorities remained on high alert for racial strife.[19]

In the South, Norfolk and Baltimore became principal landing spots for those arriving from the West Indies. Both places offered relief, but most refugees judged Baltimore to be the city of greater opportunity. Caribbean immigrants—the majority white or of mixed race—added to the culture of their new country by becoming teachers, lawyers, and business owners, or by using their expertise in such subjects as irrigation to support themselves during the region's dry seasons. In Louisiana, another destination favored by some refugees due to its French influence, former Saint-Dominguans contributed to the theater and opera of New Orleans, becoming significant contributors to the artistic nature of the Crescent City. Others moved to South Carolina, where they introduced new methods of indigo production. Throughout the southern states, immigrants who fled the collapse of Saint-Domingue influenced the South's view of the Caribbean and its perception of the Haitian Revolution.[20]

With the influx of French refugees in their towns, slaveholders found themselves in a precarious position. Although sympathy for the new white arrivals ran high among American planters, assisting them often conflicted with their attempts to hamper the spread of insurrectionary ideas from the Caribbean. Planters on the continent hoped to reduce the influence of successful black rebellion on the American enslaved population by implementing harsh black codes. In Louisiana, for example, reports of conspiracies ran rampant in the aftermath of the Haitian Revolution. In 1795, the enslaved took advantage of the struggles between the Jacobins and the royalists, along with the Spanish and the French, to strike at their bondage. In Pointe Coupée, roughly 150 miles away from New Orleans, four men and a woman were executed for plotting to overthrow the planter elite. Throughout the decade after the fall of Saint-Domingue, French slave owners used their power to terrorize black people, using torture as a check against the insurrectionary impulse coming from the Caribbean. Some of the accused felt the whip on their backs; others were tied and dragged to death behind a horse. Many more were hanged, their bodies quartered. The Gulf Coast planters left the corpses on posts as a warning to other potential rebels before eventually closing off the slave trade from the West Indies entirely.[21]

Slaveholders in the United States at large took similar measures to limit black freedom. In Georgia, proslavery politicians in the statehouse required all "free negroes, mulattoes, or mustizoes" who came into the state to register themselves and their locations at the county clerk's office. The law further absolved the state from any recompensing of slave owners for "the value of slaves legally executed." During a period of panic, black people deemed troublesome by the plantation elite could be killed with impunity by the state. The prospect of a revolution coming to their slave society made southerners wary of new people—free or enslaved—who joined the African American population.[22]

In South Carolina, slaveholding leaders obeyed the desires of their constituency to limit who entered their state. In a petition to the legislature, one group wrote, "We also recommend that all free French Negroes and all free French people of color who have come into this state since 1st January 1790 be required to depart therefrom within a limited time never to return, and that those who do not comply with the said requisitions shall be liable to certain penalties." Worrying that they might usher favorable feelings toward revolt, several citizens of the Palmetto State, both voters and politicians, feared the arrival of French-speaking immigrants. They ended their petition to the statehouse by asking for more patrols in Charleston to deter an "assemblie and conspiracies of negroes" that might "be formed with more speed and facility." Too many people with a "dangerous disposition and character" had been "continually smuggled from the French." They also stressed that black mariners might come to the port of Charleston from the West Indies and cause problems among the enslaved and asked that "proper precautions may be taken" to impede the suffusion of radical ideas fanning out from Haiti to the enslaved population of the United States. Moreover, Alexander Gardener, a Scottish botanist living in Charleston, worried about residents communicating with Les Amis des Noirs. He claimed slaveholders had heard the enslaved tell their "superiors" that "the right of freedom was theirs." Such a sense of injustice, he feared, would "produce a flame that can only be extinguished in blood" and recommended that all literature challenging slavery be censored.[23]

White Virginians also supported a redoubled state militia in the 1790s, calling for the creation of a standing army to bolster their dominion over the black community. Concern about slave revolt trumped traditional apprehensions toward a permanent military presence. Although slave resistance had been a threat long before the Haitian Revolution, including during the American Revolution nearly two decades prior, a number of slaveholders reported that the arrival of French refugees brought an increase in disturbances among the black populace. In 1793, leaders in the South warily watched for anything out of the ordinary. They took active steps to ensure that the Americans did not share the same fate as Saint-Domingue.[24]

The specter of Haiti's successful revolution appeared in everyday life for some American slaveholders. John Randolph awoke one night to find his wife complaining about noise coming from the street in front of their home in Richmond. Groggily going to the window, he found a congregation of black men gathered and "ordered them to disperse." At first, Randolph noted, "they seemed regardless of my words," but they soon left. Upon returning to bed, however, he again heard two black men talking outside his window. Curious to know what caused the commotion, the Virginian crept slowly to the window to listen again. This time he heard one say to the other that "the blacks were to kill the white people soon in this place." After asking what time the rebellion would take place, the black companion (and Randolph) heard the answer—October 15, a few months away.[25]

Peering out, Randolph heard an incredulous slave question the potential insurrectionist's claim. A third man asked why the rebels waited so long before taking action. In reply the speaker made a bet; while "pointing his finger down the street," he boasted that following the uprising two different houses would be his. The "chief speaker" ended the discussion by reminding his compatriots to remember "how the blacks has [*sic*] killed the whites in the French Island and took it a little while ago." Randolph considered the conversation sobering enough to report it to local authorities. Like many in the slave South, he feared the black population striking against those who held them in bondage. In the months that ensued, numerous accounts of other instances of slave resistance, from New York to Georgia, engendered beleaguered feelings in plantation owners who worried that their attempts to sequester Haiti's revolution to the Caribbean had faltered.[26]

Not long after Randolph's testimony in Richmond, local officials heard warnings of another threat. A note had been found discussing a plan to launch an insurrection on October 15, the exact date mentioned by the black men outside John Randolph's window. A grand conspiracy seemed to be afoot. Written under the pseudonym of the "Secret Keeper, Richmond," the letter read, "The great Secret that has been so long in the being with our Colour has come nearly to a hed [*sic*] though some in our Town has told of it, but in which the Manner it is not believed." Addressed to the "Secret Keeper, Norfolk" and allegedly carried by a black preacher named Gawin who "passed through Richmond on his way to Norfolk," the correspondence stated that insurrectionists had obtained "about five hundred Guns and plenty of Led [*sic*], but not much Powder."[27]

The conspiracy appeared to go beyond the Old Dominion. The author remarked, "Since I wrote you last I got a letter from our friend in Charleston, he tells me he has listed near six thousand men and there is a gentleman that says he will give us as much powder as want and when we begin he will help us all he can."[28] The note also referenced an ally who would begin "stirring up" as many as he could to resist the power of the planter elite. In the wake of the Haitian Revolution, the leaders of every slave state regarded threats with new seriousness. Virginia's governor promptly contacted his friend in South Carolina, Governor William Moultrie, and advised him to ready for an uprising. He worried that the Haitian Revolution had come to America.

Shortly following the warning, two other black residents presented Governor Moultrie with letters of their own. Supposedly written by someone relevant to the conspiracy, the messages seemed to corroborate the initial findings in Richmond. One message warned him to "guard against certain strangers" and to not "let your attention be directed to frenchmen alone." Finally, that note counseled Moultrie to "give the most particular orders to your own patroles [*sic*] in every part of the State, keep up the military duty till the 10th of January at least." Named a hero for his defense of South Carolina during the Revolutionary War, Moultrie took a cautious posture and placed the militia on high alert. South Carolina prepared for slaves to oppose planter authority. In the wake of the Haitian Revolution, many southerners believed, any kind of uprising could be a glint of freedom that toppled, or at least severely diminished, the power of the American slaveholding regime.[29]

Defensive measures by the state's troops were not enough for South Carolina. By the end of 1793, local leaders began working to expel all black immigrants from Saint-Domingue—along with any other free blacks—who had come to the state. Governor Moultrie issued a proclamation giving them ten days to leave. "There are so many characters amongst them, which remain dangerous to the welfare of the state," he declared. The possibility of experienced black revolutionaries living in their state left whites on edge and the slaveholding gentry found itself asking uncomfortable questions. If a multiracial coalition of insurrectionists attacked slavery in South Carolina, would the state successfully repel them? Would the new Union, merely a few years old, stay together if free staters received the call to come and defend the enslavement of blacks in the South? Moultrie had no intention of learning the answers. He took every precaution to forestall an insurrection.[30]

The "Secret Keeper" letter, along with Randolph's deposition, cultivated an existing paranoia among Virginians. Thomas Newton, a militia leader from Norfolk who first discovered the letters, thought that blacks from the West Indies planned to enter the United States and aid slaves in a fight against their masters. In correspondence to the lieutenant governor he wrote, "I suppose there may be two hundred or more Negroes brought from Cape Francois . . . they I have no doubt would be ready to operate against us." Newton implored the lieutenant governor to strengthen the defenses of Norfolk. "In case of insurrection or invasion," he warned, "we should be badly situated." The lieutenant pleaded that "a few more men" and a "small fort [in Norfolk] would keep all in order." American slaveholding required vigilance because threats could come from anywhere. It seemed sensible to southern military leaders that Haitians enthusiastically wished to extend their revolution across the Caribbean and to the United States. After all, Americans had hoped to convert a "candid world" to their ideals and believed their fledgling nation would become an archetype of democracy for the rest of humanity to follow.[31]

Despite a lack of direct contact with the Caribbean, Virginian slaveholders worried that black people in their state might identify with the revolutionaries in the West Indies. When Thomas Jefferson pondered the condition of the enslaved in the United States, he envisioned a distinctive people without a country. He judged the relationship between whites and blacks to be similar to two countries constantly at war. During the Secret Keeper scare, the author of the Declaration of Independence communicated to South Carolina officials that he too had a reliable source informing him of "two Frenchmen, from St. Domingo," who were "setting out from this place for Charleston, with a design to excite an insurrection among the Negroes." He viewed slaves in United States as potential threats to the nation. With the Haitians as natural allies, he expected the black population held in bondage to eventually strike out in an attempt to secure freedom.[32]

Proslavery anxiety about the Haitian Revolution became contagious during the latter half of the 1790s. Southern cities reported allegations of arson and other smaller forms of resistance as products of West Indian influence. In 1795, North Carolina followed South Carolina's model of racial control and barred the importation of any slaves from the West Indies. Two years later, Maryland repealed a law permitting French slaveholders to bring slaves with them when they entered the state. By the end of the decade, nearly all of the other slave states placed restrictions on immigration to the United States from the French West Indies, regardless of race or status. Although slaveholders believed they shared a connection with the planters of the Caribbean, they also worked to divorce slaveholding in the United States from the practice in the West Indies. American planters strove to seal off foreign influence from the black community.[33]

Robert Goodloe Harper, for example, felt trepidation when he thought about the security of slavery in the late 1790s. A congressman from South Carolina who once famously blustered "millions for defense, but not a cent for tribute!" during the XYZ Affair with France, he now postulated that an even larger French conspiracy threatened his nascent country. A former land surveyor in the West, the spirited South Carolinian suspected the French of planning an attack against the South by mounting a Haitian-style uprising. He claimed a French governor in the West Indies had readied "an army of blacks" with "a large supply of officers arms and ammunition" to invade the United States. Their "missionaries previously sent" already lived among the southern population, Harper warned. Similar to the discoverers of the Secret Keepers only years earlier, he alleged to have uncovered the plot by gaining information from one of the conspirators. He said that "black officers who were to be employed in the expedition" had supplied the intelligence related to the upcoming insurgency and he called upon his constituents to be on the lookout for slave rebellions being fomented by those linked to the troubled French colony.[34] Those who objected to slavery, he exhorted, intended to manufacture another Haitian Revolution, first in the Palmetto State before eventually engulfing the entire country in the flames of racial violence. Southerners connected the security of plantation system to the safety of the nation as whole.

In the House of Representatives, Albert Gallatin, then serving as a congressman from Pennsylvania, shared his concerns about the Haitian Revolution. An opponent of slavery, the future secretary of treasury worried about what kind of neighbor an independent Haiti might become. In his thick Swiss accent, he conveyed his belief that the self-emancipated slaves in the West Indies "received their first education under the lash of the whip, and . . . have been initiated to liberty only by that series of rapine pillage, and massacre" that "laid waste and deluged that island in blood." They could not "apply themselves to the peaceable cultivation of the country." Instead, he argued, the former slaves in control of the former colony would "try to continue to live, as heretofore, by plunder and depredations."[35] Believing that Haitians dreamed of passing their insurrectionary ideology to other slaveholding nations, Gallatin asked his colleagues to listen to the harried calls for protection that came out of the South. National unity needed to be the response to threats growing out of Caribbean instability. Although Gallatin and Harper eventually disagreed over slavery's expansion to the western territories, they shared the same thinking that Haiti's revolution involved the entire United States, not just the planters of the South.[36]

At the turn of the nineteenth century, a considerable number of Americans remained restive toward the Haitian Revolution. Having recently won independence in a war filled with lofty rhetoric, they understood the power of idealism and inspiration. The use of their own rhetoric from 1776 by the former slaves who took power in the Caribbean colony, along with language from the French Revolution, left many whites with the feeling that Haiti's revolutionaries wanted to spread universal liberty to the United States. In the summer of 1800, those fears almost became realized in the capital of America's oldest slave state—Richmond, Virginia.

When Absalom Johnson began renting a farm in Virginia, he believed he had begun his ascent into the ranks of the planter elite. A practitioner of human misery, the white overseer came upon a startling scene while surveying his land one night in October 1799. He stood agape as he watched Jupiter, a slave from his newly leased property, along with a couple of companions—Gabriel and his brother Solomon—stealing one of his pigs, most likely hoping to supplement their meager rations. They were running away, hog in hand. When the slaveholder tried to assert his authority as a white man, he received an unanticipated greeting. Gabriel fought back. The brief skirmish cost the white taskmaster his ear. Johnson's black rival bit a large portion of it off during the tussle. Recognizing he had lost this brief, but violent conflict, Johnson scrambled away. His retreat did not last long, and the slaveholder quickly came back with powerful reinforcements—the law.[37]

Although the guilty verdict Gabriel received from fighting a white man came with the severe punishment of hanging, the court granted him clemency when local clergy asked for his sentence to be commuted. Rather than swinging from the gallows for his crime, the rebellious slave received thirty-nine lashes and a branding of the letter "T" on his thumb. The blacksmith survived his initial strike against southern slavery. Whenever he looked at his hand he saw an indelible reminder of the power that men like Absalom Johnson held over him. Rather than be subdued by this, the blacksmith became more determined to resist the system that enslaved him and his family.[38]

Born in 1776 as the United States declared to the world that "all men were created equal," Gabriel experienced a different life than most slaves in the South. In an era where merely 5 percent of enslaved Americans were literate, Thomas Prosser, a tobacco planter and the white man who claimed ownership of Gabriel's life, taught him how to read and helped him develop a skill in pounding iron. At six feet, three inches tall, he towered above most who met him. Many in Richmond's black community saw him as a natural leader. Whites too perceived a commanding quality in the blacksmith, considering him to be enterprising, independent, and intelligent. However, few worried about his potential as a leader of rebellion. He was an American, loyal, and content with the few extra freedoms he received for having skill with the anvil and hammer, they presumed.[39]

Large slave revolts evolved over time, not from impulse as proslavery intellectuals insisted, but with careful planning. Although Gabriel actively resisted slavery when he attempted to steal from a farm and fought a slaveholder, his actions on the Johnson plantation only served as a starting point. He tested the resolve of the planters who enslaved him and believed that his survival exposed a weakness in the slaveholding class. A year later, the two accomplices who had once helped him pilfer a pig enlisted in his army. They targeted the heart of the Commonwealth of Virginia for their battle and wanted to fight for more than a few slices of ham. This time freedom stood as the final reward.[40]

Talk of overturning the status quo filled the air during the spring of 1800. White citizens openly debated John Adams versus Thomas Jefferson. Some eventually referred to the election results as "the Revolution of 1800." As the campaign occupied the thoughts of voters, Gabriel walked the streets of Virginia's capital with a different societal transformation in mind. To begin, the blacksmith concocted a way to free himself and his neighbors. Then, in his shop at Brookfield plantation, a place where he turned iron into the tools of slaveholders, the insurrectionist leader unveiled his design for liberty to Solomon and another friend. Gabriel stated his goal clearly: he planned the total overthrow of slavery in the Old Dominion.[41]

The small audience listened intently as Gabriel laid out his blueprint for toppling the master class. He appealed to the men in attendance by calling on them to protect their wives and children from slavery's terrible reach. For months, the ironworker and a few compatriots turned the blades of wheat scythes into swords for battle. When the time came, Gabriel planned to gather his army of Richmond slaves in his shop or the surrounding woods. The conspirators envisioned hundreds of soldiers carrying weapons. After wreaking revenge on Thomas Prosser and Absalom Johnson by taking their lives, the outfit of insurgents intended to ride on horseback toward the capital in the middle of the night. There, Gabriel expected his allies—emboldened by the seizure of one of Virginia's oldest cities—to join him. The fight for liberty would begin.[42]

Once inside the city, the large group would split into three platoons, choreographing their movements to make the biggest impact against the defenses of the planter elite. The first set planned to take weapons stored in the Capitol before capturing James Monroe as he slept in the Governor's Mansion. Another had to start fires, setting the warehouse district ablaze and causing a distraction on the opposite side of the city. A final detachment was assigned the task of fortifying the main entrance to the state capital, establishing defensive positions in preparation for the inevitable attempt by slaveholders to reclaim the city. Gabriel's revolution relied on timing and precision. This would be no typical uprising easily put down by plantation owners. Gabriel expected to ransom Virginia's capital for freedom.[43]

Significantly, Gabriel did not distinguish a stark racial divide in Virginia. He wanted to kill slaveholders exclusively. Like insurrectionists in the French West Indies, the insurrectionist imagined his call for citizenship to serve as a catalyst for poor whites—also excluded from the political influence—to join his rebellion. Only those who directly enslaved others would feel his wrath. Gabriel viewed white nonslaveholders as potential compatriots in a battle against the status quo. The insurrection leader planned to carry a banner inscribed with the words "death or Liberty," a phrase whites believed served as an inversion of Patrick Henry's famous comment, but may easily have come to Gabriel's mind because of its common usage during the Haitian Revolution. "Liberté ou La Mort" had been a slogan during the fighting in the French Caribbean and eventually headlined Haiti's declaration of independence written but a few years later. Gabriel understood that success offered the only way for his survival. Freedom was worth the risk.[44]

On August 30, 1800, the night designated for the uprising, Gabriel readied to meet his troops, but only a handful arrived. That evening the clouds opened and a downpour drenched eastern Virginia. Some whites in Richmond noticed that, unlike most Saturday nights when the enslaved from the rural areas came into town, many of the black Americans who lived in the city seemed to be trying to leave the capital. With resounding thunder echoing across the countryside, they paid little attention to the unusual behavior. As the river rose from the deluge, the wooden bridges connecting Brookfield to the rest of the city became impassable. Only a small number of Gabriel's recruits trudged through the muddy roads to assemble at the assigned meeting place. With fewer numbers than anticipated, the leader of the revolt decided to reschedule his plot, postponing the attack until the ensuing night. The storm had given white slaveholders an extra night of respite. The blacksmith-turned-revolutionary expected to mount his rebellion the following day.[45]

The delay caused some of Gabriel's crew to have misgivings about the plan. Making the rainy trip to the countryside only to see a handful of men mustered left some of the rebels discouraged. Pharaoh, an enslaved craftsman from a neighboring plantation, changed his mind about participating in the revolt. Unlike Gabriel and several other members of the insurrectionary conspiracy, Pharaoh had a long and close relationship with the family of the slaveholder who owned his life, Mosby Sheppard. Four years earlier, he remembered, Sheppard had consented to a slave's request to purchase his own freedom for a discounted price. Maybe, Pharaoh likely thought, the slaveholder would do it again if he revealed Gabriel's plot. He found himself with a choice: betraying his friends for potential freedom or risking his life in an attempt at striking a deathblow to slavery.[46]

Self-interest and a lingering doubt about Gabriel's plan affected the would-be insurrectionist. Pharaoh ignored warnings from the rebel leader that any informant faced death and revealed the plan. After first telling a trusted friend on the Sheppard plantation, he then unveiled the secret directly to the planter himself. He named the blacksmith on the Prosser farm as the enslaved leader of the upcoming uprising. Having lost faith that they could succeed in conquering Richmond, two other members of Gabriel's army also outed the scheme to white authorities. A rainstorm unraveled the plot to take Richmond. Gabriel would not crack the yoke of American slavery.[47]

The planter class promptly subdued Gabriel's rebellion before it began. When Governor James Monroe was informed of the conspiracy he immediately took measures to secure Richmond, ordering weapons moved away from the Capitol and into the penitentiary, a building more easily defended. Next, he mobilized a number of regiments in the state militia. Fearing that whispers of an oncoming slave revolt might generate panic, Monroe tried to mask the particulars of the situation from the public. Finally, he launched a search party for the insurrectionists, which captured collaborators working with the blacksmith. Within ten days, roughly thirty conspirators—though not Gabriel—had been found and arrested.

On September 9, James Monroe ordered the slave trials to begin. Although the governor worried that overkill might play badly in the northern press, thus hurting his friend Thomas Jefferson in the looming presidential election, the hangman received twenty people following the verdicts. Plantation owners would not tolerate threats to their system of unfree labor and they needed to be appeased by the spilling of blood. The Commonwealth of Virginia snuffed out any hope for black freedom—any challenges to the established order would be met with the full strength of the government. The state signaled to the outside world that slaveholders remained in total control.[48]

A grateful Virginia legislature granted freedom to Pharaoh and the two other informants. Moreover, some wealthy white citizens in Richmond provided a trust fund valued at a thousand dollars as part of a reward to each former slave who undermined Gabriel's revolution. Pharaoh later became an independent farmer and did some work as an overseer for the family that used to claim his future. Although his betrayal appeared to cost him standing in the black community, it also granted an economic status in Richmond's white society that few black southerners achieved during the early nineteenth century. He may have been in limbo socially, but he prospered as a free man.[49]

By the end of September, Virginia authorities captured Gabriel in Norfolk, just under a hundred miles away from the state capital he had planned to conquer. Slaveholders carried the blacksmith back to Richmond in iron manacles. He received a death sentence for his crimes against the state. Large crowds gathered to watch the prospective black general executed. Unlike his compatriots—nearly all had entered the afterlife with a fellow rebel by their side—Gabriel hanged alone. Richmond's slave owners withstood the first large and organized slave conspiracy of the new nation unscathed, but unnerved. Similarities between Gabriel's plan and the Haitian Revolution did not go unnoticed by plantation elite.[50]

The successful revolution in Haiti likely inspired Gabriel and his fellow insurrectionists to secure emancipation through violence. Unlike the exploits of George Washington, which happened when Gabriel was a small child, stories about the Haitian Revolution had run rampant in the United States during the insurrectionist's formative years. Undoubtedly, some of Virginia's slaves heard information concerning the events in the West Indies. Different from many leaders of enslaved rebellions in the New World, however, Gabriel did not adopt the title of king; rather, like George Washington and Toussaint, he designated himself as a general and curried an "army" of black rebels who fought for liberty.[51]

Throughout their testimonies, the black conspirators referred to their commander as "General Gabriel" and talked with pride about serving under his "command." Gabriel had "appointed" another as "second in command." Other leaders served as "captains" in the insurrectionist's forces while those without much knowledge of the plan acted as "foot soldiers" who had "enlisted" in the army of the enslaved. The rebel leader empowered his troops with martial ranks and treated them as military men entitled to honor and respect. By granting titles to himself and his troops, the enslaved blacksmith uplifted his entire force above their prescribed cultural stations. They were no longer slaves; they were generals, captains, and lieutenants waging a battle for liberation. They refused to be chattel and expected to fight as men and women who deserved both dignity and freedom.[52]

Newspapers throughout the United States reported Gabriel's conspiracy with shock, often noting the military language embraced by the black rebels. The *Philadelphia Gazette,* for example, remarked that the instigator of the uprising had been a "villain assuming to himself the appellation of *General.*" A Virginian newspaper mocked "General Gabriel" who "manifested the utmost composure; and with the true spirit of heroism seems willing to resign his high office and even his life rather than gratify the officious enquiries of the Governor, which may endanger the necks of his dark satellites." Although many whites derided his claim to be a military leader, Gabriel's use of the title forced whites to acknowledge the authority he wielded among his troops. A recently elected trustee to the University of North Carolina alleged that Gabriel planned to take the name Bonaparte after he killed "all the white males and elderly women." Gabriel forced his opponents to recognize him above the station that the white supremacist society had placed him. Legends and rumors respecting Gabriel's plan grew, reminding southerners of the tales that had come from the Caribbean only years before. In response, James Monroe organized the Public Guard of Richmond, a slave patrol tasked with protecting public buildings and seeking out slave conspiracies by enforcing a curfew.[53]

The southern gentry believed that slaves could only succeed in overthrowing the planter class with the aid of whites sympathetic to the cause of the enslaved. Gabriel thought his plan might stimulate a broader campaign of resistance. Avowing his Americanism, he compared himself to George Washington while standing trial in front of the white men who sat in the seats of power. The leader's brother Solomon testified to how the insurrection would have made war on the slaveholding gentry of Virginia. He told investigators that Gabriel had come into contact with a French veteran from the Battle of Yorktown who volunteered to train the insurrectionists in the arts of war. The prospect of a black rebel leader finding a version of Lafayette frightened a large portion of the planter elite in the South. Solomon's deposition struck fear into the hearts of slaveholders and led to starker racial divide in Gabriel's wake.[54]

Slave resistance—whether at home or abroad—affected American politics throughout the antebellum period. The fallout from the conspiracies for rebellion often caused politicians to blame their opponents in hopes of scoring an electoral win. The reaction to the Richmond slave conspiracy was no different.

White Americans in both slave and free states connected Gabriel's conspiracy to the Haitian Revolution. Federalists in Virginia and New England chastised their Republican opponents for supporting the ideals of the French Revolution, focusing on two Frenchmen who supposedly had allied with the insurrectionists. Just as the leveling rhetoric from Paris fueled uprising in Saint-Domingue, the Federalists claimed, so too would it inspire black slaves to rise in opposition to their masters in the South. Idealism, they believed, should not trump security.[55]

One Federalist editor sneered at Thomas Jefferson's favorable feelings toward France, arguing his election would engender a situation in which "the unhappy negroes may again be deluded by his *French alien friends* to make a general uprising." To northerners, the Federalist explained how they too needed to worry about slave uprisings. He argued that due to "the white people in the lower and middle parts of the southern states [being] very few in number in comparison to the blacks," the South relied on militia troops from New England "being dragged over 1000 miles from home to expose their lives to the cut-throat negroes." The Constitution linked the North and South together in common defense, both from threats domestic and abroad. The security of southern slavery knotted the nation together, from Massachusetts to Georgia. Americans believed that the violent collapse of southern slavery, especially if spurred on by foreign ideas, might lead to the destruction of their exceptional democracy and the Union.[56]

During the campaign of 1800, as Federalists pointed to the French Revolution and its radicalism, many Democratic-Republicans directed their barbs to an event much closer to home—the Haitian Revolution. Federalists lodged complaints about attacks from a Jeffersonian newspaper that accused President John Adams, the first president from a free state, of supporting Haiti's rebellion against France. The *Aurora General Advertiser* in Philadelphia alleged that Federalists secretly collaborated "with the British to establish an independent empire of the Blacks in St. Domingo" and that Gabriel's plot stemmed from a conspiracy between Toussaint and American slaves working in concert with the Adams administration. Absent full devotion from Washington, the publication declared, southern slavery remained at risk, leaving the entire nation imperiled by potential racial violence.[57]

Following the election of 1800, and with victory achieved, Jeffersonians across the country debated ways to strengthen southern slavery. Virginians understood that Gabriel had struck at a defective part of their society. One correspondent reported that the enslaved "could scarcely had [*sic*] failed of success" because the whites in Richmond would have been caught by surprise and without weapons. Changes had to be implemented, he wrote. Slaveholders in the United States became convinced that they needed to guard against outside influences on the region's enslaved population. In various areas of the South, slaveholding political leaders viewed the growing black population with reservation.[58]

In the aftermath of the unsuccessful uprising, Governor James Monroe pressed the Virginia legislature to take steps to stifle enslaved resistance. Members of the press urged a variety of remedies, from increasing the size of the militia to ending private manumissions. One citizen from Richmond took the opportunity created by Gabriel's rebellion to examine slavery as a whole. George Tucker published an appeal to the state legislature asking that it reexamine a gradual emancipation scheme produced by his cousin a few years before. Living in a nation that valued the ideas of republicanism gave enslaved Americans an insatiable desire for freedom, he contended. American idealism encouraged the oppressed to resist their subjugation.[59]

George Tucker did not appeal to common humanity or employ a moral argument against slavery. Instead, he focused on the safety of Virginia's white population and anticipated that introducing rigorous new restrictions on the black population would only engender "thousands of slaves" to become "vindictive and impatient." This, along with the growth of the black populace, destabilized the entire slave system. Since he believed racial desegregation could never exist without hostility between the black and white races, his plan hinged on colonization. Black residents in Virginia would be moved to the "western side of the Mississippi," Tucker explained.[60] The formerly enslaved could cause no future disturbances to the white population if they lived on reservations far away.

At the behest of the Virginia legislature, the newly inaugurated President Jefferson examined Tucker's idea. In a letter, the president admitted that Haiti, "where the blacks are established into a sovereignty de facto," offered "the most promising" place to send freed American slaves because those "exiled for acts deemed criminal by us" might be considered "meritorious" to them. However, he believed that such a solution would do more harm than good for the South and spurned the idea. Jefferson feared American slaves sent to the Caribbean might convince the Haitians to attack in "concert with their brethren remaining here." Although the president wanted to make the United States more white by sending black Americans away from the new nation, the author of the Declaration of Independence faced the conundrum of finding a place to diffuse slavery from the United States without giving the former slaves the ability to exact a revenge he presumed they wanted.[61]

Thomas Jefferson's personal attitude regarding the Haitian Revolution pervaded his administration. In 1802, Postmaster General Gideon Granger, from Connecticut, expressed concerns about employing free blacks as mail carriers. A Yale graduate and staunch Jeffersonian, he wrote, "After the scenes which St. Domingo has exhibited to the world, we cannot be too cautious in attempting to prevent similar evils in the four Southern States, where there are, particularly in the eastern and old settled parts of them, so great a proportion of blacks as to hazard the tranquility and happiness of the free citizens." Gabriel served as a tutorial for proslavery forces in the United States. If free or enslaved blacks became too empowered, Granger feared, the fires of insurrection might consume the nation altogether, ending the American democratic experiment.[62]

After pointing to various slave conspiracies, including Gabriel's, the postmaster general insisted that approving the employment of black mail carriers added to "their knowledge of natural rights, of men and things, or that affords them an opportunity of associating, acquiring, and communicating sentiments, and of establishing a chain or line of intelligence, must increase your hazard, because it increases their means of effecting their object." Granger further maintained that black post riders might communicate with other slaves, gaining information on white defenses and "becoming teachers to their brethren." The mail system had the potential to be used as a weapon to sabotage planter control. Treating all black residents as potential insurrectionists, he offered a solution to "prevent the evil [rather] than to cure it" and recommended ending the practice of black mailmen. In a society built on the bedrock of racism, privileges and opportunity for African Americans weakened white power.[63]

Initially, President Jefferson tried to limit the influence of the Haitian Revolution on the United States by asking England to block any "Kind of Navigation" or sale of arms to the new nation. At the beginning of his term—and in light of Gabriel's rebellion—the author of the Declaration of Independence initially supported Napoleon Bonaparte's brutal attempt to subdue Toussaint's sway in the Caribbean. However, he quickly changed course upon receiving intelligence that Bonaparte intended to expand his empire onto the American continent. One scenario Jefferson described to Secretary of State James Madison depicted the French sending the "most warlike" black rebels to Louisiana, bringing the black revolutionary spirit with them to North America. When Bonaparte's general arrived in America, the president decided not to support the recapture of Saint-Domingue. The South was too vulnerable, France too untrustworthy. Jefferson's stance included a refusal to change John Adams's policy of allowing American merchants to trade with Toussaint's forces.[64]

Napoleon planned to overwhelm France's formerly prosperous colony through a barbarous practice of mass murder that included live burnings, crucifixions, and the use of killer dogs trained to tear human beings apart. Fighting for their freedom, the Haitians repelled Bonaparte's army and the French soon paid a steep price for trying to re-enslave their former colony. After nearly two years of brutal conflict between the French military and black freedom fighters, Haitians officially gained their independence, showing that successful insurrectionists could win official recognition from European powers.[65]

With the defeat of his expeditionary force, from both the black army's resistance and an epidemic of yellow fever, the Little Corporal saw his dream of an American empire collapse. While French troops died on the island of Hispaniola, Spain blocked American shipping lanes at the port of New Orleans, motivating the president to send James Monroe, the former ambassador to France, with a bid of ten million dollars to purchase the city along with the Floridas. Fed up with the Americas and defeated by Haiti's stout resistance, Bonaparte abandoned Louisiana, ordering his foreign minister to offer the entire territory to the United States. For the price of just three cents an acre, amounting to a total of fifteen million dollars, Monroe returned home from Europe with a treaty that doubled the size of his country and vastly escalated the potential amount of slave territory in the United States. The Louisiana Purchase fundamentally transformed American slavery by allowing planters—often in the name of national security and the prevention of a Haitian-like revolution occurring in the South—to spread black enslavement further to the West, establishing a precedent for the future expansion of black enslavement on the continent.[66]

Although the Haitian Revolution expanded the power of the United States by opening an opportunity for the new nation to acquire Louisiana, the independent black-led country caused political headaches for Jefferson and his successors. The discussion over whether or not to formally accept the existence of the Republic of Haiti as an official nation came almost immediately after its formal independence. Once in the White House, Thomas Jefferson swiftly acquiesced to southern slaveholders who demanded a trade embargo and nonrecognition of the only other independent republic in the New World. The United States would not officially accept Haiti's sovereignty until after the secession crisis, yet, over the following decades the black republic in the West Indies frequently reentered political discussion in Washington. Southern slaveholders could not ignore the black nation so close to their shores.[67]

Since the colonial period, North American planters had long worried about importing too many slaves. They believed that the larger the enslaved community, the less secure the society. The Haitian Revolution reinforced those concerns, and the fear of insurrection influenced American foreign policy during the early nineteenth century. Some southerners identified the end of the slave trade as a way to weaken the potential for a revolt in the future. When planters examined the events of French Saint-Domingue, they distinguished its demographics as the main source of slaveholding weakness. In 1800 one Virginian who favored curtailing the slave trade stressed that "the safety of [the southern states] depend on a great accession of the white population." His idea gained currency in the Upper South as the expiration date for the constitutional ban on ending the international slave trade approached.[68]

Several Virginians viewed the enslaved members of their community as having the potential threat. For example, William Leckie, a Kingston trader whose family and dry goods business linked him to the United States, England, and the Caribbean, believed that the safety of slavery in North America was eroding. He wrote, "The other [problem] is the encreasing [*sic*] quantity of blacks, who in Virginia . . . amount to 350,000, who are all native, many of whom can read and write, will perhaps prove the bane of all the Southern States, and by this struggle for freedom and involve nearly one half the Union in Civil Wars."[69] For slavery to continue, the merchant argued, whites needed to dominate the black population; any taste of freedom might be the spark that ignited the tinderbox of plantation slavery in the South.

States in the Lower South scarcely considered the suspension of the slave trade due to moral qualms. Instead, they focused on security concerns. The calamity for plantation owners involved in the Haitian Revolution impacted the outlook of the American master class and its desire to bring more slaves into its states. As planters pondered the fate of their counterparts in the Caribbean, the possibility of a race war seemed increasingly possible, especially if non-Americans continued to join the black communities in the slave states. If former slaves could successfully battle Napoleon, the slaveholders worried, what could they do in United States? The enslavers concluded that only a large white population could allow them to escape a fate similar to that of Saint-Domingue.[70]

The dread felt over the importation of potential insurrectionists also affected Congress. Anticipating the Palmetto State to reopen the Atlantic slave trade in 1803, the federal legislature passed "An Act to Prevent the Importation of Certain Persons into Certain States, Where, by the Laws Thereof, Their Admission is Prohibited," a law that illegalized the importation of "any negro, mulatto, or other person of colour, not being a native, a citizen, or registered seaman of the United States, or seamen natives of countries beyond the Cape of Good Hope, into any port or place of the United States." Although the Constitution proscribed the federal government from curtailing the international trade until 1808, Congress sought ways to regulate South Carolina's actions and attempted to block it from bringing more slaves from the Caribbean to the continent.[71]

Moreover, in 1807 the federal legislature ended the international slave trade to the United States as soon as the Constitution permitted. During debate about enforcing the ban, one Pennsylvania congressman asked the House of Representatives "to look at St. Domingo" as a reason to end the slave trade. The Haitian Revolution illustrated that slaves might "learn the rights of man" and become "proficient in the art of war" in order to obtain their freedom. Additionally, he submitted that Europeans, who already had "armed Indians against us," might also "arm the negroes," threatening the incipient American republic. The Pennsylvanian insisted in keeping the black population "as numerous as is consistent with safety" and thought it to "be extreme impolicy to import more."[72]

By basing their arguments on the platform of national security, northerners isolated the ardent proslavery faction from the Deep South that wished to keep the Atlantic trade in human bodies open. Slaveholders in the Upper South still remembered the scares caused by Gabriel. They wished to limit the size for the black populace and joined their colleagues from the free states to end the slave trade. On March 2, 1807, believing it to be "in the best interests of our country," President Jefferson signed the prohibition of the African slave trade into law with minimal objection from southerners in Congress. Joining the British Parliament, which had barred the trade a week before, most Americans prioritized the safety of their new nation over the economic interests of the planter elite in the Deep South.[73]

Unlike the United States, where much of the debate regarding the further importation enslaved Africans revolved around national security, the English saw the international moratorium on the slave trade as an avenue to redefine their empire in a changing global landscape. Armed with the largest fleet in the ocean, the British enforced the ban on the slave trade in order to gain the moral high ground against its French enemies. Although the English saw their enforcement as a way to garner sympathy from across the world, in the summer of 1807, shortly after signing America's official end of the Atlantic slave trade, President Jefferson found his nascent nation in conflict with its former colonizer once again.[74]

During the 1800s, the Royal Navy grew to an enormous size as it defended international trade routes, colonies, and the homeland. Fighting a multicontinental war against Napoleon, Great Britain realized its need for more sailors and soon noticed how United States merchants had doubled their tonnage—and their profits—by using American neutrality to evade the English blockade of France. English admirals also understood that nearly 40 percent of sailors in the American fleet were British by birth. The impressment of American sailors, under the pretext that the seamen were actually English deserters rather than citizens of the United States, became key for British ministers looking to maintain their country's control of the ocean.[75]

On June 22, 1807, James Barron, captain of the USS *Chesapeake,* began his sail across the Atlantic. Tasked with relieving the USS *Constitution* in protecting American ships in the Mediterranean, the 38-gunned *Chesapeake* only traveled eight miles from its namesake before being hailed by the HMS *Leopard,* a 50-cannon ship of the line. Acting out his orders, the British captain demanded permission to board the American frigate and search for deserters from the Royal Navy. When Barron refused, the *Chesapeake* was met with crippling broadsides, killing three members of the crew and leaving several others wounded. In a meek rebuttal, the Americans managed to fire only a single shot before Barron struck his colors and surrendered. A British search party scoured the *Chesapeake* and captured four supposed deserters—three who were black—before letting the Americans sail their damaged rig home to Norfolk for repairs. Old Ironsides would have to wait to return home.[76]

Initially met with outrage in the United States, the crisis only deepened when Virginians called for war, attacked a British consul, and smashed casks intended for British ships. The Britons, happy to insult the slaveholding American protesters, responded by taking in runaway slaves who saw the English fleet as vessels for their emancipation. Southerners responded with even louder cries for war while American leaders quickly asserted their authority to naturalize citizens from anywhere in the world, and they insisted that Great Britain recognize the national sovereignty of American ships and the naturalization of its citizens. The British countered protests by pointing to its naval strength and insisting that U.S. diplomats acknowledge how the Crown protected the world, including the young American republic, from Napoleon's imperial designs. They urged the United States to repatriate British sailors and prayed for tolerance against the occasional, accidental impressment of those born in North America.[77]

Refusing to build more warships, but still feeling affronted by England, the Jeffersonian Republicans in charge of the federal government could only cry outrage against the British strategy on the high seas. In response to the continued impressment of American seamen—along with the British Orders in Council, which instituted commercial warfare against France and negatively impacted the economy of the United States—Republicans enacted a boycott of England. Supporters of the embargo expected to bring about pain to factory workers in Britain and plantation owners in the West Indies. They assured their constituents that without American food their enemies would starve, producing an end to the practice of impressment without firing a shot.[78]

Jefferson's tactic of economic warfare soon backfired, however, when England found alternative sources of goods from other areas of its massive empire. As the United States became more divided on the plan, New Englanders elevated their claims that the boycott had been implemented to strengthen the South and help France: the president's favored ally. After fourteen months of economic self-destruction, Congress finally repealed the ban on Jefferson's last day of office. In 1809 the Father of the Constitution succeeded the author of the Declaration of Independence into the White House. Many of his supporters desired war.[79]

James Madison's first term as president was marked by failures in diplomacy and lost national standing on the world stage. Embarrassed by his foreign policy missteps and seeing his chances at reelection becoming less likely, the president relented to the war-hungry faction in his party as the election fast approached. He was supported by the speaker of the House, Henry Clay, along with other young, expansionist, militant members of the House of Representatives dubbed the War Hawks. Madison asked for and received a declaration of war from Congress in June 1812. The United States of America entered its second war with England primarily on the votes from Pennsylvania, the South, and the new western states comprising of Ohio, Kentucky, and Tennessee—areas that served as Republican political strongholds and that often came into conflict with British-allied Native Americans. Although Madison won reelection, New Englanders promptly declared the conflict a southern, proslavery folly that placed the United States on the brink of destruction.[80]

For many southern plantation owners, the War of 1812 became a lesson: fighting on home soil threatened planter control over the enslaved and confirmed in many of their minds that the black population might become an "internal enemy." Although the British still maintained slaveholding colonies in the West Indies, the foes of slaveholders became viewed as friends by many Americans held in bondage. Throughout the fighting, and undoubtedly remembering their actions during the Revolutionary War, thousands of black southerners offered aid to the British in exchange for freedom. Several white Americans, especially Federalists, expected insurrection across the South. Building on Thomas Jefferson's legal writings that declared the rousing of insurrection to be an act against the civilized laws of war, slaveholders countered critics by employing racialized pro-war rhetoric, denouncing English alliances with Native Americans, and chastising British deployment of black military companies. They also demanded that northern troops protect their plantations.[81]

As the conflict ensued, both British war planners and their U.S. counterparts came to view the enslaved population as a liability for defending the South. Only five months after the American declaration of hostilities, Sir John Borlase Warren, the British commander of the North American squadron, proposed an operation against New Orleans as a counter against the American invasion of Canada. Instead, Earl Bathurst, the secretary of state for war and colonies, ordered an attack against the Atlantic coast. He wanted British forces to raid American towns and suggested freeing the enslaved and enlisting them in the Colonial Marines, a British black fighting force from the Caribbean. Although the initial plan only called for liberated slaves to be employed as scouts, Warren told his superior that the "Terror of Revolution" and an uprising by the enslaved would wreak havoc in the slave states. He expected American slaveholders to panic at the sight of black soldiers marching with the British.[82]

The chance of insurrection weighed heavily on the minds of white southerners during the war. American planters along the Atlantic coastline begged federal officials for more troops to stave off potential uprisings and quell the attempts of the enslaved to flee to enemy ships, especially after British commanders proclaimed that any slave who entered "into his Majesty's service" would find liberty or be sent "as FREE Settlers" to the Caribbean.[83] The English hoped to break the morale of the plantation South by evoking slave-owner paranoia about slave revolts, hoping such fears might serve as a perfect weapon against the United States.

As the war progressed, planters did indeed fear an uprising. For example, as British forces marched towards the nation's capital in 1814, Americans living near Washington pleaded with their governors for stronger defenses after hearing rumors that the enemy planned to promote black rebellion. Petitioners in the Old Dominion asked that Fort Powhatan, a major defense of the James River, be rebuilt "in case of an insurrection of negroes." While British soldiers torched important federal buildings, including the White House, slave revolts failed to materialize. Those held in bondage often had less of an appetite for revenge and longed more for a taste of freedom. Although the British general in charge of the campaign had only a minor interest in being a liberator, and thus refused entreaties from black Americans for help, some persistent slaves escaped with the invading army.[84]

As General Andrew Jackson swept across the coast from Florida to Louisiana in 1814, he routinely experienced trouble from southern fears that the British planned to spark slave insurrection. Secretary of War John Armstrong warned Old Hickory that the English planned to "free and prepare for war all of the Blacks in this quarter," and the governor of the Pelican State, William C. C. Claiborne, declared that the enemy intended to excite "the black population to insurrection [and] massacre."[85] On the verge of becoming the most famous American general since George Washington, Jackson first sought a way to quell planter anxiety that their society might explode into another version of the Haitian Revolution.

The fear of revolutionary insurrection in Louisiana stemmed from a massive uprising by the enslaved shortly before the war had begun. Newspapers from New York to South Carolina described the scene: led by "a mulatto from St. Domingo" named Charles Deslondes, enslaved and free black men took advantage of the political uncertainty on the Gulf Coast following the Louisiana Purchase and mounted an attack against their enslavers. The rebels went from plantation to plantation, destroying property near the German Coast of Lake

Pontchartrain, heading toward New Orleans. As they marched toward the Crescent City, the ranks of the rebels swelled and they organized themselves into military regiments, each having a leader and carrying a battle flag. Only after two weeks' fighting—and a number of uneasy days for the slaveholding gentry—did the militia quell the uprising and reassert white jurisdiction over the area purchased by President Jefferson less than a decade before.[86] As the Battle of New Orleans approached, those lingering memories presented a challenge to Andrew Jackson and the American defense of the Gulf Coast.

While the British advanced on New Orleans, Governor Claiborne assured Old Hickory that the free black regiments of Louisiana supported the American defense of their homeland. Moreover, recognizing that he required more soldiers to repel the British invasion, Jackson recruited slaves to join his cause by offering their liberty in exchange for military service. As a slaveholder, the future president understood how the occupation by an outside enemy exasperated concerns over insurrection. Rather than acknowledging their equality, Andrew Jackson enlisted the enslaved as a tactic to consign them to his defense of the Crescent City because he worried about them joining with the English invaders. Old Hickory viewed black Louisianans as a resource that needed to be kept out of enemy hands rather than as residents prepared to fight for their homes.[87]

During the War of 1812, black Americans—in both the North and South—often chose to side with the United States rather than assist the British. After the Battle of Fort McHenry, of "Star-Spangled Banner" fame, black sailors joined white comrades in celebrating their defense of the third-largest city in the country. After victory in New Orleans, Andrew Jackson praised his troops, including the freemen of color who consisted of roughly 10 percent of his force. Despite their military service, however, many black Americans became viewed with further suspicion by whites, and several black veterans never received the pensions or land promised for their service. In the end, fewer than six thousand enslaved Americans fled to freedom with the British. Slavery in "the Land of the Free and home of the brave" showed an endurance that caused many in the proslavery movement to view black enslavement in the South as unique.[88]

While victory in the War of 1812 preserved American independence, it also confirmed the Edwards thesis in the minds of many plantation owners. As thousands of enslaved Americans sabotaged U.S. military plans by trading information for their freedom with the British, a new generation of slaveholders experienced firsthand how an outside force disrupted their grip over the enslaved. Starting with calls for reparations from the British for liberating black Americans during the fighting, the planter elite became determined to expand their influence and worked to gain more authority in both local and national government. They intended to employ the power of the state to insulate American slavery from the growing antislavery impulse in the Atlantic.[89]

Moreover, keeping the British at bay during the War of 1812 did not stifle the notion that West Indian blacks had plans to invade the South in order to incite uprisings. Less than a decade after the Treaty of Ghent, Haiti again became associated with an insurrection conspiracy. On May 25, 1822, another panic caused by a slave conspiracy connected to Haiti unfolded in Charleston, South Carolina.[90] Peter, a slave, reluctantly told his owner's wife and son what he had heard at the market. Another enslaved artisan named William Paul had tried to recruit him "to shake off our bondage." White strength seemed impenetrable, but Paul reassured him, promising the recruit that the uprising had a leader capable of fighting the planter elite. Upon hearing the rumor, South Carolina authorities placed the city on alert and organized a committee to seek out and stop potential insurrectionists. Planters in South Carolina used the scare to emphasize their authority.[91]

City leaders immediately investigated who plotted to challenge the planter elite. They concluded that a black carpenter and preacher named Denmark Vesey and a mysterious conjurer named Gullah Jack acted as masterminds of the alleged plot. Similar to Gabriel's rebellion, the conspiracy revolved around skilled black laborers in Charleston, both the free and enslaved. A large portion of those convicted in the conspiracy had acquired skills appertaining to the shipping industry, a vital segment of the city's economy. In the aftermath, a number of black residents received the sentence of death or banishment. The state sent some of the exiles to be sold into slavery in the Caribbean, a destination seen by leading slaveholders as a place for troublemakers.[92]

Haiti played a noteworthy role in the testimony that condemned Denmark Vesey. Born in the West Indies, and having spent time in Saint-Domingue during the Haitian Revolution, the alleged insurrectionist fit the model of what white southerners envisioned an insurrectionist leader to look like. He fit the profile of a radical "fanatic." One of his charged compatriots, Rolla, testified that Vesey expected to receive assistance from Haiti and Africa. The preacher told his followers that Haitians would "come over and cut up the white people if we only made the motion here first." The testimonies seemed to corroborate the misgivings slaveholders held in regard to the small Caribbean nation.[93]

Others indicted in the alleged conspiracy also designated Haiti as an ally. According to the official account of the trials, after gaining freedom and sparking an uprising in Charleston the insurgent slaves ultimately planned to "get money from the Banks, and the goods from the stores" and "hoist sail for Saint Domingo." Once there, Vesey "expected some armed vessels" to offer protection to them as they escaped from the United States. One slave's final words before being hanged revealed that Vesey had "the habit of reading to me all the Passages in the newspapers that related to St. Domingo" along with the transcripts of speeches given by antislavery members of Congress whom the preacher named "the black man's friend[s]."[94] The conspiracy seemed to play into every fear that white southerners held regarding black insurrection.

That the testimonies of the enslaved often came after severe emotional and physical trauma should prompt modern historians to question the voracity of their forced confessions. However, even if the indicted slaves only told their slaveholding captors what they wanted to hear, the claims to which the prisoners attested display how real the perception of danger from Haiti had become in the minds of proslavery southern intellectuals. President Jean Pierre Boyer of Haiti had indeed invited free blacks in the United States to join his nation in an effort to import skilled labor into his developing country. He advertised free land for black immigrants throughout newspapers in United States, including Charleston. The small act, even though it lured black Americans away from the continent, made the planters nervous.

According to South Carolina authorities, Vesey presumably believed he could buy his way into Haitian exile. The rebel leader even sent letters to the Haitian president asking him to prepare for his arrival. Whether the conspiracy had actually been planned, and he intended to set an insurrection in motion, or simply been devised by slaveholders as a way to assert their authority, the plot's link to Haiti served as a successful bogeyman that strengthened the political standing of planters both at home and in the nation's capital. The fear of black rebellion being transported from the Caribbean to their own plantations lingered in the minds of southerners. If the scare was a fiction perpetrated by the master class, the greater public believed the hype because Haiti frightened whites in the United States.[95]

As the trial records became publicized, white southerners worried that some of the rebels charged in the conspiracy had escaped authorities and fled to neighboring states, where they planned to regroup. As part of its reporting on the South Carolina insurrection scare, the *Alexandria Herald* in Virginia wrote that "sixteen negroes of colour, supposed to have been engaged" in the Vesey affair had been caught near the northern border of South Carolina. However, the *Herald* assured its readership that "the necessary steps to secure the citizens from any accident that might occur" had been taken to "suppress every similar attempt."[96] Although the newspaper gave no account of what happened next, the article articulated how rampant the anxiety over a Haiti-like rebellion coming to the U.S. South had become. It also signaled to the white public that despite the threat of slave revolt, the planter class held total control over their society and could be trusted to maintain the racial hierarchy. If white nonslaveholders remained firmly committed to the perpetuation of slavery, the proslavery movement maintained, the southern states—and the Union—would remain secure.

As South Carolina's planter elite used fear to increase their influence, they also manipulated the Vesey scare to place tighter restrictions on free black sailors who came to their state as merchant marines. Promoted by the South Carolina Association, the Negro Seamen Act required black seafarers arriving on foreign vessels to be detained and held in jail until their ship left the city. Slaveholders considered black sailors to be the harbingers of insurrection, and they worked diligently to isolate the black community from the rest of the world. Other southern states soon followed South Carolina's lead and passed similar laws. Leaders in the South began building a culture in which only the devoutly proslavery could be tolerated.[97]

Challenged in court by the British as unconstitutional, the defense of the statute by the South Carolina attorney general Benjamin Hunt demonstrated the paranoia that free blacks, especially those from the British West Indies, engendered among American slaveholders. Hunt argued that without the law South Carolina would see "moral pestilence which a free intercourse with foreign negroes will produce." He claimed the proslavery legislature had written the law based on "the right of self preservation."[98] Two decades after the Haitian Revolution, and following the anxiety caused by the British deployment of the Colonial Marines during the War of 1812, southerners still viewed those who lived in the Caribbean with an eye of suspicion, believing they longed for black rebellion in the United States.

While many South Carolinians blamed antislavery rhetoric during the congressional deliberation regarding Missouri's status within the Union for the Denmark Vesey scare, others saw it as an opportunity for the North to display an allegiance to preserving the power of slaveholders. Because the Vesey conspiracy had allegedly been engineered in a Methodist church, Reverend Richard Furman, in an effort to protect evangelicalism in the state, released a pamphlet clarifying the need for northerners and southerners to work together to maintain the security of the South. A commanding figure of American Christianity, the aging minister told his audience that slaves must be reminded "however numerous they are in some parts of these Southern States, they, yet, are not, even including all descriptions, bond and free, in the United States, but little more than one sixth part of the whole number of inhabitants." The minister wanted the enslaved to completely understand the hopelessness of gaining emancipation through violence. Black Americans needed to know that South Carolina—along with the rest of the South—was not Haiti. Unlike Saint-Domingue, where reinforcements were an ocean away, the American military could respond almost immediately to a slave revolt. The Constitution required northerners to defend the South's peculiar institution, making the United States exceptional.[99]

Employing the same tactic that antislavery northerners used to buoy their arguments to end the slave trade, proslavery southerners used the fear of slave insurrection, pointing to Haiti's revolution as the archetype, to push northern politicians toward a proslavery foreign policy in the 1820s and 1830s. Near the end of 1825, Mexico and Colombia asked the United States to attend a Panama conference of recently independent nations from South America. President John Quincy Adams readily accepted the invitation and sought approval from Congress to send a delegation to what became known as the Pan American Conference. Proslavery politicians in the Capitol spared no energy in attacking the legitimacy of the international gathering. Decrying Haiti's independence, slaveholding politicians labored to prevent the State Department from participating in any meeting with their nonwhite neighbors.[100]

The official recognition of the Republic of Haiti brought the most vitriolic language to the floors of the House and Senate. Granting a nation ruled by black people a commensurate footing on the world stage, slaveholders worried, condoned the destructive uprising that had ended slavery in France's former colony. It threatened planter hegemony in the United States and the Atlantic. Citing fear of insurrection, most elected officials from the southern states insisted that any formal welcoming of Haiti as a member of the community of nations would lead to the repetition of its revolution in America. Invoking national security and devotion to the Union, the proslavery movement worked to undermine the president's request.[101]

Thomas Hart Benton served as one of the most vocal members of the Senate during the discussion about the Panama conference. A scrapper from Missouri who once wounded Andrew Jackson in a brawl while employed as the general's aide-to-camp, Benton became a fixture of the United States Senate for much of the antebellum period. He dismissed any formal recognition of the Caribbean republic, saying, "Our policy towards Haiti, the old San Domingo, has been fixed, Mr. President, for three and thirty years. We trade with her, but no diplomatic relations have been established between us. And Why? Because the peace of eleven States in this Union will not permit the fruits of a successful negro insurrection to be exhibited among them."[102] The slaveholding position was clear: the white North and South had to be united in opposition to Haiti's independent existence. Undermining the authority of the planter elite by vaguely recognizing the existence of the black nation eroded the safety of the United States as a whole.

Southerners felt real apprehension with respect to the black-led revolution on the western portion of Hispaniola. Thomas Hart Benton did not simply worry that granting even symbolic equality to the black republic subverted slavery; he also believed that agents from Haiti might attack southern slavery once their diplomats arrived on American shores. The senator argued that the South "will not permit black Consuls and Ambassadors to establish themselves in our cities, and to parade through our country, and give their fellow blacks in the United States proof in hand of the honors which await them, for a like successful effort on their part."[103] The Missourian alleged that all black people, despite language barriers and varied residence, formed an adversarial alliance that resisted southern slavery. In the minds of the planter class, to dignify a successful black movement for independence meant the diminishing of the American Revolution.

The sheer act of American slaves witnessing a black foreign minister from Haiti, Benton insisted, might cause devastation to the South and the death of whites in the slave states. The federal government could not reward Haitians for successfully toppling a slaveholding regime and claiming their freedom. He bellowed that southerners would "not permit the fact to be seen, and told, that for the murder of their masters and mistresses, they are to find *friends* among the white People of these United States." Although Jean Pierre Boyer offered to forbid Haitian agents from traveling south of the Potomac and promised to only send a minister whose skin color did "not offend the prejudices of the country," Benton remained unconvinced.[104] Anything deemed inappropriate according to the sensibilities of the planter elite became the national standard—a southern, proslavery formula for American exceptionalism began to take shape.

South Carolina senator Robert Y. Hayne echoed Benton's concerns. Hayne believed that if the United States sent a mission to Panama that they should "plead the cause of the South" and work to slow the revolutionary spirit of South America. The senator hoped an American mission might convince South Americans to refuse Haiti's sovereignty. He summed up the proslavery stance regarding the Caribbean nation more succinctly than his colleague from Missouri: "Our policy, with regard to Hayti, is plain. We never can acknowledge independence. . . . The peace and safety of a large portion of our Union forbid us even to discuss. Let our government direct all our ministers in South America and Mexico to protest the independence of Hayti."[105] The proslavery forces in the federal government did everything they could to deter a country of former slaves from receiving equality among the community of nations. In the end, proslavery forces in Congress successfully subverted the president's effort to send a delegation to Panama. Congress appropriated funds too late for Adams to send a meaningful delegation to the international gathering. The president's corps of diplomats arrived in Panama near the conclusion of the conference and did not participate in any significant way. Slaveholders flexed their political power in American diplomacy despite having a president who did not fully support slavery.

Realistically, the nation of Haiti had little desire to attack slavery in the United States. The likelihood of an army of black revolutionaries crossing the Caribbean for the sake of American slaves appeared remote at best and absurd in reality. As a symbol, however, the black republic struck a discomfiting chord with southern slaveholders and made them extremely wary of real insurrections. The free and independent former slaves of the Caribbean offered a startling example to American planters and the rest of the world: those held in chains could successfully strike against their masters and win their liberty. Even the richest of plantation societies were susceptible to collapse. The Haitian Revolution, along with their personal encounters during the War of 1812, suggested to powerful planters that if given the opportunity, the right environment, and inspiration from successful slave revolts overseas, enslaved Americans could achieve freedom through rebellion.

Certainly the memory, or at least idealization, of the Caribbean revolutionaries influenced Gabriel in Virginia and Denmark Vesey in South Carolina to rebel against the master class. American slaveholders took notice. These slave conspiracies, along with a number of smaller instances of defiance throughout the South, bore a close enough resemblance to the uprisings in the West Indies to give southern whites a feeling of uneasiness about their security. The anxiety planters experienced could be wielded as a political weapon as well. The slaveholding elite soon bolstered their influence by fastening the objectives of the proslavery movement to national security.

Many in the South believed that the North offered a safeguard that Saint-Domingue had lacked. The overwhelmingly white population in the free states could buttress the power of slaveholders in the event that an actual American Toussaint rose in the South. Unlike the French or English slaveholders in the Caribbean, American planters had a military close by to protect them. White reinforcements would arrive quickly to squash a slave rebellion before it could engulf the slave states because northerners had a stake in successfully putting down an insurrection. They would be fighting to save their country, not a colony an ocean away. Regardless of their opinions on slavery, the white citizenry of the free states would not stand for the massacre of other whites, nor would they assent to black people controlling any portion of their nation. This made American slavery and the Union exceptional, southerners contended. Such a notion came to reveal how proslavery intellectuals defined the national purpose of the United States government during the first half of the nineteenth century.

In the 1820s, however, slaveholders began scrutinizing the antislavery movement in more detail. Approval from northerners, whether outward or tacit, remained a vital component to the planter elite's maintenance of slavery and suppression of the black population. In the aftermath of the Haitian Revolution and War of 1812, plantation owners perceived the growing abolitionist movement as a real threat to the stability of their society. As the proslavery movement anticipated future events, they saw the proponents of universal freedom as a dangerous obstacle to the perpetuation of the South's peculiar institution, an enemy to be dealt with and vanquished. Enslavers turned their eyes to Washington as they looked for a solution.

2

"FANATICISM" AND SOUTHERN FEARS OF BLACK REBELLION

Slavery is considered a festering sore by the fanatics of the North. They believe that they are responsible before God and the world, for the sin of African slavery, and although it is within our borders, they must use all their means in their power to destroy it in the States.

—Jeremiah Morton's Secessionist Speech,
Virginia, February 28, 1861

On January 16, 1830, subscribers to the *Milledgeville (Ga.) Southern Recorder* continued their weekly practice of reading news from across the United States.[1] One column talked about dinner parties between strangers on steamboats. Another described an estate sale desperately trying to sell the property of a dead man. The newspaper advertised hogs, cattle corn, kitchen furniture, and enslaved bodies of African Americans. At the bottom of the page, the editors mentioned the release of a new book. "Webster's Dictionary," the headline read. The bulletin explained that "the officers of Yale College, who have examined this work, are said to have recommended it to the students as being superior to any dictionary of our language." The new dictionary was written and verified by Connecticut Yankees and published in London. The short, though positive, appraisal encouraged its purchase. The book seemed to do what its author intended: tie the nation together with a homogenized writing style.[2]

Born in New England, a graduate of Yale where he studied Latin and Greek, and the cousin of an American political icon, Noah Webster submitted that his dictionary was more than a new reference tool. He considered his work to be a project in nation building. The rise and fall of empires often came to the forefront of American thought at the turn of the nineteenth century, and Webster believed the United States could avoid the common pitfalls of other empires. He aspired to build connections between the scattered people of the United States by standardizing the English language throughout the republic. In discussing his famous spelling book, he wrote, "A *national language* is a band of *national union.*"[3] A dictionary—his dictionary—might cement the marriage between all regions of the country by encouraging the practice of conversation.

Newspapers all over the United States had reported Webster's headway for some time, tracking his progression. After twenty years of studying various languages, the linguist completed his magnum opus in 1828. A handful of periodicals poked fun at some of the words the Nutmegger included in his masterpiece. More than one publication joked, "Noah Webster introduces into his Dictionary as legitimate, the word *lengthy.* We should like to know whether his reason for so doing are *breadthy* and *strengthy.*" Despite the good-natured criticism, Webster's book received accolades from everywhere. After inspecting the final project, the *Connecticut Herald* said it was "the most extensive and elaborate work which, in our country, has even been executed by the persevering industry of one man."[4] The reviewer praised the new dictionary as a useful way to help

Americans understand each other. It appeared that the lexicographer from New England had succeeded in his ultimate goal.

As the political discourse over slavery began to rise in volume during the 1830s, the dictionary proved useful in defining the language of the debate. Of all the words in Webster's book used by southerners to portray abolitionists, one word stood out among the rhetoric: "fanaticism n. Excessive enthusiasm; wild and extravagant notions of religion; religious frenzy."[5] Although the lexicographer meant the definition to be specifically related to spiritual fervor, the proslavery movement broadened the usage. Members of the slaveholding class warned the rest of the nation that the antislavery movement was filled with people so blinded by their faith in black freedom that they risked the total destruction of all whites in the South, enslavers or not. By the middle of the 1830s, proslavery authors labeled abolitionists as traitors to the United States who, because of their fanaticism, happily placed "the brand and the torch in the hands of the savage negro, and, pointing to the whites, bid him rise and destroy."[6] Planters insisted the singular focus of ridding the United States of black bondage made abolitionists deranged.

When Georgians picked up the *Southern Recorder* and read about Webster's new dictionary, they also saw a column delineating the recently enacted laws aimed at undermining the antislavery movement in their state. The purpose of the new restrictions revolved around the attempt by slaveholding policymakers to quell an uproar caused by David Walker, an abolitionist a thousand miles away in Boston, who had recently mailed his own magnum opus to the South. Much of the southern gentry feared the repercussions of his incendiary pamphlet, *An Appeal to the Coloured Citizens of the World,* reaching the hands of the African American population. To maintain the security of their plantations, they determined, the abolitionist message needed to be censored.[7]

Noah Webster's desire to see his country become increasingly unified through increased communication slowly came to fruition during the 1820s. From Maine to the southwestern territories, Americans corresponded with each other by sending letters to friends and family hundreds of miles away. Between 1821 and 1831 the size and scope of the American postal system mushroomed at an astounding pace. Moreover, although literacy was mostly denied to the enslaved, the United States became a nation of readers during the nineteenth century, boasting one of the highest literacy rates in the world. By the year 1830, nearly thirty million letters and publications went through the

United States postal service, a number that dwarfed Great Britain's mail service. Americans made contact with each other easier than ever before, and magazines, filled with everything from farming techniques to political news, blossomed in both the North and South.[8]

In the 1820s, anyone willing to pay for postage had an easy means to transmit ideas, with pointed accuracy, across the country. David Walker—a seller of used clothing who had once attended church with Denmark Vesey—understood the Post Office's value in communicating to black southerners. Restrictions might be placed on ships that arrived in southern ports, but Walker vowed to pay, at his own expense, for the circulation of his antislavery pamphlet. Along with sailors heading down the coast, the abolitionist used the mail like a piece of artillery, launching his missive against American slavery from a safe distance in Massachusetts. Some slaveholders worried that Walker might become a black Thomas Paine who stirred compatriots to fight for revolution. By the end of 1830, southern authorities found the abolitionist's radical ideas appearing throughout the slave states. They vowed to employ every resource at their disposal to stop it.[9]

In December 1829, a free black man living in Richmond named Thomas Lewis opened a parcel that came with a clear return address: 42 Brattle Street, Boston, Massachusetts. Along with thirty copies of his *Appeal* was a letter signed "Yours Very Affectionately, David Walker." The antislavery author asked him to sell every copy "among the Coloured people" living in the capital of Virginia. Each copy cost twelve cents; however, the author insisted, "if there are any who, cannot pay for *Book* give them *Books* for nothing." Spreading his message superseded any profit motive. The abolitionist from Boston realized that with an address and a stamp he could render slaveholders nearly defenseless. Trailing his package to the Old Dominion, *An Appeal to the Coloured Citizens of the World* arrived at the doorstep of Henry Cunningham, the preacher of the African Baptist Church in Savannah, Georgia. Upon examining the writings sent to him, and fearing retribution from the planter class if they discovered his new literary possession, the minister alerted state authorities. What Georgia leaders read frightened them.[10]

Following in the footsteps of radical black abolitionists who came before him, David Walker participated in a pan-African international tradition that fought against enslavers throughout the Atlantic. Known in Boston for organizing celebrations of Haiti's independence, the antislavery author did not simply intend to influence those held in slavery to organize local resistance like Gabriel or Vesey. He wanted—demanded—something bigger, more exhaustive in scale. In his pamphlet, composed of four individual articles, the Bostonian addressed "the coloured citizens of the world." From Africa to Haiti, Virginia to Brazil, Walker called for massive resistance to white power. Walker disdained black people who did not aspire to a better life, whether they faced discrimination in the North or the chains of enslavement in the South. Like Thomas Jefferson, whom he lambasted for giving credence to the belief in the inferiority of Africans, Walker saw two nations living in America: one black, one white, both filled with antipathy towards each other. The oppressed had to claim freedom themselves instead of relying on the sympathy from the more powerful. Walker's *Appeal* read as a jeremiad addressed to white America, North and South, and challenged white Christianity. In similar fashion to the Haitians, the rebels of Demerara, and even Denmark Vesey or the Founding Fathers of the United States, Walker declared God to be the progenitor of natural rights to all humanity. He aspired to boost the morale of possible insurrectionists by motivating them to serve something greater than themselves.[11]

David Walker also insisted that the Almighty heard the cries of southern slaves. He prophesied that plantation owners would one day feel the wrath of an angry Lord for depriving black people from reading the Bible. Enslaved Americans fit into the history of other Christians oppressed by "heathen nations." Along with challenging them to gain more schooling, the abolitionist pleaded for blacks to "fear not the number and education of our *enemies,* against whom we shall have to contend for our lawful right; guaranteed to us by our Maker; for why should we be afraid, when God is, and will continue . . . to be on our side."[12] In a battle between the enslaved in the United States and their oppressors, the Creator would side with the meek and poor. Slaves simply needed faith and courage to claim the rights that naturally belonged to them. David Walker appealed for war and talked about the arrival of a heaven-sent African American leader commissioned with the holy assignment of toppling the master class. "The Lord our God, as true as he sits on his throne in heaven, and as true as our Savior died to redeem the world," he predicted, "will give you a Hannibal," the most famous African general of antiquity who, in the face of seemingly insurmountable odds, climbed the Alps and attacked Rome.[13]

Unity served as the main component for vanquishing white slaveholders, Walker claimed. He implored black people everywhere to quash divisions between them and pointed to "the history particularly of Hayti, and see how they were butchered by the whites, and do take warning." Walker continued, "The person whom God shall give you, give him your support and let him go his length, and behold in him the salvation of your God. God will indeed, deliver you through him from your deplorable and wretched condition."[14] He promised the arrival of a modern-day Moses who would lead the faithful to freedom. The enslaved could eventually find their Holy Land if they kept faith and stuck together as one community devoted to resisting planters and their northern allies.

The final section of Walker's *Appeal* differentiated between the southern slaveholder, who directly oppressed black people, and England, which merely tolerated the institution in its colonies. Walker wrote, "The English are the best friends the coloured people have upon earth. Though they have oppressed us a little and have colonies now in the West Indies, which oppress us *sorely* . . . they (the English) have done one hundred times more for the melioration of our condition, than all other nations of the earth put together." He most likely separated the Caribbean slaveholders from the British mainland in order to portray the connection between the American and British antislavery movements. The Bostonian reminded his audience that some members in Parliament sympathized with their plight. If the enslaved heeded his advice and rebelled, he envisioned the British approving of their cause and offering help.[15]

Upon discovering the pamphlet in their states, southern elected officials responded quickly to scotch its circulation. Both the governor of Virginia, William Giles, and the mayor of Savannah, William T. Williams, turned to the person considered an ally to slaveholders in the North—Harrison Gray Otis, the mayor of Boston. Both southern politicians asked Otis to block Walker's *Appeal* from leaving Massachusetts. Giles and Williams also asked that an example be made of the abolitionist and demanded punishment for the author. They insisted that no one should be allowed to blaspheme against the institution of black enslavement without feeling the wrath of the proslavery movement.[16]

Giles and Williams could not have wished for someone more open to their perspectives than the man in charge of Boston, a growing hotbed of American abolitionism. Harrison Gray Otis had been active in politics for decades, first as a congressman in 1797, then as a senator in the 1810s, and, finally, the Federalist stalwart became the third mayor in the history of his hometown in 1829. In the House he supported the extension of slavery into the Southwest Territory and allied with southerners who condemned antislavery petitions. As a senator, however, Otis opposed admitting Missouri as a slave state, but not because of moral qualms. The New Englander had distaste for the power espoused by Virginians in the nation's capital during the first few decades of the Constitution. He perceived the blocking of Missouri's slave status as a way to bolster his region's political strength. When the antislavery movement in Massachusetts became exceedingly radical during the 1830s, Boston's mayor urged the attacks on slavery to be toned down. Surely, the two southerners speculated, such a northern politician would deem Walker's pamphlet inappropriate and dangerous enough to warrant prosecution.[17]

A couple of months later, the reply that the proslavery duo received from Massachusetts most certainly disappointed them. Aiming to convey to their constituents that they did everything they could to hinder Walker's writing from circulation, the two white southern leaders asked the *Richmond Enquirer* to publish the response from the Bay State. In his letter, Boston's mayor responded that southerners "cannot hold in more absolute detestation, the sentiments of [Walker] than do the people of" New England. He agreed that the abolitionist's invective was filled with "sanguinary fanaticism" and aspired to "disgust all persons of common humanity." He even asserted, wrongly, that the free black population of the city regretted that the "seditious" pamphlet had derived from their community.[18]

Boston's mayor filled his correspondence with regret. The citizens of the northeast, he attested, understood why southerners feared Walker might incite insurrection. Otis noted that after a local alderman gave him a copy of Walker's *Appeal* he "perused it carefully, in order to ascertain whether the writer had made himself amenable to our laws." Unfortunately for planters, he stated that "notwithstanding the extremely bad and inflammatory tendency of the publication," the abolitionist committed no crime. No indictment, no charges of sedition, and no punishment for the seller of old clothes were leveled to silence the author of *An Appeal to the Coloured Citizens of the World.* In Boston, a black abolitionist could speak his mind.[19]

When Otis ordered an investigation into David Walker's writing, his fact finders told him that the abolitionist "openly avows the sentiments of the book and authorship" and that he "declares his intention . . . to circulate his pamphlets through the mail." The only legal action the city leader could take, he concluded, was "to publish a general caution to Captains and others, against exposing themselves to the consequences of transporting incendiary writing into your and other Southern States."[20] He did not take action to quiet Walker's personal right to free speech. While Otis explained to the people of Boston that harsh accountability waited in the slave states for those who encouraged insurrection, he also told slaveholders that they would have to mete out punishment once abolitionists entered southern borders. Planter authority held little sway in the Bay State.

A number of white Bostonians applauded their mayor for distancing their city from Walker's radical writing. The city's press praised Otis, declaring that he "exculpated the citizens of Boston from any suspicion of participating in the incendiary attempt."[21] The *Boston Courier* took things even further. Its editors stated that "curiosity induced us, a few days since, to seek out the vender of these 'seditious pamphlets,' and to purchase an article that had created so much excitement among our southern neighbors." The newspaper continued: "The thing is inflammatory enough, in all conscience; but he who believes it to have been written by David Walker, the dealer in old clothes in Brattle street, must have more abundant faith than falls to our humble share."[22] Surely, the paper argued, a black man could not have written with such eloquence. "There are too many allusions to names and incidents in ancient and classical history scattered through the pamphlet. . . . It has the appearances of being the work of an educated and well-read writer, endeavoring to conceal his real character." The *Courier* speculated that the black abolitionist only claimed ownership of the work as a way to "pocket a pretty handsome sum by the sale."[23]

Slaveholders cared very little for Bostonian sympathies. They wanted action and became determined to take matters into their own hands. Walker's *Appeal* came southward at a time when many white southerners felt unsettled about the stability of the South's peculiar institution. During the previous summer, reports of slave uprisings had raised caution among the white populace in both Virginia and Georgia. Furthermore, in July 1829, a Virginia militia commander informed the governor of a potential revolt brewing and reported, "Should this alarm be well founded, we are in a helpless situation for a want of arms."[24] A year later, whites in North Carolina asked their state assembly for military assistance because the enslaved had "become so uncontrollable as to go and come when and where they please." The local patrol feared their houses being burned by black residents.[25] David Walker exacerbated the sense of unpreparedness. Many southerners held to the idea slavery remained vulnerable to outside influence, especially from radical abolitionists.[26]

White Georgians also found themselves worrying about black rebellion. James Stuart, a former politician from Scotland traveling across the United States in 1830, reported that a dubious fire in Augusta had led to white indignation throughout the town. Most convinced themselves it had been ignited by "incendiaries among the people of colour," and plantation owners took extreme precaution. "One slave a female," the traveler noted, "was convicted, executed, dissected, and exposed, but she died denying the crime. Another, now with child, is sentenced to be executed in June, but she still denies her guilt. I fear these unhappy creatures are convicted on what we should consider very insufficient evidence." The flames left much of Augusta's arsenal in ruins and the local militia lost most of their stockpiled weapons. Fearing his slave patrols might be undersupplied, the governor asked U.S. secretary of war John H. Eaton for additional weaponry from the federal cache. A proper slave society required armed authorities to be ready at the first signs of insurrection.[27]

In light of the recent local scares and reports of insurrections in the Caribbean, planters in Georgia acted quickly to silence *An Appeal to the Coloured Citizens of the World.* Upon initial discovery of the pamphlet, state legislators enacted harsh laws they deemed essential to the safety of the state's white citizenry. By the middle of January 1830, Georgia's plantation gentry emulated South Carolina's reaction to the Vesey conspiracy and banned free black mariners from leaving port. They also imprisoned any black sailor who communicated with "any person of color residing in this State." The law, however, did not create a white and nonwhite divide. The bill explicitly affirmed, "This act shall not be construed to extend to any free American Indian, free Moors, Lascars, or other colored subjects of the countries beyond the Cape of Good Hope." White Georgians considered only black people living throughout the Atlantic—the main audience of Walker's pamphlet—to be a threat. They also revived a restriction passed in 1817 that prohibited the importation of slaves to their state except for "certain conditions."[28]

Georgia legislators went to extremes to prevent the dissemination of Walker's brochure. They enacted an ordinance that punished with death anyone who helped distribute "any printed or written pamphlet, paper or circular, for the purposes of exciting to insurrection, conspiracy or resistance among the slaves, negroes, or free persons of color." Furthermore, the statehouse banned black residents, both free and enslaved, from becoming literate, fining white teachers up to five hundred dollars and "whipping at the discretion of the court" black educators who taught "any other slave, negro or free person of color, to read or write either written or printed characters."[29]

The excessive repression implemented by the Georgia government shocked James Stuart. In his travelogue *Three Years in North America,* the Scotsman explicitly mentioned the state's new statutes. He wrote, "The laws on the subject of slavery in the State of Georgia are as tyrannical as in any of the states." Earlier in his journal he noted the differences between free states and slave states in the Americas: "The regulations in the different states as to the liberty of the press are as different as those respecting slavery. This liberty can hardly be said to exist in Louisiana, or Georgia, while in most of the northern states it is enjoyed, almost, I may say, without control."[30] For an outsider, the sectional differences between the North and South seemed stark and bewildering.

Several northern allies of slavery gave the new restrictions positive reviews. On the same day that the *Southern Recorder* documented the new constraints placed on the lives of black Georgians, the *Columbian Centinel,* reporting from Massachusetts, commented that "this act appears at first blush violent and sanguinary." However, the newspaper stated, "it appears necessary to the immediate safety of whites. We have seen the pamphlet, which is doubtless here alluded to and do not hesitate to pronounce it one of the most wicked and inflammatory productions that ever issued from the press."[31] The writer decried the calling for bloodshed by David Walker and vindicated the harsh regulations as necessary protections for the white population. Some minor liberties could be sacrificed in the name of security, the northern journalist argued, especially if those freedoms were taken from black southerners living hundreds of miles away.

Neither Georgia's new laws nor intimidation from proslavery forces impeded Walker from dispersing his work to potential partners in the South. Despite passing harsher regulations, state authorities found two missionaries to the Cherokees in possession of Walker's *Appeal.* Furthermore, a printer and newspaperman in the state capital, Elijah Burritt, made the mistake of being too curious about the mailer that had set off such uproar in the legislature. He wanted to read the object of such fuss and asked the abolitionist in Boston to send him a copy, hoping to broach the subject in a news report. Walker mailed him twenty-five. When his business partner found a message from David Walker and the included copies of the pamphlet, he reported the editor to authorities. Burritt had already crossed local officials when he spoke out against the removal of the Cherokees; finding the antislavery writing granted proslavery leaders an excuse to punish him. The journalist quickly fled for his life, leaving the South entirely and settling in Connecticut.[32]

South Carolina newspapers promptly examined how to stifle the circulation of Walker's *Appeal,* as well. In analysis of the response from Harrison Gray Otis, an editorialist for the *Charleston City Gazette and Commercial Daily Advertiser* talked about the "fanatic insolence" of Walker's writing and asked, "Will these wretches never be quiet? Have they no apprehensions that they may be destroyed in the very flames they are laboring to enkindle." The antislavery movement, the South Carolinian contended, had become so blinded by their hate of slavery that it no longer comprehended the calamity their unfettered attacks on the South's peculiar institution might cause.[33] Three weeks later, the pamphlet finally arrived in the state with the densest slave population and harshest laws to maintain the power of slaveholders. Charleston police arrested Edward Smith, a white sailor from Boston unaffected by the Negro Seamen Act, for carrying and disseminating the pamphlet into South Carolina. In his deposition, the mariner claimed ignorance of the writing's theme and insurrectionary language. He only knew that he had been tasked to deliver to "any negroes he had a mind to, or that he met" and "did not know that he was doing wrong or violating the law."[34] South Carolina authorities planned to make him an example of what happened to those who threatened the South's peculiar institution.

The attorney general of South Carolina swiftly investigated Smith, accusing him of "maliciously contriving and intending to disturb the peace and security of this State and to move a sedition among the Slaves of the people of this state with force and arms at Charleston in the District of Charleston." The indictment from the grand jury read like a laundry list of slaveholder nightmares. To implicate Smith, the prosecutor took different passages from Walker's *Appeal* that specifically asked African Americans to remember the Haitian Revolution. The State of South Carolina tried and convicted the sailor from Boston in just six days. Not wishing to evoke outrage in Massachusetts by executing one of its citizen, the court ordered Smith to pay a thousand-dollar fine—a massive sum—and sentenced him to a year's imprisonment. As they had with other attempts by abolitionists to free slaves during the 1830s, planters aimed to show lenience for a few rabble-rousers in exchange for tacit support of slavery by those in power in the free states.[35]

A few months later, the *Charleston City Gazette and Commercial Daily Advertiser* claimed Walker's writing had "recoiled upon those with whom it originated." The proslavery journalist reported that a riot between "the *brownies* and a few of the philanthropists" had occurred in the North "in which the latter have been seriously battered and bruised." The periodical gleefully claimed those in the free states might "discover in time, that mischief, like chickens, 'comes home to roost.'"[36] The message was clear: northerners friendly to slavery needed to protect the institution or face the predictable, violent ramifications of emancipation. Southerners insisted that black people would rebel if abolitionism thrived in the free states.

An Appeal to the Coloured Citizens of the World appeared in much of the South between March and October 1830. In August, for example, Walker's pamphlet appeared in North Carolina. Jacob Cowan, an enslaved tavern keeper, acted as the main agent for its distribution. Receiving the *Appeal* through the Port of Wilmington, the bartender found himself with as many as two hundred copies to pass along to the local black community who came to his establishment for a drink. Upon discovering his stock, the Wilmington magistrate of police James F. McKee reassured Governor John Owen that "every means which the existing laws of our State" provided had been "promptly used to prevent dissemination." McKee warned the governor that a "systematic" attempt "to sow sedition among the slaves at the South" had obviously been launched "by some reckless personas at the North." He recommended thwarting the conspiracy by implementing more intrusive regulations to the lives of the black population.[37] In response, North Carolina lawmakers quickly passed new restrictions on black residents that matched those of Georgia and South Carolina, primarily focusing on teaching slaves how to read.[38]

The appearance of Walker's pamphlet caused commotion in Louisiana, as well. In September 1830, officials arrested Milo Mower, a French immigrant and the editor of *The Liberalist,* an antislavery publication. To justify his imprisonment, authorities accused the abolitionist of breaking a new law criminalizing the distribution of any writing that might "excite insubordination among the slaves therein." Despite his disavowal of violence, local leaders charged Mower with distributing a "seditious circular to the free people of color at New Orleans," and he never appeared in public again. Fellow antislavery editors speculated he had been deported to Europe, but no one knew for sure.[39] The proslavery movement successfully employed the fear of black rebellion to justify using government authority to silence opposition.

Despite Louisiana's tradition of affording free black residents a higher place in their society, the state legislature forbade the entrance of free black immigrants and threatened to remove recent arrivals. The state passed its own version of the Negro Seamen Act, prohibiting black sailors from staying in the busy Port of New Orleans for more than thirty days. In reaction to the new regulations, some in the free black community asked their neighbors to "hope for better times," but others considered leaving for the West Indies. The effect of the new policy mattered too much to their lives, and they fled while they still could.[40]

White southerners barring free blacks from moving into their states raised the ire of many in the North. Similar to southerners, who viewed free black Americans as a threat to public safety, a large portion of the free states wanted little to do with African Americans. These northerners warned that banning the newly emancipated from living in southern states would compel them to seek free soil. Although several northern states had long ago placed slavery on a path toward extinction, many white northerners felt antiblack sentiment. Much of the animus toward slavery above the Mason-Dixon Line came from the desire to have nothing to do with black people, free or enslaved.[41]

Southern members of the press ridiculed the antislavery movement, which they blamed for causing the need to pass stricter laws on the black community. For instance, the *Milledgeville Southern Recorder,* reporting on an article from the *New York Journal of Commerce,* described concerns from northerners with scorn. A proslavery periodical wrote, "The Free person of color are a burden in the Northern States! They are not willing to receive more of this kind of population! What a confession! especially the Southern State for possessing a greater number than they do." The newspaper also mocked abolitionism: "The *humane* in the North, and the *truly philanthropist* will have in their power to convince, that their repeated professions of virtue, disinterested humanity for the poor degraded Africans are not empty declarations." The article ended by asking why abolitionists did not use their wealth to buy slaves and send them to Africa. If the proponents of emancipation yearned to free the enslaved, slaveholders argued, their neighbors should be the ones to reap the outcome of the fanatical harvest.[42]

Proslavery politicians in Virginia, also fearing insurrection, attempted to pass new restrictions on their state's black population after the appearance of Walker's *Appeal* in their state. As concern about the pamphlet spread throughout the slave states, Governor William Branch Giles requested a surreptitious session of the legislature to enact harsh restrictions on black residents, including a ban on teaching enslaved Americans how to read. Virginians had not been swept up in the furor revolving around David Walker's pamphlet, however. Although the proposed law passed the House of Delegates, the proposal failed in the Senate. Dissenting senators thought the ordinances to be too harsh. The Old Dominion did not go down the path of its southern neighbors from the Deep South.[43]

Newspapers in Virginia chided the secrecy of the governor and criticized his fear of the black populace. The *Richmond Whig* found itself quoted in other publications, both in slave and free states: "One would really suppose that Governor Giles imagined he was sleeping over a mine of gunpowder and that he dreamt of nothing but conspiracies and servile war."[44] One rabble-rouser in Boston did not have the ability to threaten the security of America's oldest slave system, proslavery moderates contended. For these skeptics, the scare provoked by David Walker and his pamphlet seemed overblown and politically motivated to help the governor gain higher approval from the electorate. These opinions changed drastically eighteen months later.

In the summer of 1831, in remote Southampton County, Virginia, roughly seventy miles from Richmond, Nat Turner—an enslaved evangelical preacher—mounted a violent attack against slavery. The quiet, backwater region near the Dismal Swamp suddenly became infamous as the stage for one of America's bloodiest rebellions against slaveholders before the Civil War. By the end of 1831, the Old Dominion's planter elite experienced a shock to their slave system that made a large portion of whites reconsider their objections to emancipation and the removal of black people from the state entirely. Plantation owners throughout the South tied the growing abolitionist movement in the North to the violence encountered by whites on that warm summer night. In the aftermath, the intellectual members of the southern gentry became determined to do everything they could to hamper the promotion of "fanaticism."

Throughout most of his life Nat Turner believed he was destined for something great. He came to believe that God granted him divine revelations. Like Moses and the burning bush, "the Spirit that spoke to the prophets" had revealed itself to the preacher. "For two years," Turner "prayed continually," hoping to experience "the same revelation, which fully confirmed me in the impression that I was ordained for some great purpose." Finally, on August 13, 1831, the minister became convinced that he received his last message from Heaven. The sun seemed to change colors as he gazed up into the sky. The signal to strike had come and the preacher poised himself to act in the name of the Lord.[45]

Although it is unlikely that Turner knew much about his *Appeal,* David Walker's prophecy seemed to come true during the hot summer in rural Southampton. As in Gabriel's rebellion, Turner's followers called him "General Nat," and he recruited lieutenants and other foot soldiers. The insurrectionist leader fit squarely into the tradition of mystical conjurers that often contributed and promoted resistance by the enslaved. He and his fellow warriors characterized the work they planned to do as holy. Strengthened by the belief that God's hand protected them, and fully aware of what happened to those who rebelled against the planter elite, the group of insurrectionists readied for battle. They enthusiastically "armed and equipped" themselves "and gathered sufficient force, neither age nor sex was to be spared." They preoccupied themselves with delivering vengeance to the whites holding them in bondage and living off of their labor and their future.[46]

As with Gabriel's strategy, Nat Turner's war against black enslavement started with the death of his own master, Joseph Travis, followed shortly by the slaveholder's family. In the middle of the night, the band of insurrectionists walked up to the Travis cabin carrying axes. Turner broke into the locked house through the roof, unlocking the door from the inside so his compatriots could quietly flood into the house. Sneaking softly as to awaken no one, Nat whispered to his fellow soldiers that he "must spill first blood."[47] He crept into the Travis bedroom where the head of the household laid fast asleep. Turner raised his weapon; he knew there would be no turning back. The tight-knit group of enslaved rebels he recruited readied themselves for bloodshed and its consequences.

Nat Turner's small hatchet struck the man who claimed ownership of his life. The blow only glanced off Travis's head, however. As the slaveholder sprung out of bed to defend himself he screamed for his wife before one of Turner's compatriots "laid him dead, with a blow of his axe." Sally Travis and two others met the same end—hacked to pieces. After leaving the cabin and walking "some distance," the insurrectionists remembered the final member of the Travis family, "a baby in a cradle."[48] They returned to kill the child destined to be an owner of slaves. The deed was finished and the Travis family wiped out. A new commanding general took the field in a war against the southern slaveholding regime.

After the deaths of the Travises, the group found muskets in the plantation's barn. Once inside, Turner transformed himself from a preacher into a drill sergeant. In his account of the revolt, he said, "I formed them in a line as soldiers, and after carrying them through all the manoeuvres [*sic*] I was master of, marched them off to Mr. Salathul Francis.'" Death sprang forth from the weapons the insurrectionists wielded. Throughout the night Turner and his new army of rebels went door to door: first to the Francis house, then Mrs. Reese's, then Mrs. Turner's, then Mrs. Whitehead's, and finally Mr. Bryant's. They reaped retribution from every white person they found.

Turner's troops split into brigades to be more effective in accomplishing their business. Some whites pleaded for their lives as the axes came down on them. Others cowered, whimpering as they came to their bloody end. In one circumstance, Will, nicknamed "the executioner" by Turner, dragged a woman from her house before nearly decapitating her. The black insurgents aimed at total destruction. No white person could be innocent; no absolution granted. Unlike Gabriel's targets, those who tolerated slavery received no reprieve from Turner. He and his followers meted out their outrage against their enslavers through blood and planned to destroy the white community that worked together to subjugate them.[49]

As the company of enslaved warriors marched forward they came across a vacated house. The Porter family had escaped, the alarm certainly sounded. Turner's soldiers braced themselves for combat as they spotted eighteen white men preparing a counterattack. "Immediately on discovering the whites," Turner recalled, "I ordered my men to halt and form."[50] The slave general readied his men for battle. They soon skirmished, but after surveying the field, the rebel commander spotted new proslavery reinforcements arriving. The black battalion retreated, leaving none of their casualties behind. They followed Turner as he went to Jerusalem, one of the larger towns of Southampton County. There, he hoped they would redouble their efforts and strike again, but Turner tried "in vain to collect a sufficient force to proceed." After failing to rally his troops and finding "no more victims to gratify our thirst for blood," he retreated to a cave near the Travis homestead. Four days later, slaveholders quelled the rebellion when the South's federal allies finally arrived and the U.S. army fortified the state's defenses. The white population of the small Virginian community began its dogged search to apprehend the preacher-turned-general.[51]

The media described the uprising with a tinge of hysteria. Staggered by the events that unfolded in Southampton, one publication exclaimed, "What an abandoned set of banditti these cut-throats are! Their steps are everywhere marked with the blood of women and children: An astonishing fatality seems to have attended these helpless classes. Neither infancy nor female sex is spared in their blood-thirsty wrath!" Others found the violence difficult to accept. The *Richmond Compiler* attested, "The intelligence was so awful and unexpected, that it was received with much hesitation and doubt by all whom it was communicated, until the afternoon" when a colonel from Suffolk "left no room for conjecture or uncertainty." Furthermore, Virginia's governor was presented with a letter describing Turner's actions to be part of a bigger conspiracy. In his eagerness to punish whites, the correspondence stated, the insurrectionist in Southampton had attacked too early. The note predicted a more "concerted" assault, similar to that of the Haitian Revolution, transpiring in eight days. Although the slave-led mass revolt never came to fruition, Virginia seemed to be in chaos.[52]

Descriptions from all over the state varied on how large Turner's force had been. Some newspapers reported "150 to 400, acting in detached parties"; others claimed there were only "40 to 100 deluded wretches." Turner placed the number to be between sixty and eighty. Most journalists tried to calm the public by conveying a message that white military leaders were ready to act in their defense, and that, after a few days of white nervousness, "tranquility [had] been restored." The *Norfolk American Beacon* confessed to readers that it purposely withheld some of the stories from the public in order to "counteract the many exaggerated statements with which gossip rumor, with her hundred tongues, has hourly abused the public confidence." Local officials also worked to keep white Virginians calm while they tracked the insurrectionist leader, constantly assuring the public that they remained in control of the situation.[53]

A white reign of terror against the black community shadowed Turner's revolt. Both slaveholders and yeomen hunted those charged with being part of the insurrection and viciously—and arbitrarily—doled out brutal punishment. On August 29, the *Richmond Constitutional Whig* noted that "people are naturally wound up to a high pitch of rage." Five days later the newspaper reported, "It is with pain we speak of another feature of the Southampton Rebellion; for we have been most unwilling to have our sympathies for the sufferers diminished or affected by their misconduct. We allude to the slaughter of many blacks."[54] The wave of white fury that trailed Turner's uprising saw nearly forty black Americans either shot or decapitated with scant investigation and no trial.

Proslavery panic sparked by Nat Turner went beyond the Old Dominion. In her memoir, *Incidents in the Life of a Slave Girl,* Harriet Jacobs described the "fear of insurrection" that enveloped the white population in North Carolina shortly after they learned about the violence in Southampton. Jacobs wrote, "The news threw our town into great commotion." The gentry quickly mustered the militia to assert their racial supremacy. "It was a grand opportunity for low whites," she stated; "they exulted in such a chance to exercise a little brief authority, and show their subservience to the slaveholders." A number of people paid a heavy price for having black skin as mobs attacked alleged insurrectionists. "The soldiers, stimulated by drink," she remembered, "committed still greater cruelties.... Every where men, women, and children were whipped till the blood stood in puddles at their feet, and tortured with a bucking paddle, which blisters the skin terribly." The planter elite used the scare from Nat Turner to give nonslaveholders, "who had no negroes of their own to scourge," a taste of power and absolute jurisdiction over the lives of black southerners, bolstering their loyalty to the South's peculiar institution by feeding the yeomen envy for mastery.[55]

Jacobs remembered seeing "a mob dragging along a number of coloured people, each white man, with his musket upraised, threatening instant death if they did not stop their shrieks." Among the damned was a "respectable old colored minister. They had found a few parcels of shot in his house, which his wife had for years used to balance her scales." She continued: "Staggering under intoxication, assuming to be the administrators of justice," the foot soldiers of white supremacy declared him guilty on the spot and opted to shoot him. Only after the plantation owners realized that "their own property was not safe from the lawless rabble they had summoned to protect them" did they rally "the drunken swarm" and send them "back to into the country, and set guard over the town."[56]

After the mob left, the planter elite began their own investigations into black homes, committing "shocking outrages" with "perfect impunity," Jacobs wrote. "Every day for a fortnight, if I looked out, I saw horsemen with some poor panting negro tied to their saddles, and compelled by the lash to keep up with their speed, till they arrived at the jail yard. Those who had been whipped too unmercifully were washed with brine, tossed in a cart, and carried to jail."[57] The slave patrols continued for weeks, only abating when North Carolina planters heard that Nat Turner had been captured in Virginia. The South, both white and black, had been shaken by the violence.

"Fanaticism" rapidly became the explanation for the events of Southampton. Numerous newspapers printed the same story explaining that "a fanatic preacher by the name of Nat Turner (Gen. Nat Turner!) who had been taught to read and write and permitted to go about preaching in the country, was at the bottom of this infernal brigandage." "Fanaticism" became less about religion and more about social order and politics. In a letter published in the *Richmond Enquirer,* a resident from Southampton County decried the insurrectionist leader's association with the Baptist church. God had nothing to do with the slave revolt, he argued; "those fanatical scoundrels" only "pretended to be divinely inspired." The editor of the *Constitutional Whig,* another Richmond publication, also maintained that the uprising had been inspired by "fanatical revenge."[58] Virginia experienced another Gabriel: a slave with a little more freedom than most who became a general in a war on slaveholders. This time the blood of whites had been spilled.

The insurrection in Southampton led to slave patrols being placed on high alert throughout the South. One South Carolinian told his brother that the Turner rebellion had sparked rumors and fear throughout the Palmetto State. South Carolinians were now "wide awake" in monitoring the black populace for dangerous activity. North Carolinians also asked their governor to send the militia to guard against a potential revolt by the enslaved. Moreover, panicked white citizens felt apprehensive about their safety, especially in the southwest, where some leaders challenged the interstate slave trade. Just as South Carolinians worried about importing "fanaticism" from the Caribbean after the Haitian Revolution, planter politicians in Alabama and Louisiana took legislative action to ban the importation of the enslaved from the "infected" portion of the country. The social constraints cultivated by the slaveholding class to insulate white residents from the violent resistance of enslaved African Americans seemed to be unraveling.[59]

Many whites in the southern states—like the generation that came before them during the Haitian Revolution—concluded that free blacks served as an obstacle to maintaining a peaceful system of slavery. In response, slave-state legislatures placed new constraints on the lives of black southerners, limiting liberties they had previously enjoyed.[60] Gabriel and Vesey's plots were averted without harm to whites. Language and ocean separated Americans from the fires of Haiti; the German Coast rebellion had French overtones. This time, however, those who died had been neighbors, friends, and family. Insurrection was no longer something that happened elsewhere. American slaveholders could be killed like anyone else.

After the Southampton revolt, restrictions emulating those that came after the arrival of David Walker's writing gained reconsideration in the Virginia State Capitol. State political leaders enacted a law that punished "any person" who distributed "any book, pamphlet or other writing, advising, or inciting persons of colour . . . to make insurrection, or to rebel" with "death, without the benefit of clergy." It was the same punishment that Gabriel received three decades earlier for preparing an actual slave revolt. The legislature also placed regulations on the movement of all black people, limited the ability of enslaved southerners to sell goods—regardless of how they obtained them—and prohibited all nonwhites from disbursing alcohol within a mile of "any muster, preaching, or other public assembly." The nervousness of slaveholders in the Deep South stemming from *An Appeal to the Coloured Citizens of the World* had come to the Upper South with Turner's Rebellion. Those in charge of the oldest slave society in the United States became much more risk averse. They viewed black Virginians with a jaundiced eye and became determined to temper "fanatical" ideas that threatened their power.[61]

Many white southerners cast themselves as being besieged by those opposed to slavery. Conforming to Bryan Edwards's thesis about the motivation of the Haitian revolutionaries, much of the proslavery gentry in the Old Dominion blamed the North for instigating the insurrection. Benjamin Cabell, a former lawyer from Kentucky who had risen in the ranks of Virginia's militia, warned the governor of a much larger conspiracy to overthrow the planter elite. He contended, "The Southampton insurrection was only a branch of a plan, long since laid." Expecting an escalation of violence, he requested arms to keep his village from harm because "the slave population in town and its vicinity bears a great proportion, if it does not equal that of the whites." Cabell connected David Walker to Nat Turner and blamed "the damnable spirit of fanaticism engendered by Northern publications and, perhaps disseminated by missionaries."[62] The militia leader sincerely thought that black Virginians would only violently resist their enslavement if antislavery supporters encouraged them, and he relied on that notion to continue believing that the Old Dominion should remain a slave state.

Many slaveholders sought out ways to punish northern abolitionists, hoping to deter them from "meddling" with southern slavery. In South Carolina, the "Vigilance Association of Columbia" offered a reward of fifteen hundred dollars for the capture and conviction of "any white person who may be detected in distributing or circulating within the State the newspaper called 'the Liberator'" or any other journal that had a "seditious tendency." Virginia governor John Floyd followed suit. He wrote in his diary that if the "fanatics" proceeded to be unchecked by northern governments, Virginia would "not be tied up by the confederacy from doing ourselves justice."[63] The planter class of the Old Dominion believed they could not sit idly and watch their society collapse under pressure from the antislavery movement. In the wake of Turner's uprising in Southampton, white southerners again looked to their free-state counterparts and demanded action to stem the rising tide of abolitionism. Mutual security under the Constitution fastened the nation together and allowed for the United States to be exceptional, they insisted.

Additional threats to slavery from outside the South continued to flood into the Old Dominion. In the autumn of 1831, a letter from Boston arrived at the post office of Jerusalem, Virginia, and was quickly forwarded to the governor. Speaking with a rage similar to David Walker's, bolstered by the independence of Haiti, and encouraged by Turner's rampage on the state's white residents, the author—a man named Nero and allegedly a former slave in the state—claimed that all of Turner's lieutenants had not been caught. He predicted more white blood being spilled, telling planters to expect "more than three hundred men of colour . . . who have pledged ourselves with spartan fidelity" to "avenge the indignities" placed on black southerners by "the Slave holding Tyrants." Whereas Walker summoned visions of Hannibal, Nero promised "a modern Leonidas" who would transform Virginia into an American Thermopylae. Although some thought the message to be a hoax, the governor placed the letter in his scrapbook under the label of "Liberator: Genius of Emancipation," the title of William Lloyd Garrison's radical antislavery outlet. Floyd judged it to be an abolitionist's attempt at scaring an already paranoid planter class.[64]

Nero did not stop with the prediction of more slave insurrections. He also announced that a vast conspiracy existed to dismantle southern slavery. The conspirators used a network of communication that stretched from Haiti to the United States, both in the free and slave states. The letter stated that Walker's *Appeal* had all been part of a larger blueprint for black revolution. He also identified Elijah Burritt, the editor run out of the South due to owning Walker's pamphlet, as one of the plot's agents. "Our holy cause most surely was then in jeopardy" when the printer had been caught by Georgian authorities, the note read. However, "had it not been for a most masterly maneuvre [*sic*] of our Chief

. . . Burritt would have lost his worthless life, and our fond hopes would have been blasted." Nero boasted: "We have many a white agent in Florida, S. Carolina, and Georgia."[65]

The letter also described an international element to the antislavery plot to overturn the enslavement of black Americans, connecting Nat Turner to the Haitian Revolution. He wrote that although "our beloved Chief is a Native of Virginia," he had escaped to Haiti where "his noble soul became warmed by the spirit of freedom, and an unqualified hatred for the oppressors of his race." If any truth existed in the warning, it meant that the only slaves to ever defeat a powerful planter class had taught a black American hero how to do it in the United States. The spirit of Haiti's revolution, Nero insisted, would come to the South, if not by directly supplying soldiers, then indirectly by training southern slaves in the tactics of winning a race war.[66]

The letter's explanation of how potential insurrectionists might acquire weapons unnerved slaveholders. Nero claimed, "We have assurance of arms and ammunition from Non-Slaveholding States—I mean from individuals in those states, and Hayti offers an asylum for those who survive the approaching carnage." The "approaching carnage" would be in the same vein as Turner's, the letter writer insisted. The rebels planned to "spare neither age nor sex." The mysterious Nero capitalized on the southern stereotype of northerners to undermine their trust that free staters remained faithful to the planter elite in the case of a large-scale rebellion. He said, "A Yankee, you know, will hazard his life for money." Wealthy abolitionists desired the end of southern slavery by any means necessary. They could easily buy off the North's allegiance to the proslavery movement, forcing planters to fight the enslaved warriors by themselves in a battle to the death.[67]

Nero challenged the proslavery movement's faith in American exceptionalism and the effectiveness of the Union in protecting slavery. "There are more people in Boston, [New] York, Philadelphia and Hartford," he wrote, "who know more of the circumstances of the late insurrection than any Slave holder in Virginia or North Carolina." The letter also promised that abolitionists looked forward to using the U.S. postal service as a tool to fight American slavery. Mimicking David Walker, Nero assuredly avowed, "our handbills and placards will soon be found in your streets, and there will be enough to read them; this you cannot prevent—the Post Office is free for anyone—anyone has a right to receive communications through the medium of it." He exalted the postal service as a "machinery of vast power" for the supporters of emancipation to utilize.[68] Before Virginia's gentry could worry about outsiders undermining their system of black enslavement, however, they first needed to deal with nonslaveholders who were fed up with the continual fear of an insurrection.

Just as Gabriel's rebellion prompted questions about the viability of slavery in the long term, proponents for making the state's population whiter saw Turner's insurrection as an "auspicious moment for action." Many nonslaveholders in the Old Dominion believed the best remedy for the threat of a dangerous revolt was to devise "a means by which the blacks may be removed beyond our borders, and by which too, the number of slaves may gradually be diminished." Although some challenged the enslavement of African Americans on moral grounds, several other nonslaveholders argued for Virginia to move toward becoming free soil for more pragmatic reasons. Many yeomen had already immigrated out of the state in search for greater opportunities. Along with losing potential foot soldiers for their security forces, these Virginians feared the "machanick trades and arts [were] falling fast into the hands of the black population," driving white skilled labor away and forcing their state to become too dependent on its slaves for crafted goods while also becoming a nonwhite majority.[69]

Following the violence in Southampton, a number of Virginians demanded that something be done to ensure the safety of whites from black rebellion. The elderly James Madison worried that holding so many people in slavery remained dangerous to the nation he helped create. The author of the Constitution recommended that the proceeds from the sale of public lands be used to remove the African American population from the Upper South. Other reformers proposed various solutions while the proslavery movement marshaled forces to block any attempt at putting their labor system on the road to extinction. Slaveholders professed that safeguards against insurrection merely required strengthening. The two sides debating the future of slavery in the Old Dominion did concur on one idea—whether free or in shackles, black people posed a danger to whites. They agreed that the more the black population grew in density the weaker slave owners became, undermining the social order as a whole.[70]

Other slave states—Delaware, Kentucky, Tennessee, Maryland, and North Carolina—also deliberated the role of the black populace in their society. Some legislatures banned blacks from entering their states altogether. Many in the Upper South promoted selling the enslaved southward, sending them as far away as possible to brutal slaveholding regimes on the Gulf Coast. The contentious discussion about emancipation in the early 1830s forced those most ardently in favor of slavery to shift how they defended the institution. Instead of proclaiming it a necessary evil, as much of the founding generation did, a new wave of proslavery advocates insisted that enslavement provided positive effects for both nonslaveholding whites and those held in chains. As the Atlantic world shifted towards universal freedom, Thomas Roderick Dew, a bookish scholar of history and political economy at the College of William and Mary, emerged as an audacious voice for the plantation elite of the United States.[71]

The thirty-year-old son of a Revolutionary War soldier and born to a prosperous plantation family in the Tidewater region of Virginia, Thomas Dew published his proslavery polemic as an article in the *American Quarterly Review*. After receiving acclaim throughout the slave states, the urbane professor expanded his thoughts into a book called *Review of the Debate in the Virginia Legislature of 1831 and 1832*. The Upper South, where slavery was challenged the most, supplied the planter elite with its new intellectual cornerstone. Rather than begging northerners to tolerate the South's peculiar institution, Dew contended that slaveholders should feel pride about black bondage. From Williamsburg, he laid a foundation for a new defense of slavery in the United States and, as a result, many southern intellectuals became deeply committed to slavery's expansion while simultaneously feeling more fearful about the consequences of emancipation.[72]

Widely read at the time, and eventually canonized by proslavery polemicists in the 1850s, *Review of the Debate in the Virginia Legislature of 1831 and 1832* touched on several topics that Dew associated with slavery in the United States: colonization, emancipation, Haiti, England, and insurrections. The Virginian's book served as a proslavery counterargument to *An Appeal to the Coloured Citizens of the World*. On the one hand, Walker talked about the evils of slavery, raged against its injustices, and forecasted a future in which the sword eradicated slavery from existence. Dew, on the other hand, evoked a positive spin to the enslavement of black Americans. He lamented the harmful effects that emancipation might bring to both whites and blacks in the United States. The two men understood that the destiny of slavery had yet to be determined.[73]

David Walker told his readers that slavery caused the black population in the United States to be "the *most wretched, degraded* and *abject* set of being that *ever live*." Thomas Dew proclaimed to his mostly white audience: "Slavery, we assert again, seems to be the only means that we know of, under Heaven, by which the ferocity of the savage can be conquered, his wandering habits eradicated, his slothfulness and improvidence overcome." The American institution of forced labor, the Virginian wrote, had "been perhaps the principal means for impelling forward the civilization of mankind." The southern historian insisted that the enslavement of black people offered the most progressive way for society to advance through the "three stages in which man has been found to exist," the first being "hunting and fishing," the second "the pastoral," and finally, "agricultural." What Walker decried as degradation, Dew designated the cultivation of enlightenment, contending, "Nothing but slavery can civilize such beings, give them habits of industry, and make them cling to life for its enjoyments." Like most elites throughout history, the self-declared master class thought they knew best how to shape the general public. The proslavery polymath insisted that the enslavement of African Americans promoted advancement for all of mankind and demanded that nonslaveholders, poorer and less educated, trust the guidance of the planter elite in the march toward a better world.[74]

Dew proclaimed slavery to be a progressive version of Christian morality. "We cannot get rid of slavery without producing a greater injury both to the masters and slaves, there is no rule of conscience or revealed law of God which *can* condemn us," he maintained. While David Walker predicted divine punishment for the practitioners of slavery, the Virginian anticipated commendation from the heavens. He believed white planters should expect to hear that they had been "good and faithful servants" on the day of their judgment. After all, the professor maintained, by controlling a dangerous black population slaveholders had chosen a higher good when debating the "original sin" that had been foisted up the United States by the British. Thomas Roderick Dew declared that bondage best took care of people who could not take care of themselves in a "civilized" manner. The new argument portrayed the paternalism of the slaveholding elite as a redeeming quality, something to be praised rather than scorned. That notion was transformed into a proslavery rallying cry against abolitionists who cited the Declaration of Independence to account for their activism.[75]

Dew also pointed to England's experience with slavery and asked readers to look at "the Parliament of Great Britain, [which] with all its philanthropic zeal" had "never yet seriously" contemplated full emancipation in the Caribbean.[76] Despite its antislavery movement, the British validated slavery in the United States, he maintained. If one of the friendliest nations to the enslaved still believed that ending slavery led to disaster, why should southerners move toward emancipation? Dew also relied heavily on Bryan Edwards's *History of the West Indies* to demonstrate what Great Britain thought on the subject, expanding the book's influence in proslavery thought and increasing the degree to which planters linked insurrection to abolitionism.

Review of the Debate in the Virginia Legislature, like David Walker's *Appeal,* contained passages that described the violence and destruction during the Haitian Revolution. Whereas Walker discussed Haiti to convey how the mistreatment of black people would eventually lead to the collapse of white power, Dew used the former French colony as a warning to his white readers to be leery of emancipationists. He blamed Revolutionary France's "intemperate and phrenetic zeal for liberty and equality" for causing the "the bloodiest and most shocking insurrection ever recorded in the annals of history." The naïveté of French "fanatics," he proclaimed, had cost that country "the fairest and most valuable of all her colonial possessions." However, proslavery theorist continued, once France became "convinced of her madness," it tried in vain to restore slavery.[77] The Virginian made certain that the proslavery moral of Haiti's story stood out to his white readers: once those held in slavery gained freedom, they could never be forced back into slavery. Abolitionism could not be turned from once it went awry.

Dew's defense of slavery hinged on two counterintuitive concepts—while the enslaved could be a dangerous, uncivilized, potentially threatening component that could upend society, the practice of slavery itself, which increased the black population, continued to be peaceful and morally right. The professor argued that David Walker's belief that black southerners wanted their freedom and equality, or that Nat Turner hated his master, proved to be exceptions to the general rule. *Review of the Debate in the Virginia Legislature* maintained that nearly every slave in the South "generally loves the master and his family" and expressed "unfeigned grief at the deaths which occur among the whites." Dew also argued that, while in captivity, African Americans "imbibed the principles, sentiments, and feelings of the whites," thus making them less dangerous. American slavery—and the nation—could only remain exceptional if abolitionists did not undermine the proslavery dominance over the Union, the professor declared.[78]

Review of the Debate in the Virginia Legislature contended that the enslavement of black people helped maintain racial peace in the South. Thomas Dew urged readers to subscribe to the notion that "in dealing with a negro we must remember that we are dealing with a being possessing the form and strength of a man, but the intellect of only a child." He assured slaveholders and nonslaveholders alike: "A negro will rob your *hen roost* or your *stye,* but it is rare indeed that he can ever be induced to murder you." Rather than identifying the enslaved as a source of national insecurity, he challenged the proslavery movement to keep its focus on outside forces that threatened to incite insurrections. Developing a point that came to dominate white thinking in the South, Dew said that slave rebels did not originate out of a desire to be free. Instead, only "demented fanatics," spurred on by outside forces such as David Walker or William Lloyd Garrison, attacked their masters and yearned for liberty.[79] Like tricked children, insurrectionists did not realize what they did or how their actions might negatively affect their families. Dew advised that whites view uprisings by the enslaved as emotional outbursts rather than a rational attempt at winning freedom. They were mental miscalculations by an unsophisticated group of people unequipped to make decisions of their own. Black people, the white Virginian insisted, needed to be guided by masters who knew what was best for them.

Dew warned white America, both North and South, against supporting any movement that circumvented the power of the plantation class. The Virginian professed that all antislavery proponents promoted violence. He believed that "the great evil, however, of these schemes of emancipation, remains yet to be told. They are admirably calculated to excite plots, murders, and insurrections; whether gradual or rapid in case, you disturb the quiet and contentment of the slave who is left unemancipated." Whites and blacks could not live freely together. In freedom, Dew asserted, a large black population had no ability to take care of themselves; the "worthlessness and degradation" of the enslaved, he predicated, "will stimulate him to deeds of rapine and vengeance."[80] The proslavery movement protected the enslaved from their own barbaric nature, which, in turn, also kept the white, nonslaveholding population safe.

Review of the Debates of the Virginia Legislature deeply shaped how slaveholders approached politics. When talking about western Virginians supporting legislation for colonization or gradual emancipation, Dew wrote, "The fact is, it is always a most delicate and dangerous task for one set of people to legislate for another, without any community of interests." He urged readers to realize that all whites, not only slaveholders and not merely southerners, might suffer terribly from universal emancipation, writing, "Let [Virginia] liberate her slaves, and every year you would hear of insurrections and plots, and every day would perhaps record a murder." The professor asked rhetorically: "If a convention of the whole state of Virginia were called, and in due form the right of slave property were abolished by the votes of Western Virginia alone, does anyone think that Eastern Virginia would be bound to yield the decree?"[81] During the next decade, proslavery politicians from across the nation clung to that notion as conversations about the future of slavery moved from state legislatures to the U.S. Capitol.

Dew contextualized his argument by talking about different places where emancipation had already occurred. Pointing to Central and South America, he quoted a passage from Henry Dunn's *Sketches of Guatemala,* writing "Colombia and Guatemala have tried the dangerous experiment of emancipation, and we invite the attention of the reader to the following dismal picture. . . . 'With Lazaroni in rags and filth, a *colored population drunken and revengeful,* her females licentious and her males shameless, she *ranks as a true child* of that *accursed city. . . . Not a day passes without murder.*'" The historian continued: "From the day of the arrival of the negro slaves upon our coast in the Dutch vessel, up to the present time, a period of more than two hundred years, there have not perished in the whole southern country by the hands of slaves, a number of whites equal to the average annual stabbings in the city of Guatemala." Without diligence the South could turn into Dunn's proslavery version of *Paradise Lost,* ending the exceptional nature of the United States.[82]

Review of the Debates of the Virginia Legislature painted a picture of despair and also described the Haitian Revolution and the Amis des Noirs as the prime example of the dangers of abolitionism. Dew argued that the antislavery movement promoted insurrection in the Caribbean by giving nonwhites "the same privileges and immunities as whites" and created a "strangely inharmonious" white community that could not rally to squash a potential black revolt in its infancy. Whites, regardless of where they lived, had to stick together. Holding black people in slavery was not hazardous, he instructed. However, if spurred on by "fanatics" such as David Walker, the enslaved might rebel, forcing the American military—filled with northern soldiers—to engage in a race war to quell a violent upheaval.[83]

The fear among southerners that an outside force might induce a slave uprising was real. In 1833, Virginia's governor received a note from a concerned citizen expressing uneasiness over the state's security. The letter discussed a "suspicious charlatan who is endeavoring to cause the slaves to rebel and make insurrection." According to the message, a stranger arrived with two other men and had with him "a large box supposed from the best evidence I can get to weigh from four to five hundred pounds and thought by the citizens at the closest house to contain arms. He was seen in the company of nine to ten slaves and heard by white persons to say if you will only be true you can get free."[84]

According to the correspondence, action had already been taken: "The slaves have been apprehended and brought before me." The letter writer explained that the suspected insurrectionists "state that he gave them money, treated them, and told them he had plenty of arms." The white rebel leader allegedly claimed that "he had got the negroes from Prince William County to join him and many others by some means got alarmed and immediately fled to Alexandria." The note ended with an ominous postscript: "We have no arms to defend ourselves." Nero's "Chief" did not seem distant. Although no uprising occurred, southern anxiety led to a distrust of strangers and became a key component to how southerners believed a proslavery society could be maintained. Planters labeled abolitionism as un-American and used the suspicion of outsiders to validate their power among white nonslaveholders.[85]

During the 1820s and 1830s, proslavery attempts at isolating the ideas of universal freedom and black rebellion after the Haitian Revolution seemed to have failed. Denmark Vesey allegedly cited Haiti as an ally in his upcoming war for freedom. Furthermore, David Walker's circular displayed to planters that the message of abolitionism could not be choked off completely from reaching the slave South. While Walker offered a global plea to nonwhites, his pamphlet and its distribution were entirely American undertakings. The abolitionist did not ask for a foreign entity to attack the South from the outside. Instead, he promoted undermining American slavery by toppling the slave system from within and prayed for an American version of Toussaint to rise up from the enslaved population or from the North's free black community. *An Appeal to the Coloured Citizens of the World* did not urge those under the toil of slavery to wait for Haiti, France, or even England to offer them emancipation—it called for African Americans to free themselves through violence. Qualms about a massive black rebellion being fostered by foreigners conjoined with Walker's message to unnerve slaveholders throughout the United States.

David Walker successfully relied on two vital American systems of communication to distribute his writing: sailors traveling southward and the Post Office, which had the ability to send a package nearly anywhere in the country.

Unlike the secretive outside agents, real or imagined, that southerners blamed for infiltrating their slave population and causing problems, Walker brazenly attacked slavery and openly cried for insurrection. He ensured that the packages mailed to the South clearly listed a return address, wanting the planter elite to know exactly who sent them. The black abolitionist assumed that at least some privileges granted in the Bill of Rights pertained to him, and he made use of his liberty to condemn the injustice of southerners who found his message intolerable. Despite sharing the proslavery distaste for Walker's pamphlet, Boston's mayor refused to be cowed by southern pressure and rejected the pleas of planters to censor the abolitionist. The tradition of free speech and federalism in the United States protected Walker's message from congressional intrusion and left slaveholders in Washington powerless to silence him. The refusal of Harrison Gray Otis to punish a free black author who challenged slaveholders showed southerners where the limits of the northern defense of their peculiar institution existed.

As slaveholders looked northward, they saw their once-trusted allies growing apart from them and their peculiar institution. In response to escalating antislavery sentiment among southern nonslaveholders after Turner's revolt, Thomas Roderick Dew articulated what became a foundational and piquant argument for the proslavery movement for subsequent decades. In short, black Americans had better lives as slaves and would never develop an insurrectionary impulse without the influence of outside abolitionists. Simultaneously, however, slavery also kept nonslaveholding whites safe from a population that would revert to a form of barbarism if universal emancipation occurred. Dew transformed the intellectual defense of black enslavement from one that begged for tolerance to an argument involving the security and future prosperity of white people, regardless of whether they owned slaves. Only in perpetuating the status quo against the antislavery movement could both whites and blacks live together in peace. In 1833, reports trickled into American newspapers from London that England was preparing to end slavery in the West. Enslavers readied themselves to fight the rising tide of universal liberty. As proslavery leaders thought about the future of slavery in the United States, they shifted their stance toward the purpose of the federal government and the Union.

3

ATLANTIC ABOLITIONISM AND AMERICAN EXCEPTIONALISM

You cannot depend upon the North for any guaranty she gives you. She may stipulate and promise, and make Constitutions, but so far as slavery in concerned, she will observe none of these.

—Henry L. Benning's Secessionist Speech, Georgia, November 19, 1860

The bulletin screamed across front pages all over the South: "HIGHLY IMPORTANT TO THE WEST INDIES." The end of slavery in the British Caribbean appeared to be approaching—quickly. Quoting an article from the *London Globe,* southern newspapers, in both Virginia and South Carolina, explained that freedom for the enslaved held in the English colonies was imminent. Both the *Richmond Enquirer* and the *Southern Patriot* reported that, in response to the rumors of emancipation, "a deputation of gentlemen connected with the West Indies" had visited leaders in Parliament and "requested to be informed whether it was true that it was the intention of the government to emancipate the slave population."[1] Slaveholders throughout the Atlantic waited to hear whether or not the speculation was true.

The answer given by leaders in Parliament "was in the affirmative," southern newspapers later reported. Publications throughout the United States disseminated the debate in the Palace of Westminster. American antislavery and proslavery groups understood the considerable ramifications of England ending slavery in its Caribbean holdings. Some cited sources from Liverpool, others from London. Everyone eagerly awaited official word from the Crown. American planters immediately suspected the British were developing plans for the emancipation of southern slave societies, as well. They perceived a powerful enemy being emboldened merely a few hundred miles away. Slaveholders also read that, to keep the peace, "an imposing force, composing of 15,000 men, would forthwith be sent to the West Indies."[2] Parliament presumed violent upheaval to coincide with the implementation of emancipation.

American planters also expected unrest in the West Indies. Their defense of slavery declared that insurrection automatically accompanied black freedom. Southern alarmists predicted a repeat of the violence seen during the Haitian Revolution. In June 1833, the *Richmond Enquirer* reported, "The scheme appears to us to be wofully [*sic*] harsh" and would be "ruinous in its consequences." The newspaper worried that "even our own shores may not altogether escape the hurricane."[3] Similar to their predecessors at the turn of the century, leaders in the slave states prepared for problems as another slaveholding regime in the West Indies crumbled into obscurity.

As slavery in the Caribbean came under fire in the House of Commons, American planters adopted the arguments initially developed by their West Indian counterparts and later honed by Thomas Dew: slavery had a positive influence on society generally and on the black people in particular. British abolition forced proslavery intellectuals to stride more boldly with their claims that the South's peculiar institution contributed favorably to the advancement of mankind. Like Virginia's deliberation of gradual emancipation after Turner's uprising in Southampton, an insurrection had led to a change in Parliament's support of slavery in the Caribbean. The seemingly sudden change in English public opinion startled many slaveholders in the United States and added to the fear that a revolt by the enslaved could be used as a political weapon. In response, planters attempted to popularize their cherished system of enslaved labor by turning to proslavery journals, just as Dew had in the Old Dominion a few years earlier.[4]

During the summer months of 1833, when emancipation in the British West Indies became evident, proslavery intellectuals aimed at two targets to condemn: Great Britain in general and the ideology of free labor manufacturing. In August, with the termination of slavery in the British Caribbean flooding American media, a series of articles entitled "Poor Laws and Domestic Slavery" appeared in the *Charleston Mercury,* one of John C. Calhoun's media organs and a preeminent outlet for proslavery ideas. The publication's guest editorialist, choosing the pseudonym "Pliny," compared the lives of the laboring class in England and the enslaved of the British West Indies to the treatment of black Americans held captive throughout the South. The author argued for a slaveholding version of American exceptionalism.[5]

To portray southern slaveholding as more sophisticated than free labor, the proslavery editorialist assumed the name of a Roman philosopher and offered a compassionate tone as he defended slavery and criticized England. Pliny began his series by stating, "To advance the condition of the labouring classes in comfort and security from misfortune, would be the most important improvement in human affairs." With that in mind, he asked readers to consider the lives of the working poor in London while Parliament discussed ending slavery in the Caribbean. The state of the working class, the South Carolinian contended, displayed the hypocrisy of British abolitionism. The "fanatics" did almost nothing to help white Britons living in poverty and instead devoted their energy to black emancipation half a world away. England, he contended, should examine its own shortcomings before meddling with affairs in the New World. Building on Thomas Roderick Dew's argument, Pliny argued that, despite their lack of freedom, the enslaved of the South were materially better off than the poorest of England. He took exception to abolitionist contentions that planters treated slaves like cattle, writing that although they had "no political privilege," African Americans were given "civil and moral rights."[6] Slaveholders treated those they held in chains humanely, he insisted, unlike mill and factory owners in England.

Abolitionists hardly felt compassion for the underclass in either England or the Caribbean, the proslavery editorialist claimed. Whereas the British West Indies required a steady importation of new slaves to maintain the size of its unfree labor system, American planters, on the other hand, watched its black populace increase naturally. "This fact," the South Carolinian maintained, "speaks volume in favor of the comfort of our negro population."[7] American masters took care of the people they held in chains, unlike the brutal British industrialist. Although southerners in several parts of the slave South fretted over the mounting number of people held in bondage, defenders of slavery used the population growth of the enslaved as proof of planter humanitarianism. Despite their association with the plantation owners of the West Indies, southerners resolutely held to the notion that slavery in the United States differed substantially from the one coming to an end in the Caribbean. The way of holding people in slavery in the United States was exceptional in comparison to the rest of the world.

Pliny's final article discussed Haiti. He reasoned that without the white planter class to guide them, the enslaved became "lost" to France. The "mistaken zeal" of the antislavery movement's fanatical belief that if slavery "were abolished, all evil would be redressed, and society stand forth regenerated and perfect," the proslavery author argued, had instead cultivated chaos in what used to be the world's richest colony. The South Carolinian blamed "fanatics" who did not understand the ramifications of their actions for causing trouble in both the Caribbean and the South.[8] Blinded by an emotional desire to free the enslaved, they neglected to examine the risks of emancipation in a rational way. Abolitionists, he explained, needed to understand that God had cursed black people dating back to Noah's flood; their natural state included enslavement where the white masters could tend to them, keep them safe, and help them progress toward civilization. By enacting emancipation the English had set back civilization.

Other southerners joined Pliny in worrying about the destabilizing effects of abolition in the West Indies. In 1829, Hugh Swinton Legaré contemplated the possibility of a Haitian-style insurrection occurring in the United States. American chargé d'affaires to Belgium, the young South Carolinian wrote that whites in the slave states perceived "no uneasiness at all about the event of any servile war, unless it be complicated with some other kind of war." Only outside pressure could prompt unrest. He continued: "If our Northern friends will have the goodness to abstain . . . from propagating the impracticable and dangerous doctrines about universal emancipation and equality of rights," slavery could continue to be a safe and secure institution. "Let [the slave's] conspiracy be unaided by foreign power, and it will be easily suppressed," he wrote.[9] Slavery might be dangerous, but it could only become fatal if unchecked white fanatics aided black insurrectionists in a violent struggle for freedom. The calm sense of security all changed with the number of possible friends to enslaved Americans increasing in the Caribbean.

Emancipation in the British West Indies caused proslavery paranoia to become contagious in the United States and changed how many planters viewed the world. Unlike the nullifiers of the 1820s, who seemed to turn every political conversation into one concerning slavery, Legaré was acknowledged as a rising unionist from South Carolina. The success of British abolitionism led him to reconsider his belief about the security of holding slaves. As he assessed the implications of British emancipation an uneasiness settled over him. "Added to St. Domingo," the chargé d'affaires to Belgium wrote to another emerging player in South Carolina politics, British emancipation "will present you, at the mouth of the Mississippi, a *black* population of some 2,000,000, free from all restraint and ready for any mischief."[10] Denmark Vesey, he remembered, had planned to partner with Haiti. The number of southern sympathizers seemed to be shrinking while possible partners in supplying aid to an American insurrection appeared to be multiplying.

Many southerners who examined the West Indian islands believed that demographics shaped the control of the plantation owners in the colonies and noted how the slaveholding world was changing. Several notable southerners agreed with Legaré and judged the sizable black population as a threat to the United States. The *Columbus (Ga) Enquirer* remarked that the "blacks are to the white in the proportion to 11 to 1" in the British Caribbean. In 1800, slavery not only existed but also continued its territorial expansion to the planters' east, west, and south as it became more and more profitable. The institution had existed above the Mason-Dixon Line before abolitionism gained a foothold in the North. In the span of one generation—the first after the American Revolution—the South appeared to be nearly surrounded by free soil in a geopolitical climate moving toward universal freedom. Slaveholders looked at a map and detected their area of influence shrinking: to the north by free soil and a flourishing abolitionist movement, and to the east and south by freed blacks, suddenly empowered by a nation with which the United States had already fought two wars. The community of slaveholders had significantly dwindled while, simultaneously, the opponents of slavery grew stronger and became more open in attacking the enslavement of black people worldwide. Fealty towards King Cotton from the free states became imperative to slaveholders in light of emancipation in the British West Indies, especially in regards to supplying military and diplomatic protection, or stifling the antislavery movement.[11]

Once again, southerners feared an invasion of their society from outside forces. Planters worried that the success of the antislavery movement in Great Britain might energize abolitionism in the United States. One wealthy planter summed up the problem for slaveholders, "The great Slave question has started in England, if realized will transfer a great bearing on the United States: of course the whole evil will fall on the Southern section."[12] Southerners did not consider themselves isolated from what happened in the West Indies or England. David Walker's *Appeal* had revealed to the planter elite that ideas could spread like wildfire across the ocean, affecting American culture and eroding support for the South's peculiar institution, and they worked to stop the message of freedom from influencing the slave states.

In September 1833—shortly following British leaders' formally announcing the end of slavery in the West Indian colonies—the *Charleston Mercury* reprinted a portion of articles originally written in 1827 by Robert Turnbull, a man one historian has labeled "the archradical of the lowlands." Due to his staunch approval of nullification and his participation on the seven-man panel that tried Denmark Vesey, Turnbull became a star in the radical proslavery movement. Since its original publication, Turnbull had expanded his writing into a pamphlet entitled "The Crisis," tying his own ideas to those of Thomas Paine during the American Revolution. To the planter elite shaken by the success of the antislavery movement in England, his words seemed prophetic.

Six years before emancipation in the British West Indies, the polemicist had pointed to William Wilberforce's efforts at ending the slave trade and warned that abolitionists would never be satisfied until enslavement in the colonies was ended entirely. The leader of the antislavery movement in England, Turnbull wrote, "avowed that their sole object was *abolition* of the *trade,* and no more."

However, that changed once Wilberforce accomplished his goal. "Now in the fulness [*sic*] of time," the proslavery writer noted, "he openly advocates a general emancipation." The opponents of slavery had a plan of action to rid the world of slavery. Abolitionists felt no desire to temper the institution of bondage, or make it more humane; they aimed at ending it at all cost. In response, the South Carolinian challenged the proslavery movement to create a counterargument that defended the South's peculiar institution. He sensed a slaveholding crisis occurring in the United States as the Atlantic world embraced the ideas of universal freedom and he begged his fellow slaveholders to prepare for a fight.[13]

When Turnbull originally crafted his argument in 1827, he wrote, "The minority in the British Parliament was at first trifling. I doubt if there were even twenty or ten in both Houses of Parliament who were for emancipation. But yet the West Indies are hastening, with a very quick step, towards complete ruin." After the passage of the Abolition Act in London, his next statement seemed more prescient and meaningful to slave owners: "And so will South-Carolina assuredly be ruined, if at this day, there are twenty men in Congress, who are for emancipation, sudden or gradual, and the right of Congress to take even a vote, is not RESISTED as an ACT OF WAR by South-Carolina." Turnbull asked fellow planters whether they wanted to be "like the weak, the dependent, and unfortunate colonists of the West-Indies" or be willing to loudly object to antislavery action in Washington. The proslavery radical meant to sound a clarion call. Six years later, the proslavery gentry seemed to be finally hearing it. Upon republishing Turnbull's work, the editor of the *Mercury* noted: "Let every Southern man remember that like causes will produce like effects." Abolitionism appeared to be on the march; the newspaper implored every southerner to take notice.[14]

The discussion of British emancipation stoked the smoldering fires lit a few years earlier during the nullification crisis, when President Jackson defeated a small, but loud, corps of radical South Carolinians who argued that state legislatures could void federal laws. Henry Clay, the Kentuckian who—along with President Monroe—facilitated the Missouri Compromise, saw old wounds reopening as southerners discussed news from England. He told James Madison, "The political malcontents in the South seem to have adopted a new theme to excite alarm and to disseminate Unfriendly to the Union." The Sage of Ashland worried that emancipation in the West Indies "may give some aid to the efforts" of the defeated nullifiers, boosting their prestige and culminating in another controversy.[15] The former speaker of the House presumed the proslavery movement might find it easier to rally against England than the popular Old Hickory residing in the executive's mansion.

Clay's instincts soon proved correct. In response to British emancipation of the Caribbean, ideas regarding American exceptionalism and the purpose of the nation's unique form of government, which initially came into the public conversation during the nullification crisis, resurfaced to the forefront of political conversation in the South. Two media outlets typified the diverging sides: the *Richmond Enquirer,* edited by unionist Thomas Ritchie, and the *Charleston Mercury,* which built on Turnbull's concepts by arguing that the unique nature of the Union rested wholly on its ability to protect slavery. Throughout 1835, proslavery southerners divided on how best to perpetuate the practice of black enslavement in a world rapidly growing more amenable to universal liberty. The conversation between the two newspapers illustrated how the slave states shared varied expectations about the future of the nation's expanding democracy and the purpose of federal authority.

By the 1830s, Thomas Ritchie had become one of Virginia's leading journalists. Having purchased the *Richmond Enquirer* in 1803, a period in which journalists often wound up dead in Virginia's rugged capital, he quickly turned it into a financial success, making it a must read for those living in the Old Dominion. Thomas Jefferson once quipped, "I read but a single newspaper, Ritchie's Enquirer, the best that is published or ever has been published in America."[16] The *Enquirer* had covered insurrection scares before and remembered the dangerous and violent panic that struck Virginia's white population following Turner's rebellion. Ritchie recalled the savagery unleashed in its aftermath—a frightened mob could do ghastly things.

Throughout the 1820s the veteran newspaperman strongly advocated for slavery's expansion. Proving his proslavery credentials in a region increasingly becoming more hostile to abolitionism, Ritchie criticized the Missouri Compromise, arguing slaveholders conceded too much in the deal. He also noted the abandonment of black enslavement by nonslaveholders during the debate to end slavery in the Old Dominion's legislature. Despite those events, the journalist still insisted that slavery in Virginia remained secure from both violent uprisings concocted by the enslaved and the antislavery impulse coming from the North and across the Atlantic. The *Richmond Enquirer* remained steadfast in its belief that the Constitution still fortified slavery against an antislavery movement growing in power, even as British emancipation became finalized.

Thomas Ritchie encouraged moderation in southern attacks on the antislavery movement and asked his proslavery readers to remain confident in the United States system of government and the Union—the source of American exceptionalism.[17]

Ritchie insisted that the South differed greatly from the West Indies and suspected predictions of southern calamity to be overwrought. On the cusp of Caribbean freedom, he published a story with the headline, "ENGLISH EMANCIPATION." The article, parts of which were borrowed from other newspapers, argued that the Founding Fathers forged a democratic government different from the one in Westminster. The British Parliament possessed "a power in the dearest points, over the lives and fortunes of thousands, when those who are most affected by their measures are unable to regulate or control them."[18] In other words, West Indian planters had no real representation in the British democracy. Most of the members of Parliament experienced minimal contact with slaveholders while, at the same time, they often spoke with the antislavery movement based in England. American plantation owners, however, lived under a more representative form of government. The Constitution allowed for the United States to be different from other countries because slaveholders had a direct say over the power and authority in national affairs.

The *Enquirer* contended that the United States had purposely been constructed differently. The Constitution, Ritchie wrote, produced "an inherent and insoluble difficulty in the legislation concerning slave-holders and their property, by those who are not only not slave-holders themselves, but cannot be made to comprehend the nature of that relation." The discussion of slavery, the Virginian explained, was "left so exclusively to the legislation of the several States, that the Congress of all the States cannot touch [slavery] without a palpable usurpation" of constitutional restrictions. "The silence" about the South's peculiar institution left by the Founders stemmed from a "most wise" decision to put slaveholders in charge of their own destiny.[19] This allowed for American slavery to be unlike that of England, where people who had never seen a slave decided the future of the planter class in the West Indies. With northern allegiance to that principle, slavery would be safe and abolitionism scorned, Ritchie said. He assured readers that Americans eschewed radicalism and that the antislavery movement, as with the nullifiers, would gain only a limited amount of traction in popular culture. Citizens of the United States valued the Union more than both the proslavery and the antislavery movements. The public admonished disunionists of all stripes as traitors to the American Revolution and the purpose of the federal government.

After the passage of the Abolition Act by Great Britain, the *Enquirer* published a statement signed by "A Pennsylvanian" that contrasted the deliberations in England about slavery's future with the one being held in the United States. The writer stated, "The Anti-Slavery People, Tappan, Garrison, and Co. will find more difficulty in creating an excitement in the middle and Northern States for immediate abolition, than they did in England." The northerner continued: "In that country, the position of the various parties gave a fatal facility to combinations in Parliament favorable to the measure. The fanatics, the whigs, the liberals all found it their interest to unite against the West Indian proprietors; the latter could only count on the tories."[20] The lack of approval from nonslaveholders a thousand miles away doomed the plantation owners in the British West Indies. Things differed in America; slaveholders shared a government filled with checks and balances of power while having fewer political liabilities than their Caribbean counterparts.

Like the letter writer whose note he publicized, Ritchie contended that the uniqueness of the American system inherently permitted southern slavery to be distinct from the rest of the slaveholding world. America's exceptional form of government, he explained, shielded slavery in the United States from abolition and insurrection. Northerners like "A Pennsylvanian" would stand with the southern gentry to resist the rising antislavery movement in the free states. The writer finished by discussing the distinguishing nature of the United States. He wrote, "In this country, the state of the political elements is altogether different [than England]. The southern States have an independent existence in Congress, besides having their rights expressly secured to them by the Constitution. The coalition of parties at the North is peculiarly hostile to any agitation of the slavery question. No tears, therefore, can grow out of the insane efforts of the agitators."[21] The Constitution balanced regional interests rather than ideological factions. Free staters, he maintained, would always love the Union more than they hated slavery. They believed the former made the United States the most remarkable nation in the world.

Despite Ritchie's persistence in defending the Union, many in the proslavery movement remained unconvinced by his confidence about the future. As the *Enquirer* centered squarely on the exceptional qualities of the American system of government, Calhounites, spearheaded by the *Charleston Mercury,* drew on concepts developed during the nullification controversy. The proslavery publication expanded its radical understanding of American federalism and what should be done to shelter slavery from the winds of change. For Ritchie, the Constitution served as a fair rulebook that forced partisans to get along. The *Mercury,* however, contended that the constitutional rules only acted as an honest broker if they remained enforceable and unchanging—something the paper found unlikely.

During the mid-1830s, in an extraordinary transition from their earlier arguments based upon states' rights, the proslavery movement claimed that the founding documents did not have the capability to protect slaveholders from a persistent majority in favor of the abolition. In response, the eager custodians of proslavery ideas decided to promote the active national defense of black enslavement in Congress, giving little concern to the notion that they were adding credibility to federal involvement with the South's system of unfree labor. The *Charleston Mercury* became one of the first publications to advance the notion that the Constitution needed to be more than just a set of guidelines that balanced northern and southern interests. The periodical maintained that slaveholders required Washington to actively support and promote the enslavement of millions of African Americans. Anything less, the newspaper intimated, allowed the antislavery movement to incite black rebellion that threatened the southern white population.

The *Mercury* challenged Thomas Ritchie by publishing an article from one of the *Enquirer*'s rival newspapers. Entitled, "SLAVERY—WEST INDIES: State Rights," the write-up read, "True, [Ritchie] may say that Virginia has representatives in Congress, which the West India Planters have not in Parliament—but what that?" For much of the proslavery movement, representation hardly provided a reassurance of slavery's perpetuation in the United States. Without sway of both chambers, proslavery members of Congress could not "control those persons who can control their lives and fortunes." Instead, the *Mercury* contended, southern "voices are merged in the clamors of the majority. They are neither heard nor felt."[22] The majority, the planter elite of the Deep South believed, always had the ability to crush the minority. It was only in commandeering the federal government, by establishing proslavery prevalence in Congress, that slaveholders could find safety for the future.

According to the editor of the *Charleston Mercury,* and those who contributed to its ideas, the Constitution of the United States did not provide a unique legal system for an exceptional nation. The Founding Fathers, they asserted, had not constructed a government that greatly contrasted with the English model that ended slavery. The proslavery author proposed a hypothetical: "Suppose the Federal Government, should do as the British Parliament has done, and bring out its scheme of Emancipation?" The editorialist then mocked the *Enquirer's* defense of unity and equality between the states:

> What is Virginia to do?—"Remonstrate," says Mr. Ritchie. What next? "Protest," says Mr. Ritchie. What Next?—"Rush to revolution," says Mr. Ritchie.—What next? "Be hanged like dogs," says A. Jackson, Esquire. And pray, may not the W. India Planters do these very things?

Nullification created a lasting effect on much of the slaveholding elite, but British emancipation transformed planter intellectuals. Prominent defenders of slavery no longer saw a weak national government as being the key to slavery's perpetuation. For these strident defenders of slavery, the South required more than the Constitution and its abstract protections. Rather, the master class insisted on their ability to use the authority of the federal government against abolitionism, both in the North and throughout the Atlantic.[23]

In light of English emancipation, many proslavery radicals argued that Andrew Jackson had spoiled the Constitution during the nullification controversy. The columnist in the *Mercury* contended that "the Jackson Van Buren Party," deserting "the principles of the Constitution," had caused the United States to abandon its republican ideals and embrace a world ruled by kings and tyrants—or worse, the mob. "The doctrines of these men," the South Carolinian wrote, "are of the very essence of monarchy, and must speedily reduce the States to the abject condition of the West India Colonies, unless their progress be arrested."[24] The only option left for the planter elite was to claim the crown of the national government and use its authority to smother their opposition.

After 1831, more proslavery radicals adopted the idea that the Constitution and the Bill of Rights did not preserve southern slavery. Following the Southampton revolt, Virginia governor John Floyd discussed his frustrations about states' rights in his diary: "We are gravely told there is no law to punish" abolitionists such as William Lloyd Garrison, who "express intention of inciting the slaves and free negroes in this and other States to rebellion and to murder the men, women and children" of the South.[25] Merely two years later, what Floyd had written privately became a foundational part of the mainstream proslavery argument. Old Hickory proved the Constitution to be more flexible than southern Unionists cared to admit. Without taking action in the nation's capital, slaveholders would be doomed to follow their Caribbean counterparts into obscurity.

Unlike Ritchie, who put faith in the anti-abolitionist rhetoric coming from above the Mason-Dixon Line, several radical proslavery intellectuals asserted that northerners spoke in a coded language. Worked-up slaveholders offered high-pitched claims about "fanatical" conspiracies, branding antislavery northerners as confidence men who masked evil intentions with idealism. As the sole translators of the coded language, zealous planters could take anything said, or unsaid, by northerners and turn it into evidence that they supported black rebellion. The belief in coded language operated as a device used by slave owners to win acceptance from nonslaveholders. It enabled them to turn northerners into ideologically driven monsters who could be dismissed as unreasonable. As these ideas became popularized, distrust of the North escalated in the slave states. The paranoid contention by proslavery elites that coded language existed allowed enslavers to tighten their grip over the politics of the Deep South.

The *Mercury* treated the North as a foreign entity that needed to be infiltrated to gain information about the antislavery movement. In the opinions of the most ardent members of the proslavery movement, organized abolitionism and the northern population at large had become synonymous. They could not be detached from each other. In the summer of 1833, the newspaper published a letter from "A Spy in New York" that read like an intelligence briefing. British emancipation had boosted the morale of the antislavery movement, he stated. "The Gladiators are in extasies [*sic*] at the latest news from England, viz: that all the slaves will be let loose on the Kings birth day. They have an idea that emancipation of the slaves in the West Indies will have a very great influence on the south." The spy claimed "fanatical rascals" were "continually at work, with a zeal worthy of a better cause" and explained that members of the American Colonization Society lied to southerners when they tried to raise funds. The ACS told northerners that emancipation served as their chief goal. However, "when the agents of the society are begging for money in the slaveholding States, their tone is changed: then they beg money to carry off the *free* negroes who are contaminating the slaves with notions of liberty."[26] The reporter reminded southerners to stay alert—fanatical abolitionists might say anything to get their way and to seem less dangerous.

The Charleston publication also reprinted an article from the *New York Commercial Advertiser* written by "An Anti-slavery Citizen." The northerner defended immediate emancipation, but also stated that it could not be forced on southerners. He argued that slavery should be debated as a social issue instead of as a civil one, writing, "As political men then anti-slavery men must be quiet." The opponents of slavery were not a monolithic group. The large majority of them, he maintained, did not want to set "the slave free to roam without restraint, to live in idleness; to butcher the whites, and to be lawless." Many in the North accepted the premise that a freed black population compromised the safety of all whites. Moreover, this northern proponent of abolitionism still presumed that southerners alone should shape the future of slavery, telling slaveholders that they could still expect free staters, even some who supported antislavery ideals, to promote local authority over the slave system and work to keep it secure from insurrection.[27]

Explaining why they had republished an article written by a member of the antislavery movement, the editors of the *Mercury* wrote, "We give place to the following communication as a temperate and well expressed article upon the subject which it treats; and are fully confident that our correspondent is sincere in his aim to act upon the consciences and hearts of slaveholders *only,* and not interfere with the political compact between the States." However, northern sincerity held little sway over the southern gentry. The Charleston newspaper continued with a question: "By what process then are their mouths to be opened in such a manner as that the principles they utter shall be divested of their political effect?" If all of free speech were to be protected under the Constitution, the effect of abolitionism on northern culture could not be divorced from its influence on northern politics. Slaveholding leaders in South Carolina determined that as long as proponents of the antislavery movement shared their message freely in public, the "fanaticism" they preached would continue to threaten to southern society. Abolitionists became more than an ideological adversary; they became the domestic enemies of the planter elite, ones who peddled foreign ideas to undermine the United States and the Union that preserved proslavery American exceptionalism.[28]

Two years later, the planter class insisted that federally protected speech could not be consistent with a secure slave system. During the last week of July 1835, filled with passengers and parcel, the *Columbia* glided down the East Coast from New York until it finally slipped into its destination in Charleston Harbor.

Those in the city who expected to receive news from across the Atlantic were disappointed. The *Southern Patriot* disclosed that the ship's cargo "had no further intelligence from Europe, and that the papers are commonly barren in information of any novelty or importance." However, what the *Columbia* did haul southward became a flashpoint of controversy. The steamship, the Charleston periodical reported, had not been "merely laden, but literally overburthened, with the Newspaper 'The Emancipator' and two Tracts entitled 'The Anti-Slavery Record,' and 'The Slave's Friend," destined for circulation all over the Southern and Western Country."[29] Proslavery commentators predicted trouble.

Hoping to convince southerners to give up slavery, and with the help of wealthy donors, William Lloyd Garrison raised thirty thousand dollars for mailing antislavery tracts to white southerners. During the summer of 1835, abolitionists mailed over 170,000 antislavery tracts to addresses found in city directories and newspapers. The number equaled the entire output of southern publications. The *Columbia* carried one of the initial mailbags filled with antislavery messages to the South. Hoping to draw attention to the story, the *Southern Patriot* decried Garrison's actions immediately with the headline "INCENDIARY TRACTS AND PAPERS," labeling his campaign a "monstrous abuse of the privilege of the public mail" and the antislavery writings a "moral poison." The publication insisted, "Some mode of prevention should be adopted to abate this nuisance" and claimed if nothing legally could be done by the postal service, angry members of the proslavery movement would make it "impossible to answer for the security of the Mail in this part of the country, which contains such poisonous and inflammatory matter."[30]

Most Charlestonians looked to their postmaster to decide the fate of the unsolicited pamphlets. An alumnus of Princeton University, Alfred Huger originally planned to practice law until he abandoned jurisprudence to become a planter. He was a unionist during the nullification crisis, and President Jackson rewarded his loyalty with a position at the Post Office in 1835. The arrival of the *Columbia* found him facing a decision he had no desire to make. Instead, Huger sent word to Washington and waited for a reply. The postmaster in South Carolina had no protocol regarding unsolicited mail, especially correspondence that might engender unrest among the oppressed slave population. He waited, hoping for guidance that might relieve him from making a decision.[31]

Others in the city, however, did not stand by for an official strategy from Jackson's White House. Only a few hours after the *Southern Patriot* broke the news, leading slaveholders in South Carolina devised a plan to take the matter into their own hands. In the darkness of night, members of a proslavery organization named the Lynch Men used a crowbar to break a shutter, open a window, and gain access to the Charleston post office. Once inside they quickly discovered their loot. Earlier, Huger had separated the tracts from the rest of the mail as he awaited word from Postmaster General Amos Kendall on how to treat the unwanted mail. Once in possession of the bag filled with antislavery pamphlets, the burglars departed, leaving the ordinary mail no worse for the wear. Garrison's addressees would not be hearing from him.[32]

The thieves made no attempt to hide their crime. As dusk settled over Charleston the next night, a smell of burning paper filled the air as smoke floated towards the sky on the parade grounds. With the white marble buildings of what later became South Carolina's military academy—the Citadel—standing in the background, angry defenders of slavery lit thousands of the pamphlets ablaze. Others burned effigies of Garrison and his supporters. Hundreds looked on, standing around the bright orange glow as the message of universal freedom turned to ash. The Lynch Men knew no one had the nerve to stop their spectacle, not even Huger. Supporting the cause, the *Southern Patriot* proclaimed, "Extreme cases require extreme remedies." Southerners, the newspaper proclaimed, could not "fold their arms and permit the poison to circulate through all the veins and arteries of society at the South and West." Proslavery leaders meant to send a warning: when the message of emancipation came to the slave states it would be met with force.[33]

The *Charleston Mercury* surprisingly condemned the actions as rash and "premature." Although insisting that "none could blame" those who broke into the post office, the editors argued that slaveholders missed an opportunity. Instead of immediately burning the pamphlets, the abolitionist mailings could have provided a test to see if the federal government would "protect us in our rights." Furthermore, the *Mercury* continued, "We think it would have been better had the pamphlets been allowed to reach their destination, to put the whole Southern community on their guard." Abolitionists gave the proslavery movement a chance to join southern whites together. Unlike the nullification crisis, when South Carolina alone challenged federal authority, the antislavery mailings united much of the South in fear that abolitionism might unravel the security of slavery.[34]

As pamphlets denouncing slavery poured into the South, local politicians urged northern counterparts to pass laws disciplining the antislavery movement. Virginia, for example, asked free-state governments to "make it highly penal to print, publish, or distribute, newspapers, pamphlets, or other publications, calculated or having a tendency to excite the slaves of the southern states to insurrection and revolt." Mississippi's state legislators offered a plan to "suppress, and restrain" inhabitants "from associating, plotting or conspiring to undermine, disturb or abolish our institutions of domestic slavery, in any manner or by any means, and under any pretext whatever" and suggested a prohibition that restrained "writing, speaking, printing or publishing sentiments and opinion, expressive of advice or suggestion to the public or others, calculated in temper and spirit, to induce disaffection among our slaves." Alabama's legislature prayed that such regulations might "finally put an end to the malignant deeds of the abolitionists, calculated to destroy our peace, and sever this Union."[35] Each resolution that southern legislatures promoted acted as a reminder for those who lived in the free states that they had no domain over slavery.

The antislavery mailings seemed to be everywhere in the South. In Tennessee, the *National Banner and Nashville Whig* reported, "In our town the excitement has become great. . . . A handbill of the most insidious and inflammatory nature was last week posted up at the corners, evidencing that the miserable fanatics are moving with concern, and that their plan of operations if wide spread." The *Richmond Whig* gave an account of a steamboat passenger in Kentucky who found a copy of "Human Events" and declared, "One example of a coat of tar and feathers would be more effective than any argument, in cooling the zeal of these incendiaries." In Norfolk, the *Herald* discussed "a bundle of incendiary missiles from the abolitionists' pandemonium in New York" and maintained that, despite antislavery claims otherwise, "20 or 30 copies mailed for this post office, *were directed to free negroes* in the borough and vicinity," thus giving credence in the southern mind that abolitionists intended to foment a rebellion. One of the most popular news magazines in the United States, the *Niles' Weekly Register* also reported, after reprinting a handful of southern complaints, that "many other southern newspapers" had "paragraphs of a similar character." While abolitionists claimed their right to free speech, and indicated plans to continue their attack on slavery, vigilance became the watchword among the planter class.[36]

Garrison's mail campaign provoked white southerners of all stripes to rally in objection to the antislavery movement. Thomas Ritchie's *Enquirer* joined the call for the slave states "to guard, by the severest punishment, against the circulation of such papers from the Post Office," and it argued for regulating the mail. Sticking to its editor's devotion to the Constitution and Union, the *Enquirer* pleaded with northerners to maintain the federal compact by keeping the discussion of slavery outside the scope of Congress and national politics. Only two years earlier, Thomas Ritchie had fought with ardent supporters of slavery over the exceptional nature of America's national government and the purpose of the Revolution. This time, the Virginian gave abolitionists a heavy admonition, "We warn the North again and again—to guard the Union and strip the Fanatics of all power and the Factions of all excuse."[37]

Ritchie also worried that the actions of abolitionists would embolden the more radical wing of the proslavery movement. South Carolinians had already used the mailings to justify an attack on a post office. He fretted that more confrontations might follow, unraveling the authority of the federal government. The Virginian asked his readers to be leery of both the "Fanatics" and the "Factious," the former being abolitionists, the latter being the radical members of the slaveholding elite. In keeping the middle ground, he said that "both are equally worthy of scorn and indignation of every honorable man."[38] Each side, blinded by ideology, he claimed, threatened the very core of America's exceptional nature—the Union. By ignoring the Constitution's silence on the subject of slavery, both camps only offered to sabotage America's democratic experiment.

Despite its large impact on the political conversation about slavery, Ritchie knew the antislavery movement consisted of only a small portion of the northern population. The *Enquirer* cited a publication from Massachusetts as more proof that northerners still supported the South's control over its peculiar institution. The *Boston Atlas* demanded a meeting of city leaders to discuss the abolitionist postal campaign: "Let the Websters, and Otises, and Adamses . . . be invited to attend, to vindicate the fair fame of our city. Let a manifesto go forth declaratory of our sentiments, as to the rights of the South, and of our abhorrence of the conduct of those combinations . . . encouraging the worst of all possible calamities which can befall a nation—A CIVIL AND SERVILE WAR." Other southern members of the press published similar anti-abolitionist outcries from northern publications. The ideas of Bryan Edwards remained relevant in the United States. Northern outlets showed that much of the white population above the Mason-Dixon Line saw abolitionism as a risk to the Union and threat to national security. Moderate southerners assured themselves in

William Lloyd Garrison's inability to change the inherent racial antipathy of northerners. In a zero-sum game of racial antagonism, black slaves would never gain a preference over southern whites in the minds of free-state voters and politicians. So long as northerners rejected the idea of having a large, free black population living in the United States, slavery remained safe.[39]

Many southerners genuinely believed that antislavery tracts fueled black rebellion. Anti-abolitionist meetings sprang to life in the wake of the literature attacking slavery that arrived in South Carolina. The gatherings typically held two intentions: to paint the abolitionists as fanatics who cared very little about the ramifications of their actions and demand an increased presence from the local militia and slave patrol. Both concepts were thought to be essential to mitigating the possibility of slave revolts while "fanatical" pamphlets circulated throughout the southern states.[40] Emancipation would devastate the South, many in the slave states predicted. At one meeting in Georgia, an anti-abolitionist group passed a resolution asking those in attendance to recall the violence experienced by the French planters during the Haitian Revolution, classifying American abolitionists as "bloody Jacobins—worse than the St. Domingo rioters and cutthroats." The Richmond Vigilance Committee, for instance, proclaimed, "There is no means of removing the coloured ones—and the consequences, therefore, of the scheme of the abolitionists, must be the destruction of our race by force, or, what is yet more odious and detestable, by 'amalgamation,' or the merciless extermination of the black." The proslavery movement aimed to change the question. Instead of discussing the legitimacy of slavery in a country that declared "all men are created equal" in its founding document, slaveholders positioned themselves as defending America's white republic and attempted to stigmatize abolitionism, calling on northern allies to join them in ensuring African Americans never obtained equality.[41]

Several leaders in the free states confronted the burgeoning antislavery movement. Only a few years before, Harrison Gray Otis protected David Walker from southern calls to stifle his right to publish and mail *An Appeal to the Coloured Citizens of the World* to the South. Garrison's mail campaign caused the former mayor of Boston to change his mind. He came to view the radical opponents to the enslavement of millions of Americans as a threat to the United States. At the famous Faneuil Hall in the summer of 1835, Otis classified antislavery societies popping up throughout the North as "imminently dangerous" and "hostile to the spirit and letter of the constitution of the union." Perceiving these new groups as a revolutionary force that threatened to disrupt the stability of the nation, he argued the claim that the mailings "are for the master and not for the slave" was "a pretext" that insulted common sense.[42]

The legendary leader of New England Federalism titled his speech "Abolitionism Is Equal to Revolution" and concluded: "They may as well believe that they can set all the bells in Richmond ringing so as to arouse and alarm the white inhabitants, and affect the slaves only as a tinkling lullaby to soothe them to repose."[43] Individuals such as David Walker could write pamphlets and use their money to launch broadsides against the South, he surmised, but organizations gathering money for the large-scale promotion of universal emancipation differed from the black abolitionist's work entirely. Size and scale mattered—the abolitionist postal campaign threatened the status quo and the stability of both the Constitution and the Union it created.

Many allies of slavery responded to the calls issued from the South to challenge abolitionism in the free states. Upon receiving a request from Alfred Huger for help, the son-in-law of James Monroe and postmaster of New York, Samuel Gouverneur, asked Arthur Tappan, the president of the American Anti-Slavery Society, to suspend the mailings "until the views of the postmaster general be received." Tappan declined. In response, Gouverneur refused to send the mail anyway. When the American Anti-Slavery Society changed the sending point and mode of transportation for their pamphlets in August 1835, dockworkers in Philadelphia found and confiscated thousands of "incendiary pamphlets," which they deemed "calculated to excite and inflame the mind of the slave,—and to poison his already embittered feelings against his master." After consulting the southern "gentleman to whom the aforesaid box was directed" and hearing that he "had no such knowledge" of the package being sent him, officials in the City of Brotherly Love declared the writings to be "torn to ten thousand pieces and scattered upon the waters" of the Delaware River.[44]

At town gatherings from Maine to Pennsylvania northerners passed gestures of support that, despite recognizing slavery as immoral, condemned the abolitionist mailings. One Philadelphia resolution read: "That we respond to the call of our brethren of the south, that we are their brethren and, as such, sympathize . . . and view with regret and indignation the incendiary measures which have disturbed their tranquility." Furthermore, the meeting promised that "the young men of the north are prepared to meet the danger" in assisting the South if the abolitionists provoked slave rebellion. The Pennsylvanians concluded their statement by affirming their loyalty to the nation: "We regard the union of this country as inseparable from its freedom, greatness, and glory; that we consider no sacrifice too great to maintain it."[45]

The *Ohio State Journal and Columbus Gazette* also denounced emancipation in the South as "the mischievous schemes of designing fanatics." The newspaper reminded its readers that northerners and southerners had sworn an oath to protect each other: "If it was believed for a moment that the fanatic could injure the people of the South, the men of the North would put their feet upon them and crush our their venom; and if servile war should ever arise in the South, let the men of the north be but called upon and they will trample it down at once."[46] The purpose of the Union was to keep the United States stable and safe. Patriotic Americans had to stop the radicals who wanted to fracture the bonds that held the country together. For many in the North, supporting slavery was the price to pay for keeping their country, and the Constitution, exceptional.

Some anti-abolitionist northerners turned angry words into pugnacious action. Although violence often occurred during antislavery rallies in the 1830s, mob action against abolitionism increased in the aftermath of the antislavery postal campaign. Several well-known crusaders for emancipation received injuries during the furor that followed the abolitionist mailings being sent to the South. On October 24, 1835, Boston merchants threatened William Lloyd Garrison's life at a meeting of the Massachusetts Anti-Slavery Society. A month later, another angry mob, this time in Troy, New York, stoned Theodore Weld, a leading member of the American Anti-Slavery Society who had already encountered other brutal run-ins as an activist. Following the rioting, Troy's mayor—who a year earlier had declared that the South should leave the Union if abolitionism did not become illegal in the North—ordered Weld to leave the city. Challenging the morality of slavery garnered a meager amount of toleration in the hometown of Uncle Sam.[47]

Whether fueled by antipathy toward black people or by commercial attachments to the cotton economy of the South, a number of people in the free states defended American slaveholders from the antislavery movement. For the most part, southerners viewed the North's reaction optimistically, seeing the assaults on abolitionists as a sign of loyalty. For the proslavery movement, however, the strongest attack on those who mailed antislavery tracts to the South came from the man they had denounced as a despot a few years before. President Andrew Jackson wanted to shut down the antislavery mailing campaign entirely.

Unlike David Walker's *Appeal,* the size and scope of the abolitionist mail campaign, along with the government-run Post Office being used as the main courier of the pamphlets, became sensationalized in the nation's capital. The incipient federal response to the crisis came from Postmaster General Amos Kendall. Born in Massachusetts, educated in New Hampshire, but settled in Kentucky where he thrived as an editor of a Jacksonian publication, the wiry government official worked in the background of American politics for the bulk of his career. During his time in Washington, Kendall held a place in Andrew Jackson's "Kitchen Cabinet," an unofficial retinue that advised the president. Kendall wrote a large portion of the president's addresses and wielded heavy influence in the administration. Concerning Kendall's more than a decade of service to Old Hickory and to his successor, Martin Van Buren, former president John Quincy Adams remarked in his diary that the two presidents had been "the tool of Amos Kendall, the ruling mind of their dominion." As head of the postal service, and a trusted adviser to the White House, Kendall found that the responsibility of dealing with the question about the antislavery pamphlets naturally fell to him, and he quickly strategized a way to impede the antislavery movement from attempting to change minds in the South.[48]

Shortly after receiving the urgent request from the panicked postmaster in South Carolina, Kendall responded by telling Alfred Huger, "Upon a careful examination of the law, I am satisfied that the postmaster general has no legal authority to exclude newspapers from the mail, nor prohibit their carriage or delivery on account of their character or tendency, real or supposed." He explained that the administration did not "want to confer to the head of an executive department a power over the press, which might be perverted or abused." However, despite his reluctance to censor the mail directly, Kendall told the postmaster in Charleston that he was "not prepared to direct you to forward or deliver the papers." He stated his reasoning plainly: "The post office department was created to serve the people of *each* and *all* of the *United States,* and not to be used as the instrument of their *destruction.*"[49] The postmaster general argued that the Constitution did not protect those who worked to undermine the Union by sowing sectional dissension about slavery.

Despite knowing that the law said otherwise, Kendall felt compelled to defend slavery and searched for a way to warrant his actions. He sent a message to the Palmetto State, "We owe an obligation to the laws, but a higher one to the communities in which we live, and if the *former* be perverted to destroy the *latter,* it is patriotism to disregard them. Entertaining these views, I cannot sanction, and will not condemn the step you have taken" by refusing to deliver the mail. Civil disobedience in the name of security could be justified, both for the white population against black rebellion and for the sake of the Union. One of the leading Jacksonians thus endorsed his own version of nullification—federal appointees could refuse to execute the law in the name of maintaining the peace. The postmaster general granted each of his local deputies the authority to determine what should and should not be delivered through the American mail service. The postal bureaucracy became a censorship board.[50]

Kendall's actions engendered intense northern protest. The *New York Evening Post* condemned the postmaster's actions and called for him to resign. "Who gives him a right to judge of what is incendiary and inflammatory? Was there any reservation of that sort in his oath of office," the newspaper asked. The *Boston Atlas,* which had condemned the abolitionists, also chastised Kendall's response, writing, "What *higher duty* can we owe to the community in which we live, than to obey the laws which that community has framed? Is an individual, or class of individuals, to say—we deem such a law to be unjust, and it is *patriotism* in us to disregard it?" It continued: "There was but one course for the postmaster general to have pursued; and that it to have directed his subordinate officer to follow the law as it was laid down, and leave the result to the law."[51] To these northern publications, the head of the Post Office lent credence to anarchy. A key to American success, they argued, was the strident devotion to the rule of law.

Proslavery members of the northern media praised Kendall's actions. The Albany *Argus* dubbed the postmaster's decision to be a "prompt, liberal, and just reply." An Ohio outlet contended that laws could not be enforced in the absence of the people's will and advised discretion. The *New York Commercial Advertiser* took censorship of the antislavery movement even further, writing, "If the madmen who are scattering fire-brands, arrows and death, cannot be persuaded, or 'rebuked' to silence, we see no other alternative, than for the slaveholding states to protect themselves, by establishing all the odious machinery of passports and examinations, to which travelers in Europe are subjected."[52] Prominent planters still kept friends in the North.

Southern journalists varied in their responses to Kendall's conception of a "higher law." A Louisianan asked with bluster, "Where is the man in the South who would not rather receive a bushel of abolition trash, (which can easily burn,) than to have his own private affairs pried into by every rascally deputy postmaster, or clerk, who might choose to say he suspected they contained incendiary matter?" For this southerner, his privacy trumped concern that the pamphlets might cause trouble among the enslaved. Despite some planter puffery, though, whites in the South generally supported the postmaster's work, saluting Kendall for trying to prevent the message of universal freedom from entering the slave states. The *Athens (Ga) Southern Banner* wrote, "In the justice to Mr. Kendall's views, and the propriety of the course he has adopted . . . there is, we believe, but one opinion here; and that is one of *unqualified appropriation.*"[53] The nation waited to see the official reaction from President Andrew Jackson.

As part of dealing with the attacks on the Charleston post office, Amos Kendall sent a copy of Huger's letter, along with an explanation of his motives, to the White House. He told the president that he expected that "these steps carried out will pacify the South."[54] Kendall insisted that he obtained the peace by refusing to send all of the mail, allowing the administration to act as it saw fit. He told the chief executive there could be no other way to continue regular postal operations in the face of angry proslavery assaults on the Post Office.

Old Hickory agreed, and the Garrisonians promptly faced the fiery ire of the seventh president. Jackson replied to the postmaster general, "I have read with sorrow and regret that such men live in our happy country—I might have said monsters—as to be guilty of the attempt to stir up amongst the South the horrors of servile war—Could they be reached, they ought to be made to atone for this wicked attempt, with their lives."[55] The president, a plantation owner, concurred with the idea that talk of abolitionism aroused insurrection in the slave states. To ensure the safety of the South, Jackson hoped to find a way to obstruct the antislavery mailings from reaching their targeted audience.

Unfortunately for Andrew Jackson and his postmaster general, the Constitution hampered immediate action against the antislavery postal campaign. Recognizing his legal restrictions, the president lamented to Kendall, "But we are the instruments of, and executors of the law; we have no power to prohibit anything from being transported in the mail that is authorized by law."[56] Under both the Constitution and his oath of office, he could not ignore rightfully enacted regulations simply because he found the current law to be inconvenient. Once painted as sharing kingly ambitions by the Whigs, Andrew Jackson told fellow Democrats that only tyrants would arbitrarily waive the enforcement of laws through the executive fiat. When Congress reconvened after summer recess, he asked them to provide his administration with the authority to regulate what could and could not be sent through the postal service. The "incendiaries" from William Lloyd Garrison and his antislavery fanatics, the president maintained, had to be deterred before they impaired planter control and instigated an uprising by enslaved Americans held captive throughout the southern states.

Although the postal campaign convinced few, if any, southern planters to give up slavery, the abolitionists applied a different reading of the founding documents of the United States as a pretext to nationalizing the discussion of human bondage in America. In an open letter from the Massachusetts Anti-Slavery Society, the group explained, "We have said, in the words of the Declaration of Independence, that 'all men are created equal,' and that liberty is an unalienable gift of God to every man. We know of no clause in the constitution, which forbids our saying this."[57] The major figures in the fight to end slavery wanted to shift the discussion to the halls of the Capitol by developing a different meaning for the American Revolution and a different purpose for the Constitution and Union. They offered a different path for American exceptionalism.

Furthermore, just as free speech laws protected David Walker in Boston, the antislavery society insisted that the Bill of Rights preserved antislavery speech at the national level, even while they stood accused of fomenting insurrection. The abolitionists argued, "It is said that the constitution of the United States forbids our acting, in any way, on this subject. Admit, for a moment, that slavery is, as is so confidently asserted, *guaranteed* by the constitution; is not the liberty of speech and of the press also explicitly guaranteed?" Mirroring the *Charleston Mercury,* the organization's letter asked, "If it be found that they cannot co-exist, the question is before the country—which of them is best worth preserving?" The members of both the antislavery and proslavery movements admitted that they thought free speech and black enslavement—and, at least for slaveholders, a secure slave population—could not exist in harmony. Yet, many Americans considered both the freedom of expression and slavery to be issues Washington should leave alone. Congress became burdened with performing a tedious balancing act between slavery and the First Amendment.[58]

In his seventh State of the Union, President Jackson asked Congress to confront the delivery of antislavery literature through the mail. "I invite your attention to the painful excitement produced in the South by attempts to circulate through the mails inflammatory appeals addressed to the passions of the slaves, in prints, and in various sorts of publications, calculated to stimulate them to insurrection and to produce all the horrors of servile war," his letter to the legislature stated.[59] Taking the opportunity to regain the confidence of slaveholders he had lost during the nullification crisis, Old Hickory postured himself as a defender of the planter class who ensured the security of the entire nation by limiting the reach of abolitionism.

After paying respect to "the state authorities to whom it properly belongs" for censoring the antislavery tracts, Jackson continued, "it is nevertheless proper for Congress to take such measures as will prevent the Post Office Department, which was designed to foster an amicable intercourse between all the members of the Confederacy from being used as an instrument of an opposite character." The president urged Congress to pass "a law as will prohibit under severe penalties the circulation in the Southern states through the mails of incendiary publications intended to instigate the slaves to insurrection."[60] The proslavery movement insisted that the fear of slave revolts should trump the free speech rights of the antislavery movement.

The Senate moved first in attempting to comply with the White House's request. John C. Calhoun led the way for the proslavery movement in Washington. Jackson's former vice president, who had recently returned to the Senate, asked for the creation of a special committee to write new regulations for the postal system. Despite some objections, the Senate voted to form a group of four southerners and one northerner to examine and develop legislation related to "incendiary publications." The South Carolinian served as the committee's chairman and took up the job of using federal authority to silence antislavery voices.[61] Calhoun's special committee announced its findings a few months later. However, its concluding report and suggested remedy had the oddity of not being endorsed in the whole by a majority of the committee members. Calhoun and North Carolina senator Willie Mangum supported the special committee's work in its entirety. The other three members took issue with portions of the proposal. As Chairman Calhoun read the long report on the Senate floor, he explained that they "fully [concurred] with the president as to the character and tendency of the papers which have been attempted to be circulated in the south. But, while [the committee members] agree with the president as to the evil and its highly dangerous tendency, and the necessity of arresting it, they have not been able to assent to the measure of redress which he recommends."[62] Few senators who studied the issue wanted to circumvent the Bill of Rights by allowing Washington to monitor what was sent through the mail.

Despite concerns from its own members, the special committee offered a bill to bar the Post Office from being used as a way to "excite insurrection among the slaves of the slaveholding States." The proposed legislation made it unlawful "for any deputy postmaster knowingly to receive and put into mail any pamphlet, newspaper, handbill, or other printed, written, or pictorial representation touching the subject of slavery, directed to any person or post office where, by the laws thereof, their circulation is prohibited."[63] Following Amos Kendall's pattern, Calhoun's proposal would empower postmasters to judge the appropriateness of mail, making them the agents of proslavery censorship. To justify these additional granted powers to Washington, the South Carolinian couched his argument in the language of state rights: the bill used federal authority to reinforce state laws. Slaveholders got the best of both worlds; they could claim consistency with the ideology that slavery was a state issue while Washington's active commitment to the protection of slavery continued to expand its federal scope.

Throughout the early half of 1836, the Senate discussed the bill without a sectional tendency. Many northerners offered their approbation while several slave state senators—though none from the lower South—expressed disapproval. Support for the potential regulation of the postal service focused mostly on the reasoning expressed by President Jackson. Did the prevention of slave revolts trump free speech? The president's party men in the Senate answered with resounding affirmation; knowing that the New Yorker Martin Van Buren was going to be their presidential nominee, many Democrats hoped to shore up their party in the South for the upcoming presidential election.[64]

Pennsylvania senator James Buchanan parroted Old Hickory and implored colleagues to pass Calhoun's bill. The future president professed to the Senate that censorship was "absolutely necessary" to protect the South from "servile insurrection." He insisted the security of the nation rested on stifling the cause of abolitionism and admitted that "unless in extreme cases, where the safety of the Republic was involved, we should never exercise this power of discrimination between what papers should and should not be circulated through the mail." This was no ordinary situation, though. Buchanan added, "The Constitution, however, has conferred upon us this general power, probably for the very purpose of meeting these extreme cases, and it is one which, from its delicate nature, we shall not be likely to abuse."[65] They could not allow the antislavery movement to inspire an American version of Haiti's revolution. The proslavery movement in Congress argued that fanatical abolitionism threatened the

Union, and therefore American exceptionalism. As the antislavery movement advanced a different purpose for the Union and the Constitution, Jacksonians tied the safety of the country to the security of slavery more closely than ever.

A number of senators attacked the Post Office bill, arguing that the First Amendment shielded all publications from censorship by the government, including those that slaveholders found dangerous. The most effective reply to Jackson, Calhoun, and the supporters of censorship came from Henry Clay. The former speaker of the House and fierce opponent of Old Hickory, the Kentucky senator was troubled by the proposal coming out of the White House. Despite Democratic pretensions that stated otherwise, he insisted that Americans did not want the federal government filtering the circulation of newspapers. He opposed the Jacksonians because "it was unconstitutional; and, if not so, that it contained a principle of a most dangerous and alarming character."[66] Delivering tracts to the addressed postal office did not threaten slavery. Local law dealt with them once they arrived. Under the principles proposed in the bill, state laws trumped federal laws; therefore, local legislatures that passed draconian regulations could shape the nation's legal system. If state laws decided how mail circulated, they could also eventually use the same premise to attack antislavery speech in the North directly. It opened the door for a national political system dictated by radical activists. Granting censorship authority to states damaged the nation, Clay argued. It beckoned the extremes, encouraged anarchy, and went against the principles of the American Revolution and the purpose of the Union.

After the debate, the Great Compromiser and his supporters ruled the day. When it came time to vote, the Senate disapproved Calhoun's attempt to regulate the circulation of antislavery newspapers through the mail, voting 24–19 against the bill. The federal government would not define what could and could not be sent through the mail. The United States Post Office remained open to everyone, delivering anything with the right postage to any destination in the country. Despite objections from prominent members of the proslavery movement, abolitionists pressed on with their mission, knowing they were protected by the Bill of Rights.[67]

When it came to discussing the sectional controversy caused by the abolitionist mail campaign, the House of Representatives operated much differently. In the Senate, one member could initiate a heated discussion. In the lower chamber, however, the speaker of the House held more sway over who could propose a bill or address the floor. The House of Representatives heard scant talk about the issue and chose to stay away altogether. The representatives refused to create a special committee to write a bill because its members believed the issue needed no particular attention. The people's House followed the ideas of Henry Clay: the Constitution protected slavery and the freedom of the press—no clarification required. If antislavery writings sparked unrest in the South, the federal government could quell black rebellion.[68]

After debating issues related to the postal service in an ordinary fashion, the House of Representatives passed a bill divided into forty-six sections that organized how the postal service operated. Only one referenced the antislavery pamphlets. The section forbade anyone working for the Post Office from detaining "any letter, package, pamphlet, or newspaper with intent to prevent the arrival and delivery" and punished "any postmaster" who might "give a preference to any letter, package, pamphlet, or newspaper over another" with a fine and possible imprisonment. In June 1836, the House passed its Post Office bill. The Senate assented to the proposal a few weeks later. Congress rejected Andrew Jackson and John C. Calhoun's attempt to prohibit works that criticized slavery from being sent through the mail. The president had no choice but to sign the legislation when it arrived on his desk.[69]

The abolitionist postal campaign magnified the growing divide between slavery and the Bill of Rights. Moderates won the day when Congress eventually determined that the federal government should stay out of actively supporting slavery against a growing abolitionist movement. By sticking to a strict version of the Constitution, which granted minimal authority to Congress to act on the behalf of slavery in the outright, the United States might secure both free speech and the safety of slaveholders from insurrection. In continuing to keep national authority regarding the issue above the partisan fray, moderates hoped to save the Union from being torn apart by radicals on both sides of slavery's future.

Circumstances began changing for slaveholders both within the United States and internationally during the 1830s. British emancipation frightened southern plantation owners and empowered a new outspoken proslavery movement in the United States. With the freeing of the enslaved in the British West Indies, American planters viewed the world as an increasingly dangerous place. Rather than being firmly ensconced in the middle of Atlantic slavery, the American master class found itself representing the institution's western edge. Instead of serving as a reservoir for rebellious slaves, the Caribbean became occupied by hundreds of thousands of free blacks who white southerners expected to seek revenge. More important, losing England as a justification for the morality of the South's unfree labor system undermined a key rationale for theorists who defended slavery.

However, the changes to Atlantic slaveholding also opened a new avenue for the proslavery movement to expand its strength and created an issue that dominated politics in the United States for nearly a decade. During the southern discussion of British emancipation and the debate over the postal campaign, many slaveholding politicians withdrew from a limited government approach to defending the South's peculiar institution. For many planters, the rise of the abolitionists in the House of Commons showed the naïveté of those who believed the Constitution alone could safeguard slavery, especially as moderates allowed radical abolitionists to share the liberties expressed in the Bill of Rights. The majority, they claimed, always defined constitutional limits.

A new proslavery strategy came to the fore in the aftermath of English emancipation of the West Indies. Although some ardent defenders of slavery initially criticized planters who asked for federal legislation to censor David Walker's *Appeal,* the situation changed five years later. The size of the abolitionist postal campaign, along with the success of English abolitionism, led to the former nullifiers' spurning the laissez faire approach to federal influence over the South's peculiar institution. The proslavery movement intended to expand the scope of Washington's relationship to slavery, and slaveholding nationalists undertook the task of seeking new ways to justify federal intervention for the sake of conserving slavery.

Hostility toward Great Britain seemed to be the answer. Although slavery's defenders could no longer point to the English as justification for the morality of the institution of black enslavement, the nation with which the United States had already fought two wars served as a target for prominent slave owners. Proslavery leaders quickly labeled abolitionists as anti-Americans who not only advocated slave uprisings but also sympathized with America's traditional foe. Under the banner of patriotism, the planter elite called for northerners to defend the southern institution of human bondage. Leveraging the power gained from the rising value of King Cotton, enslavers looked to Washington and the federal government as the answer to their escalating concerns about the strength of Atlantic abolitionism. They claimed American exceptionalism and the purpose of the Union were at stake.[70]

4

PROSLAVERY FEAR AND THE RISE OF THE ABOLITIONIST POWER

San Domingo, so often referred to, and so little understood, is not a case where black heroes rose and acquired Government. . . . Do you wonder, then, that we pause when we see this studied tendency to convert the Government into a military despotism? Do you wonder that we question the right of the President to send troops to execute the laws whenever he pleases, when we remember the conduct of France, and that those troops were sent with like avowal, and quartered on plantations, and planters arrested for treason . . . and brought away that insurrection might be instigated among their slaves?

—Jefferson Davis, January 10, 1861

In the immediate aftermath of the abolitionist postal campaign, southern planters went on an offensive to reshape the nature of the conversation about slavery in the United States.[1] Prominent slaveholding politicians began promoting their region's peculiar institution through the expansion of federal authority. As this aggressive new proslavery movement plunged into the debate, however, it also caused waves in the North. In January 1836, Charles Sumner noticed how the exploits of the invigorated proslavery movement in Washington had led to a change in the free states. Then a young lecturer at Harvard Law School, the future antislavery senator wrote to his mentor, Francis Lieber, "We are becoming abolitionists at the North fast; the riots, the attempts to abridge the freedom of discussion, Governor McDuffie's message, and the conduct of the South generally have caused many to think favorably of immediate emancipation who never before inclined to it."[2]

A German by birth, Francis Lieber won fame in Boston during the 1820s for his intellectual prowess. A burly man who had been wounded at the Battle of Waterloo, he left Massachusetts to teach economics at South Carolina College less than a year before receiving his letter from Sumner. Lieber came to the South at a time of much commotion about the antislavery movement, and slaveholders greeted his arrival with suspicion. They forced the new professor to pen an article declaring that he felt little sympathy for the enslaved. Lieber offered a public announcement that he was not a secret abolitionist trying to instigate black rebellion. The state's governor had recently condemned abolitionism in a powerful message, causing a stir across the United States that reverberated enough to be read by his former student in Cambridge.[3]

South Carolina, as it had during the nullification crisis and the onset of the Civil War, functioned as a lapidary that polished radical proslavery ideas before these were disseminated to the rest of the South. In response to the abolitionist postal campaign, Governor George McDuffie, once named the "orator of nullification," addressed the slavery question in his annual report to the state legislature. Mentored by John C. Calhoun, who found him working in a blacksmith shop and turned him into a politician, the governor remained loyal to Cast-Iron Man throughout his life. McDuffie usually cast a dour mood, and an acquaintance once described him as "a grim-looking man, who was an admirer of Milton and who was never known to jest or smile." He had long championed slavery, fighting in the House of Representatives in objection to the Panama diplomatic mission in 1825, and using any platform he could find to expand the influence of the slaveholding class. His fiery speech circulated in publications across the country, gaining him national attention—both praise and scorn. The executive of the Palmetto State used his address to draw a line in the sand regarding the acceptance of abolitionism in the United States.[4]

McDuffie launched his diatribe because he believed the antislavery movement placed southern security at risk. The governor classified abolitionists "wicked monsters and deluded fanatics" who masked their true beliefs with religion to trick northerners into obeying their calls to end the white republic established in 1776. The whiteness of the United States, not just slavery, was what "fanatics" desired to overturn by fulfilling "the fiend-like errand of mingling the blood of the master and the slave, to whose fate they are equally indifferent, with the smoldering of our peaceful dwellings." The South Carolinian claimed antislavery northerners embraced an "unholy creed." Even "murder itself," he bellowed, became "a labor of love and charity" for those who supported universal freedom.[5] Their actions could not be tolerated anywhere, let alone in the slave states.

The governor echoed the sentiments of Robert Turnbull from a decade earlier. He adamantly appealed to the biases of white southerners, asking them to remember history as they contemplated the future of slavery in the United States. He passionately told the legislature, "The experience of both France and Great Britain fearfully instruct us, from what small and contemptible beginnings, this *amis des noirs* philanthropy may rise to gigantic power."[6] The push for emancipation could only gain strength if white southerners remained disengaged from the fight. He argued that American planters needed to be more assertive than their Caribbean counterparts. The recognition of why West Indian planters failed served as the first requirement for southern slaveholders hoping to withstand Atlantic abolitionism. By taking lessons from the experiences of the Caribbean plantation owners and applying them to make changes to strengthen the institution at home, the planter elite on the continent might be able to change their fate.

The South Carolinian continued his defense of slavery by branding abolitionism as anti-American. McDuffie asserted that foreign elements lusted over acquiring more influence in the country by fostering the antislavery movement in the free states. Referring to the postal campaign and the British condemnation of the Negro Seamen Act, he said, "The crime which these foreign incendiaries have committed against the peace of the States, is one of the highest grade known to human laws." They required harsh treatment: "It is my deliberate opinion, that the laws of every community should punish this species of interference by death." Anything less was unacceptable because the antislavery movement consisted of the "enemies of the human race."[7] All white Americans, not just slaveholders, needed to remain vigilant to protect the independence of the nation from English designs at empire.

Expecting his speech to garner great attention throughout the South, George McDuffie also told the proslavery movement in Washington that they had to do more to dispute the antislavery movement in the nation's capital. The obvious flaw in relying on the states' rights defense alone, he maintained, was that "any laws which may be enacted by the authority of this State" could only "punish or repress offences committed within its limit."[8] David Walker, William Lloyd Garrison, and the rest of the activists who supported emancipation could not be stopped while they resided in free states. All government—both locally and nationally—needed to be wholly devoted to the preservation of slavery, he contended. The planter elite could not simply accept antislavery ideas flowering in parts of the country they did not control: they required stronger northern allies.

The governor also acknowledged the risks associated with slavery. The millions held on plantations were like a tinderbox waiting for a match, he said. As northerners refused to suppress the antislavery movement, "the authors of all this mischief" continued to "concoct their schemes, plant their batteries, and hurl their fiery missiles among us, aimed at that mighty magazine of combustible matter, the explosion of which would lay the State in ruins."[9] If such a calamity came to pass, he said, the entire state, not slaveholders alone, might fall to the flame. McDuffie's language purposely included all whites living in South Carolina and throughout the slave states. He wanted nonslaveholders to believe that abolitionists, and the inevitable uprising caused by their protests, placed everyone in a dangerous situation. Only together, under the common banner of defense, could slaveholders and nonslaveholders unite against black rebellion sponsored by abolitionists.

According to the proslavery state executive, southerners had the "imperious duty" to "demand of our sovereign associates the condign punishment of those enemies of our peace, who avail themselves of the sanctuaries of their respective jurisdictions to carry on schemes of incendiary hostility against the institutions, the safety, and the existence of the State." However, that did not go far enough for his liking. He also explained that the times necessitated taking the proslavery message national. "If we go no farther" than passing laws in the slave states to repress abolitionism, the governor alleged, "we had as well do nothing" because "the outrages against the peace and safety of the State are perpetrated in other communities."[10] The time had come to take control of Washington and use the authority of the federal government to advance slavery's perpetuation. He demanded that southerners holding federal office employ every tool at their disposal to slow the rise of abolitionism throughout the Atlantic.

George McDuffie realized he needed to win approval from outside the South if the proslavery movement hoped to remain a powerful force in the country. He aimed to convince Americans, both northern and southern, that the antislavery movement would hurt the entire nation if left unopposed. As part of his defense of slavery, the governor portrayed the planter elite as the defenders of a white American republic against emancipationists who wanted to surrender white control over the nation. He contended that the "state of political amalgamation and conflict, which the Abolitionists evidently aim to produce, would be the most horrible condition imaginable, and would furnish Dante or Milton with the type for another chapter illustrating the horrors of the infernal regions."[11] Instead of creating Heaven on Earth, the South Carolinian maintained mockingly, the religious antislavery movement portended to summon Hell—or at least the Haitian Revolution.

The difference between social amalgamation in the South and "political amalgamation" with the North had to be sharply drawn for those living in antebellum America. Similar to their southern counterparts, most white northerners abhorred miscegenation, but the issue had a more abstract meaning. Most lived hundreds of miles away from sizable black communities, leaving many northerners unconcerned about proslavery predictions about social intermixing between white and black Americans. However, "political amalgamation" inherently affected northerners, who shared the same Constitution with southerners. For many whites living in the free states, granting the black population power to influence elections and head to Washington was unacceptable, a threat to American democracy and exceptionalism. Antislavery success marched the country down a wayward path, McDuffie argued, and impugned national destiny. Garrisonians routinely chanted the motto of "no Union with slaveholders." South Carolina's governor countered by supporting no Union with black people.[12]

McDuffie wanted slave-state legislatures to issue a "disclaimer" emphasizing that Congress could not "interfere in any manner" with slavery. He insisted, "Though the right to emancipate our slaves by coercive legislation has been very generally disclaimed by popular assemblages in the non-slaveholding States, it is nevertheless important that each of those States" be given such a notice "as a permanent record for our future security." If proslavery southerners pushed hard enough, the South Carolinian reasoned, they could bully northerners into having no option but to fortify black enslavement below the Mason-Dixon Line. He welcomed Washington's support of slavery, but wanted to ensure that the federal government could never use its authority to undermine the South's peculiar institution. He balanced the expanded national protection of slavery with a states' rights approach, all for the benefit of the planter elite.

McDuffie ended his speech by saying, "The liberal, enlightened and magnanimous conduct of the people in many portions of the non-slaveholding States forbids us to anticipate a refusal on the part of those States to fulfill these high obligations of national faith and duty." The destiny of the Union and security of the nation rested upon the North's protection of the South from antislavery interference. If slavery ended, "ten millions of poor white people would be reduced to destitution, pauperism and starvation," he predicted.[13] His forceful speech resonated with proslavery southerners—both those who already owned slaves and those who hoped, one day, to climb the economic ladder on the backs of the oppressed. In the weeks afterward, another South Carolinian answered his governor's call, pushing northern allegiance to its limit.

A few months prior to his proslavery address to the state legislature, Governor McDuffie visited the plantation home of James Henry Hammond, a man desperate to win approval from South Carolina's master class. The governor spoke with the new member of Congress about the future of American slavery. Half bald, but fully ambitious and egotistical, Hammond gained fame during the nullification crisis as an eager supporter of John C. Calhoun. Hoping to find a place in the firmament of the proslavery intellectual elite, Hammond had defended slavery wholeheartedly during discussions over the emancipation of the West Indies and the abolitionist postal campaign, seeing it as a way to win recognition from his peers. In the heated summer of 1835, he wrote the editor of the *New York Evening Star* demanding that free-state governments employ threats of "Terror" and "Death" against the antislavery movement. To exhibit his seriousness, the congressman-elect compared southern planters to the recently abolished slave owners in the West Indies. The young planter wrote,

"The Northern Fanatics must not expect to find in us the unrepresented colonial subjects of an arrogant monarchy."[14] American slaveholders, unlike their Caribbean counterparts, aimed to forcefully shut down those who dreamed of ending the institution of slavery. He became determined to ensure that Washington never followed the path of Westminster.

Having studied Thomas Roderick Dew's defense of the South's peculiar institution, Hammond believed, like his governor, that strengthening black enslavement required proslavery action in the nation's capital. He insisted that planters stop being "abject apologists of slavery." Instead, they needed to "openly, manfully erect and roll back the misdirected tide of public sentiment" and establish a "ground selected for battle as will cover us best both behind and before and make the triumph as bloodless as possible."[15] The halls of Congress offered the perfect arena for this clash of ideologies. It also gave James Henry Hammond a stage on which to strut in the spotlight and burnish his proslavery credentials. During the postal campaign, proslavery and antislavery forces argued about free speech and slaveholding security under the First Amendment. When Hammond arrived in Washington he hoped to carry the conflict on to the floor of the House of Representatives.

In North America, the right to petition the government for grievances long antedated the Bill of Rights and the Constitution. The first recorded act of the colonial government of Connecticut, for example, was a petition regarding a grievance between neighbors. Before the American Revolution, the reception of petitions from the populace originated more bills in the colonies than any other source of legislation. However, in December 1835, Hammond led an attempt at changing the meaning of the right "to petition the Government for a redress of grievances" in the United States forever. Understanding the significance of his scheme, the callow South Carolinian took an opportunity to make a name for himself by challenging centuries of precedent in English-speaking democracy.[16]

For over forty years the House of Representatives had dealt with petitions in a customary fashion: one day every week, while in session, the House received and dispersed them, divided by subject, to the committees responsible for the concerns expressed by the citizens who sent them. Sometimes this arrangement varied, but mostly it did not. On December 16, 1835, a little more than a week after the first session of the new Congress convened, four congressmen presented petitions from their constituencies back home, but only one induced serious conversation on the House floor. John Fairfield of Maine, one of 155 freshmen members of Congress, envisaged minimal turmoil when he "presented the petition of one hundred and seventy-two ladies residing in his district, praying for the abolition of slavery in the District of Columbia" and followed it with "a similar petition" from "one hundred and seventy-two gentlemen residing in his district."[17] Usually, the submission of such petitions to the House—also referred to as memorials—aroused scant discussion on the floor. This time, however, things changed.

Fairfield requested that his submission be moved to the Committee on the District of Columbia. However, before a motion to table the bill could proceed, thus dismissing it from further discussion, the antislavery representative from Middlebury, Vermont, William Slade, asked that the memorial be printed and distributed to every congressman. He wanted the House of Representatives to debate the merits of the petition from the citizens of Maine. The Constitution, after all, granted Congress the power to "exercise exclusive Legislation in all Cases whatsoever, over such District (not exceeding ten Miles square) as may, by Cession of particular States, and the Acceptance of Congress, become the Seat of the Government of the United States."[18]

A former bookstore owner and future governor of the Green Mountain State, Slade contended that the issue of the slave trade in Washington, D.C., could be separated from the practice of human bondage in the South. He insisted that his colleagues consider the memorial because the Constitution granted Congress the authority to dictate the laws of the nation's capital. However, succeeding a short discussion about whether the merits of slavery in Washington could be debated, an overwhelming majority, 180 in favor and merely 31 voting nay, chose to ignore Slade's request and tabled the antislavery petition. Abolitionism remained nearly voiceless on the House floor. Immediately after the vote, various congressmen presented nine other memorials with minimal commotion.[19]

Two days after Fairfield presented his petition to Congress, another congressman—this time from Massachusetts, where abolitionism continued to gain momentum in the public mind—asked the lower chamber to accept a request to end slavery in the District of Columbia. Sensing his chance, James Henry Hammond seized the opportunity to confront the antislavery movement and assert congressional power in favor of plantation owners. The South Carolinian moved that the people's House formally shun antislavery petitions entirely rather than simply receiving and then ignoring them. He stated, "The large majority by which the House had spurned a similar petition a few days ago had been very gratifying to him, and no doubt would be very gratifying to the South."[20] Congress, the new member proclaimed, should prove to northern abolitionists that it had no jurisdiction over slavery. His action served as an announcement that the proslavery movement had changed its approach to defending against attacks on the South's peculiar institution.

In his initial request that the House refuse to receive antislavery petitions, Hammond explained he could not "sit there and see the rights of the southern people assaulted by the ignorant fanatics from whom the memorials" came to Washington. He insisted that his motion did not pertain to constitutional rights, but instead to "sacred" ones, which went beyond the rules of the Constitution.[21] Several southern congressmen viewed obstructing the memorials as a way to defend their region's honor while attacking abolitionism. Blocking the requests from antislavery petitioners became a way for the proslavery politicians in Congress to assert authority over the antislavery movement at a time when northern governments refused to acquiesce to planter demands.

The South Carolinian challenged House tradition by insisting on a proslavery interpretation of the First Amendment. Stunned by the actions of the South Carolinian, the speaker of the House and future president James K. Polk tried to resolve the crisis without starting a sectionalized fight over slavery in the halls of the Capitol, something he claimed that most of his congressional colleagues "desired to avoid."[22] As the House of Representatives fell into disorder debating the validity of Hammond's request, Polk failed to quell the rising anger over the antislavery memorials. Slavery again became part of the national political conversation. Hammond had carried the new proslavery movement with him to Congress.

At the end of 1835, sectional discord about the enslavement of black Americans again raged inside Congress. When a representative from New York implied that Hammond's move had proven the existence of "fanatics and incendiaries at the South, as well as the North, who hoped to profit by agitation," one of Hammond's fellow South Carolinians enthusiastically defended him. Francis Pickens, a cousin of John C. Calhoun, said, "We desire [discussing slavery] because we believe we have been foully slandered before the world; and I stand here prepared, at any time . . . to vindicate the institutions of the people I have the honor in part to represent, from the foul aspersion and calumny thrown upon them."[23] The congressional delegation from the Palmetto State took their governor's call for action to heart. As Christmas recess arrived, some in the

House of Representatives prayed that the time away from Washington might temper sectional fighting over the petitions. Members of the proslavery movement had other ideas, however, and their motivations went beyond hurt feelings from abolitionists calling their region's peculiar institution immoral. They saw sectional friction as a chance to attack abolitionism and, unlike during the antislavery postal campaign, planters unified in dissenting to the memorials, scoring a victory for the federal perpetuation of black enslavement in the United States.

At the dawn of 1836, the House of Representatives became further consumed with the limits of the First Amendment's guarantee of the right to petition. James Henry Hammond took a straightforward approach to justifying the defense of slavery with the power of the national government: the antislavery memorials jeopardized the security of the South, and thus the country as a whole. During the recess, the freshman congressman admitted to friends that he acted impulsively when he initially challenged the antislavery movement's right to petition Congress. However, upon returning to Washington in January, the South Carolinian was poised to explain his actions. In the words of one Hammond biographer, the perfervid defender of slavery wanted to "show that the most fundamental issue at hand was not the right to petition, but the South's right to survival."[24]

Roughly two weeks later, the determined South Carolinian got his chance to speak to publically explain his actions. In a two-hour speech, the twenty-eight-year-old made a case for the federal government's active defense of slavery. A new generation of slaveholders appeared ready to lead the planter elite's fight against the antislavery movement, taking up the cause where Robert Turnbull and Thomas Roderick Dew had left it years before. They intended to turn the future of human bondage into a national issue that forced northerners who did not support abolitionism to prove their faithfulness to the South. They tied the Union and American exceptionalism to the safeguarding of slaveholders from the antislavery impulse growing throughout the Atlantic.

James Henry Hammond's long-winded speech served as an announcement to the country that the proslavery movement was willing to do battle in Congress. Many slave owners had become convinced that, following the English model, an Abolitionist Power, or as the South Carolinian called it, "a systematic plan of operation intended to subvert the institutions of the South," had been initiated to influence the politics in the United States. "If carried into effect," Hammond predicted the result to "desolate the fairest portion of America, and dissolve in blood the bonds of this confederacy"[25] He saw a worldwide conspiracy to create chaos among plantation societies coming into form. Echoing George McDuffie, the South Carolina congressman declared to his southern colleagues—and their northern allies—that the time had come to challenge the antislavery movement inside the Capitol.

Hoping to portray the antislavery movement as inherently anti-Union and a domestic enemy of the United States, the young slaveholding radical quoted abolitionist newspapers that echoed "no union with slaveholders," the motto of William Lloyd Garrison. After that, Hammond read a letter he received from a proslavery northerner from western New York, identifying the man as a "shrewd observer of events passing around him." The New Yorker explained that some abolitionist organizations conspired to change the question from "emancipation of the slave to that of the continuance of the Union."[26] Hammond, a former nullifier, argued that the nation was under a concerted attack by fanatics who sought to weaken the constitutional bonds between the states in order to subvert southern slavery. Their loyalties lay outside of the United States political tradition and threatened America's distinctive form of democracy.

The letter's author also told Hammond that the supporters of southern emancipation circulated tracts at prayer meetings and worked "to unite [the northern] people against you." The antislavery movement wanted sectionalism to reign because disunion would leave southern planters on their own to fight insurrection. The northerner pleaded with his representatives in Congress, "I endeavor to convince my neighbors that these pamphlets are false in every particular, and that if they join the cry of abolition, they must partake of the enormous sin of bringing on a civil war, of destroying our Union, and of causing the renewal of the horrors of St. Domingo."[27] Once again, the echoes of the Haitian Revolution sounded in the halls of the Capitol. If it could happen in the Caribbean, merely a few hundred miles away from the South, the proslavery representative implied, it could happen in the United States. The only ingredient missing for the creation of a massive uprising mounted by the enslaved was the northern acceptance of "fanaticism," the slaveholder warned. He called for Washington to take action—the nation's special standing in the world was at stake.

The writer from the Empire State ended his note by telling Hammond, "Congress will be the ultimate scene of the struggle." The South Carolinian used the message to justify the creation of an active proslavery coalition in favor of using federal authority to ensure slavery's perpetuation. When a New York congressman demanded the name of the author, the brash representative replied, "I cannot give it. I will vouch for his character. But such is the state of society around him, I hear it would prove dangerous if not fatal to him, if I disclose his name."[28] Reversing reality, the proslavery congressman argued that abolitionists routinely employed violence to drown out dissenting viewpoints. He refused to put his friend at risk of recriminations. Fanatics, he insisted, could do terrible things.

James Henry Hammond continued his speech by adumbrating three ways slavery might end in the United States: "Through the medium of the slaveholder—or the Government—or the slaves themselves." He then reviewed the potential for each contingency coming to pass, starting with the chance of slave owners, on their own volition and fearful of the black population, emancipating the African Americans they held in bondage. Echoing Thomas Roderick Dew, Bryan Edwards, and other proslavery polemicists, the proslavery representative maintained that slavery could be practiced safely only if the planter elite remained completely in charge of its security. "There may be nervous men and timid women whose imaginations are haunted with the unwonted fears, among us, as there are in all communities on earth; but," Hammond boasted, "in no part of the world have men of ordinary firmness less fear of danger from their operatives than we have."[29] Plantation owners had little to fear so long as those they enslaved never thought they could win white acceptance in the North for their freedom.

Furthermore, Hammond considered moral suasion to be a dead end for abolitionism. He asserted, "In the whole history of the question of emancipation, in Europe or America, I do not remember a dozen instances of masters freeing their slaves, at least during their lifetimes, from any qualms of conscience." Proslavery theologians had already explained why slaveholding violated none of God's laws. The president of the first national Baptist association, Richard Furman, the same man who defended evangelicalism in the wake of Turner's rebellion, preached that, "the right of holding slaves [was] clearly established in the Holy Scriptures." Moreover, in response to the abolitionist postal campaign, southern religious leaders consecrated the defense of slavery from the pulpit as much as elected officials had defended the institution on the stump. "The abolitionist can appeal only to the hopes or fears or interest of the slaveholder, to induce him to emancipate his slaves," Hammond told Congress.[30] Calls for universal liberty that rested on moral grounds fell on deaf ears in the slave states.

Next, Hammond challenged the idea that American abolitionists might mimic the model of the English in the West Indies. He asked Congress to consider the "probability of success [that the abolitionists] can call upon the Government to emancipate our negroes." The southerner believed West Indian–style emancipation, which reimbursed slaveholders for freeing enslaved southerners, could never become a practical solution in the United States. He estimated the number of people held in slavery to be about "2,300,000" and "their annual increase" to be "60,000." Even using British standards for compensation, which Hammond complained had been "about sixty per cent of their value," the United States Treasury would have to pay an astronomical figure to southern slaveholders in order to free every enslaved man, woman, and child in America. The government money necessary for such an undertaking "would amount to upwards of nine hundred millions," a sum nearly thirty-times the size of the entire federal budget.[31]

Slaveholders often dreaded military conflict on their own soil because it frequently triggered a climate of instability that threatened their control. However, radical members of the proslavery movement often predicted civil war if antislavery politicians wielded the authority of Congress against proslavery interests. Hammond continued the trend, pledging that "the moment this House undertakes to legislate upon this subject, it dissolves the Union" and promised to "go home and preach, and if I can, to practice, disunion, and civil war if need be." He reasoned that if the slaveholding elite could no longer dominate the enslaved, "a revolution must ensue, and this republic sink in blood."[32] War, with planters in charge of a military force, appeared better than a federal government operated by abolitionists. The freshman congressman contended that only one way existed for emancipation to happen in the United States: through a deadly and massive slave insurrection, like the Haitian Revolution.

The South Carolinian speculated abolitionists understood that black rebellion offered the most probable way to end bondage in America. He told his fellow congressmen, "the only remaining chance for the abolitionists to succeed in their nefarious schemes will be by appealing to the slaves themselves; and say what they will, this is the great object at which they aim." The plan of the antislavery societies of the North was clear, he said; "all their meetings, publications, lectures, and missions" revolved around one goal: to "excite a servile insurrection" and to teach "the slave to cut his master's throat."[33] Vociferous members of the proslavery coalition insisted that abolitionists, with their moralistic and fanatical tendencies, did not merely intend to end slavery in the United States; they also wanted to deliver a gory punishment to southern planters by fomenting a black revolt against the white South.

Nevertheless, Hammond believed the antislavery attempts to undermine the loyalty of the enslaved had a meager chance at success. He clarified for his free-state colleagues: "there is not a happier" population in the world. Unlike northerners, he said, "I have been brought up in the midst of them, and, so far as my knowledge and experience extend, I should say they have every reason to be happy." Rebels were the outliers in the black community. Hammond declared a few "drunken wretches had caused Turner's insurrection," nothing more. The South Carolinian also challenged the contention submitted by John Quincy Adams that slave owners routinely separated families by selling black Americans to the highest bidder and insisted the enslaved were part of the master's family. They would never participate in "the horrid process of burning and assassination" supported by abolitionists. Although he admitted that some of the enslaved might have a "secret" wish for freedom, the overwhelming majority never desired to attack slaveholders.[34]

Hammond argued that if, by chance, abolitionists succeeded in "drawing the slave into his fiendish purposes, our never sleeping watchfulness would speedily detect every conspiracy that might be formed." Southerners constantly drafted emergency plans in case of insurrection. He explained, "Our habits in this respect have become second instinct. Our vigilance is prompt and personal as our courage." Hammond insisted that it "did not arise from fear," but "from the fact" that southerners guarded "against minor evils" so thoroughly that they would "not fail to discover every danger of great magnitude." So long as the South maintained its "own police," the slaveholder told the House of Representatives, "every insurrection which has yet been meditated—and there have been very few—when not discovered by some faithful slave, has been soon discovered by the whites."[35]

For years, black abolitionists labored to prove that the African American population could be self-reliant, pointing to the emancipated Caribbean—including Haiti—as a rebuttal to white claims of their inferiority. The garish young member of Congress attempted to push those notions aside by making blunt appeals to racial prejudice. He read aloud an article entitled "Abolition" from an Ohio newspaper. The *Cincinnati Gazette* described a settlement of "emancipated slaves" in which "each family has a farm." However, because the former slaves were "excessively lazy and stupid" and could not "raise produce enough on their own lands to feed their families, much less to have a surplus for sale abroad," the town had failed. Free black Americans, according to the tawdry story, lacked the ability to have liberty. "The negro settlements are dead weight . . . that space of country might as well, to this day have remained in possession of the Indians," the *Gazette* reported.[36] To the delight of the slaveholder, the abolitionist plans to help former slaves in the Buckeye State did not succeed.

During the final minutes of his fervent defense of slavery, he posed a hypothetical question: What if slavery could be erased peacefully? Would white Americans be "prepared for the consequences which must follow?" He asked,

> Are the people of the North prepared to restore to them two fifths of their rights of voters, and place their political power on an equality with their own? Are we prepared to see them mingling in our legislation? Is any portion of this country prepared to see them enter these halls and take their seats by our sides, in perfect equality with the white representatives of an Anglo-Saxon race—to see them fill that chair—to see them placed at the heads of your Departments, or perhaps some Othello, or Toussaint, or Boyer, gifted with genius and inspired by ambition, grasp the presidential wreath.[37]

Hammond argued that the white population of the United States, regardless of where they lived, would never accede equal standing to black residents.

James Henry Hammond's long-winded address ended with what he believed to be a frightening thought for the white public. The gradual freeing of enslaved black southerners, he argued, could never be implemented while immediate emancipation proved too costly and dangerous. He pointed to the Caribbean, specifically Jamaica, as an example of a failed gradual emancipation scheme, and the congressman implied that white abolitionists did not fully understand black people. The South Carolinian finished by saying, "Those who know the negro character cannot doubt, what the recent experiments in the West Indies fully prove, that the first step you take towards emancipation bursts at once and forever the fetters of the slave." Universal freedom "would not last a day, an hour" before a "civil war between the whites and the blacks" broke out, "the result of which could not be doubtful, although it would be accompanied with horrors such as history has not recorded." "The blacks," he insisted, "would be annihilated . . . such a catastrophe would be inevitable."[38] In order to stop such calamity and bloodshed, slaveholders, alongside their northern allies, needed to direct the federal government. Painting his movement as moderate, the young proslavery leader argued that blocking antislavery petitions in the House of Representatives acted as a preventative measure to fend off the calamity of racial warfare and the extremism of black revolution.[39]

Debating the acceptance of antislavery petitions revealed a small change in how southern proslavery politicians perceived the growing movement in support of abolitionism. They no longer viewed abolitionists as moralists who, so consumed by their beliefs, did not understand the consequences of their actions. Instead, several southern representatives depicted the opponents of human bondage as evil enemies who purposely wanted to kill whites in the South indirectly by provoking slave revolt. An outspoken representative from northwestern South Carolina, Waddy Thompson moved past simply classifying abolitionists as "fanatics." He angrily bellowed to his colleagues: "The fanatics? Fanatics, did I say sir? Never before was so vile a band dignified with that name. They are murderers, foul murderers, accessories before the fact, and they know it, of murder, robbery, rape, infanticide." He classified his antislavery opponents as wicked—traitors to the country who collaborated for the death of the white South.[40]

Antislavery members of Congress, however, stood up for themselves. William Slade wondered why, if slaveholder assumptions were correct, there had been no insurrections in Virginia after the Old Dominion discussed emancipation following Turner's Rebellion. The Vermont congressman asked: "If it was 'glorious' and safe for Virginia to 'grapple with the monster' in 1832," why would not it be the same for Congress?[41] The answer he received exhibited how different the proslavery movement had become in the wake of abolitionist success in the British West Indies and the antislavery postal campaign.

James Garland, a Virginia Democrat, rose to respond to the Vermonter, saying, "On former occasions there was no extraordinary feeling of alarm . . . of danger, spread throughout [the South]." He emphasized how much the world had changed since Turner's revolt. "The spirit of insurrection and insubordination was not then abroad. It was reversed for the last summer's campaign of a few fanatics," he explained. Like Thompson, Garland no longer accepted the idea that abolitionists did not understand the ramifications of undermining the power of slaveholders in the South. He continued, "My colleagues called them blood-hounds, but that term is too mild. I call them fiends of hell."[42]

Furthermore, Garland pressed for northern allegiance to the proslavery movement. He told his colleagues from the free states that simply opposing abolition no longer fulfilled their commitment to the South; they had to actively work with slaveholders in Congress to protect slavery. The Virginia representative stated, "These abolitionists (I class them all together) have excited a feeling of alarm in the South which cannot easily be quieted. The safety of our wives and our children is endangered by their mischievous and incendiary attempts to produce a servile insurrection among our slaves." The petitions, he claimed, were "calculated to encourage, if not to excite, the slaves themselves to insubordination and insurrection." Black Americans held in southern slavery, he stated, "know everything that transpires here."[43] Discussions in Congress mattered as much as its actions did.

Garland also appealed "to our brethren of the North in behalf of our wives and our children, and for the protection and security against the instigators of midnight murder and assassination." In regard to the ever-present fear of black slaves by white southerners, the proslavery member of the House argued that those in the free states could never "realize our true situation; they are distantly removed from our slave population, and know but little of their character and disposition." The congressman asked northerners for empathy regarding the dangers of slaveholding and defined the federal compact in strictly proslavery terms: "Knowing our danger, and feeling it, too, we appeal . . . to the North to do their duty to the South, and to the Union by discharging their obligations to the constitution." The time had come for the North to display whether they sided with the white South or not.[44]

Despite the contentious argument in the House of Representatives, the proslavery movement did not get exactly what it wanted. Rather than directly violate the First Amendment—or at least redefine it—the lower chamber of Congress, led by the Democrats, passed a new rule proposed by South Carolina's Henry Laurens Pinckney, the former mayor of Charleston who won his seat by running as a member of the Nullifier Party. Named the "gag rule," it stated that the House still maintained the obligation to accept every antislavery memorial, but upon receiving them, the Committee of the Whole would immediately table the petitions, thus sequestering them from further consideration.[45] This automatic rejection of abolitionist petitions caused uproar from antislavery members of Congress, especially former president John Quincy Adams, who had won a seat to Congress in Massachusetts in 1830. Proceeding from his anger at the gag's passage, the sixth president spent the rest of his life fighting the notorious rule at the beginning of each congressional session.[46]

Unsatisfied with the gag rule, extremists within the proslavery movement went even further in asserting their authority. Deemed a traitor by the Calhounites who helped elect him, in the next election Henry Laurens Pinckney lost the nomination for his party to Hugh Swinton Legaré. Opponents claimed he had not done enough when he allowed the House of Representatives to accept the dangerous petitions in the first place. They replaced the author of the gag rule with someone even more radical on the issue of free speech. Despite claims by some slaveholding politicians, the proslavery movement won a significant victory. Northern Democrats joined a nearly concordant southern congressional delegation—just three dissented—in voting in favor of the new rule. The Senate also adopted a softer version of the rule at the behest of John C. Calhoun. By the 1840s, the proslavery movement grew increasingly influential, and the gag rule became further extended to include additional topics deemed unacceptable to be discussed in Congress out of deference to the slaveholding class.[47]

Southerners in state offices also believed that congressional acceptance of antislavery petitions directly led to insurrection. Kentucky—not Alabama, Louisiana, South Carolina, or other Deep South states well known for a total devotion to slavery—offered a succinct explanation of why free speech laws needed to be slanted toward defending slavery. Its own petition to Congress read: "The freedom of the press is one thing—its licentiousness another; whilst the former is justly dear to every freeman, the other is the object of deep reprobation. It cannot be that the right of discussion at the North carries with it the right to excite a portion of the population of a sister State to rapine and murder."[48] The members of the proslavery movement did not merely win a symbolic victory with the establishment of the gag rule. Instead, many saw it as a proper balancing of the freedom of expression and the maintenance of a secure slave system. Emboldened, prominent southerners considered other ways to exercise congressional power to promote the South's peculiar institution nationally.

In the aftermath of the clash over the petitions, the Democratic Party became an effective vehicle for the planter elite to shape American politics and culture. With approval from Vice President Martin Van Buren, a New Yorker whom Andrew Jackson had chosen as his successor, a strong majority of northern Democrats joined every southern representative, besides those who chose not to vote as a protest against the technical acceptance of the petitions, in supporting the gag rule. James K. Polk, then a slaveholding speaker of the House from Tennessee, explained, "the unanimous vote of the friends of Mr. V. Buren (with less than half of dozen exceptions) on Pinckney's resolutions must satisfy that they are sound upon that subject [of slavery]."[49] The House that only a few months earlier had rejected censoring the mail voted to ignore all antislavery petitions sent to Congress.

Northern Democratic support for rejecting the antislavery petitions did not stay confined to the halls of Congress. New York governor William Marcy, a former senator closely connected to Martin Van Buren's political clique named the Albany Regency, also took on the antislavery movement in 1836. According to Marcy, "The very first act in this scheme of abolition, which is carried on under the guide of religion, morality, and love for mankind, would open with insurrection, massacre, and servile war, in which, if the slaves triumph, their masters must be victims." He also thought, "If slave-owners ever concur in any plan for the abolition of slavery, it must arise from a better motive than fear." The notion that the discussion of emancipation led to insurrection had become conventional wisdom. The governor argued that abolitionism made southern slaveholders more determined "to maintain the institution of slavery" and stated that if southerners did not feel protected under the Constitution, they would surely leave, destroying the Union. Many Americans believed that the purpose of the American Revolution was to create a unique nation that proved a republic could peacefully exist. If the nation fell apart over slavery, the exceptional nature of the United States would languish and the Spirit of 1776 might be seen as a failed experiment in democratic governance.[50]

Many in the free states agreed with southern denunciations labeling the antislavery movement as a foreign attempt to spoil American exceptionalism. The novelist James Kirke Paulding, for example, named William Lloyd Garrison a traitor to his country after the radical abolitionist traveled to Britain seeking help from English antislavery leaders. Furthermore, in his book *Slavery in the United States,* the New Yorker wrote, "abolitionists have been stimulated by an impulse derived from abroad." Americans did not endorse the effort to rid the nation of slavery. "English abolitionists," he claimed, "came, red hot with furious zeal, to light the fires of contention, insurrection, disunion, and massacre," while northern abolitionists were influenced by foreign money "because it is otherwise incomprehensible how they obtain the means of gratuitously distributing so many papers, pamphlets, and pictures, or of supporting such a number of brawling incendiaries who are every day disturbing the peace of communities by their disgusting and inflammatory harangues." Patriotic northerners needed to stand with the proslavery movement and protect against "abolitionist fanaticism" that threatened "the existence of civil government and the principles of liberty, in their enlarged and liberal construction."[51]

The proslavery movement evolved as the English-speaking world moved toward emancipation. Slaveholders in Congress, along with northern allies, planned to widen their influence over American foreign policy and national defense. Southerners classified England as a partner in an international plot to attack southern slavery in order to "produce jealousies and heart-burning in a united and happy country." Alfred Cuthbert, a Georgia Democrat, explained why abolition frightened him; "For this plain and obvious reason, that the spirit of abolition was not an American spirit; it was transplanted from a foreign soil; it belonged not here, and was a base mockery of what had passed in another country, whose relations to their slave populations were not similar to ours, but stood in absolute contrast with them."[52] He believed that foreign powers promoted the antislavery movement in order to degrade a Union that existed to defend slavery.

The Georgia senator exemplified how the ideas of Thomas Ritchie and Robert Turnbull had fused into one proslavery vision. The defenders of slavery tied the idea of American exceptionalism to the federal government's defense of black bondage. Our people," Cuthbert explained, "had evinced that patriotism in resisting with energy and success that wide-spread and wild spirit of fanaticism." Although abolitionists aimed "to weaken the bonds of Union," their attempts had failed and only demonstrated "its durability and its strength. . . . As the lofty pine on the mountains becomes more firmly rooted as it is shaken by the tempest, so had the love for this Union taken deeper roots in our hearts." Southerners defined the Union as meaning the overall defense of slavery against anyone who objected—domestic or abroad. They interpreted the constitutional compromise that created the federal government as granting authority regarding every issue that conceivably affected slavery, both nationally and locally, to the planter elite exclusively. The international tinge of abolitionism gave justification to using an exaggerated foreign policy agenda to attack the northern antislavery movement.[53]

Emancipation in the British West Indies caused American planters to consider their future with a sense of trepidation. Many proslavery southerners identified the British Empire as the worst combination imaginable—a powerful nation merged with a substantial population of newly freed blacks, located just hundreds of miles off the American coast, and driven by "fanaticism." Southern planters labeled England a state sponsor of abolitionism intent on dispersing its message with no regard for the safety of white Americans. England, and Europe in general, they feared, planned to extend the Haitian Revolution's racial violence to the United States. "The armed monarchies of Europe, with all the powerful elements both on this and the other side of the Atlantic," one congressman said, were "already in incipient commotion, already rumbling in their deep crater" to end the Union and force their will on the country. Planters insisted that abolitionism operated as Europe's apparatus to undo American exceptionalism and undermine United States democracy.[54]

Planter suspicion toward English abolition was far from new. A few years before West Indian emancipation, a southern diplomat to Jamaica named Robert Monroe Harrison warned his friends back home about the possibility of the Caribbean islands serving as a launching pad for antislavery attacks on American slavery. Born in Virginia to an aide-to-camp of George Washington, Harrison worried that Great Britain might pressure other slaveholding nations to free their slaves, as well. When other countries refused, he contended, England might enact policies to foment insurrection, bringing its rivals to their knees. The Jamaican consul believed the English could use free blacks from the West Indies to "poison the minds of the *Negroes* in the *Slaveholding States*!" England's hunger for empire, he estimated, might prompt another war against the United States.[55]

A large number of slaveholders saw a free Caribbean as unwelcome news for the stable perpetuation of United States slavery. Whether by offering hope to enslaved people in the South or by serving as a base for abolitionism promoted by the full force of the British Empire, a new enemy had appeared off the borders of the South. From June 1833 to August 1, 1844, the day of emancipation, Harrison sent seven dispatches asking for the American Navy to patrol the Caribbean. Each letter predicted a new round of violence similar to the Haitian Revolution. The English might urge insurrection and light a spark that caused another Haitian-style revolution on the continent, he said. Unlike the Haitian revolutionaries, the English could easily communicate with the enslaved of the South and they had exhibited a willingness to free black people held in American servitude during the War of 1812 and afterward. Harrison's correspondence urged stronger defenses in the Gulf of Mexico as a deterrence to England's potentially quenching its "fanatical" urge by attacking slavery in the United States of America.[56]

Apprehension about ending up like the feckless planters of the Caribbean became a constant theme in proslavery rhetoric as the 1830s came to a close. In 1838 another junior congressman from South Carolina, Robert Barnwell Rhett, argued that Europe actively tried to defy slaveholding interests. Having bought the *Charleston Mercury* a few years before, the thirty-seven-year-old told a South Carolina audience that he worried about England and France's influence over the free states. He asked those listening to him to "mark this history of fanaticism in foreign nations. Born in atheism, and baptized in the blood of revolutionary France, it accomplished its purpose there. In England it has sprung up under the guise of religion and it has accomplished its purpose there. It has never yet failed, and never will fail, in accomplishing its purpose, where the slaveholder does not control his own destinies."[57] A radical member of the planter elite, Rhett talked of the "blood" that had "baptized" abolitionism in France, but he did not mean the Reign of Terror in Europe. He meant the death of whites in the Caribbean. The congressman hoped that such a fear might strengthen the resolve of the proslavery movement of the United States, both in the North and South, to employ federal authority against the burgeoning antislavery movement.

Haiti, as it always had, remained a threat in the minds of the planter elite. During his lone term as a representative of South Carolina, Hugh Swinton Legaré gave a speech that publicized how much the white proslavery movement feared the black Caribbean. A week before Christmas in 1838, the man who replaced the creator of the gag rule in the House of Representatives challenged the reception of a petition offered by Leverett Saltonstall, a Whig from Massachusetts who also sat on the Harvard Board of Overseers. Unlike the calls to end slavery in the nation's capital that James Henry Hammond challenged, Saltonstall's petition had no direct relationship to slavery in the United States. Rather, the memorial submitted by the northern representative merely prayed "for the recognition of the Republic of Hayti, and the establishment of international relations with her," a foreign policy request from the people of New England.[58]

Following in the footsteps of southerners who blocked America's delegation from attending the Congress of Panama in 1826, Legaré considered the petition from Saltonstall's constituency to be dangerous. The former chargé d'affaires to Brussels had always eyed Haiti with suspicion and worried about West Indians helping to lead black rebellion. He considered Saltonstall's submitted petition to be part of the abolitionist conspiracy to eradicate slavery in the United States by any means necessary. He proclaimed, "The memorials before you, as I understand, are but another step in the war which a band of wicked conspirators are daring to wage upon the constitution and the peace of the country." The petition, Legaré contended, "[aimed] at *abolition*" and was "part of a system" that intended "the ruin of the South."[59] For the more paranoid members of the proslavery movement, the gag rule required an extension to foreign policy requests. Recognizing Haitian sovereignty might turn the slave states, "from the Susquehanna to the Red river—from the capes of Virginia to the recesses of the Missouri," into a place "with indignation and alarm" because it "involves their life and being." The federal defense of slavery needed to reach further into national policy making, and the mixing of resentment toward a former foe in England with a latent belief in the possibility of a Haitian-type revolt occurring in the slave states created a recipe for proslavery supporters in the Capitol to try and win more southern military defense installations from Congress. Believing the expansion of America's ocean fortifications in the Gulf of Mexico served as the best way to deter an English attack coming from the Caribbean, slaveholding southerners focused their attention on growing naval resources like never before.[60]

The thought of black troops wearing the red coats of the British army freeing slaves as they marched through the South horrified plantation owners in the United States. Nearly three weeks after Legaré's attempt to block a petition to officially recognize Haiti, Congress talked about bolstering the nation's southern defenses. Afraid that an assault on slavery might come from the Gulf of Mexico, proslavery forces in Washington demanded additional military installations in the South. A debate involving where to build a new dry dock, in Philadelphia or Pensacola, proved to be a perfect vehicle for slaveholders on Capitol Hill to flex their political muscles. The congressional discussion demonstrated where planters perceived American weakness and how they expected to shore up their peculiar institution from outside interference.

Waddy Thompson opened the discussion for the proslavery side. The congressman referenced the former secretary of the navy Samuel Southard, who with his "enlarged and enlightened patriotism which has illustrated his whole public life" had urged Congress to fortify Florida because "The whole country from Alleghany to the Gulf is interested in establishment of a naval station at Pensacola. With whatever nation we may be at war, the principal theater will be the Gulf of Mexico, and the object of attack the commerce of the Mississippi."[61] Hardly a proslavery radical, before becoming the head of the navy Southard had been a senator and the governor of New Jersey. The South Carolinian hoped a northerner's words might help gain support from the free-state delegation in Congress to further bolster the defenses of the southern states.

Legaré also put himself in the middle of the fight. He told members of the House of Representatives that the United States needed a stronger naval presence in the Gulf of Mexico because the West Indies might serve as "either the strongholds of the great powers, with a view to hold us in check, or dens of picaroons and bucaniers [*sic*]" who would threaten the South.[62] Slaveholders in Washington plainly expressed that outside forces undermining their system of unfree labor kept them unsettled. They argued that any kind of the lack in their authority might diminish the security of the white population as a whole. Any attack on the South, even from pirates, could be a spark that inflamed their plantations with the fires of insurrection. It fell to Congress to implement more protection from outside abolitionism, the proslavery movement argued.

South Carolina newspapers supported their congressman. An editorialist for the *Charleston Southern Patriot* also discussed the importance of a naval station in Florida to guard against possible invasion from the West Indies. The writer stated that Key West could function as an "avenue of entrance to the enemy—to the black regiments of [England's] cruel policy."[63] If the English planned to spark a new Haitian Revolution in America, the Gulf of Mexico would be the avenue on which they traveled. Planters demanded that more be done to fortify the slave states against abolitionist attacks being launched from the Caribbean.

Many northerners concurred with their southern colleagues. In 1837, for example, Captain Charles Stewart, a Philadelphian who worked in various positions within the United States Navy throughout his life, described his concerns relating to the threat posed by America's former enemy. He published a letter to the secretary of the navy contending, "The new principles of European policy and reform in relation to their American colonies, aided by the fanatics spread over our own country, exciting an insurrectionary spirit among a numerous class of our south-western populations . . . admonish us not to trust too far our own peaceful habits and passive disposition, but to apply all means . . . for the permanent defense of that interesting portion of the Union."[64] Placing a naval station in Pensacola served the interest of national defense in a period of time that necessitated a defensive national posture. Abolitionism was an aggressive force willing to attack even if Americans did their best to continue their "peaceful habits" in foreign policy, he warned. Throughout the 1850s, the size and scope of the United States armed forces grew even larger while southern politicians used their leadership positions in Congress to turn the American military into an instrument of slavery's protection. Planters gained policy victories in Washington by convincing enough northern allies to believe that the antislavery movement cared little about justice or peace and held anti-American ideals.[65]

Tensions between the American proslavery movement and England continued to mount during the 1840s as Great Britain rigidly enforced the international ban on the African slave trade. As during the 1810s, many southerners complained about the English searching American ships, this time for slave smugglers. The tentative peace appeared to crack in 1841 when American slavery came into confrontation with British West Indian emancipation. On the night of November 7, 1841, Madison Washington led a mutiny on the slave ship *Creole* as it carried him from Virginia to the New Orleans slave market. With eighteen fellow slaves, Washington overtook the crew and gained command of the vessel, guiding it to the English Bahamian Island of Nassau where he hoped freedom awaited. Arising from an investigation that took nearly a week, and despite American protest, British authorities declared the slaves on board to be free. More than a hundred people received their natural right to liberty and a precedent became set: The English in the West Indies granted any American slaves their liberty whenever possible. Leading planters howled and made pleas for restitution from Great Britain. Slaveholders in the South feared England had upped the ante in the battle between American slavery and Atlantic abolitionism.[66]

In the 1840s, to blunt the growing antislavery influence in their hemisphere, the advocates of slavery's expansion developed a strategy to solidify their sway in the United States. Supported by the newly ascendant Tyler administration, proslavery politicians positioned national military and foreign policy in opposition to the international antislavery movement. The new president perceived English abolitionism, which he estimated would encourage black rebellion, as a danger to national security. With yet another slaveholder occupying the White House, the proslavery movement again directed the federal government and implemented a program focused on the strengthening of southern defenses and acquiring more slave territory slavery in the West.

One of the main proponents of military expansion for the defense of slavery was the new secretary of the navy, Abel P. Upshur. A man once expelled from college for partaking in a riot, the Virginian paid little mind to taking risks and concentrated his efforts on strengthening the United States Navy's presence in the Caribbean. He believed that only a stronger show of naval force in the Gulf of Mexico could keep southern plantations secure. In a report to the Senate, Upshur wrote, "The nature of our institutions presents a very strong appeal upon this point. A war between the United States and any considerable maritime Power would not be conducted at this day as it would have been even twenty years ago." The English, with the strongest naval power in the world, fell under the category of "any considerable maritime power," and they had a history of fighting unfairly. The head of America's fleet expected the British to again employ southern slaves as a weapon against the United States. "It would be a war of incursions aiming at revolution," he told Congress. "The first blow would be struck at us through our own institutions."[67] Slaveholders understood that the "revolution" which Upshur hoped to avoid would be one formulated by the enslaved, who, emboldened by British antislavery sentiments, might follow the example of the Haitian rebels decades before.

Wanting to defend slavery and secure its future in the South, Upshur openly discussed the dangerous liability that a large enslaved population posed to the safety of the United States as a whole. Craving to overthrow southern plantation owners, he reported, abolitionists wanted to unleash "the hostile elements of our social system against one another." While a potential invasion by English steamships endangered every portion of the nation, he explained, "in the southern portion of our country they might, and probably would be disastrous in the extreme."[68]

While discussing naval strategy, other members of the proslavery movement overtly expressed fears that black soldiers from the Caribbean could be used to attack the United States South. In 1841, for example, Alabama congressman Thomas Butler King, sitting on the Committee of Naval Affairs, wrote that the South's "unprotected harbors might be entered by fleets of armed steamers, loaded with black troops from the West Indies, to annoy and plunder the country."[69] It was not just the prospect of the British attacking the United States again that unnerved southern slaveholders. Rather, the feasibility of England using black troops provoked plantation owners to ask for more military fortifications in the Gulf of Mexico. While the increase of federal authority seemed to some to be antithetical to the South's states' rights dogma, in the 1830s it coincided with increased antislavery pressure both from the North and England. The planter class willingly gave up a fraction of local authority to protect slavery from outside threats. Promoting the power of slaveholders became the priority, not maintaining a pro-states' rights relationship between the South and the federal government. Maintaining the Union and defending slavery from criticism molded into a single idea for the practitioners of proslavery ideology and caused them to support the growth of federal power to protect the South's peculiar institution. They refused to accept the notion that the former could exist without the latter and this defined the planter elite's understanding of American exceptionalism.[70]

For many southern planters, the expectation of extending the South's peculiar institution of black enslavement to the Pacific became essential for maintaining a stable system of slave labor. The proslavery movement also identified westward expansion, implemented with the backing of a federal government directed by the proslavery elite, as the best way to ensure that American plantation owners never became like their counterparts in the West Indies: hemmed in by limited land and dependent on a hostile government for protection. Unlike in the Caribbean islands, slavery on the continent could continue to broaden its territorial scope, stopping the enslaved from becoming too densely populated to dominate and control. Many came to argue that expanding slaveholding territory served the national security interests of the United States.

In the 1840s, slaveholders considered the American West to be vital for their peculiar institution—it offered a place to send excess slaves, especially under the circumstance of the black population becoming too large for whites to oppress, and it prevented England from using Mexico as a way to invade the United States. One military officer, writing for a New Orleans journal, shared his concern about "the unscrupulous fanatics of England" joining forces with Mexico in order to colonize "the Californias with her colored allies" from the Caribbean. The author said, "Let Great Britain succeed in planting her colored battalions in the [Californias], and she will then have the Union surrounded by a chain of posts from New Brunswick to Honduras."[71] Being encircled by free soil meant that whites in the South should expect the eventual end of slavery and the anticipated violent consequences of emancipation. The editorialist admitted, "all the energies of the Southern States" would be needed "to resist" if a black colony became established in the western part of the North American continent.

To thwart the Atlantic antislavery impulse, planters sought to join the safety of the nation and the security of slavery. In the early 1840s, however, California did not become the priority for slaveholders who wanted new land in which to expand the United States institution of human bondage. Instead, the proslavery movement looked closer to home, across the Sabine River from Louisiana. In Texas, American slave owners hatched a revolution and demanded independence from Mexico. If annexed by the United States, the Lone Star Republic offered a massive amount of new land for American planters. Stretching from the Gulf Coast to the Rio Grande, Texas could shore up the defense of the slave states by allowing slave owners to move west without sparking sectional tension that came from creating new slave territory. With an energized proslavery class using the Democratic Party as an apparatchik, the debate concerning the annexation of Texas launched a conversation about slavery's expansion, how the federal government could be used as an instrument of slaveholding power, and the purpose of the Union and the Constitution.

5

TEXAS ANNEXATION AND THE PROSLAVERY PROMISE

WHEREAS, The recent developments in Federal affairs make it evident that the power of the Federal Government is sought to be made a weapon with which to strike down the interests and property of the people of Texas, and her sister slave-holding States, instead of permitting it to be, as was intended, our shield against outrage and aggression, THEREFORE . . . Texas is of right absolved from all restraints and obligations incurred by said compact, and is a separate sovereign State, and that her citizens and people are absolved from all allegiance to the United States or the government thereof.

—Texas Ordinance of Secession, February 1, 1861

The craving for western land became ravenous in the United States during the late 1830s and 1840s.[1] As Americans trekked toward the Pacific in search for opportunity, visions of their country reaching across the continent filled the heads of policy makers in the nation's capital. In 1836, proslavery forces established a new republic on the Gulf Coast; Texas offered southerners a feast to satiate their appetite for more slaveholding terrain. For the first time since the emancipation of the British West Indies, Americans considered adding more territory. Politics quickly became consumed with the question of slavery's role in westward expansion and the meaning and purpose of the United States of America and the Union that governed it.

During the twilight of the eighteenth century, the Spanish, followed by the newly independent Republic of Mexico, began to face immense pressure in Texas from a growing empire in North America—the Comanche. During the 1820s, the Native American nation, which had associated itself with Spanish business for decades, turned its eyes toward the United States for trade and established new commercial networks with American traders, disavowing pledges to the Spanish not to raid ranches and villages in New Mexico or Texas. Due to the lost alliance with the Comanche, Mexicans inherited a bankrupt and hamstrung province when they gained independence from their Spanish rulers in 1821.[2]

Between 1822 and 1825, and despite Mexico's objections to the institution of slavery, many immigrants who ventured to Texas came from the American South, spurred on by Mexican land grants and the new, booming trade with the Comanche economic network that extended throughout the Great Plains. During the decade before their revolution, Texans routinely found ways to skirt Mexican laws prohibiting the enslavement of human beings. Stephen F. Austin, regarded as the "Father of Texas," believed his new colony required slavery to survive. Although Austin echoed the sentiments of his fellow colonists, the Texas leader described his ambivalence toward increasing the number of enslaved black people in his colony. In a letter to his business partner in 1831, Austin—born two years after the advent of the Haitian Revolution in Virginia—wrote, "I sometimes shudder at the consequences [of slavery] and think that a large part [of] America will be Santa Domingonized in 100 or 200 years." Slavery, he believed, carried inherent danger: the larger the black population, the escalated chance of a massive rebellion. White immigrants demanded slaves, however, and, Austin concluded, "I am now in for the question and there is not retreat." Like the American founders, he placed the establishment, prosperity, and success of his new country ahead of dealing with slavery's potential risks and the natural rights of black residents in Texas.[3]

In April 1834, relations between Mexico and its northeastern province deteriorated. Antonio Lopez de Santa Anna came to power and repudiated the national constitution, proclaimed himself dictator, and created a centralized government. By September 1835, Texans held a convention to discuss how to respond. They perceived the expansion of Mexican federal authority as a threat to slavery. A month afterward, a group of Texans clashed with Santa Anna's forces in the Battle of Gonzales. Slaveholders acted preemptively to strike against potential emancipation and its feared consequences. The independence movement and the protection of slavery became entwined.[4]

As war in the southwest started, leaders in Washington waited for news. Just as southern plantation owners once agonized about the possibility of insurrections being inspired by an English or Haitian invasion, their counterparts in Texas worried that Mexico's armed forces planned to foment black rebellion, using the enslaved as a weapon to quell the white-led movement for independence. One Lone Star colonel voiced concern that Santa Anna might introduce "the sickly philanthropy of the abolitionists in the United States." While they worked to build a successful revolution, the founders of the Lone Star Republic tried to mitigate black rebellion by illegalizing "any free negro or mulatto" who came "within the limits of Texas."[5] Moreover, when the white revolutionaries gathered to frame a national government, they enshrined the prohibition of additional residencies for free-black immigrants without the consent of the Congress. Similar to their counterparts in South Carolina and Georgia, the architects of the Texas Revolution viewed the black population—both free and enslaved—as a hazardous element of society, a national problem that required the power and attention of the national government.

As fighting continued between Texas and Mexico, forty-two-year-old Stephen F. Austin tried to win independence through an American alliance. In a letter to Senator Lewis F. Linn, a Democrat from Missouri, Austin pleaded for help, posturing Texas as a sister to the United States and claiming its revolution to be important to American safety. He wrote, "For fifteen years I have been laboring like a slave to *Americanise* Texas—to form a nucleus around which my native countrymen could collect and grow into a solid body that would forever be a barrier of safety to the Southwestern frontier, and especially the outlet of the Western world—mouth of the Mississippi—and which would be the beacon-light to the Mexicans in their search after liberty."[6]

The Texas War of Independence, Austin warned, had devolved into a "war of extermination against anglo-Americans, and their principles and interests." He did not believe, however, that leaders in the United States should worry only about a Mexican invasion in the western frontier. Instead, basing his opinion on the often-violent conflict that broke out between Texas and the Comanche nation, which laid claim to the western portion of the Lone Star Republic, the revolutionary leader argued that Americans had to be wary of "the peril of an Indian and servile war—the murder of women and children, and the loss of civilization of Texas."[7] Recognition of an independent Lone Star Republic, he assured Senator Linn, served as a necessary, preventative measure to stifle potential black rebellion in the southern states. Slaveholders of the world needed to unite behind a common defense.

Many proslavery advocates considered Texas the perfect vehicle for maintaining the principles of a white republic in the United States. Austin contended: "The Americanism of Texas, is of more real service to the protection of Louisiana, Arkansas and Missouri." The United States had a responsibility to "march into Texas, and say to the pirate Santa Anna, 'stop,' a great and philanthropic and free people, will not stand tamely by and see justice, constitutional right and humanity, wantonly violated at her door; nor can a paternal Government tolerate such a state of things on its most vulnerable and important frontier." Any other alternative, he wrote, might "bring the bloody tide of savage war, and the horrors of negro insurrection" to the American South.[8] Without action from Washington, Austin insisted, the fires of slave rebellion, fanned by the Mexican army, would swallow Louisiana and Arkansas before enveloping the entire Gulf Coast. Austin did not live to see his wish fulfilled, however. The United States finally acknowledged Texas independence in 1837, a few short months after he had died of pneumonia.

In the wake of the Battle of San Jacinto, where Texans captured the Mexican president and forced him to sign a treaty granting them independence, the new Lone Star Republic immediately requested to join the United States. Sam Houston, the general who defeated Santa Anna and became the first president of Texas, wrote to the White House in November 1836 expressing a "great desire . . . that our country, Texas, shall be annexed to the U. States." Houston told Old Hickory that his new nation, despite gaining its sovereignty, would be unlikely "to sustain ourselves against any power who are not impotent." He asked President Jackson to be a "friend of liberty," using his sway to garner congressional approval to grant Texas a place in the Union.[9]

The White House examined statehood for Texas differently than it had official recognition of Texas independence. Andrew Jackson, as well as his successors Martin Van Buren and William Henry Harrison, believed that any plan for annexation could not be implemented without disturbing the nation's diplomatic relationship with Mexico. Despite trying to purchase Texas earlier in his term, Andrew Jackson delayed his decision to acknowledge its national sovereignty until long after the capture and capitulation of Santa Anna. Americans did not want to precipitate a war with their southwestern neighbor. Both Presidents Jackson and Van Buren decided to tread lightly around the issue. The division caused by the abolitionist postal campaign and the gag rule led both presidents to attempt to soothe the controversial issue of slavery in national politics. Sectional politics necessitated that expansionists wait for a political opening to support the annexation of the new proslavery republic on the Gulf of Mexico.[10]

By the late 1830s, the long-standing posture of Jackson and Van Buren toward Texas seemed to be a wise one. Hostility toward adding another slaveholding star to Old Glory intensified in the free states throughout the decade and a financial crisis crippled the economy in 1837. No one summed up the antislavery resentment toward the proposal to annex Texas better than William Ellery Channing. Born in New England and the son of a signer of the Declaration of Independence, Channing first gained fame in 1819 as a Unitarian minister living in Baltimore when he challenged the tenets of Calvinism. At that time, his antislavery conviction had not fully blossomed. As he matured, however, the theologian concluded that the enslavement of black Americans was a moral cancer in need of removal from the soul of the United States. His conversion to abolitionism came after spending time in the Danish West Indies on the cusp of British emancipation. Having seen human beings treated like animals, he could no longer sit idly by while turning a blind eye toward the suffering of the enslaved. Once Channing committed to the abolitionist cause, he joined John Quincy Adams as a commanding voice against the proslavery movement's influence over the American government.[11]

In 1837 Channing drafted "A Letter on the Annexation of Texas to the United States" that he addressed to Henry Clay, the presumed frontrunner for the Whig nomination in 1840. His writing received attention in numerous publications throughout the free states, and the minister established a framework for the antislavery movement's opposition to the annexation of Texas. Channing told Clay, the former president of the American Colonialization Society, that if he used his political power to "promote" Channing's "views on the subject of this communication," it would "accomplish a good, to which, perhaps, no other man in this country is equal."[12] He implored the Kentucky senator to utilize his popularity to become the leading voice of dissent toward adding the slaveholding republic to the Union.

Channing disputed the legitimacy of Texas's proslavery revolution against Mexico. He insisted the event had been "criminal" in exercise because the Texan colonists deliberately disobeyed the oaths they took when they acquired Mexican land grants, specifically restrictions against the importation of slavery. The New Englander maintained the consolidation of the government under Santa Anna did not warrant an independence movement. Rather, the Mexican dictator's move "was ratified by the National Congress according to the rules prescribed by the Constitution, and was sanctioned by the Mexican people." Taken altogether, he declared, "Texans, a handful of strangers, raised the standard of revolt, because the government was changed by a nation of nine millions without their consent."[13] Unlike the American Revolution, which established an exceptional nation, the Texas revolutionaries perpetrated a fraud—an overt power grab by the planter elite.

Channing provided additional statistical evidence for the illegitimacy of the Texas Revolution. He challenged the actual number of revolutionaries who lived in the Lone Star Republic, portraying the drive for independence as a coup d'état launched by a small cadre of planters rather than a major revolution consented to by the people. To him, it seemed more like an "insurrection" than an actual freedom movement. He wrote that those who raised "the standard of war" against Mexico in Texas were fewer than the discontents residing in the "suburbs of London," insisting that "their revolt may be compared to the rising of a county in Massachusetts or Virginia for the purpose of establishing a separate sovereignty."[14] Dissent by such a small group should not be allowed to turn into legitimate revolution simply because it coincided with the interests of slaveholders.

Slavery served as the cornerstone for the New Englander's critique of the Texas Revolution and its possible annexation by the United States. He admonished southerners who partook in "the project of dismembering a neighboring republic" in order to extend the South's peculiar institution westward.[15] The antislavery leader felt ashamed for his country, claiming that the American government supported the breaking of international law when it agreed to let private citizens fight against Mexico. Adding Texas as another slave state gave the proslavery movement a reason to instigate an increased number of "revolutions" throughout the world, the theologian feared. It established a precedent that emboldened planters to seek out extralegal ways to spread slavery.

Channing anticipated that allowing Texas annexation would alter the American model for declaring war. He wrote, "Texas is a country conquered by our citizens; and the annexation of it to our Union will be the beginning of conquests which, unless arrested and beaten back by a just and Kind Providence, will stop only at the Isthmus of Darien." He also warned that the consequences of Americans—especially those in free states—accepting land for slavery by conquest meant never-ending war. If America added Texas, he asked, then why not seize all of Mexico? If conquering Mexico succeeded, why not try to control of Central America as well? He wrote, "Our Eagle will whet, not gorge, its appetite on its first victim, and will snuff a more tempting quarry, more alluring blood, in every new region which opens southward." In summation, he said, "[to] annex Texas is to declare perpetual war with Mexico."[16] Slaveholders never shied away from pushing for greater expansion. They simply moved from one target to the next, devouring territory and spoiling land for those who hoped to live on free soil.

William Ellery Channing's letter to Henry Clay alerted those in the free states that if they accepted the growth of slaveholding territory by the barrel of the gun, they should also be prepared for continual war, not only with their neighbors to the South, but also in Canada. Adding Texas to the Union, he argued, put the country on the path toward another fight with England. The "collision with the West Indies will be the most certain effect of the extension of our power in" the Gulf of Mexico, he predicted. American planters would never allow West Indian freedom to influence the slaveholding South; therefore, they would never "cultivate friendly sentiments towards communities whose whole history will be a bitter reproach to their institutions, a witness against their wrongs, and whose ardent sympathies will be enlisted in the cause of the slave."[17] Instead, he expected the planter elite to use foreign policy for the promotion of their own interests rather than for that of the country as a whole. If nonslaveholders tired of their nation being dominated by slaveholders, Channing pointed to Texas annexation as the political hill worth dying upon.

Channing understood how the proslavery movement had changed during the 1830s. He wrote, "In opening to ourselves vast regions, in which we may spread slavery, and in spreading it . . . the slave-holding States may bear rule in the national councils, we make slavery the predominant interest of the State." Adding territory did not just broaden the evil of slavery across the North American continent; it also consolidated the strength of slaveholders within the federal government. He predicted that with "the basis of power, the spring or guide of public measures, the object for which the revenues, strength, and wealth of the country, are to be exhausted. Slavery will be branded on our front as the great idea, the prominent feature of the country. We shall renounce our high calling as a people, and accomplish the lowest destiny to which a nation can be bound."[18] Channing maintained that if northerners acquiesced to the addition of more slave states they could no longer blame their forefathers for planting the seed of black servitude in the United States. Free-staters would share culpability with the planter class rather than being bystanders to their nation's original sin of human enslavement. Instead, the institution might remain imprinted upon the soul of Americans forever, an eternal blight waiting for God's judgment. The minister hoped to fight the growing Slave Power in Washington, and he did not stand alone.

While William Ellery Channing attempted to sway leaders like Henry Clay to oppose Texas annexation, John Quincy Adams worked inside the halls of the Capitol to block the addition of the Lone Star Republic to the Union. Sent back to Congress by his Massachusetts neighbors in 1831, the former president emphasized the unpopularity of granting Texas statehood by pointing to petitions from roughly one hundred thousand Americans who disagreed with it. He prepared for another fight over the influence of the First Amendment on the floor of the House of Representatives.

In response to Adams, however, proslavery forces once again exerted their congressional muscle by extending the gag rule, this time to incorporate anything that discussed the expansion of slavery.[19] The planter elite's censorship of antislavery memorials grew in scope, fending off new challenges to the proslavery movement. What began as a tool to silence talk about emancipation in the nation's capital became a weapon used by slaveholders to undermine any negative reaction to adding slave territory to the United States. Plantation owners in Washington leveraged their power in the national capital to expand their political strength, quieting those who opposed slavery in any way.

Small in stature, but as brilliant and ferociously articulate as his father, John Quincy Adams became the recognized antislavery leader of the House of Representatives, earning him the nickname of Old Man Eloquent from his congressional colleagues. The former president stated that obstructing the addition of slave territory to the United States would eventually end the practice in North America altogether. Objecting to Texas, he told his fellow antislavery supporters, eroded the power of slaveholders, making it exceedingly difficult for them to continue holding millions of people in chains. "I believe," he said, "if Texas is not annexed to this Union that the time is not remote when there will not be a slave either in these States or in Texas." The rationale was straightforward: "If Texas is excluded, in the first place she will operate as a drain for the slaves from South Carolina; and that State will be so drained of its slave population that the white inhabitants, including [slaveholders], will be the first to urge the propriety of abolition."[20] He expected most nonslaveholders in the South to hold little objection to the notion of exporting the threat of insurrection—and their economic competition—to an independent Republic of Texas.

Southerners in the audience laughed at Adams, but he ignored their derision. He sincerely believed that if Texas stayed out of the Union the South's peculiar institution would eventually die in the United States. The perpetuation of slavery depended on its expansion under the American flag. The former president argued that the debate about incorporating Texas revolved around whether slavery would be a regional or national aspect of the country's future. What neither Adams nor Channing anticipated, however, was how their arguments might be co-opted by expansionists. By mere happenstance, the proslavery cause soon found itself in the position to do just that shortly after the inauguration of a new president in 1841, setting off a heated battle of words that became tinged with sectionalism and racial outlook while creating a contest over the belief of American exceptionalism and the purpose of the Union.[21]

The election of 1840 saw the Whig Party have their first serious opportunity to win the White House. Rather than nominating their founder and standard-bearer, Henry Clay, however, the chief opposition to the party of Jackson chose an Ohioan as their champion, William Henry Harrison. A sixty-seven-year-old retired general who gained national acclaim fighting Native Americans in the Midwest, "Old Tippecanoe" became the favorite in the race after the two nominating conventions. The economic trouble stemming from the Panic of 1837 dominated American politics during the presidential contest. The title of one of the Whig pamphlets summed up their strategy for defeating the eighth president's bid for another term: "Harrison and Prosperity or Van Buren and Ruin."[22]

In 1840, talk of adding Texas to the United States gained scant traction as a contentious campaign issue. The two candidates refused to risk losing votes by discussing such a divisive, sectionalized topic. Harrison did something, however, that Van Buren did not. He, along with popular party figures such as Henry Clay and Daniel Webster, actively canvassed for votes by presenting their nominee as a common man who related to ordinary people. They offered a choice to Americans: "the log cabin and the palace, between hard cider and champagne." Despite being labeled a political hack by Democrats for running what became known as "the hard cider campaign," Old Tippecanoe became the first Whig president, defeating Van Buren in a landslide by winning the Electoral College 234 to 60.[23]

In his two-hour inaugural address, which he delivered on a cold and rainy day in Washington, the second-oldest president elected in American history never mentioned Mexico, Texas, or the expansion of American landholding in the West. Instead, the former general focused on his principles, paying particular attention to the role of government in economic development. Much to the delight of his party, the new occupant of the White House told onlookers that internal improvements would be the major focus of his administration. For the first time in over a decade a different party than the Democrats found itself in charge of the federal government. The Whigs considered their triumph to be a turning point for the nation. Finally, they could implement their plan to shape America's future.[24]

A month later, the party of Clay stumbled into crisis when illness struck the new president weeks into his term. William Henry Harrison probably contracted pneumonia from the multitude of office seekers who packed the White House begging for federal employment. After a brief, final battle, the ninth executive of the United States breathed his last breath on April 4, 1841. While succumbing to his sickness, Harrison's final words were for his successor: "Sir, I wish you to understand the true principles of the government. I wish them carried out. I ask nothing more." For the first time in history an American president died in office. President Harrison was initially buried in the Congressional Cemetery in the nation's capital. His remains, however, eventually found their final resting place in North Bend, Ohio, where his wife, Anna, had been packing for her move to the White House merely weeks before. In the span of thirty-one days, three different people served as president of the United States. With three years and eleven months left in the presidential term, John Tyler, a Virginian aristocrat and former Democrat, served in Harrison's place.[25]

The death of the president so soon after the inauguration stunned the country. Although Henry Clay initially believed Tyler might remain loyal to the Whig cause, John Quincy Adams privately expressed uneasiness about Old Tippecanoe's passing. He estimated that slavery still "festered" below the surface of American political life and felt distressed about the role it might play in the policy and politics of Harrison's successor. The sixth president detested the tenth. Harrison originally offered the vice presidency to Daniel Webster, a Whig stalwart, but the Massachusetts senator declined, choosing to serve as secretary of state instead. Adams viewed the general's second choice as a man so unsuited for the office that he refused to grant him the actual title of President of the United States, referring to the Virginian instead as "Acting President of the Union."[26]

In the least, Adams expected John Tyler to actively work to preserve the power of slaveholders. At worst, he might seek to expand it. On the day William Henry Harrison died, Adams wrote in his diary that the vice president was "a political sectarian, of the slave-driving, Virginia, Jeffersonian school, principled against all improvement, with all the interests and passions and vices of slavery rooted in his moral and political constitution—with talents not above mediocrity, and a spirit incapable of expansion to the dimensions of the station upon which he has been cast by the hand of Providence, unseen through the apparent agency of chance." The weather seemed to fit Old Man Eloquent's mood. The former president ended his entry by noting, "This day was in every sense gloomy—rain the whole day." He knew the inaugural address read just over a month before suddenly became meaningless. The man moving into the White House, he suspected, never believed in the plan Harrison had set forth. Tyler had once declared abolitionists to be the supporters of "midnight assassination" who were influenced by foreign enemies of the United States. John Quincy Adams expected the new president to be less of a Whig and more of a slaveholder.[27]

As Adams predicted, the new president promptly found himself at odds with his own party. Upon the death of President Harrison, Henry Clay trivialized Tyler's ascension to the seat of the chief executive, dubbing the new commander in chief with the sobriquet of "His Accidency." Although Clay had been left off the top of the ticket in favor of Harrison, the Sage of Ashland still expected to have a role in shaping the policy initiatives of the first Whig administration. Furthermore, the presidential cabinet remained filled with appointments loyal to the party's ideals. At long last, Clay thought, the national government could build infrastructure and create a centralized banking system, both of which had been maligned while Democrats held power.[28]

John Tyler, however, quickly revealed his rather less than monogamous relationship with Whig ideas. The labeling of the new president as a "Jeffersonian" by his own party's detractors proved quite accurate. During the early months of his term, Tyler vetoed a bill that resuscitated the Bank of the United States, an institution despised by the devotees of Jackson and beloved by those faithful to Clay. In his veto message, the president wrote, "I regard the bill as asserting for Congress the right to incorporate a United States Bank, with power and right to establish offices of discount and deposit in the several States of this Union, with or without their consent, a principle to which I have always heretofore been opposed, and which can never obtain my sanction."[29] The Democrats might have lost the election in 1840, but they had not lost their policy emanating from the White House.

The president stayed true to his personal principles. When Clay ushered through a second banking bill that he presumed would satisfy the president's states' rights proclivities, Tyler vetoed it, too. In response, all but one of the president's cabinet resigned in protest. The president lost the minimal loyalty that remained from the party of Clay. A longtime acquaintance and colleague of Tyler from the Virginia state legislature, Abel P. Upshur, believed the beleaguered president should create a coalition of his own. The Virginian advised Tyler to concentrate less on domestic policy, which required congressional approval, and implored him to take up westward expansion instead—an issue that fell more broadly to the discretion of the executive branch. With Upshur as a key adviser, John Tyler looked to the proslavery movement to help him build a new political party and win a presidential term of his own.[30]

Born in Virginia and experienced in practicing both law and politics in the Old Dominion, Abel Upshur epitomized the protean nature of the proslavery movement in the aftermath of Nat Turner's revolt and the abolitionist postal campaign. In the 1820s, the lawyer from Richmond predicted that universal emancipation would eventually come to the Old Dominion. During the 1830s his expectations shifted, however. As with a number of other slaveholders, Thomas Dew's defense of slavery heavily informed the presidential adviser's ideas regarding the enslavement of black people in the United States. In a span of a year, Upshur wrote two articles: one defending states' rights from what he believed to be incursions of the federal government; the other contending that slaveholders should manage the authority of Washington. Rather than strictly adhering to the states' rights principles of the Jeffersonian school, he advocated the creation of a strong federal government that used its influence to protect slavery nationally while maintaining direct regulation of the South's peculiar institution locally. Only then, he contended, could the United States be truly exceptional.[31]

In 1840, Abel Upshur joined the chorus of slaveholders appealing for the proslavery movement to claim the mantle of the federal government. The first step, he wrote in the *Southern Literary Messenger,* was for southern politicians to turn slavery into a matter that concerned more than just the planter elite. "We have been in the habit of contemplating [slavery] rather as a domestic than as a political institution," he said. "It is fortunate for us that we are no longer permitted to view [slavery] in so imperfect a light. It is as a political institution that it possesses the highest interest to us."[32] The proslavery politicians in Congress needed to take the antislavery movement head-on because only the power of Washington could stop them.

The Virginian based his ideas on expectations for the future. A pessimist, Upshur proclaimed in "Domestic Slavery" that all free societies eventually perished. The real project for a free people, he argued, was to lengthen the time before the fall into tyranny. Americans had designed a unique way to forestall collapse, however—the Constitution. "In contemplating the future decline of liberty in the United States," he wrote, "it cannot escape us that there is a want of perfect analogy between our republics and those of every other age and country. . . . Our form of government has no example among [the rest of the world]." Upshur argued that America's "peculiar" federal structure made the nation "more solidly founded and better balanced." The exceptional nature of the founding, he said, allowed the United States to avoid the pitfalls that former empires had experienced in the past.[33]

The composition of the government and the unique nature of the country's founding did not safeguard American freedom alone, Upshur argued. Slavery played an essential role, as well. He explained to the readers of the *Southern Literary Messenger* that U.S. slaveholding was exceptional. While ancient civilizations acquired slaves through war with neighbors, southern plantation owners found class stability in the explicit racial division of the workforce. He wrote, "Our safety is in the color of the slave; in an external ineffaceable distinction of nature. With us, there is no margin in the word *manumitto,* which transmutes the slave into the free citizen."[34] The implication of his statements was obvious to those who read his message: abolitionists pushed ideas that ruined free republics of the past. Radical abolitionists tried to ignite the flames of extremism rather than remaining loyal to the political tradition of moderation; thus Upshur labeled their policies regressive and in contrast to the progressive model of slavery based on white supremacy practiced by the planter elite in the South. In an offensive against abolitionism in the North, slaveholding intellectuals fused slavery to American exceptionalism and the purpose of the Union.

Abel Upshur judged black enslavement to be the fountainhead of liberty for whites in the United States. Slavery allowed the country to be distinct on the world stage because it limited the tumultuous class revolution seen in places such as France. "The last man with whom the slave would unite," he explained, "is his overseer." However, that did not mean the institution was entirely safe, especially in times of war. To quell those concerns, the Virginian reassured readers that "a very small squadron, prepared to march promptly and rapidly to any point of danger, would be sufficient to put down the best planned servile insurrection."[35] As long as the military defended the South from black rebellion, freedom for whites could last in America. This ideology played a substantial role in the Virginian's thinking while he counseled President Tyler.

When Upshur started in Washington as the new head of the navy, many in the political class believed him to be both an extreme states' rights disciple and an ardent defender of slavery. They expected him to use his federal authority sparingly because he viewed a centralized, national government to be a potential threat against the South's peculiar institution. One Ohio member of the press described him as someone who "has zealous ideas of the beauty and utility of the slavery system, and can knock down any man living upon the theory of that point." Political watchers soon discovered Upshur's worldview rested less on a devotion to decentralized government and more on his determination to protect the South's peculiar institution at all cost. Once on the job, he actively employed reforms that erected a stronger military presence in the South because he feared an attack from the Caribbean. The Virginian hoped to make Washington the epicenter of proslavery power.[36]

After settling a border dispute with Canada, Secretary of State Daniel Webster, Harrison's lone cabinet member left in the Tyler administration, resigned from his post. Tyler chose his old friend Upshur to lead America's foreign policy, and together the two began promoting proslavery ideas that stretched constitutional limits. The president understood that the people—or at least an electoral majority of them—could only resist the temptation of territorial expansion for so long. Americans considered the addition of land to be part of the nation's destiny, but no political party adopted expansionist policies. President Tyler believed he could transform the voting coalitions that held the American two-party system together. Texas offered a convenient way for the president to gain popularity among the voting public without approval from Congress. Foreign policy rested almost completely with the presidency. Shortly after taking occupancy in the White House, the new proslavery president sent an agent to England with the task of gauging British interest in tying itself closer to Texas. The man no one thought would be president devised a plan to add massive amounts of new territory to the United States. Despite the concerns of his predecessors, John Tyler became devoted to turning the Lone Star Republic into the Lone Star State.[37]

Prodded on by the president and his supporters, Texas annexation reemerged in public consciousness in 1843. The issue first came to the forefront of American politics in a letter published in the pro-administration newspaper *The Daily Madisonian.* A dashing, up-and-coming Whig congressman, Thomas Gilmer, offered the first signs that the proslavery movement tied slavery's expansion with the defense of the Union. Having entered politics at the age of twenty-seven, and elected governor in 1840 at the age of thirty-eight, the Virginian saw supporting the president as the natural progression of his statesmanship. After being elected to the House of Representatives, he enthusiastically worked to bring Texas into the United States of America.[38]

As they had during the Haitian Revolution, British emancipation of the West Indies, and the abolitionist postal campaign, the proslavery movement looked to win support from those who held little moral qualms about the enslavement of black Americans. Gilmer explained how much the North, especially the Midwest, gained from annexation. He contended that adding "the unusually fertile territory" benefited the free states more than the slave South because Texas would "be rapidly peopled" by U.S. immigrants who would "open a market at home for the manufactures and agricultural products of all the non-slaveholding States." The former Virginia governor asserted that only southerners could oppose the incorporation of Texas due to economic concerns, writing that Texas fostered "a competition for which it could find no immediate equivalent, except in the vast acquisition of national wealth, prosperity, and harmony which would result."[39] Annexation served the interests of the common man.

Thomas Gilmer portrayed slaveholders as patriotic supporters of annexation who placed the good of the country above all else. However, he also unwittingly fulfilled Channing's prophecy that expansionists might not be satiated with only Texas. The congressman insisted that Americans stood at the threshold of greatness, and thus, should be poised for unlimited territorial expansion: "Our federative Union, in the spirit of its adoption, is capable of indefinite extension. Space and numbers will only add to its blessings."[40] He prayed that, despite being slave territory, national pride might inspire northerners to approve the incorporation of Texas into the Union.

Patriotism alone, however, did not convince northerners to join Tyler's new coalition for acquiring more western land. Two particular issues combined to prompt many free-staters to accept territorial expansion. The first was antiblack sentiment, which often drove the opposition to expanding slavery westward. Gilmer understood that the South's peculiar institution could not be altogether avoided when talking about annexation. After all, the planter elite had devised and initiated the Texas Revolution. His letter turned on its head the opposition to slavery's extension. He reasoned, "The culture of cotton and sugar in the United States has done more to withdraw slavery southward, than all the expedients which the wisdom of this or other generations could devise."[41] He told northerners that acquiring additional slave territory forced black people held in bondage to move away from the Upper South and the North. Diffusion went from being an antislavery plan in the 1820s to a proslavery argument in the 1840s.

Following in the footsteps of his proslavery predecessors, Gilmer also discussed national security, focusing on the British emancipation in the West Indies. "The prejudices of England against slavery are philosophically confined to sympathetic meetings, popular harangues, and a neighborly disposition to see us dissolve our union on account of it," he wrote. Every American needed to worry because "England, whose possessions and jurisdictions extend over so large a portion of the globe, whose influence is felt every where, will either possess or control Texas, if it does not come under the jurisdiction of the United States."[42] Thomas Gilmer argued that Americans should expect another war if the British took charge in the Lone Star Republic. Peace and prosperity required American leadership in the southwest.[43]

The misgivings of the Tyler administration about English machinations in Texas did not derive from a twisting of facts or proslavery daydreams. The cornerstone of American diplomacy in the Gulf of Mexico revolved around concerns that slaveholders held for nearly half a century. Remembering the *Creole,* the White House assumed that the English aimed at controlling Texas as a way to promote abolitionism in the United States. In the early months of his term, President Tyler asked Duff Green to be America's agent in England. An eccentric Kentuckian who served in Andrew Jackson's Kitchen Cabinet, Green earned a small fortune in patronage from editing the *United States Telegraph,* the administration's mouthpiece in Washington. However, things changed quickly for Green when he backed John Calhoun in a spat with Jackson involving the wives of the president's cabinet. The irascible Old Hickory admonished the editor for supporting the South Carolinian, but his loyalty to Calhoun made Tyler trust him. Planning to capitalize on the issue of Texas annexation, the new man in the White House tasked Green with traveling to Europe to gauge the mood in England regarding the Lone Star Republic. Would the British people support a war over Texas and slavery?[44]

Arriving in England merely a month after the *Creole* incident, Green reported that the British Empire planned to create a commercial monopoly by commanding the oceans and expanding its landholdings in North America. Their strategy involved enveloping California and Oregon in the empire, giving England a stronger foothold in the Pacific. He speculated that the English feared both American manufacturing in the North and the power southern cotton gave the United States on the world market. He wrote that the English designed to shrink American influence in the Western Hemisphere.[45]

Maintaining loyalty to the South Carolina senator, Green informed John C. Calhoun of his work for the president, telling him that England found "it impossible to maintain her commercial and manufacturing superiority, because she cannot raise cotton, sugar &c., as cheap in India as it can be raised in the United States, Cuba, and Brazil." He sent news that the British planned to use their military strength to destroy American slavery and reshape the composition of the global economy. Abolitionism had hardened the British Empire, Green wrote, "Her war on slavery and the slave-trade is intended to increase the cost of producing the raw material in the United States, Brazil, and Cuba.... You will find that England has much more than a work of benevolence in the suppression of the slave-trade."[46] He advised leaders in Washington to be on guard. England might do anything to keep their economic superiority.

By 1843 Calhoun made it his priority to find a way to exercise federal authority and add Texas to the Union. Throughout the next year, the South Carolina senator collected other worrisome letters pertaining to the growing Abolitionist Power. Secretary of State Upshur echoed the distress of slaveholders, telling Calhoun, "There can be no doubt, I think, that England is determined to abolish slavery throughout the American continent and islands, if she can. It is worse than childish, to suppose that she mediates this great movement, simply from an impulse of philanthropy."[47] From the vantage point of the proslavery movement in charge of the federal government, Texas served as the perfect place for them to exert their influence against the burgeoning antislavery impulse in the Atlantic. Risking war with Mexico seemed to be a better option to slaveholding politicians than doing nothing and waiting for insurrection inspired by British abolitionism.

Besides receiving messages from Duff Green and Abel Upshur, Calhoun also heard from Ashbel Smith, the Texas minister to England and future regent of the University of Texas. A doctor from Connecticut who had traveled previously through much of Western Europe, Smith warned that the English planned to dismantle slavery in Texas and create a nightmare for southern planters, especially in Louisiana, Arkansas, and Missouri. He wrote, "I sincerely believe that the ultimate purpose is to make Texas a refuge for runaway slaves from the United States, and eventually a negro nation, a sort of Hayti on the continent" backed by the might of the military British Empire.[48]

Scenes of black soldiers marching through Louisiana most likely filled John C. Calhoun's imagination. When the South Carolinian had been a young boy, suspicion about Haiti's revolution caused southern planters to use their power to steer the course of national diplomacy toward undermining the black-led republic on Hispaniola. The dismay experienced by slaveholders from the collapse of Saint-Domingue had undoubtedly been seared into the former vice president's memory. The prospects of the slave states being neighbored by black nations to the southeast and west—along with the abolitionist threat leavening in the free states to the north and the British West Indies to the south—caused the planter elite to worry about their future. Calhoun and other influential members of the proslavery movement became convinced that annexation served as the only way to ensure that abolitionism did not destabilize the southern plantation system.

While serving as President Tyler's chief diplomat, Upshur also perceived pressure from England's expanding antislavery presence in the Atlantic. He sent an urgent letter to the U.S. minister to Great Britain, Edward Everett, "The movements of Great Britain, with respect to African slavery," he stated, "have at length assumed a character which demands the serious attention of this Government." The secretary of state contended, "There are many and strong reasons for believing that the abolition of domestic slavery throughout the continent and islands of America is a leading object in the present policy of England." Although the White House "would be reluctant to believe that any design unfriendly to this country . . . enters into the policy of England," Upshur saw it as a necessity to convince the president otherwise. "The bare suspicion" that England desired to free enslaved Americans, he thought, was "calculated to excite, and in this instance has actually excited a very strong sensation among our people."[49] Abolitionists could undermine the system of slavery simply through language and without using force. The slightest inkling among the black populace that they had white allies might motivate them to strike against the master class. To crush such notions, slaveholders needed to assert further influence over American foreign policy and national expansion.

Planters believed that slavery's perpetuation depended on keeping England out of Texas. Upshur wrote, "It is obvious that slavery could not easily be maintained in a country surrounded by other countries whose Governments did not recognize that institution." While many in the free states were "as much opposed to the institution as England itself," northern objection to slavery remained restrained in comparison to British abolitionism. The American Constitution had, from its inception, safeguarded slavery by making it a reserved right of each state, he argued. The free states had to acknowledge slavery's existence below the Mason-Dixon Line, unlike America's Canadian neighbor, "whose Government did not recognize" the South's peculiar labor system. Because the Constitution protected property rights, "the absconding slave, therefore, has many chances against him before he can reach Canada." While relying on the concept of localism to protect the existence of slavery in the states from federal intervention, Upshur also insisted that the purpose of the Union was to protect the South's peculiar institution from outside influence that undermined the slaveholding class. For the proslavery movement, the Constitution served as a tool for planters, not as a neutral referee that balanced regional interests.[50]

Without expansion and annexation, however, Upshur maintained that the situation might turn against southern slaveholders. He wrote, "Texas, however, lies immediately on the border of Louisiana and Arkansas. The slave would have nothing more to do than simply to cross the Sabine or the Red River, and he would find himself a free man." The *Creole* incident remained fresh in the mind of the Virginian in charge of America's diplomacy. Without British cooperation in returning fugitive slaves, Upshur predicted "scenes of violence and collision between the people of the two countries would be of almost daily occurrence; resentments would be kindled; and a war *de facto* would prevail."[51]

Abel Upshur understood that admitting Texas as a slave state "would be received, at first, with a brush of repugnance" from northerners. To put his plan into effect, he determined that annexationists needed to explain the necessity of protecting white southerners from insurrection promoted by England and its antislavery influence in the Gulf Coast. He expected that "the more the subject is reflected on, the more clearly will [northerners] see that the measure is absolutely necessary. To the South, it is a question of *safety*; to the North, it is one of interest."[52] The planter elite had to find a way to regain support from those in the free states who did not object to slavery on moral grounds. Committed moralists would never change their minds, but white supremacists might.

The threat of war with the British Empire, along with the knowledge that a large swathe of people in the free states felt little sympathy for blacks—enslaved or free—functioned as the rationale for annexation. Upshur never realized his goals, however. Just days after pressuring President Sam Houston of Texas with an ultimatum that eventually added the Lone Star Republic to the Union, the secretary of state decided to join President Tyler, the newly appointed secretary of the navy Thomas Gilmer, and hundreds of others on a convivial tour of a new sloop-of-war named the *Princeton* as it sailed the Potomac in February 1844. Fate prevented the two leading annexationists from seeing the results of their handiwork.

On a winter day, the dignitaries gathered to celebrate America's burgeoning naval power. The *Princeton's* Peacemaker, described as the largest naval gun in the world, exemplified the growing might of the United States. Most of the political heavyweights mingled below deck, enjoying the festivities and hoping to have a few words with the president. For Secretaries Upshur and Gilmer the cannon provided the real fun. President Tyler had offered a toast halfway through the trip: to the *Princeton,* its captain, and its Peacemaker. Wanting to pay respects to George Washington, Gilmer talked the captain into firing the gun one last time—a thunderous salute to the Father of the Nation. Calling down to the chattering collection of grandees below deck, he encouraged those in attendance to join him in watching one last blast. As Tyler walked toward the stairs a guest used the opening to speak to him. Grabbing the president's arm, he urged him to stay for one more drink. Politely, the commander in chief acquiesced, missing the spectacle about to go on above.

Grinning with excitement and ready for the show, Gilmer and Upshur stood near the Peacemaker. They both wanted to see the ship's largest cannon up close. Gilmer encouraged onlookers to hold their mouths open to avoid a concussion from the shock wave produced by the weapon and then ordered the captain to fire. With a bright flash, the untested gun exploded like a bomb. The secretary of state, the secretary of the navy, a few members of Congress, along with several sailors, died instantly. The president remained unharmed, saved by his courteousness. Annexationists suddenly lost two key figures, but the momentum for their movement could not be stopped.[53]

Following the tragedy on the Potomac, other members of the proslavery movement picked up where Upshur and Gilmer left off. Born to an influential family in the upcountry of Pennsylvania, and married to the granddaughter of Benjamin Franklin, Robert J. Walker became the voice for annexation after the *Princeton* disaster. The Mississippi politician served as a perfect candidate to bridge the divide between North and South over expansion. A top graduate from the University of Pennsylvania, Walker initially practiced law in Pittsburgh. However, after a few years at trying his hand at the bar, he fostered another ambition; the lawyer from the Keystone State wanted to be a plantation owner and in 1826 the Pennsylvanian became a Mississippian. Less than a decade later, voters in the Magnolia State sent him to Washington, where he led the push for western territory, particularly Texas annexation. The senator knew, as Upshur and other pro-annexationists did, that adding more slaveholding territory could only prevail with the help of a large contingent of northerners.[54]

In 1844, Robert Walker became the spokesman for annexation by publishing the cornerstone argument for the proslavery effort to bring Texas into the

Union. A charismatic figure, a number of his colleagues in Congress—friends and foes alike—said that the senator could induce the most reluctant opponent to join his side of a debate. Similar to Channing with his anti-Texas message a few years before, Walker published a letter arguing his position. In a roughly thirty-page response to a group of Kentuckians who inquired about expansion, the Mississippi Democrat laid out a bold argument that successfully convinced many northerners in his own party, which now held a majority in the House of Representatives, to back annexation. Copies of Walker's letter spread across the country like wildfire. The proslavery movement also adopted the tactics of their opponents. Wealthy southerners devised a "Texas Fund" to finance the publication of Walker's writing and developed a pro-annexation mail campaign that circulated his message across the country by the thousands.[55]

Letter of Mr. Walker, of Mississippi, Relative to the Annexation of Texas demonstrated how proslavery ideology changed during the first half of the nineteenth century. During the decades after the framing of the Constitution, slaveholders eyed the federal government with circumspection, worrying that a powerful national government might eventually ban slavery. However, by the 1840s the planter elite adopted a new stance, declaring it the responsibility of Washington to preserve the South's peculiar institution by any means necessary. Drawing from the ideas of proslavery intellectuals, the Mississippi senator molded a defense for annexation that transcended sectional lines. He claimed that adding Texas secured the exceptionalism of the United States from foreign aggression and influence. Only by accepting the Lone Star Republic into the ranks of the Union could Americans maintain their freedom and independence from outside influence.

Robert Walker quickly immersed himself in a public conversation on slavery, race, and the role Texas could play in protecting the future of the Union. For the first time, he created a singular, synthesized argument that could be repeated by annexationists anywhere. The Mississippi senator imitated the example of Thomas Jefferson, who in the Declaration of Independence charged the British Crown with stirring "domestic insurrections amongst us" and endeavoring "to bring on the inhabitants of our frontiers, the merciless Indian Savages." He claimed that without Texas the United States would "surrender" the "Red river, and Arkansas, and their numerous tributaries, for thousands of miles, to a foreign power. It brings that power upon the Gulf, within a day's sail of the mouth of the Mississippi, and in the interior, by the curve of the Sabine, within about one hundred miles of the Mississippi." The proximity of Texas to the South made it imperative for Americans to be responsible for the area. Leading slaveholders feared that if the Lone Star Republic joined the English empire the slave states would find themselves "in immediate contact with sixty thousand Indian warriors of our own, and with very many thousand of the fiercest savage tribes in Texas, there to be armed and equipped for the work of death and desolation." Annexation meant peace.[56]

Senator Walker also disputed the American antislavery movement's loyalty to the United States. He wrote, "The avowed object of this party is the immediate abolition of slavery. For this, they traverse sea and land; for this, they hold conventions in the capital of England; and there they brood over schemes of abolition in association with British societies; there they join in denunciations of their countrymen, until their hearts are filled with treason; and they return home, Americans in name, but Englishmen in feelings and principles."[57] The Mississippian additionally charged abolitionists with aiming to overthrow the government and dissolve the Union. They not only challenged the existence of American democracy, but also its exceptionalism. The opponents of slavery wanted to transform the United States into a North American version of England, an empire from which their forefathers had seceded.

Antislavery politicians continued to voice opposition to adding Texas to the Union. With the possibility that the territory could be divided into many slave states, they feared the planter elite gaining an upper hand in federal politics. They worried the entire nation's balance of power between the free and slave states might collapse in the wake of annexing the slaveholding republic on the Gulf Coast. The Massachusetts legislature, for example, passed a resolution demanding an amendment to the Constitution that removed the three-fifths compromise, believing that Texas gave slavery overrepresentation in Congress. While Walker promised a national godsend that promoted sectional unity if Texas joined the United States, radical abolitionists went as far as calling for disunion if more slave territory came under American control.[58]

Robert Walker stood ready to respond to antislavery attacks. He promised northerners to expect "only change [in] the locality of the slaves, and of the slaveholding states, without augmenting their number" with the annexation of Texas. Antislavery advocates, he insisted, did not include expectations of black immigration away from the Upper South and toward Mexico. In fact, Walker guaranteed the dissipation of disunionism because the new state in the southwest would act as a magnet, drawing slaves—and slaveholders—away from the nation's capital. "That question, which now occupies so much of the time of Congress, and threatens so seriously the harmony . . . would be put at rest by the annexation of Texas," he stated. Supporting annexation functioned as the single option for those who wanted a balance of power in American politics. His plan maintained American exceptionalism produced by the nation's unique Constitution.[59]

The proslavery movement in Washington happily let Walker lead their mission to take possession of Texas, employing his argument as a template for defending annexation against the congressional antislavery caucus. "I yet feel a strong repugnance, by any act of mine, to extend the present limits of the Union over a new slaveholding territory," James Buchanan told Congress. Then a senator from Pennsylvania, he also insisted, "The acquisition of Texas would ere long convert Maryland, Virginia, Kentucky, Missouri, and probably others of the more northern slave States into free States, I entertain no doubt."[60] The Texas talking point became established. Every member of the proslavery movement used it to sway possible northern compatriots to join them. Texas joining the Union increased the strength of the free states, annexationists claimed. If the promises of Robert Walker came true, adding territory in the southwest meant the creation of more free states than slave states.

The plantation owner from Mississippi also decried the economics of emancipation. The North, he wrote, could expect "one universal bankruptcy" that "would overspread the country, together with all the demoralization and crime which ever accompany such a catastrophe" if abolitionists prevailed in stopping slavery's reach to the Pacific. The senator calculated that poverty and homelessness followed antislavery success.[61] Walker exploited anti-black sentiment in the North to win support for annexation. He insisted that if African American laborers migrated northward because slavery had not moved to the West, the price of wages for white workers would diminish while "the poor-house and the jail, the asylums of the dead and dumb, the blind, the idiot and insane, would be filled to overflowing; if, indeed, any asylum could be afforded to the millions of the negro race whom wretchedness and crime would drive to despair and madness."[62] The "immense free black population" would have almost no preparation for a life of liberty, he predicted. Northern city dwellers could expect free blacks to be a drain on their society, making whites poorer as a result.

The Mississippi senator further estimated that the loss of the Texas market would cause pay to "be reduced until they would fall to ten or twenty cents a day, and starvation and misery would be introduced among the white laboring population." Walker bolstered his statement by citing two speeches given by free-state politicians during the last session of Congress. He wrote that even northerners understood "the abolition of slavery in the southern States must be followed by a deluge of black population to the North, filling our jails and our poor houses, and bringing destruction upon the laboring portion of our people."[63] The expansionist assured free-staters that allowing slavery to move to the southwest would lead to a future with a whiter North.

Robert Walker's writing went beyond simply promoting annexation. Instead, he developed an entire doctrine regarding the purpose for expanding slavery's borders. By avowing that the extension of black enslavement to the southwest siphoned away excess, and potentially rebellious slaves—therefore making southern bondage distinguishable from the practice in the Caribbean—the senator developed a model for the proslavery movement to challenge its critics. Walker's safety-valve thesis succeeded because his proposal not only pertained to the slave states but also emphasized keeping the free states as white as possible. He wrote, "The slaves being emancipated, not by the South, but by the North, would fly there for safety and protection; and three millions of free blacks would be thrown at once, as if by a convulsion nature, upon the States of the North."[64] Texas, he claimed, could act as a vessel that kept black people away from northern cities. Annexation encouraged slaveholders to immigrate to the southwest, bringing a large portion of the enslaved population with them.

For proslavery crusaders, the genius of Robert Walker's *Letter* was its ability to make the entire nation accountable for slavery. The senator connected the spreading of slavery to positive consequences for the entire country without forcing slavery onto free territory. Having grown up in Pennsylvania, Walker understood the racial sensibilities of the North. He knew that white workers in the free states, cherishing their whiteness and the status it gave them, felt resentment toward black laborers who competed with them for jobs. Walker acknowledged that much of the North wanted to exclude African Americans from the American Dream because they viewed economic success as a racial zero-sum game. For white supremacists in the free states, a Lone Star State was a dream come true.

The Mississippian intimately laced the nation together. He referenced Alexander Duncan, a Democrat and doctor from Cincinnati, who warned Congress that "no man's fireside, person, family, or property would be safe by day or night" if slavery's expansion was blocked or emancipation enacted. The Ohioan predicted that the success of the antislavery movement "would be to inundate the North with free blacks," whom he labeled as "paupers, beggars, thieves, assassins, and desperadoes, nearly all penniless and destitute, without skill, means, industry, or perseverance to obtain livelihood."[65] Walker declared that fears of insurrection should transcend sectionalism. Years before, during the Haitian Revolution, northerners worried about the dire outcomes of their sons going south to fight against a rebellion mounted by the enslaved. In the 1840s, Walker argued that whites in the free states could not shelter their lives from the repercussions of not supporting slavery in the South. If racial warfare came to the slave states, the senator intimated, northerners would find themselves on the front lines.

As a way to win trust from whites living in the free states, Walker assured northerners that Texas would lead to a day where they rarely came into contact with slavery or black people. The Mississippi senator promised that with expansion to the southwest, the black population would move southward: "Much if not all of this great evil, will be prevented by the reannexation of Texas. Since the purchase of Louisiana and Florida, and the settlement of Alabama and Mississippi, there have been carried into this region, as the census demonstrates, from the States of Delaware, Maryland, Virginia, and Kentucky, half a million of slaves, including their descendants, that otherwise would now be within the limits of those four States." He also added that annexing Texas "must recede to the same extent from the northern of the slaveholding States, from the expulsion into them of free blacks, by abolition, gradual or immediate, would thereby be greatly mitigated, if not entirely prevented."[66] If free-state white laborers wanted nothing to do with slavery or black people, they needed to accept Texas as a slave state.

Walker's *Letter* ended with a prediction, "The African being from a tropical climate, and from the region of the burning sands and sun, his comfort and condition would be markedly improved, by a transfer from northern latitude to the genial and most salubrious climate of Texas. There he would never suffer from the exposure to cold and frost, which he feels so much more severely than any other race." He guaranteed that accepting the Lone Star Republic as a new member of the Union would lead to fewer black people and more free territory. "There is but one way in which the North can escape these evils; and that is the reannexation of Texas, which is the only safety-valve for the whole Union, and the only practicable outlet for the African population, through Texas, into Mexico and Central and Southern America."[67] Annexation became characterized as colonization without the cost. Those in favor of adding another slave state had no qualms saying that Texas, as a new member of the Union, would funnel black Americans away from the free states. Slavery, they pledged, would naturally move southward if political leaders in the free states supported expansion.

Walker's promise rapidly became a favored talking point for Democratic politicians. James Buchanan epitomized the application of this new tactic, restating his colleague from Mississippi's claims repeatedly in Congress. He believed slavery could only move toward South America. "Spaniards, Indians, and negroes, blended together in every variety," the Pennsylvanian told the Senate, "would receive our slaves on terms of perfect social equality." The Rio Grande seemed to create a natural partition that divided "the Anglo-Saxon and Mexican races," allowing a boundary between white and nonwhites, who instinctively felt hostility toward one another. "Providence," the future president stated, "generally produces great changes by gradual means. . . . May not, then, this acquisition of Texas be the means of gradually drawing slaves far to the South, to a climate more congenial to their nature; and may they not finally pass off into Mexico, and there mingle with a race where no prejudice exists against their color?"[68] In trying to persuade other northerners to join him, Buchanan marked the southwestern boundary of Texas as the western edge of slavery in North America.

Following Walker's pledge, the belief that slavery, along with the American black population in the North, might decline with the addition of Texas helped the annexation movement withstand Secretary of State Calhoun's attempts to sectionalize the issue. Having replaced Abel Upshur after the *Princeton* tragedy, the South Carolinian became the full-throated spokesman for the radical wing of the proslavery movement. In a series of letters to the British minister to the United States in April 1844, he concluded that the "Federal Government" had the "imperious duty" to add Texas to the Union as a way to protect the slave states from British abolitionism, undermining Robert Walker's moderate, nationalist pitch in favor of an ardently sectional outlook. Despite garnering protests from the antislavery movement, however, Calhoun did not spoil the chances for annexation. Walker's message proved too powerful nationally. Both in the North and the South, white Americans supported the idea of a western siphon for excess slaves and the principle that Texas could serve as a buffer to stanch black rebellion caused by overpopulation.[69]

The annexation movement received another boost in the spring of 1844. Andrew Jackson, who had once declined Texas pleas to join the Union, published a letter embracing the addition of the Lone Star Republic to the United States. Old Hickory warned about the possibility of Great Britain introducing chaos into the southern lifestyle, undermining national security and the role that the United States might play in the Atlantic. He echoed Walker's idea that the Sabine River could be used to stir "the negroes to insurrection," causing "the lower country" to fall "and with it New Orleans" while "a servile war rages through the whole South and West." By annexing Texas, the South's border became the Rio Grande, "which is itself a fortification, on account of its extensive, barren, and uninhabitable plains . . . such a barrier on our west." The seventh president believed that expansion made the United States "invincible."[70]

Walker's safety-valve thesis overturned conventional wisdom and became a political liability for the leading presidential candidates in 1844, Democrat Martin Van Buren and Whig Henry Clay. Both initially opposed annexation. The *Bridgeport (Conn) Republican Farmer* exemplified how much traction the push for Texas had gained among the electorate, both North and South. A correspondent wrote, "The last time I traveled on the Western waters was May, 1840. Then, everybody, almost, seemed in favor of Harrison; now, almost all seem in favor of the Democratic nominees. I have met numbers of well informed persons on my route, from Ohio, Indiana, Illinois, Missouri, Kentucky, Tennessee, Alabama, Georgia, and Louisiana."[71] Tyler succeeded in making an issue on which to run for re-election. However, the president did not reap the rewards of his work. Emanating from a successful convention rule change initiated by Robert Walker, the party successfully dumped Van Buren and replaced him with an ardent proponent of western expansion—the former speaker of the House who established the gag rule and ninth governor of Tennessee, James Knox Polk.

Walker also added more to the national political discussion as Election Day approached. In a pamphlet entitled *The South in Danger*, written to win Democratic votes in southern states, the Mississippi senator contended that only the party of Jackson served as a vehicle for slavery's expansion. Using speeches from Henry Clay, William Slade, and John Quincy Adams, Walker stated, "There was never a period when the South was in so much danger as at this moment." He argued that the party of Clay, controlled by northern abolitionists, would do everything they could to halt the annexation of Texas. They wanted the North to dominate both chambers of Congress and enact emancipation. He begged for proslavery Clay supporters to stand with annexationists: "Reflect, then, Whigs of the South, our brethren and fellow-citizens, pause and consider well all the dreadful consequences before you sink us all together into one common abyss of ruin and degradation."[72]

Democratic leaders realized that annexation served as a way to renew their party, which had lost power for the first time in decades. Expansionists viewed the addition of Texas to the Union as fulfilling the party's ideology of economic independence. Many northeastern Democrats worried that crowded cities led to lower wages for the working class. They contended that cheap land in the West offered city laborers, who depended on employment from others, a pathway to prosperity and economic independence. Tyler successfully created an electoral base out of the issue of Lone Star statehood. However, when Democrats welcomed plans for adding western territory without nominating Tyler as their standard bearer, the president removed himself from the campaign altogether.[73]

Despite being outmaneuvered electorally, Tyler still had one more move to make before leaving the White House. Under a cloud of controversy, the president shepherded the Lone Star Republic into the Union, striking another victory for the proslavery movement. When antislavery members of the Senate blocked the final treaty between the United States and the Republic of Texas that authorized annexation, the president found a way around the Constitution. He supported a joint resolution in the House and Senate that required a simple majority vote rather than the two-thirds required to ratify a treaty. Although Whigs—including southern members—remained committed to their principles and mostly voted against the bill, fearing that it would disrupt national unity, Democrats forced the annexation bill through Congress and turned Texas into another star on the American flag, expanding slavery's borders once again.[74]

Prominent members of the press supported the ploy and tried to squeeze out the final votes from reluctant members of Congress. The bill passed by the slimmest of margins. Having only a limited concern about the expansion of slavery in the southwest, several Democrats in the free states supported the congressional resolution, believing that the addition of Texas might indeed end slavery or, in the least, draw the black population away from the North. During the final days of his term, the president signed the bill that formally invited Texas to become the twenty-eighth state. "His Accidency" ushered slavery back onto the main stage of American politics and his legacy forever became linked with the Lone Star State.[75]

Northern Democrats who voted to approve annexation did not forget the proslavery guarantee from Robert Walker. They came to expect Texas to serve as a funnel for the black population to move southward, away from their homes and cities. Southerners also embraced the need for a safety valve. When plantation owners contemplated the future, however, they wondered whether the addition of Texas would be enough to protect the slave states from the bane of having an overpopulated slave system. They continued to believe that a densely populated enslaved underclass would hamstring their security. Proslavery intellectuals extrapolated that eventually the slave states would need even more territory as the black population naturally increased. Subsequently, they proceeded to seek ways to gain more power within the federal government.

As tensions grew with Mexico, James K. Polk campaigned on national expansion to the Pacific. The Tennessean won a close election that hinged on Henry Clay's losing a few thousand votes in Michigan and New York to James G. Birney, the nominee for the antislavery Liberty Party. In the election of 1844, ardent abolitionists punished the Great Compromiser for waffling over the extension of slavery and the annexation of Texas. By thwarting the Sage of Ashland's bid for the White House, supporters of emancipation coincidently promoted another member of the proslavery movement to the highest office in the land, strengthened the grip of planters over American federal policy, and opened the door for the pursuit for more slave territory.[76]

Polk's victory became a crucial turning point for America's march across the continent because it validated territorial expansion as a winning campaign issue. Those who desired more western lands held a mandate after the election of 1844. Both northerners and southerners believed that the principles of the American Revolution and the Constitution allowed their country to construct a unique form of empire. Expansionists aimed to see the day where the United States stretched from the Atlantic to the Pacific. The eleventh president entered the White House with dreams of fulfilling his nation's destiny and proving American exceptionalism to the rest of the world.

6

WILMOT'S PROVISO AND THE SLAVEHOLDING CRISIS

If you confine the slaves to the cotton States within their present limits, you will compel the white population of that region either to abandon it to the black, or to endure the debasing consequences of an admixture of races. Thus they have to decide a question both of existence and civilization, as well as of liberty.

—John Holcombe's Secessionist Speech, Virginia, March 20, 1861

The clouds opened and the sky boomed with thunder on March 4, 1845.[1] A dreary man working on a bleak day, Chief Justice Roger Taney stood, Bible in hand, ready to swear in the next president of the United States. The temperature had fallen to the forties, but the president-elect straightened defiantly against the cold, wet wind. Behind them rested the white columns of the U.S. Capitol's East Portico, a place where the newly elected commander in chief had served as speaker of the House. The marble columns sharply contrasted with the ocean of umbrellas flowing before them. Thousands of citizens stood in inches of mud to hear their new president's first address. Few had expected him to win the nomination of his party; even fewer thought he could beat the nationally renowned Henry Clay. With help from the Liberty Party, James Knox Polk of Tennessee, nicknamed "Young Hickory" because Andrew Jackson had mentored him, repeated the oath to protect and preserve the Constitution. A new family moved into the White House.[2]

Near the dank and huddled crowd, telegraph operators tapped descriptions of the scene, sending a rhapsody of electronic clicks to newspaper editors back home. A man reputed to be one of the best speakers on the stump, Polk in his inaugural address expressed his vision for the future of the United States. At the age of forty-nine, the youngest president in the country's short existence, Polk recognized his youthfulness might engender some uneasiness and assured the nation that he understood what allowed the Union to be special. Calling it the "most admirable and wisest system of well-regulated self-government among men, ever devised by human minds," Young Hickory told the audience, "every lover of his country must shudder at the thought of the possibility of its dissolution."[3] He pledged to preserve the uniqueness of the American system of government, which he declared to be the wellspring of national exceptionalism.

A steadfast member of the proslavery movement, James K. Polk viewed abolitionism as a serious threat to the Constitution and the Union. He proclaimed to the persistent crowd of onlookers, "It is a source of deep regret that in some sections of our country, misguided persons have occasionally indulged in schemes and agitations, whose object is the destruction of domestic institutions existing in other sections." Holding firm to his conviction that northerners loved national unity more than they hated slavery, he said, "I am happy to believe that at every period of our existence as a nation, there has existed, and continues to exist, among the great mass of our people, a devotion to the Union of the States, which will shield and protect it against the moral treason of any who would seriously contemplate its destruction." The entire country shared a "common destiny," and the new president insisted that "peculiar interests of sections or classes, must operate to the prejudice of the interests of their fellow-citizens, and should be avoided."[4]

Like Robert Walker, whom the new president appointed to head the Department of the Treasury, James Polk contended that acquiring land in the West served as the best way to unite the country behind the twin goals of security and national greatness. Texas remained crucial to maintaining the Union because "the safety of New Orleans and of our whole south-western frontier against hostile aggression, as well as the interests of the whole Union, would be promoted by it." However, to prove his devotion to the entire United States, Polk also focused on the "re-occupation" of the American northwest, affirming: "Our title to the country of Oregon is clear and unobjectionable."[5] He thought his fellow citizens might rally behind expansion if they considered the nation—altogether—as the beneficiary of additional territory, regardless of their personal stance towards the perpetuation of black enslavement.

Nearly a year before, during their convention in May 1844, Democrats took a revanchist posture toward the West, supporting "the re-occupation of Oregon and the re-annexation of Texas at the earliest practicable period are great American measures which this Convention recommends." In the months preceding Polk's inauguration, expansionist Democrats drafted a slogan to represent their goals: "Fifty-four Forty or Fight!" The catchphrase referred to the extreme northern latitude of the Oregon Territory, which today is the southern border of Alaska. Americans hungering for more territory in the continental northwest believed that controlling the entire area could hinder the establishment of a British naval port on the Pacific. A diminished Britain meant a stronger United States. They anticipated the president to fulfill his pledge quickly.[6]

Those craving a skirmish for Oregon were left disappointed. Shortly into his term, the Polk administration negotiated a settlement that gave only half of the northwestern territory to the Americans, granting United States landholding over what eventually became Oregon and Washington. Instead, the "fight" that so many expansionists anticipated occurred nearly two thousand miles away from 54°40.[7] As several abolitionists foresaw, the United States found itself embroiled in a tense standoff with its southern neighbor. After the annexation of Texas, a growing, youthful, and optimistic nation readied for battle with the Republic of Mexico.

The American acquisition of former territory enraged leaders in Mexico City. Several newspapers demanded war, exhorting that a fight served as the only method to restore national honor. Despite hoping to avoid conflict, Mexican president José Joaquín de Herrera asked for states to fill their troop quotas and told his diplomats in France and England to explain that his homeland had no choice but to fight the United States. Stressing relations to the brink of conflict, President Polk demanded the border of Texas be acknowledged as the Rio Grande—not the Nueces River, as Mexico claimed—and in response authorized nearly eight thousand troops, headed by General Zachary Taylor, to travel to the area. He told the general to garrison in the disputed territory, ensuring it remained under American control. Polk planned to intimidate the Mexican government into selling the United States the northern half of its country: modern-day sections of New Mexico, Arizona, Nevada, and California. Young Hickory offered Mexico forty million dollars for the land, condescendingly believing that Mexicans might happily sell an enormous portion of their country. Unsurprisingly, Mexico declined.[8]

Early in 1846, American and Mexican troops squared off on the contested border. By April, the standoff turned into open conflict. General Taylor received intelligence of a Mexican corps crossing the river and sent a reconnaissance team led by Captain Seth Thornton to scout the area. As Thornton and his battalion of seventy soldiers wandered twenty miles away from camp, they stumbled onto an ambush. Eleven Americans died during the short skirmish. Six others were wounded. The rest of Thornton's men had been captured, and Mexico won a resounding victory. Everyone expected more fighting to quickly follow the shedding of blood. Both nations scrambled to make the encounter on the Texas border an official war.[9]

The Mexican general in charge of the battle expressed joy in starting a clash with the United States. On the American side, however, Ulysses S. Grant, then a little-known lieutenant in Taylor's army, offered a different perspective. After the shooting began, he wrote, "We were sent to provoke a fight, but it was essential that Mexico should commence it. It was very doubtful whether Congress would declare war; but if Mexico should attack our troops, the Executive could announce" a war of defense. Two weeks later, upon receiving the news from Texas, Polk urged Congress to announce formal hostilities toward the nation's southern neighbor, calling for volunteers to be aroused and a "liberal provision . . . made for sustaining our entire military force and furnishing it with supplies and munitions of war."[10] The president readied the United States for a full-fledged military conflict with a neighboring nation.

Congress immediately took up the measure proposed by the White House, and the Democratic majority in the House of Representatives passed the declaration of war almost immediately. Only seventeen members dissented; few shared any desire to protest an armed conflict that most Americans viewed as being started by Mexico. The Senate, however, hesitated to involve the United States in a military conflict. Both Whigs and some Democrats wanted to discuss the issue. Despite having been a staunch supporter of Texas annexation, John C. Calhoun intended to slow down the nation's march toward armed engagement. The South Carolinian believed there should be a distinction between "hostilities" and "war" with Mexico, differentiating between a short-term clash and a long-term military confrontation.

A few days before the vote, Calhoun wrote to an acquaintance, "I deplore [warring with Mexico] every way." Taking lessons learned from the War of 1812, the former war hawk worried "that it may arrest, or even defeat the settlement of the Oregon Question, [and] introduce the interference of both England [and] France before it is concluded." Going into war with Mexico, he feared, opened the possibility of a larger military contest between the Abolitionist Power in England and the United States. Despite Calhoun's best attempt, however, the Senate assented to a declaration of war with a vote of 40 to 2. Three senators, including Calhoun, refused to vote. For the first time in history, the United States prepared to fight almost exclusively on foreign soil.[11]

Merely a few months after the opening of armed conflict on the Texas border, and following pivotal victories by American soldiers led by Winfield Scott and Zachary Taylor, the president asked Congress for two million dollars to negotiate lands away from Mexico. The two generals had smashed the enemy forces and American soldiers marched toward Mexico City. Military success created an opening for expansionists to create a continental American republic. James K. Polk aimed to quadruple the size of the United States by acquiring half of Mexico's land claims in North America.[12]

The legacy of the Mexican War drove deeper the political wedge of westward expansion between Whigs and Democrats. Whigs took the same stance that they held during the argument about Texas annexation: to stop sectional tension, the country should avoid acquiring new territory altogether. Instead, party leaders argued that the federal government should focus on internal improvements. Democrats, however, confidently made the addition of western territory a national issue by reiterating Robert Walker's political template for expansion. Despite victory not being won entirely, President Polk called for money to pay for Mexican land, which became known as the Mexican Cession. The White House intended to be ready to seize the opportunity when victory finally arrived. Polk having won the presidency and a majority in Congress by promising more land for the white working class in the North and the yeomen in the South, the Democratic appropriation of federal funds fulfilled a campaign pledge. As the end of the congressional session neared, the president's request seemed an easy assignment for Democrats to perform.[13]

Speaker of the House John Wesley Davis spent his entire career being a devoted Democrat, which helped him earn his leadership position following the election of 1844. The doctor from Indiana once wrote to a critic, "My friend, to save you trouble and me annoyance, I will say now that I endorse everything the Democratic party ever has done, and everything it that it will ever do."[14] Complying with President Polk's political wishes took little convincing for the man in charge of the House of Representatives. The White House expected to receive its appropriation as soon as possible, hoping to cement the president's legacy as that of the man who made the United States a continental nation. Not wanting to take too much time on such an anodyne task, House leadership limited discussion of the president's proposal to a couple of hours.

The debate started as expected and the conversation seemed procedural. Two Whigs attacked President Polk's expansionist plan and challenged his need for such an exorbitant amount of money. Robert Winthrop of Massachusetts expressed concerns about "a bill to place two millions of dollars at the disposal of the President 'for any extraordinary emergencies which might arise out of intercourse with foreign nations'" without "a word about peace" or Mexico. The congressman worried that the broadness of the appropriation might fulfill William Ellery Channing's prediction and perpetuate a never-ending proslavery push for wars of conquest. Afterward, two Democrats spoke, both in support of the measure. The president asked for flexibility to end the war, they insisted. American negotiators required money to secure a lasting tranquility and fulfill American destiny. To onlookers watching the talk on the House floor, it appeared to be politics as usual.[15]

Wishing to keep the prosaic discussion moving, Davis next recognized a dutiful congressman with a record of loyalty to the administration. He assumed that Polk's request risked nothing from allowing a fellow member of his party some time to address the floor. A lawyer from northeastern Pennsylvanian, David Wilmot first told his fellow House members that unlike the Whigs, he "believed [the war with Mexico] a necessary and proper war." The Democrat insisted that the members of Congress who labeled the action in Mexico as a war for conquest were mistaken. He trusted that the White House was "sincerely ready to negotiate for an honorable peace." Furthermore, he was "most earnestly desirous that a portion of territory on the Pacific . . . should come into our possession by fair and honorable means."[16] The congressman, who voted with the White House on nearly every issue—from the Oregon border to the tariff—defended the president from harsh criticism.

However, after professing his confidence in Polk's war effort, Wilmot dropped a bombshell. Having discussed his plan with friends beforehand, the congressman expected to rouse a sectionalized ire from those in attendance. *The Congressional Globe* described the scene: calmly, the Pennsylvanian said to the chamber, "whatever territory might be acquired, he declared himself opposed, now and forever, to the extension of this 'peculiar institution' that belongs to the South." Wilmot reminded the House of Representatives of his vote in favor of Texas annexation because "slavery had already been established there. . . . But, if free territory comes in," he said, "God forbid that he should be the means of planting this institution upon it."[17] Gasps filled the gallery. Uneasiness hung over the House floor like a dark cloud as southerners shuffled to refute Wilmot's charges and defend slavery's extension across the continent.

As the Pennsylvania Democrat continued his speech, some members stood agape as the seemingly torpid monster of sectionalism rose back to life in the United States Capitol. Wilmot promptly turned his words into actions by offering an amendment to the president's spending request. Modeled from the familiar language Thomas Jefferson employed in authoring the Northwest Ordinance, the Democratic newcomer proposed "as an express and fundamental condition to the acquisition of any territory from the Republic of Mexico by the United States . . . neither slavery nor involuntary servitude shall ever exist in any part of said territory, except for crime, whereof the party shall first be duly convicted."[18] This motion forever after became known as the Wilmot Proviso.[19] President Polk's dreams for a unified, national march toward the Pacific started to unravel. The thirty-one-year-old from Pennsylvania changed the course of American politics with a ten-minute speech and a rider to an appropriation bill.

News of the Wilmot Proviso spread quickly throughout the District of Columbia. Panicked agents of the administration rushed to Capitol Hill, hoping to lobby faithful Democrats into killing the amendment. Before long, the urgency grew great enough to bring three cabinet members to the House. They planned to twist arms and pat backs in the cloakrooms of the Capitol while party commanders desperately tried to keep their coalition together. Time for deliberation remained limited, however. As scheduled, voting on the appropriation bill began shortly after Wilmot finished speaking.

In a last-ditch effort to avert the bill's passage, a Democrat from Indiana offered his own addendum to the appropriation, replacing the proviso with an extension of the Missouri Compromise Line of 36°30' all the way to the Pacific. The House quickly voted down the Hoosier's eleventh-hour attempt at moderation 89 to 54. Next, Wilmot's amendment to block slavery from all lands acquired from Mexico passed 80 to 64. Only three dissenting votes to the proviso came from congressmen outside of the South. Northerners from both parties rejected postponing consideration of the appropriation while southerners worked to prevent the bill—with the antislavery rider attached—from winning final passage and reaching the president's desk.[20]

Taken off guard, the proslavery movement in the House of Representatives frantically sought to stop the prohibition of slavery's westward expansion from moving forward. Once the Wilmot Proviso survived the amendment process, southerners attempted a parliamentary procedure to table the measure in its entirety, but they failed. The appropriation bill, which now banned slavery in thousands of square miles south of the Missouri Compromise Line, came to the floor for a vote. The legislation passed 85 to 80. Every vote in favor came from the North. A simple request for funds opened a small fissure in the two-party political system of the United States. Antislavery politicians quickly thought of a way to sneak the amended spending bill through the Senate and onto the president's desk to be signed into law. If Polk wanted to satisfy his appetite for more American territory, northerners expected him to accept the new land as free soil.[21]

Democratic unity regarding the federal protection of slavery had been decaying for years before the Wilmot Proviso. This was especially true for the New York contingent of Van Burenites known as the Bucktails. These New Yorkers believed the proslavery movement had become too powerful in the party. The fracture in the Democratic caucus first became apparent in 1844 when John

Quincy Adams finally found a sufficient coalition of congressmen, including fifty-four Democrats, to repeal the gag rule. Proslavery mastery of the party of Jackson generally, and the House of Representatives specifically, declined after the annexation of Texas. The commitment to the southern gentry reached its tolerable limit for many northerners on Capitol Hill after Tyler had found a way around the Senate's treaty ratification process. David Wilmot and his supporters merely continued the trend that had been years in the making.[22]

The appropriation bill functioned as the perfect vehicle for restricting the expansion of American slaveholding. Having already proclaimed that adding California to the Union was paramount for the nation's future, Polk desperately wanted funding from Congress for negotiating land away from Mexico. The Senate did not take up the amended appropriation until two days later, the last day of the congressional session. The antislavery movement desired a political showdown over slavery's western boundary. Massachusetts senator John Davis, a Whig, tried to speak until the last moments of the session, forcing a vote rather than sending a changed proposal back to the House. However, the clocks in Congress spoiled any chance of passing the Wilmot Proviso. The timepiece in the House ticked ahead of the one in the Senate, and Davis spoke too long. With eight minutes left in the Senate's session, a clerk informed the senator that the lower chamber of Congress had already adjourned. The first session of the Twenty-ninth Congress expired without passing Polk's spending bill. The Bay Stater unwittingly filibustered the chance to stop slavery from heading into the Mexican Cession. With a sigh of relief, those in favor of keeping slavery out of the debate in the U.S. Capitol went home.[23]

After such an anticlimactic resolution to the sectional tension triggered by the Wilmot Proviso, public reaction remained quite muted and Democratic leaders in Washington worked to regain authority over their caucus. The White House became convinced that it could lean on enough rogue members of the party to wrangle vote changes from them, preventing additional sectional clashing over American expansion to the West. Polk wrote in his diary that the Wilmot Proviso was a "mischievous [and] foolish amendment," and he wondered, "What connection slavery had with making peace with Mexico it is difficult to conceive."[24] The president still graded the acquisition of northern Mexico as a national mission rather than as a method to further the interests of slave owners.

Furthermore, James Polk did not expect slavery to ever exist in the southwest, believing the institution to be unsuitable for the arid landscape. During the congressional recess, in hopes of changing Wilmot's mind, Polk spoke with him personally. In their meeting, the president expressed little "desire to extend slavery" and indicated that the administration "would be satisfied to acquire by Treaty from Mexico the Provinces of New Mexico and the Californias, and that in these Provinces slavery could probably never exist." During their conversation, Wilmot acquiesced to the White House's request to not reintroduce a bill to restrict slavery in land acquired from the war. However, the Pennsylvanian did not back away from his principles, telling Polk that if a congressional colleague brought the legislation to the floor he would feel "constrained to vote for it."[25]

Wilmot stayed true to his word when Congress reconvened in December. Only a few short weeks after his visit with the president, Preston King reintroduced the Wilmot Proviso as an amendment to a bill asking for three million dollars in negotiating money for the Polk administration. Feeling stung from taunts that the proslavery movement dominated free-state Democrats, the rotund congressman from New York State's northernmost congressional district took things further than Wilmot. Instead of prohibiting slavery in any of the lands acquired from Mexico, the Bucktail's version banned slavery from "any territory which shall hereafter be acquired by or be annexed to the United States."[26] Northerners demanded freedom be the national ideal that shaped the future of the United States.

After years of keeping antislavery ideas out of national politics, members of Congress found themselves in an intense sectional controversy. Northerners used the Wilmot Proviso to flex their political muscles against a proslavery caucus they deemed too powerful. Again, the votes split according to section, with many northern Democrats joining Whigs in attacking the expansion of slavery. Wilmot's Democratic supporters became dramatically more determined to keep black slaves from the West while antislavery Whigs took the opportunity to subvert the institution that undermined the American promise outlined in the Declaration of Independence. Two political interests, with two drastically different reasons to oppose slavery, formed a seemingly improbable bipartisan coalition to stop the expansion of slavery.[27]

Unlike during the Haitian Revolution, the anxiety elicited from Denmark Vesey and Nat Turner, or the abolitionist postal campaign, southerners met the Wilmot Proviso with a united voice of condemnation. Whereas northern doughfaces—who routinely voted to help proslavery interests—or southern moderates, such as Henry Clay, had attempted to ease sectional tension through compromise during the 1830s, the prohibition of slavery in all newly acquired territory became a yes or no proposition for most American politicians. The differences between North and South coarsened in the wake of the Wilmot Proviso. Members of the proslavery movement decided to take their complaints directly to the nation's capital. The *Times Picayune* of New Orleans reported, "Efforts are making to obtain a subscription with a view to establish a Washington paper which 'shall reflect the public sentiment of the South on the abolition and Wilmot proviso question.'" Banning black bondage in the western territories cultivated paranoia among the slaveholding class that transcended political division. Proslavery Democrats and Whigs unified to fight for the expansion of slavery—anything less, they contended, would eventually light the fires of insurrection on southern plantations.[28]

Following the lead set by their proslavery predecessors, slaveholders in the 1840s implied that voting for the proviso assaulted the legacy of the founding generation and American exceptionalism created by the framers of the Constitution. For example, David Kaufman, a Texas congressman, tried to convince his northern colleagues that they were attacking the very core of American democracy. "Our constitutional union," he said, "was based upon compromise, and by compromise alone can it be preserved. But when you depart from this principle; when you take the lion's share of the common stock, and appropriate it to one portion of the Union, and leave nothing for the other, you at once destroy that equality which is the basis of all lasting unions."[29] Born in Pennsylvania and a graduate of Princeton, Kaufman argued vigorously that the antislavery movement weakened the United States by undermining the Constitution. The uniqueness in American government relied on the federal government devoting its authority to protecting slavery even if that meant extending bondage across North America.

The proslavery press posted headlines warning that restricting slavery in the West threatened the security of the slave states. The *Richmond Enquirer* splashed the words "THE WILMOT PROVISO!" in the middle of its front page. The article instructed readers that abolitionists had decided to disrupt national unity and American exceptionalism: "The tocsin, 'the fire bell at night,' is now sounding in our ears; the madmen of the North and North West have, we fear, cast the die, and number the days of this glorious Union," the publication cautioned.[30] Editorialists throughout the slave states declared that fanatics, blinded by their hatred for slavery, happily risked tearing the country apart by enveloping the South with free soil and causing the enslaved population to become too large for slaveholders to control.

Regardless of section or party, members of Congress often gave buncombe speeches as a way to please their core voters back home. For months at a time, congressmen spent days rattling off addresses aimed less at swaying fellow congressmen and more targeted to help win re-election, hoping that getting their name in print—as campaign season approached—might win them another term. Much of the talk about the Wilmot Proviso, as one historian has noted, "tended to lean toward political theatre," especially the vibrant rhetorical flashes in which planter politicians called for disunion if Wilmot and his allies succeeded in preventing the spread of slavery to the territories.[31] Although they understood that their speeches would have little effect in Washington, members of Congress felt the urge to weigh in on the expansion of slavery because they saw that it offered their only chance at winning re-election. Buncombe addresses have always been useful to those in Washington because the very nature of the speeches, and the reasons for delivering them, have inherently revolved around the beliefs of the electorate. In effect, the floor discussions served (and still do serve) as the few times that the elected officials brought the ideas, or at least feelings, of the country writ large into the isolated halls of the Capitol. The speeches conveyed what politicians in Washington believed their constituents wanted to hear. What looked like pandering acted as an articulation of what voters expected their elected representatives to say and do in the nation's capital. The speechifying about the Wilmot Proviso revealed a polarized nation that considered the question of whether or not slavery could enter the West to be of utmost importance for the future of the country.

In Washington, David Wilmot and his antislavery cohort received austere rebukes. On the floor of the House of Representatives, Robert W. Roberts, a plantation owner and Democrat from Mississippi, admonished the passage of the Wilmot Proviso. The South, he stated, had been "betrayed by our friends, and are to be robbed of our rights by those on whom we have reposed our confidence and trust." Leaders of the proslavery movement insisted that free-state congressmen broke a sacred compact forged during the American Revolution when they voted to keep the institution of slavery from moving toward the Pacific. Despite clear language that gave the federal legislature authority over the territories, they maintained that the Constitution prohibited any kind of constraint on slaveholding in the Mexican Cession. Shelton Leake, a member of

Congress from Virginia, compared restricting slavery's expansion to limiting certain well-known constitutional rights. He asked, "Can you abolish the trial by jury in the Territories, or in the District of Columbia?" The understanding of rights, and the purpose of the Union, came to be defined differently in the free North and slave South.[32]

During the 1830s, those in the proslavery movement questioned whether the Union offered a government that differed from the Parliament of England. Often fearful of becoming like their Caribbean counterparts, planter politicians argued that the federal government held the duty to perpetuate the South's peculiar institution. They debated the meaning of the American Revolution and contended that the Union existed to secure the South's peculiar institution against instability. Southern slaveholders worried that the mainstream political climate was moving away from a definition of American exceptionalism that placed the safe perpetuation of slavery at the forefront of the Union's purpose. They viewed antislavery political maneuvering regarding the West as a radical change that required a large consensus to be enacted. A simple majority in the House of Representatives could never suffice without undermining the American political tradition of negotiation and compromise.[33]

Proslavery forces portrayed those who stood against the expansion of slavery as practicing a politics antithetical to the Founding. They presumed that northern Democrats—simply caught up in a temporary furor provoked by the Wilmot Proviso—would eventually feel uneasy with their new allies. George W. Towns, the governor of Georgia and a unionist during the nullification crisis, stated in his inaugural address that the Wilmot Proviso was "an act repugnant to the Constitution, destructive of our rights, and dishonorable to George Washington as one of the parties to the Federal Compact." J. C. Dobbin, a North Carolina Democrat elected to Congress in 1845, told the House of Representatives that the framers of the Constitution, who "compromised their personal opinions on the altar of patriotism," would be appalled by the members from the free states. The future secretary of the navy believed that northerners who wanted to restrict the extension of slavery to the Pacific subverted the spirit of the American Revolution, the purpose of the Constitution, the uniqueness of the United States, and the Union.[34]

The *Southern Patriot* also deemed the Wilmot Proviso to be un-American. The South Carolina newspaper stated, "The great founders of this country entered into a deliberate compact and understanding, as a fundamental condition of the Union, that in its *federal capacity,* the government should never, directly or indirectly, meddle with the question of internal slavery."[35] According to plantation owners, David Wilmot and his supporters in the House and Senate worked to transform the United States into an ordinary nation, weakening the role that the nation might play in world affairs. Abolitionism, southerners declared, promoted ideas that counteracted American values and the goals of national—and local—stability.[36]

A significant number of slaveholders in Congress did indeed feel slighted by their northern colleagues after the Wilmot Proviso passed the House of Representatives. Supreme Court justice Peter V. Daniel, who later joined the majority in the *Dred Scott* decision overturning congressional restriction of slavery everywhere, railed that it "pretends to an insulting exclusiveness or superiority on the one hand, and denounces a degrading inequality or inferiority on the other; which says in effect to the Southern man, Avaunt! You are not my equal, and hence are to be excluded as carrying a moral taint with you. Here is at once the extinction of all fraternity."[37] Slaveholders took Wilmot's proviso less as a disparagement of their manhood or morality and more as a challenge to their status as citizens of equal rank under the government established at the nation's founding. Southerners viewed making the territories only free soil to be an admission that they no longer held a balanced standing in federal politics. Banning slavery in the Mexican Cession made them no different from the West Indian planter elite who, merely a decade before, lost their power when a distant parliament enacted emancipation.

After the Wilmot Proviso, slaveholders became forced to reconcile the contention that the framers of the Constitution wanted Washington to not "meddle with the question of internal slavery" with the empowered national government they used to attack abolitionism. Planters justified their outlook with claims that "indirect attacks" on slavery—from British emancipation to the abolitionist postal campaign—fell under national defense and that antislavery sentiment sapped national strength. The planter elite still intended to use the dual nature of American governance to promote their peculiar institution, and as American politics changed during the 1840s, they still planned to turn the federal government into armor that shielded southern slavery from transatlantic abolitionism while also insisting Congress held little authority over slavery.[38]

The proslavery movement feared the ramifications of a federal government managed by those who did not prioritize the perpetuation and stability of American slavery. The distress originally caused by West Indian emancipation matured with the passage of the Wilmot Proviso. Radical slaveholders began to balk at the idea that the United States Constitution fundamentally differed from the English Parliament their forefathers had shrugged off in 1776. The planter elite had opened Pandora's Box when they used the authority of the federal government to oppress the enslaved and attack northern abolitionism in the 1830s. Proslavery intellectuals labored to establish a line of thought that harmonized the federal power they helped establish with the growing political strength of the flourishing antislavery movement on the verge of claiming congressional dominance. Channeling Robert Turnbull, John C. Calhoun argued that the southern states could not abide losing influence in the nation's capital. In the spring of 1847, having returned to the Senate, the former vice president and secretary of state proclaimed that the people of the South "are in a minority in the [House of Representatives], in the electoral college [*sic*], and I may say, in every department of this Government, except at president [and in] in the Senate of the United States."[39] The South Carolina stalwart predicted catastrophe for American slavery if the Mexican Cession became free soil.

The Cast-Iron Man used his time on the Senate floor to call for proslavery unity. "I say for one, I would rather meet any extremity upon the earth, than give up one inch of our equality—one inch of what belongs to us as members of this great republic," Calhoun exclaimed in response to the Wilmot Proviso. Angered, he bellowed, "What! acknowledge inferiority! The surrender of life is nothing to sinking down into acknowledgement of inferiority."[40] Although the South Carolinian considered defending his region's honor a necessary aspect of his condemnation, the bulk of his opposition to the antislavery amendment rested on other grounds. Slaveholding indignation about the Wilmot Proviso derived from sentiments developed throughout the slaveholding South during the first half of the nineteenth century. When the planter elite discussed potential repercussions of emancipation in the Caribbean, and prognosticated the effects in America, they became more sensitive to the idea of losing political balance between the free and slave states and worried about the consequences of not extending slave territory to the Pacific. The proslavery movement trembled at the thought of becoming similar to their West Indian counterparts. When they imagined their future under laws like the Wilmot Proviso, they envisioned the fires of a new Haitian Revolution consuming their plantations.

Calhoun had the abolitionists on his mind when he spoke about the possibility of southern subordination within the Union, proclaiming: "I have examined this subject largely—widely. I think I see the future if we do not stand up as we ought. In my humble opinion, in that case, the condition of Ireland is prosperous and happy—the condition of Hindostand is prosperous and happy—the condition of Jamaica is prosperous and happy, to what the southern States will be if they should not now stand up manfully in defense of their rights."[41] The South Carolina senator zeroed in on England, and the recent emancipation in the Caribbean, when he spoke of preserving equality within the Union and under the Constitution. Significantly, the three places he listed sarcastically as "prosperous and happy" were part of the British Empire. Calhoun told the rest of the South to "stand up manfully," as free adult citizens in the American Republic rather than be subjugated by a distant capital that did not have the South's best intentions in mind.

The proslavery luminary's speech painted a dreary image for the South. He argued that the refusal to fight for the territorial growth of slavery meant American planters would find themselves in the same situation faced by their former counterparts in the West Indies nearly a decade before: bankrupt and outnumbered by the enslaved—a mere colony reliant on help from outsiders, who held slavery in contempt, for the protection of their personal security and wealth. Southern self-determination vanished if Wilmot and the congressional antislavery movement got their way. The South Carolina stalwart told southerners that to accept the northern proposal was to watch their political power dwindle while, simultaneously, their states became surrounded by an ocean of free soil filled with whites who wanted little to do with African Americans, free or enslaved. The result would be a black population escalating in density, undermining both the value of slavery and the safety of every white person in the South.

Throughout August 1847, the *Charleston Mercury* sketched how Wilmot and his antislavery supporters planned to ruin America's unique form of government by turning Congress into a replica of the British Parliament. In bold print, the newspaper declared, "The Wilmot Proviso is Abolition, Aggressive, Revolutionary, and subversive of the Constitution and its guaranties to the Slaveholding States." The South Carolina periodical, along with many other proslavery outlets, contended that restricting the boundaries of slavery specifically tried to alter the character of the nation. In their minds, northerners who voted for the proviso desired a change that put "the Constitution itself in the hands of Abolition." The *Mercury* finished by explicitly saying, "A revolution is in progress by the Wilmot Proviso. The equality of states and of American citizens is destroyed. . . . The guaranties of the Constitution, often disregarded, are about to be utterly overthrown and rendered useless; and the Constitution and Slavery are being transferred by the Wilmot movement to Abolition and its allies." The radicals in the antislavery movement, the plantation class argued, wanted to reverse the American Revolution.[42]

The English had emboldened abolitionism in the United States by ending slavery in the Caribbean, the Charleston periodical stated. The attacks on American exceptionalism began when Massachusetts attempted to undercut the Negro Seamen Act of South Carolina following the Denmark Vesey scare in Charleston. The *Mercury* described the event as "a most dangerous insurrection . . . planned and instigated by foreign colored persons (St. Domingo) who had seduced the colored natives, free and slaves, into a bloody plot to murder the whites." Caribbean emancipation, the newspaper averred, awoke "a kindred spirit at the North." Fanatics from free states sent "agents with her commissions to invade the territories of South Carolina and Louisiana, to brave their authority, and to break the laws enacted to shelter themselves from domestic insurrection and servile massacre."[43] For the proslavery movement, the Wilmot Proviso provided evidence of the Abolitionist Power's monumental conspiracy to sabotage American slavery, and with it, risked the lives and the future security of all white southerners.

The *Mercury* prognosticated that, long before coming into full dominance, the abolitionists would try to petrify the South. "The end aimed at is to get the power granted by the Constitution, not perhaps to exercise it at once, but to hold *in terrorem* over us, and by it to rule and subject us to whatever measures of taxation, revenue, or expenditure their interests may dictate; and eventually perhaps, at some moment of fancied interest, or under the excitement of feeling or fanaticism, to end our suspense by consummating the act," the proslavery authors predicted.[44] South Carolina's master class believed the "fanatics" did not simply want to end the enslavement of black Americans. Instead, they aspired to treat the South as though it were a colony of the North, taking the region's wealth before finally crushing the planter elite in the name of universal justice and exacting retribution for the enslaved.

Conspiracy theories have often served as the liturgy of dying ideas, and the Wilmot Proviso fit squarely into proslavery feelings of paranoia about the changing political landscape evolving in the Atlantic in the 1840s. The *Macon*

Weekly Telegraph, for example, connected antislavery Democrats directly to a larger, transatlantic abolitionist movement that shared the wish of destroying the Constitution in an attempt to end slavery in the United States. The approval of Wilmot's proposal did not just grow from a few abolitionists, the newspaper reported. Rather, the scheme had a radical and global tinge: "They are brothers to the 'red republicans' of Paris," the Georgian paper wrote. "They have their allies with the British; and they are not wanting friends in the dominions of England, to render assistance to their fellow-devils in the United States, by way of the West Indies."[45]

The rise of Atlantic antislavery deeply affected the way that American slaveholders perceived the world. Proslavery political theoreticians projected southern distinctiveness onto the United States as a whole and insisted that the goal of their opponents was to erode American freedom and way of life. The apprehensions of slaveholders that originally arose after the Haitian Revolution, and then during emancipation in the British West Indies, again came to the forefront of the proslavery mind as those who read the Wilmot Proviso considered the ramifications of it becoming law. A large number of southerners believed that cordoning off the slave states and surrounding them with free territory threatened not only prospective prosperity in the West for slaveholders, but also the entire security of the white South for generations to come. In response, many from the slave states viewed the right to bring the enslaved into the Mexican Cession as a necessity for racial stability. They identified the West as a way to both sustain political dominance of the Union and fortify slavery where it already existed against potential slave uprisings. To be different from the Caribbean, planters believed their region's peculiar institution had to become continental.

Several members of the proslavery movement took the nearly unanimous acceptance of the Wilmot Proviso by northern representatives as proof that abolitionism had gained a powerful foothold in the free states. Others suggested that northerners supported the proviso as a way to gain a political edge, cynically using antislavery sentiment to win re-election. Shelton Leake, a member of the House of Representatives from Charlottesville, pointed to a colleague who opposed the original appropriation for negotiating with Mexico before changing his vote once it banned slavery in territorial expansion. The Virginian maintained that the "spawned fanaticism in the North" led to his friend switching stances.[46] What most southerners misunderstood was that the Democratic vote in favor of the Wilmot Proviso had less to do with slavery and more to do with the black population of the United States. These free-staters had not forgotten what had been promised to them by Robert Walker a few years before.

As the House of Representatives became embroiled in controversy by the reintroduction of the Wilmot Proviso, its original author explained to Congress why he stoked sectional strife while Americans remained on the battlefields of a foreign war. David Wilmot wished to "vindicate" himself from charges of abolitionism. As his fellow representatives listened, the Pennsylvanian reassured Democrats that he was, indeed, one of "the friends of the Administration." He stated, "I have stood at home, and fought single-handed—no, I was not single-handed, because my party was with me—but I have stood at home, and fought time and again, against the Abolitionists of the North.... I have met them at their meetings and assailed them."[47] Wilmot refused to be construed as a "fanatic" intent on ending slavery where it already existed, let alone American exceptionalism.

The Pennsylvanian challenged slaveholders who demanded northern moderation, saying, "I would go as far as any man in this House for compromise. Were it a question of concession and compromise, I might perhaps say to the North, Concede again, as you have done before, bow to the South, as you have done on all previous occasions." The argument stirred by the proviso, in his mind, rested on the question of fairness and equal protection under the federal government, which he believed the free states no longer received. Wilmot continued: "What, then, do we ask? Sir, we ask for neutrality of this Government on the question of slavery."[48] Free-staters, many of whom despised the expansion of slavery because it carried black people into new territory, no longer surrendered to the South's stranglehold over the national government and the future of the United States.

Like the Mississippi senator who promoted adding the Lone Star State to the Union, Wilmot cast himself as a defender of the white republic. He reminded his colleagues, "I was in favor of the annexation of Texas. I supported it with the whole influence which I possessed, and I was willing to take Texas in as she was." Robert Walker's letter and the promises he made to the citizens of the free states took the brunt of the Pennsylvanian's ire. "We are fighting this war for Texas and for the South," he said, "Now, sir, we are told that California is ours. And all we ask in the North is, that the character of its territory be preserved." The member of Congress turned the tables on the proslavery argument for adding Texas as a new slave state, asking, "Shall the South make this Government an instrument for the violation of its neutrality, and for the establishment of slavery in these territories, in defiance of the law?"[49]

Wilmot told his audience that he held minimal sympathy for the millions of African Americans held captive in the South. The Pennsylvanian disapproved the spread of slavery because he wanted the West to be for white workers, not planters and their black slaves. Instead, he wanted to promote sending the enslaved away from the United States to Central America, as the proslavery movement had promised a few years before. The congressman insisted that his proviso forced Robert Walker and his pro-annexation supporters to keep their end of the bargain struck in 1844. He reminded his colleagues, "Why, Mr. Walker told you, when he was urging the annexation of Texas, (and I admit the force of his argument,) annex Texas, and you open a frontier of two thousand miles bordering Mexico, where this slave and black population, as it shall increase and press upon the country, can pass off, and become mingled up with the mixed races of Mexico and South America."[50] The Pennsylvanian considered himself to be holding the planter elite accountable, but as he began to finish, the Speaker's gavel came down, disrupting him. The representative's time on the floor expired, leaving the transcription of his floor speech incomplete.

Robert Walker triggered a perfect political storm in the North when he argued that the addition of Texas to the United States would lead to the black population being shifted away from the free states. In politicizing anti-black sentiment to justify the addition of the Lone Star State to the Union, he manufactured a political environment that allowed for the creation of a coalition between those who opposed black Americans heading to the West and those hostile to slavery on moral grounds. David Wilmot merely completed the political bridge between the two groups. Preventing enslavers from planting their institution in the West gave each faction something to rally behind—a vision for their nation's destiny grounded in the end of slavery and the promotion of the white, independent farmer.

Although he did not finish delivering his speech, David Wilmot revised and extended his remarks for the record, placing them in the *Appendix of the Congressional Globe.* He wanted his voters in Pennsylvania to know the purpose of his actions. The congressman clarified his stance: "I have no squeamish sensitiveness upon the subject of slavery, no morbid sympathy for the slave." Instead, his goals stemmed from serving his constituency. For Wilmot, creating slave territory to the west of Texas excluded a numerous portion of his voters from the spoils of the Mexican War. While planters said they could never relocate to the new land without the ability to bring the enslaved with them, many white nonslaveholding migrants insisted upon living in an area without slavery, or for that matter, black people in general. "I plead the cause and the rights of white freemen. I would preserve to free white labor a fair country, a rich inheritance, where the sons of toil, of my own race and color, can live without the disgrace which association with negro slavery brings upon free labor," he wrote.[51] The Pennsylvanian ensured that his intentions were clear. He aimed to force the proslavery practitioners of Robert Walker's brand of territorial expansion to keep their promise.

The Wilmot Proviso touched the heart of proslavery fears. Many of the planter class rigorously studied history and judged the past as an indicator for future outcomes. What made Wilmot's plan doubly menacing for much of the slaveholding South was the idea that the federal government, managed by an antislavery coalition hostile to human enslavement, might not help enslavers sustain their grip on the lives of those they held in bondage. White southerners considered the actions of Congress to be an encouragement of slave uprisings. They also thought that the abolitionists within the federal government would happily withdraw American forces during racial unrest, abandoning the principles of the Union that insured "domestic Tranquility" and "common defence" and replacing them with "fanaticism" and instability.[52]

Violence was inherent to American slavery, and often, to match their anxiety and paranoia, plantation owners preemptively enacted brutality upon the enslaved. Both white planters and yeomen believed their slave society could erupt into racial combat under certain circumstances. They presumed that the beaten and broken of the South's brutal institution wanted revenge along with freedom. Most southerners understood that an insurrection affected the lives of everyone. Nonslaveholding whites fled Saint-Domingue in the same way that the planter class had and many white southerners recalled how Nat Turner killed children. Status meant next to nothing during the upheaval of racial combat. Often pointing to the gruesome warfare in Haiti at the turn of the nineteenth century, the intellectual class of the South firmly believed and propagated the notion that African Americans became barbaric without effective governmental mechanisms in place to preside over them. As the slave populace grew, many white southerners anticipated their authority over the black community to wane, leading to disastrous consequences. The problem seemed to be escalating when Wilmot and his supporters voted to surround the South with free territory. Slaveholders insisted that the inability to expand their borders forced them to hold a ticking population time bomb. Proslavery prophets forecasted doom without total slaveholding control of the federal government.[53]

Robert Walker's argument for Texas annexation worked almost too well. He had convinced a considerable amount of people in the South that the expansion of slavery offered the only reliable method for keeping their region safe. For example, South Carolina congressman Isaac Holmes explained to the House of Representatives that if surrounded by free states, the South would be "smothered and overwhelmed by a festering population that was forbidden to migrate, pent in and walled around on the exhausted soil—in the midst of [an enslaved populace] strong in idleness." It would only be a matter of time before abolitionists instigated slaves to "revolt and murder." Holmes and many of his fellow southerners came to see the idea of a safety valve for the excess slave population as the only plan capable of maintaining the viability of slavery in the United States.[54]

Expectations about the future played a significant role in the southern reactions to the Wilmot Proviso. Many in the slave states held a Malthusian understanding of population theory. This caused whites living in the slave states to view an increasing number of black people as a source of not only economic disruption but also physical insecurity. As northerners united in opposition to extending the boundaries of slavery in the 1840s, retaining the ability to manage the size of the enslaved populace became a slaveholder obsession. In both the North and the South—whether proslavery or antislavery—it became conventional wisdom that the institution of black enslavement needed to expand to survive and remain durable in the South.[55]

Slaveholders routinely felt misgivings about the world they left to their descendants. Several members of the planter class theorized about the long-term consequences of slavery being constrained to the South, thinking deeply about the future, long after their own deaths. As part of its response to the Wilmot Proviso, the *Charleston Mercury* published an estimation of future population statistics for the slave states that extended all the way to 1950—more than a hundred years into the future. The journal expected the residency of the region to reach 90 million. Thirty million would be slaves who could not participate "in the improvements of the white race."[56]

Throughout the Palmetto State, plantation owners mobilized their communities to stop the Wilmot Proviso, arguing that the law might lead to the total destruction of the South. "The lower classes of whites," one slaveholder dreaded, "will have gradually passed off into the Free States, retreating before the cheaper labor of the blacks," leaving the slaveholding class without foot soldiers to help quell black rebellion. The *Mercury* expressed this anxiety clearly: "When a great body of the white population will have emigrated, as we have shown, the remainder, impelled by a sense of insecurity or disgusted with a land abandoned to hopeless barbarism, will follow in the footsteps of the first, and the country be finally abandoned entirely to blacks."[57]

Without slavery's territorial expansion, the white South would find itself totally desolated by a black majority, the journalist alleged, because "their habits have never entirely forsaken their descendants in America; and left to their own control, they would rapidly return to barbarism, and invite for themselves the fate of the Aborigines of America." According to the *Charleston Mercury,* the remaining whites living in the southern states would, without "a reasonable doubt," work to "exterminate" the African American population to save their homes.[58] Slaveholders contended that life without territorial expansion meant genocide and expectations about such a grisly future went beyond radicals in South Carolina. In Alabama, the *Montgomery Advertiser* envisioned "a war if extermination against the whole negro race" if the South became bordered "on the North, West, and Southwest by a chain of nonslaveholding States." The newspaper predicted that by 1871 "the negroes will become insupportable when they shall have doubled and trebled the white population South, with the sympathies of three-fourths of the whites in the United States against the institution. The sequel may be easily discerned. We have an illustration in point in St. Domingo. This is an imperfect picture of the prospect before us. Gloomy, indeed—but is it not true?"[59]

A number of whites in the South concluded that northerners who opposed slavery intended to foment slave uprisings. To them, the proviso served as the first step in the Abolitionist Power's plan to destroy the slave states and the plantation owners who governed them, not just the institution of slavery. One Mississippi congressman, for instance, said that Wilmot encouraged the "canting Abolitionist, who secretly and stealthily, openly and fiendishly, overleaps the barriers of the Constitution, and tramples up its sacred guarantees, in order to undermine your rights and obliterate your privileges, scatters fire-brands, arrows, and death among you, envelops your house in flames, and murders your wife and children before your eyes, to him this soil is free. It is a city of refuge where he may [include] the avenger of blood."[60] The debate about the expansion of black enslavement went beyond immediate politics and became focused on slaveholding posterity.

Southern journalists labeled the members of the antislavery movement unreliable allies in the event of a massive rebellion launched by the enslaved. The *Mercury* declared that "security of the slave institution, even within our own States . . . can only be secure in our own hands" and worried that the South would soon "be surrounded by a population hostile to us. On every side girt round with those who will continually excite our slaves to insubordination and revolt, which it would be folly to suppose would forever be resisted."[61] Either the strength of the federal government—including control over the United States military—needed to rest in the hands of plantation owners or Washington's influence required a culling. Both potential situations granted the proslavery movement total domination of their society. Abolitionists in power, planters averred, could never be trusted to protect slavery from its natural risks.

The intellectual leaders within the planter elite came to believe that antislavery northerners might not send reinforcements to fight an insurrection. Long gone were the days when the free states supported slavery out of concern that their sons might be fighting against a Haitian-style revolt. With antislavery leaders directing the federal government, the publication concluded, "we may see a servile war with all its horrors. If the white triumphs, victory itself will be death. If foreign aid make the slave the victor, misery far greater than death will follow him whose unbridled passions will find in the contempt of all restraint human and divine a theatre for its that will make humanity shutter."[62] When slaveholders looked at a map, they found themselves surrounded by hostility while, simultaneously, it appeared they were losing command of the U.S. military. The South's boundaries began to resemble the Caribbean of the 1830s. Rather than a detached island surrounded by water, however, American plantation owners saw the southern states being encircled by free soil—a habitat more threatening to their peculiar institution and their personal safety.

Other slave-state media outlets joined the *Charleston Mercury* in expressing a sense of uneasiness about a potential antislavery federal government. Many proslavery writers insisted that abolitionists, emboldened by the Wilmot Proviso, purposely attempted to induce racial upheaval. A Florida journalist argued that southerners simply needed to "look at [abolitionists] as intending to be true to their pledges; as the deadly enemies of the dearest interests of your constituents and of the South; as the chosen leaders of those fanatics who will, if they can, liberate your slaves, even by fire and sword . . . prepare the way for the grand drama of Abolition, at whatever hazard, throughout the slaveholding states."[63] The old binding of national security and slavery unraveled.

The passage of the Wilmot Proviso in the House of Representatives brought the Haitian Revolution back to the vernacular of southern popular culture. With a large enslaved majority, white South Carolinians took extraordinary precaution against slave uprisings. A British-born actress who married a Georgia planter, Fanny Kemble described Charleston as similar to a town on the frontier "where the tocsin is sounded, and the evening drum beaten, and the guard set as regularly every night as if an invasion were expected. In Charleston, however, it is not the dread of foreign invasion, but of domestic insurrection." She also claimed that the enslaved black population served as "a threatening source of constant insecurity, and every southern *woman* to whom I have spoken on the subject, has admitted to me that they live in terror of their slaves."[64] Due to her opposition to slavery, Kemble's description of the South later became a widely regarded asset for the abolitionist movement's message.

James Henry Hammond also wrote about having similar suspicions regarding the antislavery movement gaining sway in the North. He worried that with the addition of more free states northerners planned to "ride over us rough shod, proclaim freedom or something equivalent to our Slaves and reduce us to the condition of Hayti. . . . If we do not act now, we deliberately consign our children, not our posterity, but *our* children to flames."[65] Slaveholders continued to advance the notion that extending slavery to the West was the only means of stopping a bleak and violent fate for their descendants.

Many planters openly worried that preventing the spread of slavery in the territories might prompt white yeomen farmers to leave the region. Waddy Thompson, who formerly served as chairman of the House Committee on Military Affairs, wrote that an antislavery "victory is worse than fruitless—its ultimate result will be to convert [the South], the fruitful mother of heroes and statesmen, into another San Domingo Pandemonium—[where their] children will be forced to leave a soil consecrated by the blood of patriot ancestors . . . and see the marble on their tombs converted into hearth stones, and their graves ploughed over by a free negro proprietor."[66] For many, especially in the Deep

South, the restriction of slavery's expansion transformed the slave states into a continental version of the Caribbean. It left the plantation class powerless in a society ready to explode with racial recriminations while the faraway capital, unaffected by the chaos and morally opposed to slavery, refused to send aid, causing the South to collapse into racial pandemonium.

Slaveholders in the Upper South joined South Carolinians in associating the Wilmot Proviso with attempts to inspire a North American version of the Haitian Revolution. Thomas Bayly, a Virginia Democrat who owned a plantation on the Delmarva Peninsula, believed that Wilmot intended to cause race war. The Virginian asked his fellow House members to "look at Santo Domingo. It was almost a paradise. It was one of the most beautiful and prosperous portions of the earth. By the means of a servile insurrection, instigated, and aided by British fanatics, the terrors of which no pen can describe, and no heart can contemplate... there was indiscriminate massacre of the whites, without regard to age, sex, or condition."[67] Bayly predicted turmoil if the proviso became the law of the land. Similar to the *Charleston Mercury*, he vowed that any large uprising by the enslaved would lead to the "extermination" of either the white or black race in the United States. He envisioned a day where "the South is deluged in blood, and is made one vast scene of desolation" if the antislavery movement took power in Washington.[68]

For decades, abolitionists worked to undermine the white supremacist notion that Haiti was filled with barbarism and tyranny, hoping to undercut the proslavery message that emancipation led to social instability. Treating such considerations with a touch of paranoia, Bayly and his southern colleagues refused to be swayed by pretensions that former slaves might live a peaceful coexistence with the planter elite. They claimed that the antislavery movement was foolhardy to insist that racial equality could be achieved in any real manner. Despite the best attempts of black-owned and -operated antislavery periodicals to argue otherwise, the planter elite persisted in pointing to the Haitian Revolution as proof that the races could not live peacefully in an integrated and free society. Mankind, they declared, could never truly be treated as equal. Prominent members of the proslavery movement framed the discussion so that whites in the North had to choose between their own race and African Americans.[69]

The sectional disposition of the vote to block slavery in the western territories pushed many southerners to reconsider disunion. During the nullification crisis Benjamin F. Perry sided with Andrew Jackson and the federal government. A journalist, editor of a pro-Jackson newspaper, and a leader in Palmetto State politics, Perry's unwavering devotion to the Union had been so strong that he once killed a pro-Calhoun rival in a duel. A decade later, however, the South Carolinian decried the restriction of slavery's expansion as an antislavery plot to destroy the white South. He postulated that the enactment of the Wilmot Proviso meant eventual freedom for the black population, subsequently leading to their domination of the electorate because "in most of our Districts and Parishes in South Carolina, there is a majority of Slaves, and being set free, [they] could carry all the elections, and fill all the public offices." Once the former slaves became the preponderance of the state's voters, Perry predicted, black southerners would "intermarry with [white] children" and serve in Congress.[70] Without slavery in the West, he concluded, the white man's republic would collapse.

Following the House's second adoption of the Wilmot Proviso on February 1847, John C. Calhoun portrayed a scenario in which the continuation of antislavery attacks led to the violent destruction of the slaveholding South. Regaining clout that he lost for disapproving of the Mexican War, the former vice president became the chief spokesman for the proslavery movement in Washington. From the starred, carmine carpeting of the Senate floor, the South Carolinian explained why southerners needed to resist the prohibition of slavery in Arizona and New Mexico. "Our opposition rests on the ground that they will be ruinous to us, if not effectually resisted. We know what we are about," he said; "we foresee what is coming, and move with no other purpose but to protect our portion of the Union from the greatest calamities—not insurrection, but something worse. [The expulsion] in time [of] the white population of the Southern States" that would leave "the blacks in possession [of the South]."[71] He continued, if "those influences on the other side be permitted to go on, the result of the whole will be, that we shall have St. Domingo over again."[72] Calhoun pleaded with his northern colleagues to disregard abolitionism's call to turn the South into an island encircled by free territory. He asked them to join him in fighting for a proslavery interpretation of American exceptionalism.

Calhoun told followers to take the fight to the North instead of merely reacting to antislavery forces in Congress. While also maintaining that northerners held the obligation to attenuate insurrections, he recommended a proslavery boycott of goods produced in the free states. Earning his nickname of the Cast-Iron Man, the senator alerted northerners, "If your vessels cannot come into our ports without the danger of such piratical acts . . . you have caused this state of things by violating the provisions of the Constitution and the act of Congress for delivering up fugitive slaves, by passing laws to prevent it, and thus make it impossible to recover them when they are carried off by such acts, or seduced from us, we have the right, and are bound by the high obligation of safety to ourselves."[73] Although such an embargo might prove detrimental to the South's economy, Calhoun expected his plan to bring moderates in the North back to defending the interests of plantation owners. For slaveholders, economic security remained less important than physical safety. The South Carolinian presumed Yankees to be more interested in money than morality.

The South Carolinian called upon all southern state governments to pass legislation repudiating the proviso. As a model for local politicians to imitate, he offered a Senate resolution that explained the proslavery position on the expansion of slavery. In response to the senator's request, the Virginia legislature unanimously passed a denunciation of David Wilmot and his supporters from the free states. Naming it "The Platform of the South," and basing their action on Calhoun's legislative language, the Virginians resolved, "the government of the United States has no control, directly or indirectly, mediately or immediately, over the institution of slavery, and that in taking any such control, it transcends the limits of its legitimate functions by destroying the internal organization of the sovereignties who created it."[74] The statehouses of Alabama and Georgia promptly followed suit, passing similar condemnations of the despised ban of slavery in the West.

The proslavery movement lashed out against the authority of the federal government to regulate slavery in any land acquired by the nation. The Platform of the South resolutions further stated: "That all territory which may be acquired by . . . the United States . . . belongs to the several states of this union, as their joint and common property, in which each and all have equal rights" and called any "enactment by the federal government of any law which should directly or by its effects prevent the citizens of any state from emigrating with their property of whatever description into such territory" a "derogation of that perfect equality that belongs to the several states . . . and would tend directly to subvert the Union itself."[75] Only after the antislavery movement began its ascent to the seat of federal authority did the planter elite give a full-throated denunciation to Washington's jurisdiction over American domestic policy.

Once the Missouri Compromise no longer served the proslavery movement, prominent slaveholders simply discarded it. Many proponents declared that the compromise line drawn in 1820 had always been unconstitutional. The reactions by the plantation class to the Wilmot Proviso helped to create the intellectual foundation for the radical defense of slavery in the 1850s. Only when planter politicians realized they could no longer employ federal power to overtly defend and expand the enslavement of black Americans did they decide to make an effort to weaken Washington's authority altogether. Once a bulwark that guarded the antislavery movement from congressional censorship, federalism and the notion of states' rights came to the forefront of proslavery ideology only when slaveholders realized their influence had begun to wane in Washington.[76]

Although Polk and the Democrats eventually found a way to garner enough votes to negotiate lands away from Mexico without the Wilmot Proviso, its initial passage in the House of Representatives, by a sectional vote, became a crucial turning point in American political history. The negative proslavery reaction to the proviso did not arise from resentment or merely economic disadvantage. Rather, southerners contended that such strong support from the free states for the Wilmot Proviso signaled the enhanced influence of the antislavery movement. Planter theorists believed that stifling slavery's expansion turned the southern states into a nursery for insurrection. With England as an ally, planters expected abolitionists to transform the South into a continental version of the West Indies. Slaveholding leaders raged in response. For example, Calhoun called for white southerners to stand up to protect "your property, prosperity, liberty, and safety."[77]

Much of the anxiety of plantation owners originated from the historical memory of the Haitian Revolution. Without territorial expansion, slaveholders anticipated their enslaved population growing too large to control, especially as the federal government—directed by the antislavery movement—undermined the authority of plantation owners. Planters expected a bloody upheaval of their society if slavery became restricted to the fifteen states and the District of Columbia. As slave owners reacted to various insurrection plots, real or imaginary, domestic and abroad, intellectuals within the proslavery movement linked the future of slavery to its geographical expansion to the Pacific.

The Wilmot Proviso became a tipping point in the politics of slavery because it granted slaveholding radicals the opportunity to tarnish the trust between the proslavery movement in the South and northerners who for years had supported slaveholders for political gain. In the late 1840s, the most ardent members of the proslavery movement began to have reservations about whether the U.S. system of government had formed an exceptional nation. They questioned the Constitution as a source of national uniqueness and labeled the southern institution of slavery as the exceptional characteristic of the country instead. From 1846 until 1860 the Wilmot Proviso became a political litmus test in the United States, both in the free and in the slave states. Every candidate hoping to win a seat in Congress became obliged to engage with the expansion of slavery as American landholding grew toward the Pacific. Political leaders tried to find a way to bridge the divide, but they were fighting several decades of history and preconceptions. Influenced by national and world events since the 1790s, dreams and expectations about the future could not be changed easily.

THE PROSLAVERY TURN AGAINST AMERICAN EXCEPTIONALISM

Experience has proved, that slaveholding States cannot be safe, in subjection to non-slaveholding States. Indeed, as no people can ever expect to preserve its rights and liberties, unless these be in its own custody. To plunder and oppress, where plunder and oppression can be practiced with impunity, seems to be the natural order of things. The fairest portions of the world elsewhere, have been turned into wildernesses; and the most civilized and prosperous communities, have been impoverished and ruined by anti-slavery fanaticism.

—The Address of South Carolina To Slaveholding States, December 25, 1860

H. L. Mencken once wrote, "There is something about a national convention that makes it as fascinating as a revival or a hanging. It is vulgar, it is ugly, it is stupid, it is tedious, it is hard upon both the higher cerebral centers and the gluteus maximus, and yet it is somehow charming. One sits through long sessions wishing heartily that all the delegates and alternates were dead and in hell—and then suddenly there comes a show so gaudy and hilarious, so melodramatic and obscene, so unimaginably exhilarating and preposterous that one lives a gorgeous year in an hour."[1] Party politics has often been a harrowing affair, but the internecine battles between political operatives on the convention floor have frequently signaled atmospheric change in America's democracy. Following the passage of the Wilmot Proviso by the House of Representatives, a reorganization of the two-party political system began in the United States.

In 1848, a few decades before the Sage of Baltimore's birth, Whigs and Democrats went to their respective national conventions facing sectional predicaments. Each party planned to demonstrate how they could be trusted to preserve slavery without disenchanting northerners and unraveling the Union. While revolutions erupted throughout Europe, the two major parties in the United States worked to dodge the sectional ramifications of victory in the Mexican War. To do so, unlikely alliances formed to nominate those considered the least offensive to the electorate. The traditional blueprint for American political compromise began to falter.[2]

Whigs and Democrats also faced new competition in the free states. Driven by the positive reception of prohibiting black enslavement in the Mexican Cession in the North, a coalition of northern Whigs (who disapproved of slavery mostly because of moral reasons), northern Democrats (who mostly disapproved the expansion of slavery on racial grounds), and former members of the Liberty Party created a third political organization. Meeting in Buffalo, the party announced that they gathered "as a union of freemen, for the sake of freedom, forgetting all past political differences in a common resolve to maintain the rights of free labor against the aggressions of the Slave Power, and to secure free soil to a free people" and supported "the National Platform of Freedom, in opposition to the sectional Platform of Slavery."[3] The Wilmot Proviso breathed life into the Free Soil Party.

Content with fighting for votes exclusively in the North, Free Soilers picked former president Martin Van Buren as their champion. In a remarkable display of the changes that occurred in American politics during the 1840s, the party named Charles Francis Adams, the son of the recently deceased John Quincy Adams, as their nominee for vice president. Although Van Buren and Adams had been political rivals for decades, they joined forces to stop the extension of slavery under the banner of "Free Soil, Free Labor, Free Speech, and Free Men." While the Liberty Party spoiled the election of Henry Clay in 1844, the Free Soil Party looked to win elections outright by pledging to curtail the power of slaveholders in Washington.[4]

Trying to compete in the South without losing the North, Democrats aimed to find a way around the Wilmot Proviso when they met in Baltimore at the end of May 1848. In a heated debate, delegates concentrated on three potential presidential nominees: Levi Woodbury, a former senator from New Hampshire and associate justice of the Supreme Court; Secretary of State James Buchanan, a former senator from Pennsylvania; and Lewis Cass, senator from Michigan and former secretary of war for Andrew Jackson. None of them owned slaves. To quiet complaints from the southern wing of the party, leaders aimed to balance the ticket by selecting for vice president William Orlando Butler, a Kentuckian known more for his credentials as a commander in the Mexican War than for his loyalty to the proslavery movement.[5]

As part of a strategy to garner southern votes, the Democratic platform stated, "Congress has no power under the Constitution to interfere with or control the domestic institutions of the several States." Furthermore, to prove its commitment to the Union, the party also resolved, "all efforts of the Abolitionists or others made to induce Congress to interfere with questions of slavery, or to take incipient steps in relation thereto, are calculated to lead to the most alarming and dangerous consequences." They depicted themselves as nationalists who protected the sanctity of the Constitution and the uniqueness of the American system while simultaneously assuring planters that Democratic rule meant their enslaved property would remain safe from federal intervention. By focusing scant attention on the role Congress played regarding slavery in the territories, the Democrats intended to tiptoe around the issue.[6]

Lewis Cass, however, knew that finding a substitute for the Wilmot Proviso meant winning his party's nomination and potentially moving into the White House. The Michigander planned to walk a fine line between sectional hostility during the convention. Following a long tradition in American democracy, he supported an ambiguous form of popular sovereignty that granted jurisdiction over slavery to those who lived in new territories. A few months before the convention, Cass answered an inquiry from a Tennessee Democrat about extending the South's peculiar institution to the West, writing, "I am opposed to the exercise of any jurisdiction by Congress over this matter; and I am in favor of leaving to the people of any territory, which may be hereafter acquired, the right to regulate it for themselves, under the general principles of the Constitution."[7] A week later, the *Washington Union* published his letter for all to read. The prospective president hoped that taking authority to regulate slavery in the territories away from Washington might satisfy both antislavery northerners and proslavery southerners.[8]

However, the senator's platform pushed in Baltimore did not go far enough for the most radical slaveholders. Many in the proslavery movement considered Cass unacceptable. Months earlier, the Democratic Party of Alabama, spearheaded by William Yancey, developed a proslavery platform of their own and commanded their state delegation to vote against any candidate who might hinder the perpetuation of slavery. Yancey demanded that the federal government promote and defend the enslavement of black southerners actively, as it had in decades before. The Alabama platform unequivocally also stated that Congress had no authority to regulate the status of the territories—directly challenging supporters of the Wilmot Proviso and popular sovereignty. A number of planters cautioned that without the expansion of slavery the white population of the South would continue to dwindle, leaving a larger, increasingly dangerous enslaved populace behind that was ready to employ violence to overthrow their oppressors.[9]

Not confident that a president from the Great Lakes State could defend white southerners, supporters of the Alabama platform demanded more from Cass. Yancey's backers argued that slavery needed to be legal in all territories and that only a state could eliminate the enslavement of the black Americans within its borders. While the Free Soilers championed freedom as the national ideal and slavery as sectional, the planter elite offered a mirror image—slaveholding defined the Union and made the United States exceptional. Although the southern press praised the motion, Democrats in Baltimore overwhelmingly rejected the radical platform 216 to 36. Yancey and his supporters responded by leaving the convention in protest. After the drama of the Alabama walkout, the convention adopted Cass's plan. Democrats became the party of popular sovereignty.[10]

The Whigs adopted a different strategy than their Democratic counterparts. As the party of John Quincy Adams and other antislavery leaders in Congress, they approached the presidential election with considerable mawkishness toward slavery's expansion. Party leaders understood they had to keep their core supporters happy while extending their reach to voters in the South. In the weeks before its national convention, the party searched for someone who might rise above the sectional infighting caused by the Wilmot Proviso. Still stinging from the loss of a close election four years prior, Henry Clay failed to gain support when the delegates gathered in Philadelphia on June 7, 1848. Instead, they chose to differentiate themselves from the Democrats by running a candidate who connected to the voters in a superficial way. Zachary Taylor, the hero of the Battle of Palo Alto, became their man for 1848.[11]

A grizzled old soldier whose face appeared as if it were made of leather, General Taylor had spent four decades serving in the United States Army. Despite being bereft of political experience or parliamentary acumen, his fame earned from fighting in Mexico made him the presumptive nominee at the convention, though this did not come about without concerns. Some Whigs worried about his fitness for the White House. One party leader who knew the nominee described him as "an honest, plain, unpretending old man who, if left to his own course, would be as honest as it is possible for a man to be, but about as fit for the President of these United States as any New England Farmer that one might select out of a thousand, with his eyes shut." Another Whig, Congressman Horace Mann, wrote that the former general "talks as artlessly as a child about affairs of State, and does not seem to pretend to a knowledge of any thing of which he is ignorant."[12] Nicknamed Old Rough and Ready from his success in the Second Seminole War, Taylor proved that in volatile times a lack of relevant knowledge or skill does not hamper a candidate from running a successful presidential campaign. During a political crisis, voters often placed their hopes in a person without political achievement, praying that untapped potential might solve the problems at hand.

The general's nomination produced a sizable resistance within his party. Frustrated by his front-runner status, opponents feared their presidential nominee did not actually hold Whig principles. Brushing aside concerns that Old Rough and Ready might be another version of John Tyler, Taylor's political managers thwarted dissent and controlled the convention floor. The general never trailed on a ballot for the nomination despite only partially committing to

Whig ideas. He had a single asset his challengers lacked: he was a slaveholder whose status as a war hero resulted in his being highly regarded in the North. Electability trumped policies. To balance the ticket, Taylor initially offered Daniel Webster the chance to be his vice president. The former secretary of state had turned down William Henry Harrison's same offer eight years before, missing the ascension to the highest office in the land. In 1848, he still wanted nothing to do with the vice presidency. After Webster declined, Taylor eventually offered the job to Millard Fillmore—a little-known former congressman from Buffalo who had opposed Texas annexation and once complained about the South's power in Congress. The Whigs set their presidential ticket with dreams of riding back into the White House on a wave of public enthusiasm for another military hero.[13]

Speaking in generalities related to internal improvements and other policies, Zachary Taylor's quest for the presidency primarily relied on his personal story. By refusing to advocate specific solutions on the campaign trail, he cast himself as someone who transcended the sectional divide. Old Rough and Ready spoke vaguely about the issues the electorate cared about, believing that specifics only produced opposition. In his quest for the White House, Taylor promised America that he would be a different kind of commander in chief, a post-partisan leader whose presidency would be a panacea to sectional tension. His supporters proclaimed him "the people's candidate," a man more loyal to his country than to any political party or sectional interest.[14] One pro-Taylor leaflet stated, "To love him, it is only necessary for his countrymen to know him, not alone as a soldier, but as a man and a citizen." The campaign material went on to share stories from his time in the army, including a section about "his morality and temperance" and "his modesty and unassuming manners." The pamphlet also praised his familiarity "with human suffering" because "General Taylor's heart is filled with the tenderest sympathies, and quickens to the noblest impulses."[15] Old Rough and Ready refused to be cornered by the national issues derived from the war he helped win. His patriotism, supporters declared, superseded any discussion of the Wilmot Proviso.

By refusing to engage in a debate, the old general functioned as a blank political canvas on which sectional partisans could project their beliefs, telling themselves that he supported their political positions. Standing for nothing meant he could potentially be for anything. Massachusetts Whigs, for example, painted General Taylor as unreservedly in favor of the Wilmot Proviso, knowing that his path to victory hinged on undermining the Free Soil Party and stealing its votes. Northern Whigs also attacked Martin Van Buren, calling him a "Northern man with Southern principles" and reminding free-staters of his efforts to censor press during the abolitionist postal campaign. Taylor's party did everything they could to stop the antislavery movement from spoiling their election chances again.[16]

When Democrats in the South attempted to tie Old Rough and Ready to the Wilmot Proviso, Whigs simply pointed to him being a slaveholder. Slave-state advocates successfully contrasted Taylor and his southerness with the Democrat from Michigan. James Henry Hammond put his ruminations about the election in his diary: "Taylor, a slaveholder, pure, firm, and patriotic and of sound judgment, I still prefer him and would vote for him." Slaveholders placed confidence in one of their own, the creator of the congressional gag rule continued. "As a Southern man and slaveholder, I thought the South should support him without regard to party, especially as Cass was openly anti-slavery." Hammond agreed with the former general's explicit promise to rise above party politics and "to be a moderate Whig and an Independent candidate who would accept support from all parties, but bind himself to none."[17]

Many in the proslavery movement distrusted the Whig nominee. Democrats in Virginia, for example, hoped to exploit planter paranoia by declaring that Taylor's election might lead to "your homes, and your fields" flowing "with the blood of yourselves and your neighbors, shed by servile hands in a civil war." They argued that only the complete and total fidelity to increasing slaveholding territory could keep southern homes safe from insurrection. Proslavery Democrats charged that the Whigs, who allowed the antislavery movement a voice in party matters, could never be fully committed to the total protection of slavery in the United States.[18]

When Election Day arrived, proslavery southerners faced a choice: the Democratic Party, with its record of protecting slavery, which now nominated a northerner; or the Whigs—a party filled with those morally opposed to slavery that nominated a slaveholding war hero. When the votes were tallied, they split evenly. Cass and Taylor each won six southern states. Taylor, however, won the Electoral College majority in the North, dividing the free states between east and west. The Michigander won in the northwest while Taylor stood victorious in every state in the northeast except Maine and New Hampshire. The Free Soil campaign launched by Van Buren gained nearly 10 percent of the popular vote, but played a minimal role in the outcome. The cause of excluding slavery in new territory could not yet galvanize the support required to produce a winning campaign. Old Rough and Ready became the twelfth president of the United States by running as a man who transcended sectional division. He also became the last slaveholder to reside in the White House. Subsequently, no national party nominated a candidate solely from the South until 1964 when Democrats nominated President Lyndon Johnson.[19]

Meanwhile, as the two major parties organized conventions to choose their nominees for the upcoming 1848 electoral contest, James W. Marshall chanced upon a few flakes of glistening metal from his water wheel thousands of miles away in California, a place where David Wilmot wanted to prohibit slavery. The carpenter immediately knew what he found: gold. At first, news in the East of Marshall's discovery came with skepticism. However, the mad dash began after President Polk officially affirmed the find in his State of the Union address. The former Bear Republic became a national—even international—sensation. Hundreds of thousands of fortune seekers migrated to the new American territory on the Pacific.[20] The number of people living in the territory swelled seemingly overnight. As settlers traveled towards the American Pacific, the planter elite waited to see how the new president handled the issue of slavery in California—a large portion of which laid south of the Missouri Compromise Line. As a slaveholder, they expected him to remain true to the political priorities of the proslavery movement.

Polk anticipated that the gold rush would produce a massive population boom in California, and he asked Congress to organize the territory despite political reservations about the Wilmot Proviso. The president worried that Californians might hatch another revolution, this time against the United States. Polk explained to leaders on Capitol Hill that he sat ready to sign the extension of the Missouri Compromise Line or any similar alternative that passed a divided House and Senate. His main imperative became ensuring that California remained under American jurisdiction as thousands from all over the world went to the Pacific Coast in search of striking it rich. The gold needed to belong to Americans, Young Hickory insisted; it signified the nation's destiny.[21]

One alternative to furthering the Missouri Compromise Line came from Stephen A. Douglas, the recently elected senator from Illinois. On the day Polk asked Congress to organize California, the senator sponsored a proposal that ushered the entire Mexican Cession into the Union as one state, thus avoiding the Wilmot Proviso altogether. Although Polk supported the idea, a large contingent in Congress concluded that such a large state could never be properly managed, killing the plan. Antislavery northerners declared their stance boldly: free soil only or no direct statehood in the Mexican Cession. The proslavery movement castigated the Douglas bill as an attempt to pass the proviso by another means. The Polk administration could not resolve the sectional conflict and the task fell to his successor. President Taylor, a novice in the realm of political negotiation, found himself as the chief arbiter of sectional compromise over the future status of an American territory that seemed to be filled with gold.[22]

Like Polk, Zachary Taylor accepted the trope that slavery could never exist in the West. He believed the slaveholding opposition to a free California derived from politicians trying to score political points rather than having any real fear about the destabilization of slavery. Whether from a lack of political experience or his arrogance as America's latest war-hero president, Taylor believed he could rise above the Wilmot-generated sectional partisanship that deadlocked Congress. The former general convinced himself that he was incapable of falling into the same traps caused by slavery's expansion that torpedoed Polk's presidency. Like many new presidents, Old Rough and Ready overestimated his ability and discounted the struggles of the man he followed into the White House, viewing Young Hickory to be an incompetent. Taylor adopted a policy toward western expansion that made many in the South think that they had been played for fools. The twelfth president proved himself less of a slaveholder and more of a Whig. His time in office instigated a crisis that nearly split the Union in 1850, grew distrust between the North and the South, and empowered the radical proslavery movement.[23]

Taylor underestimated the slaveholding paranoia that followed the passage of the Wilmot Proviso. In August 1849, only months into his term, the president sent a commission to California with instructions to help create a new state government that, most likely, would request entrance into the Union as a free state. Realizing that an antislavery stance might help his party win seats in the midterm elections, the president announced in Mercer, Pennsylvania: "The people of the North need have no further apprehension of the extension of slavery." He promised the audience that the Whigs operated as the vehicle for free soil and issued an executive order warning against any efforts to enkindle revolution in Cuba, which several in the proslavery movement believed might offset a free California in Congress. Old Rough and Ready, the heroic planter many southerners had relied on to block the Wilmot Proviso, abruptly condemned attempts by proslavery southerners to annex additional slave territory to the United States. Plantation owners immediately derided him as a renegade. They prepared to dig in their heels and fight the entrance of a free California as the thirty-first state. Slaveholding leaders believed that adding the Golden State to the Union turned the South into an island surrounded by free soil, placing southern slaveholders in the same predicament that their failed counterparts in the Caribbean had faced years earlier.[24]

The proslavery movement judged Taylor's time in the White House to be an archetype of how an administration unfaithful to slavery might sabotage southern security. As he had in his reaction to the Wilmot Proviso, John C. Calhoun warned that the policy pushed by Old Rough and Ready might turn the South into a mere colony of the North and undermine white power over the enslaved. The South Carolina senator wrote a letter, which he begged every southern congressman to sign, condemning the impetuous actions of antislavery members of Congress. Antislavery northerners "disturbed" the "tranquility" of the South with "systematic agitation," the former vice president told the nation. He tried to convince his compatriots to join his cause, arguing that the efforts to prohibit the extension of slavery and abolish the slave trade in the District of Columbia would, in effect, allow the North to hold "the white race at the South in complete subjection."[25] Calhoun insisted that Zachary Taylor served as the perfect dupe. The proslavery stalwart promoted the notion that the South needed to sound their objections in unison, but his endeavor ultimately failed. Although several southern legislatures approved the ideas behind his letter, only 48 out of the 121 southern members of Congress signed the document. Most wanted to give the new president a chance to lead, allowing him to facilitate a compromise solution.

Many planters viewed President Taylor's actions as a hostile betrayal. More by ineptitude than antislavery motive, the president seemed to fulfill Robert Turnbull's prophecy from the 1830s. His tactics magnified how the antislavery movement might use the federal government to sabotage slavery and erode the security of the white population against black rebellion. Slaveholders believed their fears to be substantiated when Horace Mann, a Massachusetts Whig, responded to southern cries for disunion by telling Congress, "The state of slavery is always a state of war" and that an uprising by enslaved Americans was both inevitable and preferable to the extension of slavery. Without the president uttering a word of disapproval, Mann challenged radical proslavery ideology by relishing the idea of civil war, claiming, "With the creation of every human being, God creates this love of liberty anew. The slave shares it with his master, and it has descended into his bosom from the same high source. Whether dormant or wakeful, it only awaits an opportunity to become the mastering impulse of the soul. Civil war is that opportunity." With Taylor in the White House, proslavery leaders exclaimed, abolitionists now willfully spoke about establishing a second Haitian Revolution in the South. Several leaders from the slave states feared that the president might spur a revolution similar to those spawned by Europeans in 1848, toppling the slaveholding status quo and allowing for the long-predicted race war to finally begin.[26]

By the end of 1849, political comity in the United States deteriorated. By re-electing Henry Clay back to his old position, leaders in the Bluegrass State believed they could provide a hero to safeguard national unity and preserve American exceptionalism. Reluctant to fill his former role in the upper chamber after a seven-year absence, the Great Compromiser nonetheless returned to ply his trade in the art of negotiation. Throughout the early months of 1850, Clay formulated a plan that acceded to California entering the Union as a free state in exchange for concessions to the proslavery elements of Congress, such as a stronger Fugitive Slave Law and the assumption of the debt accrued by Texas during its revolution. For nearly a year, the voices of legends echoed in the Senate chamber. Three aging political titans, Henry Clay, Daniel Webster, and John C. Calhoun, along with two new entrants into the political arena, Jefferson Davis and William Seward, all gave brilliant speeches. Clay and Webster fought for unity and compromise, Seward attacked slavery, and Davis and Calhoun defended the South's peculiar institution. They all agreed on one aspect of the debate, however—the meaning of America and the future of its democracy hung in the balance.[27]

As the discussion continued, the proslavery movement's champion orator became so weakened by illness he could no longer speak in the Senate. Rendered feeble by tuberculosis and looking half dead already, John C. Calhoun listened as his friend, Virginia senator James M. Mason, read his closing argument in favor of slavery's expansion. The moribund Calhoun testified like a convert who now believed that the American government had lost its distinctiveness when compared to the rest of the world. The "long-continued agitation of the slave question on the part of the North," he wrote, had sapped the Constitution. Following the Revolution, the Founders had established an equilibrium that "afforded ample means to each [section] of protecting itself against the aggression of the other." However, as the population of the free states outpaced the slave states, that symmetry of power wasted away, he insisted. Northerners now dominated southerners, both in number and in the Electoral College. Calhoun blamed the federal ban of slavery in the Northwest Ordinance and the funneling of tax money from imports from the South to the North for creating the sectional discrepancy. The Abolitionist Power had worked behind the scenes for decades, Calhoun contended. Their scheming in Washington had finally flowered, bearing fanatical fruit.[28]

The pallid South Carolina senator argued that the emerging population dominance of the free states came at a time when "every portion of the North entertains views and feeling more or less hostile to [slavery]." While "fanatics" saw slavery "as a sin, and consider themselves under the most sacred obligation to use every effort to destroy it," the "not so fanatical" still regarded the southern institution "as a blot and a stain on the characters of what they call the nation, and feel themselves accordingly bound to give it no countenance or support." Alternatively, Calhoun claimed, "the southern section regards [slavery] as one which cannot be destroyed without subjecting the two races to the greatest calamity, and the section to poverty, desolation, and wretchedness; and accordingly they feel bound by every consideration of interest and safety, to defend it."[29] Without northern allies, the proslavery movement once again hypothesized that outside "agitation" would destroy "the existing relation between the two races of the South," causing a battle between the races while abolitionists sat on the sidelines unwilling to enforce the established racial hierarchy of the slave states.

Calhoun believed that the failure of Congress to squelch the abolitionist mailings had allowed them to gain "a position in Congress from which agitation could be extended over the whole Union." The gaunt senator insisted that Robert Turnbull's prophecy had ultimately come true. He alleged, "Instead of being weaker, all the elements in favor of agitation are stronger now than they were in 1835, when it first commenced, while all the elements of influence on the part of the South are weaker."[30] According to Calhoun, the Wilmot Proviso was another tear in the fabric of the nation. Now that slaveholders found themselves losing grip over Washington, he insisted the constitutional protection of liberty from the power of the majority had been eroded, and he opposed Clay's plan. From the vantage point of enslavers, the compromise seemed to be another step toward curtailing black enslavement and ending the proslavery Union that sustained American exceptionalism.

Less than a month later, the longtime head of the proslavery movement went to his grave. Calhoun's intellectual heirs, however, a group of southern radicals labeled the "fire-eaters," continued his legacy. Robert Barnwell Rhett articulated their ethos succinctly: "The South must protect itself, no slaveholding communities can be safe but by their own energies." The Constitution meant nothing if slavery could be influenced, even in the abstract, by antislavery northerners directing the authority of the federal government and American military. As the Senate talked about Henry Clay's sectional bargain, the fire-eaters called a meeting of proslavery leaders in Nashville, Tennessee. They desired to portray a unified front of opposition toward abolitionism, but only five states sent official delegations—Texas, Georgia, Virginia, South Carolina, and Mississippi. Most of the South still favored the Union.[31]

One speech delivered by Nathaniel Beverley Tucker, a legal scholar and political commentator from the Old Dominion, revealed how the twin worries of being encircled by free soil and enduring a Haitian-style insurrection persistently hounded the fire-eaters. In an address appealing for the creation of a new slaveholding nation, Tucker argued, "But let a place be found nearer home, where a colony of free blacks may be established under a provincial government, protected, regulated and controlled by a Southern Confederacy, open to all who will go to it, and from its proximity accessible to all. . . . The folly and madness of France have prepared it. It is Hayti."[32] The most ardent members of the proslavery movement firmly believed that having a large black population—especially with a free black class—proved dangerous to southern whites. Some ambitious slaveholders thought that seizing the black-led nation and turning it into a safety valve for "excess" slaves could serve to keep a close watch on a nearby enemy while also mitigating black rebellion at home. In suggesting a preemptive war of conquest against Haiti, radical planters revealed slaveholding paranoia as the antislavery movement increased its sway in Washington.

Meeting in June 1850, the timing could not have been worse for the zealous proslavery delegates hoping to draft a significant statement in Nashville. Although some fire-eaters sought to galvanize the slave states to oppose any congressional action, most convention attendees preferred compromise to secession. Fearing the possibility of being branded as disunionists, they waited as the Senate discussed Clay's measures, and most favored extending the Missouri

Compromise Line to the Pacific, refraining from endorsing Calhoun's stance that slavery should be legal in every territory.[33] Without formal delegations from each slave state, the convention had almost no chance of success. As with the nullification crisis, most southerners advocated a wait-and-see posture, hoping to stay loyal to the Constitution—the government of their forefathers. They still believed that American exceptionalism made them different from the other slaveholding nations of the world.

Zachary Taylor spoiled the opportunity for an amicable settlement. Rather than giving Clay's bargain the crucial support it required from the White House, the president acted on his own. Unlike the Missouri Compromise, which President Monroe quietly ushered through a sectionalized Congress, Clay's strategy did not sufficiently measure up to Taylor's expectations for the West. Despite understanding the political uproar his actions would cause, the president encouraged Californians to adopt a state constitution. Old Rough and Ready judged himself to be a new Andrew Jackson and expected to be adding a new addition to his legacy as a national leader. Filled with hubris, the president believed the issue of slavery's expansion could be his version of the nullification crisis. The former general planned to bend the recalcitrant to his will just like Old Hickory. With a divided Congress and the threat of a veto, the compromise failed to pass either chamber of Congress.[34]

In effect, Taylor's inflexible stance enacted the Wilmot Proviso through executive order. Plantation owners now identified two branches of the federal government—the presidency and the House of Representatives—as cheerfully restraining the extension of slavery, thus creating an environment for mass insurrection. Unlike the confrontation between Jackson and Calhoun over nullification in the 1830s, Taylor's actions broadened opposition to the White House. Every slave state held a sizable objection to the Wilmot Proviso. Old Rough and Ready's clumsy threat of military force simply increased talk of civil war and strengthened the influence of the radical proslavery movement in the South. For an increasing number of southerners, the possibility of free soil surrounding their states served as a fundamental threat to both their safety and way of life. They believed their homes and families to be at risk along with their pocketbook.[35]

President Taylor never got the chance to oversee his plan, however. The seventy-fourth anniversary of the signing of the Declaration of Independence in the nation's capital was a sunny day filled with heat and humidity. The District of Columbia felt as if it were returning back to its natural state: a swamp. Fascinated with the construction of the Washington Monument, the president looked forward to watching the builders raise the marble obelisk, stone by stone. The nation's birthday gave him a chance to satisfy his curiosity. Organizers invited special speakers to commemorate the occasion. Most attendees only stayed to listen to the main event—a speech delivered by Senator Henry S. Foote, a Mississippi senator who supported Clay's compromise—and to witness the dust from the tomb of Tadeusz Kościuszko, a Polish hero of the American Revolution, be deposited inside the unfinished monument. The more ambitious lasted much longer, and sweating through the festivities, the president stayed to hear George Washington's step-grandson speak. Merely days earlier, medical officials had advised the inhabitants of the District of Columbia to avoid both milk and cherries, fearing a contaminated recent shipment. The former general paid no mind. Enjoying his time, Taylor sat in sweltering weather, drinking chilled milk and eating cherries for two more hours.

Following his afternoon of relaxation, the president fell ill. Doctors diagnosed him with gastroenteritis, the stomach flu. On July 9, 1850, the second Whig president to be elected to the White House, like William Henry Harrison before him, died in office. Millard Fillmore became another improbable president. Unsettled by the sudden turn of events, the political class in Washington wondered how the man placed on the ticket to satiate the antislavery wing of his party intended to handle the growing sectional crisis over California and the future of slavery in the West. Those on both sides of the divide held their breath as the man one proslavery periodical declared to be "an abolitionist, pledged in favor of the abolition of slavery in [Washington], and the interdiction of the slave trade between the States" moved into the White House.[36]

During his first tumultuous days in office, the *Richmond Enquirer* wrote, the new president would "have the glorious opportunity of enrolling his name high on the list of patriots," and that those who knew him best expected him to "effectually tranquilize the public mind and insure the perpetuity of the Union." Millard Fillmore proved his friends correct. He changed course from Taylor immediately, becoming the best hope for negotiating a settlement over the status of the territories. Determined to start his administration without influence from his predecessor, the New Yorker accepted the resignation of Taylor's entire cabinet. The new president promptly appointed Daniel Webster, Clay's chief ally, to his former position as secretary of state and threw the full weight of the presidency behind passing the proposed compromise. He also masterfully defused the escalating border stand-off between Texas and New Mexico, telling the slaveholders in charge of the Lone Star State to expect any aggressive action toward their neighbors to be met with executive force.[37]

Fillmore proved that effective presidents have the ability to rise above partisan rancor and forge an agreement between divided parties, at least for a time. In August, after the threat of a veto to the compromise bill was removed, but with the aging Clay away from Washington while on the mend from an illness, Stephen A. Douglas began reworking the failed resolutions in an attempt to save the nation. Remembering that the Missouri Compromise had never been voted on as a single piece of legislation, the Illinois senator used parliamentary tricks and political tact to dissect the omnibus bill into digestible portions for Congress. The Senate voted separately on each aspect of the Kentuckian's plan. By the first week of September each part of Clay's compromise lay on the desk of President Fillmore, where he happily signed them. It appeared that the Union had once again been saved from the destructive nature of the debate over slavery, stifling fire-eaters who hoped a congressional impasse might lead to more radicalism in the South.[38]

Nicknamed the Little Giant because of his short stature but imposing political skill, Douglas managed to garner an affirmative vote on every aspect of Clay's bill by cobbling together a small coalition of moderates who desired compromise and the sectional stalwarts. Only three northern senators supported the strengthening of the Fugitive Slave Law. However, unanimous northern votes carried the bill for the admission of California as a free state despite its receiving just six votes from southern senators. The House of Representatives acted in similar fashion. Clay's agreement passed with a meager appetite for a bargain being found in the halls of the Capitol. Merely four senators and twenty-eight congressmen voted in favor of each resolution of the Compromise of 1850.[39] The Wilmot Proviso drove a wedge into national politics that separated the United States into regional factions. Northerners believed they were in a fight against the Slave Power. The South saw a conspiracy initiated by an Abolitionist Power. Neither side was entirely wrong.

Members of the House and Senate celebrated the passage of the Compromise of 1850, believing they had saved the Union. Lewis Cass declared, "I think the question is settled in the public mind." The former Democratic nominee for president vowed never to give another oration on the topic. Stephen Douglas echoed Cass's sentiments, promising to "never make another speech upon the slavery question in the Houses of Congress." Journalists reporting from Capitol Hill encouraged Americans to celebrate the perpetuation of national unity. The Wilmot Proviso and the questions it raised had been resolved. Following the tradition of political negotiation, which had originally created the Union, Congress preserved American exceptionalism.[40]

In the ardently antislavery areas of the country, however, the Whig coalition began to break down. Under the headline of "We Give It Up," The *Milwaukee Free Democrat* reported, "Not a single Whig press in this State has approved [Fillmore's] position, but, on the contrary all have decidedly condemned it." The newspaper believed that if the president did not become a more outspoken voice in opposition to slavery, "nothing but divisions, defeats, and disasters await the Whig party.... The curses of a free people, deep and loud, and universal will be the only welcome to the new Executive."[41] Antislavery northerners searched for a party that supported their interests wholeheartedly.

The sectional confrontation over the Wilmot Proviso had been decades in the making. Throughout the 1850s, the fear of slave revolts intensified as southern power waned within Congress. The compromise measures hardly eased the concerns of slaveholders. For many southerners, the belief they had avoided civil war by passing Clay's compromise changed little about their expectations for the future. They still thought slavery required expansion to keep the white population safe from black rebellion. The sectional conflict stemmed from one important difference: while most northerners outside of the abolitionist movement believed that slavery's expansion and slavery's continued existence in the states could be discussed independently of each other, the proslavery movement perceived them as one and the same. Northerners did not share the southern concerns about potential insurrection. They saw it as bluster from proslavery demagogues desperately clinging to political influence in Washington. Planters, however, came to view the diffusion of slavery as a life or death matter, and many actively schemed to add slaveholding territory to the United States. Instead of concentrating exclusively on the West, they turned their attention to the Caribbean and Central America, identifying the growing tensions between the English, French, Russians, and Ottoman-Turks over the Crimea as the right time to expand the nation by taking territory from the old powers of Europe.[42]

From 1848 to 1854, southern leaders encouraged four different presidents—James K. Polk, Zachary Taylor, Millard Fillmore, and Franklin Pierce—to purchase Cuba from the Spanish. After the election of 1852, they believed Spain might assent to President Franklin Pierce, a northern Democrat sympathetic to slaveholders, submitting a bid for their colony in the Caribbean. Pierce actively participated in the Young America Movement, a group of youthful politicians with the goal of rapid U.S. expansion. He seemed to be the perfect man for the job. Faithful to the proslavery movement, the Granite Stater routinely stalled on a treaty with Spain regarding the American renouncement and prosecution of filibusters, privately funded military outfits who worked to detach the Spanish colony through revolution in order to eventually add the island—and with it, more slave territory—to the Union.[43]

The commitment to taking action in the Caribbean became greater, however, when the Spanish, under pressure from both Great Britain and France, considered emancipation in Cuba and the arming of black troops to ward off American invaders. When news of the plan hit southern shores, slaveholders demanded action in Washington. The Louisiana legislature petitioned Congress, calling potential abolition in the Spanish colony "a most pernicious influence upon the institutions and interests, social, commercial, and political of the United States." They alleged that a predominantly free-black Cuba would mean "the sacrifice of the white race, with its arts, commerce and civilization, to a barbarous and inferior race." The Louisianans argued that it was the responsibility of the federal government to "adopt the most decisive and energetic measures to thwart and defeat a policy conceived in hatred to this republic, and calculated to retard her progress and prosperity."[44] Leaders from the Upper South joined the Louisiana legislature, as well. In a ninety-minute speech, Robert M. T. Hunter, a senator from Virginia, declared that America needed to preserve a stable international racial order as a way to maintain peace and prosperity in the Western Hemisphere.[45] The sudden threat of a large free-black population less than a hundred miles from the coast of Florida made Cuban annexation an immediate priority for the proslavery movement.

As northerners began to protest the passage of the Kansas-Nebraska Act, which implemented popular sovereignty north of the Missouri Compromise Line, the American ministers to France (John Y. Mason), Spain (Pierre Soulé), and England (James Buchanan) devised a scheme to annex Cuba. During a meeting in the coastal town of Ostend, Belgium, and at the suggestion of Secretary of State William Marcy, they drew up their plan, which became known as the Ostend Manifesto. The three ministers explained why they believed the United States had to acquire the Caribbean island off the coast of Florida. They contended, due to its "wretched financial condition," that Spain would happily accept an offer from the Pierce administration for $130 million. If Spain refused, the United States could also "afford to disregard the censures of the world" and rightly attack Cuba in the name of national interest.[46] Conquering the Spanish colony would serve to defend slavery in the South in the name of "self-preservation."

The proslavery diplomats declared themselves to be on the right side of history. The term "self-preservation" became their watchword to vindicate an American war to seize the island. As during the decades before, national security again came to the forefront of political debate as powerful slaveholders attempted to use federal policy to gain more slave territory. The three foreign ministers maintained, "We should, however, be recreant to our duty, be unworthy of our gallant forefathers, and commit base treason against our posterity, should we permit Cuba to be Africanized and become a second St. Domingo, with all its attendant horrors to the white race, and suffer the flames to extend to our own neighboring shores, seriously to endanger or actually to consume the fair fabric of our Union."[47]

The old method of tying proslavery foreign policy to national security found limited success when it was applied to Cuban annexation. The Wilmot Proviso had changed the ambience of American politics. Northern politicians no longer genuflected toward slaveholding political leaders who decreed the work of universal freedom to be the leading cause of slave insurrection. The Ostend Manifesto, along with the Kansas-Nebraska Act, received a harsh rebuke from those who lived in the free states. Fearing a backlash from their constituencies more than the anger mustered by their southern colleagues, Democratic leaders in the North, such as Lewis Cass, furiously denounced it. Voters kept them in their jobs, not friendships developed on Capitol Hill. In the midterm election of 1854, President Franklin Pierce and his fellow Democrats paid a heavy price for supporting the Slave Power, losing seventy-three seats in the House of Representatives. Whether through popular sovereignty or conquest of slaveholding territory in the Caribbean, a winning coalition of northern voters no longer tolerated the extension of slavery. David Wilmot revealed the political weakness of the planter elite when he introduced his antislavery proviso. Following the rejection of territorial expansion to Cuba, the United States did not add and organize another large piece of territory until the 1890s, when Congress finally organized Alaska, purchased in 1867.[48]

As Democrats took their lumps at the polls, the party of Henry Clay dissolved entirely. Southern Whigs joined their Democratic counterparts while northerners left for two new political organizations: the American Party, which became known as the Know-Nothings, and the Republican Party. Both courted the northern electorate by portraying themselves as the party of the antislavery movement. The latter adopted a slogan similar to the Free Soilers, "Free Soil, Free Labor, Free Men," and successfully became the party most associated with fighting against the Slave Power. The free states organized politically to safeguard their own interests, much like the South decades earlier. Expressing approval of slavery's expansion became toxic for northern candidates at the congressional level. The planter elite recognized that their grip over the federal government was slipping away faster than ever.[49]

In the 1856 presidential election, Democrats took advantage of the demise of the Whig Party while the Republicans and Know-Nothings still worked to forge competitive national tickets. By nominating the last ardently proslavery northerner left on the national stage, the party of Jackson gained unanimous support from the slave states. A man with an extensive resume, James Buchanan rustled up enough backing in the North to win a solid majority of the Electoral College despite gaining only 45 percent of the popular vote, defeating the Republican nominee, John C Frémont, and the Know-Nothing nominee, former president Millard Fillmore. The failed presidency of the Buchanan administration, however, served as one of the final confirmations for the planter elite that abolitionism had become a force in American politics.[50]

A Pennsylvanian who encouraged the expansion of his country's landholding to include both Cuba and Texas, along with the censorship of antislavery tracts in the 1830s, James Buchanan during his time in the White House supported two proslavery measures that doomed the Democratic Party in the North. As his inauguration came closer, the president-elect corresponded with a few justices of the Supreme Court in an attempt to influence the outcome of the controversial court case *Dred Scott v. Sanford.* For over a decade the enslaved Dred Scott had been suing for his freedom. He maintained that he deserved freedom because he had been taken to a free state. Scott contended that free soil acted as a tonic that relinquished him from his enslavement—once his feet touched the North, he deserved his natural right of liberty. The newly elected president expected the decision to stop sectional discord over the expansion of slavery. The established political power of Washington hoped the Court would give federal legislators a pass from controversy by ruling that slavery's extension fell outside of the purview of Congress.

Days before his swearing in, the president-elect received word that the ruling favored the proslavery movement in the South. Knowing the outcome, Buchanan used his inaugural address to specifically identify the question of slavery as belonging "to the Supreme Court of the United States, before whom it is now pending, and will, it is understood, be speedily and finally settled." Two days later, in a 7 to 2 decision, the court issued a broad ruling that, in essence, legalized black enslavement nationwide and undermined local determination over the status of the enslaved. The fifteenth president hoped that the issue of slavery in the territories could be laid to rest.[51]

In his opinion, Chief Justice Roger Taney announced that black Americans received no protection under the Constitution. Free black people living in the United States, he determined, could not be considered citizens—the rights outlined in the Declaration and Bill of Rights could never be ascribed to them. The chief justice wrote in his opinion of "beings of an inferior order, and altogether unfit to associate with the white race, either in social or political relations, and so far inferior that [black Americans] had no rights which the white man was bound to respect." The Supreme Court also invalidated the Missouri Compromise, declaring the bargain struck in 1820 to be unconstitutional. Neutering congressional authority, Taney's opinion defined slavery as a national institution. The Tenth Amendment's guarantees of states' rights defended freedom in the North, not slavery in the South. Only an amendment to the Constitution could overrule the decision.[52]

Antislavery proponents immediately attacked the Court's ruling, and the Republican Party found itself with a political object for its voters to rally against. The decision heightened the sense in the North that the Democrats preferred pandering to slaveholding interests to promoting the free states and the white working man. Moreover, the proslavery movement could no longer attract a majority of northern support by portraying its concerns as an issue of national security. The president's party, especially in the Midwest, became viewed as puppets of the Slave Power rather than as representatives of their own constituents. Pressure from the debate about slavery's expansion led to the party of

Jackson fracturing in the old northwest. Two rival and incompatible visions of American exceptionalism formed: one supported extension of the boundaries of slavery while the other worked to make freedom national. Both sides of the divide saw their opponents as provincial and unfit to lead the United States into the future.[53]

Buchanan cemented the belief that Democrats were the party of slavery with his actions following the *Dred Scott* decision. With the passage of the Kansas-Nebraska Act, the territory of Kansas became both the rhetorical and physical battlefield between the proslavery and antislavery movements. In an attempt to quell the confrontation over slavery and settle the question once and for all, the president searched for a leader with the ability to use a strong hand on the Great Plains. He finally designated his longtime friend Robert Walker as territorial governor, selecting the man who had convinced northerners to accept Texas annexation for the task of bringing the future Sunflower State into the Union—preferably as a slave state.

Upon his arrival, however, Governor Walker found the situation in Kansas perilous and his inaugural address stunned slaveholders. He believed in democracy, he said. Most Kansans supported free soil and Walker endorsed their ability to choose their fate. The governor announced that any constitution submitted to Congress ultimately required ratification from the "actual *bona fide* resident settlers of Kansas." It took little time for his former proslavery friends to attack the idea, labeling him a southern version of a doughface. The *Charleston Mercury* declared, "General Walker is a native of Pennsylvania. He immigrated to Mississippi, and represented that State in the Senate of the United States. He is now a Pennsylvanian again. Neither the Constitution of his native State, Pennsylvania, nor that of his temporarily adopted State, Mississippi, ever submitted to the electorate for ratification after being adopted in Convention."[54] The proslavery movement expected ratification by the people to turn the territory into a free state. The Slave Power, both in Washington and in Kansas, did everything in their waning ability to shape the outcome.

The vote to create a state constitution hardly embodied Walker's goal of honest representation. Despite heavy financing by the planter elite to supplement the immigration of yeoman southerners to the Great Plains, the 1857 population of the state was estimated at seventeen thousand antislavery settlers to just seven thousand proslavery migrants. Any true balloting would have indicated the majority's favor of a free Kansas. A couple of years prior, however, before the mass immigration of free-soilers to the territory, proslavery citizens from Missouri had ventured to Kansas to declare themselves citizens for one day: Election Day. These daylong residents elected a legislature heavily populated by the proslavery movement to a two-year term. As the defenders of slavery saw their stay in office coming to an end, they expected the new legislature—dominated by new antislavery arrivals—to turn the territory into another free state. Time seemed to be running out on the idea of a slaveholding Kansas.[55]

Walker's inaugural provoked the Kansas proslavery movement to react quickly. The expiring legislature voted to create a state constitutional convention that convened before the 1857 election. Because of the previous election fraud by southerners, Kansans who favored free soil mistrusted the process for choosing delegates and boycotted the vote, resulting in a dominant proslavery contingent at the convention. Predictably, delegates in Lecompton drafted a constitution that permitted slavery in the new state. They also adopted a maneuver around the electorate while technically staying within the framework of Walker's ultimatum. The convention decided to place only the constitutional clause relating to the importation of future slaves on the ballot. Those already held in bondage in the Great Plains would remain in that condition. Ratification of the Kansas constitution revolved around the future of slavery, not its present status in the territory.[56]

Antislavery northerners disparaged the Lecompton constitution as a farce. Slaveholders, they insisted, could easily ignore a ban on importation even if voters barred more slaves from entering their state. In response to what they considered a sham, antislavery Kansans boycotted the ratification vote. Instead, they held a separate election that measured support for the entire draft sent from the slaveholders. Division reigned and the consent of the governed became contested. The official election ratified the Lecompton constitution's admittance of slavery into the territory while the unofficial vote overwhelmingly rejected the proslavery document in its entirety.[57]

Believing the base of his party resided in the South and that promoting the expansion of slavery helped Democrats remain in power, President Buchanan foolishly supported the Lecompton constitution. The fifteenth president paid the full political price for his error. In protest, Robert Walker quit his post. Meanwhile, Stephen A. Douglas, angry at Buchanan's obvious abrogation of local democracy, rallied northern Democrats to refuse the admission of Kansas. When Congress took up the issue, a stark sectional divide ruled the day.

The Senate admitted Kansas into the Union as a slave state by a vote of 33–25; however, the House of Representatives demurred, voting 120–112. In both cases, a majority of the North and a handful of southerners in the Upper South voted against the proslavery position. The people's House again undermined the machinations of the proslavery movement to extend black enslavement westward.[58]

Southern radicals came to believe the exceptional nature of the Constitution had fallen to the wayside as abolitionism gained credence in northern politics. Slaveholders held that "Black Republicans" used it as a "stratagem" to "divert attention from the occupation of an advanced position towards securing Southern subjection and Northern rule. Under the way of an increasing and overshadowing Northern majority, agitation is to go on." Echoing Robert Turnbull nearly three decades before, the newspaper inferred that the majority had started the process of stamping out slavery in North America. No longer did the American system seem different when compared to the British government. Many planters presumed that antislavery politicians wanted to foster violence by the enslaved in an effort to weaken slavery in the South. Without expansion, the *Mercury* warned, "the cordon of hostile sentiment" would slowly strangle slavery to death, "perhaps after a desperate and bloody struggle."[59]

In the fall of 1859, a man deemed the most fanatical of the fanatics carried the battles of Kansas to the East. In an event that shocked the nation, John Brown and his companions—inspired by the Haitian Revolution—attempted to launch a massive uprising in the South. During the aftermath of the revolt, Brown's son told the *New York Times,* "It is, then, only the body of Toussaint L'Ouverture which sleeps in the tombs; his soul visits the cabins of the slaves of the South when night is spread over the face of nature.... The despots of America shall yet know the strength of the toiler's arm, and that he who would be free must himself strike the first blow." The white northerner who had brutally killed Kansas slaveholders during the conflict over the Lecompton constitution intended to ignite a revolution. The abolitionist attacked the oldest slave state in the Union, designing to stab the heart of the slaveholding ethos. Emulating Gabriel Prosser, Denmark Vesey, and Nat Turner, Brown came to Virginia with the aspiration to break slavery in the United States.[60]

Following the rejection of the Wilmot Proviso in the Senate, John Brown became convinced that southern slavery could be ended only through violence. While planters lodged complaints about slavery's exclusion from California, the radical abolitionist dwelled on *Dred Scott* and the Fugitive Slave Act. After readying himself and gaining financial aid from other antislavery radicals, the abolitionist chose Harpers Ferry, Virginia, as the place to start his war. He planned an ordeal that would force Americans—both North and South—to face the question of human bondage in a nation that declared the inalienable rights of life, liberty, and the pursuit of happiness. The insurrectionist expected to serve as slavery's reckoning.

Harriet Tubman wanted to join John Brown in order to help him recruit the enslaved in Virginia to his ranks, but she had been difficult to locate and taken ill and the insurrectionist could no longer delay his plan. Before leaving, Brown and eighteen followers wrote farewell letters to their families. None expected to live, but in death, they aspired to be the moral nourishment required for change. Five members of Brown's band of raiders were black, including one whose wife and children still fell under the heavy yoke of southern bondage. The plan centered on seizing the federal arsenal at Harpers Ferry and using the weapons stored there, along with hundreds of handcrafted pikes, to arm enslaved southerners as they rose to strike against their masters. A student of the Haitian Revolution, John Brown carefully chose the town in western Virginia because of its proximity to the Appalachian Mountains. Just as Toussaint utilized the Cahos Mountains in his war on the French, the American insurrectionist planned to conduct guerrilla warfare throughout the mountainside.[61]

The insurrectionist leader truly thought his attack on the armory would cause the enslaved in the area to join him in spurring revolution in the South. His "Declaration of Liberty" proclaimed, "In the course of Human events, it becomes necessary for an Oppressed People to Rise, and assert their Natural Rights." While much of the opening resembled the Declaration of Independence, the rest of his statement echoed David Walker's *Appeal,* laying out a history of human injustice and calling for a unified opposition to slaveholders. Brown declared that American planters broke the law of God requiring the universal and natural freedom of all people.[62] The abolitionist expected to punish the slaveholders for their crimes against humanity, bathing the slave states in the blood of tyrants.

On the night of October 16, 1859, John Brown started his war with a yell to the night watchman guarding the armory, demanding he open the gate. When the sentry refused, Brown's men used a crowbar to get in, taking captive the lone guard and seizing the stored weapons and ammunition. The insurrectionist leader looked at his hostage with unforgiving eyes and calmly said, "I came here from Kansas, and this is a slave State; I want to free all the negroes in this State; I have possession now of the United States Armory, and if the citizens interfere with me, I must only burn the town and have blood."[63] Brown hoped to renew the spirit of the Haitian Revolution, this time on the continent.

The raid did not ultimately turn out as the insurrectionist planned. No massive slave revolt sprang into action. No revolutionary army appeared. Upon news of the attack, President Buchanan dispatched a detachment of Marines to Virginia. Led by Colonel Robert E. Lee, the American military secured the town. Following thirty-six hours of skirmishing, and a handful of casualties, the federal forces attacked Brown's encampment, a small brick engine house at the train station. After a short standoff, J. E. B. Stuart led a squadron of soldiers as they rushed into the building. Amidst the chaos the insurrectionist leader fired one final shot, sending a Marine to his final resting place.

Lt. Israel Greene first encountered John Brown in the engine house. He smashed the cold blade of his military saber against the abolitionist's head, not killing him, but causing injury. During the battle, four of Brown's men died along with two Marines. Stuart ensnared the wounded rebel, taking him and the rest of the survivors as prisoners. Although the Haitian Revolution did not come to Virginia, the raid at Harpers Ferry made a lasting impact on the United States. Freedom found its martyr. Before swinging on the gallows, he used the time he had left to perform the role of a prophet who portended the coming end of slavery in the United States of America.[64]

White-haired and scarred, John Brown faced his earthly judgment a few weeks later. Despite his having attacked a federal armory, the state of Virginia put him on trial instead of the federal government. Although his defense lawyers worked desperately to paint their client as insane—in hopes of receiving a more lenient sentence—the Kansan had none of it, challenging their claims in front of the entire courtroom. He demanded the world understand that he had acted thoughtfully. His violence was not the undertakings of a lunatic, but rather pensive action that came from years of reflection about how to end slavery. The insurrectionist prayed that others might adopt his approach, both in the antislavery movement of the North and those held captive in the South. He thought of himself as a forerunner for future leaders of rebellion. Following five days of proceedings, the People of the State of Virginia declared John Brown guilty of murder and treason. The noose would be knotted around his neck one month later.[65]

Initially, northerners evinced little pity for the abolitionist, and the press in the free states lambasted his tactics. One Connecticut resident noted, "We pity the weakness that has made him a fanatic."[66] Many of his ardent supporters deserted him as he awaited death. Members of the Secret Six—a collection of prominent northerners who funded Brown's expedition—fled the scrutiny of an angry public. Proslavery publications in the North claimed success in putting down another enslaved uprising. They indicated to their readers that Brown had indeed intended to start a revolution in the mountains of Virginia, but that the American military insulated slavery from the horrible results of fanaticism. The *New York Herald* wrote, "Old John Brown made a foray on Harpers Ferry; but he is not likely to repeat the experiment. . . . The enemy's camp is broken up; their leader is in a Virginian prison; their arms and munitions of war have fallen into the hand of the victors; and three or four survivors of the provisional government have fled promiscuously, with prices set upon their heads."[67] For the proslavery movement, Harpers Ferry appeared to be a victory, a triumph that proved the power of slaveholders, both in Virginia and Washington.

Investigators soon realized the massive scale of John Brown's plan when they found maps of slave states drawn by the insurrectionist leader. Each drawing was marked with crosses and census figures indicating counties with black majorities, which served as his main targets. Some of the data he used came from the slave states, supporting the notion that the insurrectionist had allies helping him in the South. Descriptions of both Brown's cartography and his belief in fueling a Haitian-style rebellion circulated quickly in the southern states. In response, slaveholders formed vigilance committees to patrol the black population while southern correspondents reported the arrests of suspected abolitionist agents purported to be part of the insurrectionist's company. Although the planter elite claimed to have everything under control, they prepared for rebellion.[68]

Proslavery journalists also connected the raid to the Haitian Revolution, portraying how dangerous someone like John Brown could be to the white South. Others offered evidence to northerners that they needed to embrace the planter class in order to prevent the millions of enslaved from revolting against their bondage. The *Baltimore Sun* wrote, "Brown wanted the citizens of Virginia calmly to fold their arms and let him usurp the government, manumit our slaves, confiscate the property of slaveholders, and without drawing a trigger or shedding blood permit him to take possession of the Commonwealth and make it another Hayti." The Union would work only if the free states fully supported the South's system of unfree labor, including its expansion to the West.[69]

In the aftermath of the raid on Harpers Ferry, several proslavery newspapers chastised Republicans, claiming that the freedom fighter acted as one of their agents to undermine the Union. "If our Northern Browns *shoot* 'freedom' *into* the South, and make slaves masters of *their* masters, as was done in Hayti, then the South will turn out to be as productive as Jamaica or Hayti," the *Washington Constitution* squealed, using Harpers Ferry to continue its recent stories on the strife in the Caribbean. "If we are not countrymen," the newspaper desperately said, "New Yorkers, Marylanders, and Virginians—we are neighbors. Our *farms* are near together. . . . Is it right to be scattering firebrands into neighbors' houses, to preach principles in neighbors' households that certainly lead to servile if not civil war?"[70] In the same way the Federalists tied the party of Jefferson to the Haitian Revolution at the turn of the century, the Democrats in the 1850s tried to associate the Republican Party with violent insurrection. Most proslavery writers characterized John Brown as a fanatic who merely acted out what many others in the North actually believed. The slaveholding class called for their northern friends to temper abolitionism before it led to more violence in the South. Slaveholders predicted that Brown would not be the last member of the antislavery movement to encourage the enslaved to resist the planter elite who held them in chains.[71]

As Brown awaited the hangman's rope, southerners guarded him cautiously, expecting his followers to attempt a rescue mission. Virginia governor Henry Wise effectively declared martial law throughout much of his state after the raid at Harpers Ferry. Claiming he received credible sources indicating another impending attack, Wise sent notices to President Buchanan and the governors of Pennsylvania and Ohio informing them of his plan to seal the northern border of his state from potential antislavery incursions. Moreover, he notified them, "Necessity may compel us to pursue invaders of our jurisdiction into yours."[72] Virginia's governor told his northern counterparts that his state expected "the confederate duty to be observed, of guarding your territory against becoming dangerous to our peace and safety, by affording places of depot and rendezvous to lawless desperadoes who may seek to war upon our people."[73] Those in charge of the slave states no longer trusted northerners to defend the South from attacks launched by radical abolitionists. Instead, the proslavery movement viewed the leadership of the free states as tacitly supporting the destabilization of planter control over the enslaved.

More pragmatic slaveholders warned against making John Brown a martyr. They supported a commuted sentence where he lived the rest of his life in a Virginia prison cell. Despite those objections, the radical proslavery movement favored revenge over strategic thinking, and Governor Wise granted no pardon. Brown was hanged on December 2, 1859. The fears of white southerners did not fall away when his lifeless body hit the ground. Instead, the northern responses to the insurrectionist's execution seemed to vindicate southerners' belief that the free states had embraced fanaticism and, in the minds of the planter class, moved away from a true understanding of the purpose of the Union and the meaning of proslavery American exceptionalism.

Brown mailed letters to supporters and curiosity seekers who contacted him during his final months, using the short time left to craft a benediction that might empower his antislavery cause. As moderate southerners had feared, northern anger and veneration only intensified when reports of Brown's calm demeanor as he walked to the gallows flooded newspapers throughout the free states. One New York journalist reported that the freedom fighter kissed a black baby held up to him as he left his jail cell. John Brown understood that his legend would be more meaningful than any action he had taken at Harpers Ferry, and he played his role perfectly. The warrior prophet of abolitionism became extraordinarily more powerful in death than he had ever been in life. Universal liberty found its American sacrificial lamb.[74]

On the day of Brown's death, church bells tolled a mournful song throughout northern cities and villages. Some attended prayer meetings or listened to local politicians deliver glowing oratories in praise of the insurrectionist. Ordinary citizens throughout the free states held vigils in memory of the fallen abolitionist. More than one town offered a hundred-gun salute to the antislavery icon. Newspapers in the North ran full-page stories about the day's events. Antislavery authors recited poems and hymns celebrating Brown's life. A hero had died—Brown's violence became sanctified.[75]

The planter elite perceived northern celebration of Brown as an obscene support for creating a Haitian-style uprising in the South. They worried that more might join the abolitionist's cause, prompting attempts to instigate revolts in the slave states. The proslavery movement predicted calamity if they lost grip of the White House and the American military, especially in a political climate that turned Brown into a paragon. Without the complete devotion to slavery by the armed forces, the planter elite worried about a rebellion against slavery transforming itself into a revolution that engulfed the South in insurrectionary violence.[76]

The entire country seemed to feel as though John Brown's raid, capture, and eventual execution changed things and the memory and purpose of his actions became contested. As the proslavery movement discussed the ramifications of being surrounded by free soil, they could not easily forget the distress caused by the abolitionist, while radical abolitionists contended that Brown's attempt to topple the master class had been justified. The election of 1860 proved that sentiment to be appropriate. The first sign of the collapse of the American political system came at the Democratic National Convention. Following the raid on Harpers Ferry, the proslavery movement demanded more guarantees from the federal government to protect slavery's stability and perpetuation. At the opening of Congress in 1859, Senator Jefferson Davis had issued a demand, which the Senate Democratic caucus adopted, that called for a national slave code fulfilling the *Dred Scott* ruling. When Democrats convened in Charleston a year later, Alabama delegates remembered their instructions to walk out of the convention if the Davis resolutions were not specifically included in the party's platform. The delegations of the South likewise vowed to block the nomination of the frontrunner, Stephen Douglas—the man who had ushered the Compromise of 1850 through Congress—if he failed to include an unwavering promotion of slavery's expansion in the party's platform.[77]

Striking divisions emerged during the Democratic meeting in South Carolina. Riven with sectional ill will, the convention lasted ten days, but it closed without naming a nominee for president. When they reconvened in Baltimore, Democrats remained divided by section. However, this time the supporters of Douglas forced through his nomination. In protest, the proslavery southern delegations abandoned the national party and held their own convention, nominating Vice-President John C. Breckinridge for the presidency. In 1860 no candidate for the White House offered an acceptable vision to both Free Soilers and slaveholders. The representative government of the United States fell into crisis.[78]

For decades the antislavery movement contended that the meaning of American exceptionalism did not lie in the Union's ability to defend black enslavement or in the maintenance of sectional comity, but rather in the Declaration of Independence. On July 5, 1852, the black abolitionist Frederick Douglass epitomized this idea by offering a speech entitled, "What to the Slave is the Fourth of July?" at a New York meeting of antislavery advocates. In the beginning of his oration, the former slave stated, "I have said that the Declaration of Independence is the ring-bolt to the chain of your nation's destiny; so, indeed, I regard it." However, as he continued, Douglass proclaimed that the principles of the Revolution remained unfulfilled. He asked his mainly white audience, "Fellow-citizens, pardon me, allow me to ask, why am I called upon to speak here to-day? What have I, or those I represent, to do with your national independence? Are the great principles of political freedom and of natural justice, embodied in that Declaration of Independence, extended to us?" and he argued that "this Fourth of July is yours, not mine."[79]

Douglass spoke about the future of the country through the lens of the nation's founding document, pointing out the hypocrisy of whites who celebrated the concept of all men being created equal while slavery and prejudice remained in the United States. He also insisted that those principles could be used to guide American destiny. He stated, "Notwithstanding the dark picture I have this day presented of the state of the nation, I do not despair of this country. . . . While drawing encouragement from the Declaration of Independence, the great principles it contains, and the genius of American Institutions, my spirit is also cheered by the obvious tendencies of the age." Frederick Douglass articulated a vision for the United States—based on the ideals of the American Revolution—that directly challenged the planter elite and perpetuation of slavery. In 1860, his vision finally found a presidential candidate to articulate it.[80]

In May, Republicans met in Chicago and chose a surprise candidate to lead their party: Abraham Lincoln. A former Illinois congressman who most considered to be a moderate, the Republican nominee based his opposition to slavery on the ideals of the Revolution. He crafted a message that challenged the proslavery formulation for American exceptionalism. Born in Kentucky, Lincoln ardently spurned expanding slaveholding territory. However, the former rail-splitter from the Midwest did not have the political baggage that the original Republican frontrunner William Seward carried. Abraham Lincoln could win the White House, party leaders believed, because he articulated an alternative for the future of the United States—one that involved a different purpose for the Union and significance of the United States as an example of a free democracy for the rest of the world.[81]

A few years before, Massachusetts senator Harry Wilson had explained the Republican strategy regarding the South's peculiar institution: "We shall blot out slavery from the national capital. We shall surround the slave states with a cordon of free states. We shall then appeal to the hearts of men and consciences of men and in a few years we shall give liberty to millions in bondage."[82] If not as immediate as Wilson declared, Lincoln planned to do the same. For decades southerners linked the expansion of slavery with its existence in the slave states. Antislavery northerners did the same. The planter elite required little convincing that the Republican nominee supported abolitionism and intended to enact policies that would eventually destroy the institution of black enslavement entirely.[83]

Although Abraham Lincoln, along with numerous other Republicans, promised to not confront slavery where it already existed, both sides of the sectional divide understood his ultimate objective included eventual emancipation of the South. Republicans continuously discussed their goal of making "freedom national" by banning the enslavement of black Americans in all lands organized under the authority of the national government, including federal property held within slave states. Antislavery politicians planned to surround the slave states with free soil until, "like a scorpion girt with fire," southern legislatures succumbed to outside pressure and drafted emancipation plans themselves. Without slavery's expansion, meanwhile, the proslavery movement only imagined a scenario akin to the Haitian Revolution as their states transformed into territorial islands of slaveholding. They considered the Republican plan to be an attempt at making the South more susceptible to insurrection.[84]

Throughout 1860, slaveholders became paranoid about insurrection being spurred on by antislavery infiltrators of the South. In Texas, planters blamed the spirit of abolitionism for mysterious fires that occurred. They worried that the flames portended an upcoming insurrection. The hysteria allowed the ardently proslavery, pro-expansion organization Knights of the Golden Circle to establish a secret police that primarily monitored the black community. No longer able to use the idea of national security to remain in control of public policy, radical members of the proslavery movement cast themselves to be the true defenders of the South who protected their fellow white citizens from a barbaric black population slowly being unleashed by abolitionism.[85]

The disquiet felt in Texas spread as the election approached. Journalists across the South declared that abolitionists "infested" the slave states in order to rouse chaos on the southern plantations. The Knights of the Golden Circle recruited more proslavery squadrons to guard against possible slave revolt. Harkening back to the American Revolution, the Knights organized "minute men" to guard the slave states as they anticipated sectional tension over slavery to instigate racial violence. Laurence M. Keitt, a congressman from South Carolina, wrote to James Henry Hammond with grave concerns about the future of the slave states. Known mostly for perpetrating violence against his antislavery colleagues on the floor of Congress in the 1850s, the congressman told Hammond—currently serving in the Senate—that the nation was changing: "Our Negroes are being enlisted in politics. I confess this new feature alarms me, more even, than every thing in the past. If Northern men get access to our Negroes to advise poison and the torch, we must prevent it at every hazard." The presidential election, he said, "is life or Death."[86]

As sectional conflict over the future of slavery's expansion increased during 1859, former Whigs in the Upper South worked to create an opposition party against Democrats to forestall the mounting political divide over slavery's future. Sensing "a change has come over the spirit of our politics," and seeing the country being rent apart by slavery's expansion, Senator John J. Crittenden, Henry Clay's successor from the Bluegrass State, called for a convention of moderates to meet in Baltimore. Naming themselves the Constitutional Union Party and nominating John Bell—a senator from Tennessee and former speaker of the House—the new third party aspired to offer an alternative to the proslavery and antislavery visions of American exceptionalism. Their platform centered squarely on the American tradition of political compromise and negotiation.[87]

Campaigning on "the Constitution as it is," Bell and his supporters argued that the basis for America's unique form of government rested on compromise between sectional interests. They maintained "the fact that our Union is composed in part of slaveholding States, and in part of non-slaveholding States, imposes grave duties upon both sections—duties of forbearance, concession, and conciliation."[88] The institution of slavery, these southern Unionists believed, had already reached its natural limits. The Unionists continued Thomas Ritchie's tack from nearly three decades before: the Union was being torn apart by radical sectional zealots and political demagogues who lusted for power, not perpetuation of American exceptionalism. The Tennessean Bell offered himself as an alternative to secession and potential civil war, aiming to send the choice for president to the House of Representatives by impeding any candidate from winning a majority of the Electoral College.

In 1860, the perfect political storm hit the United States of America. The sectionalized division between the Democrats allowed the Republicans, with their platform of stopping slavery's expansion, to win the presidency and the majority in the House of Representatives without a single southern vote. While Unionists found victory in only three states in the Upper South, Bell failed to win any free state. Stephen A. Douglas won only Missouri while Breckenridge won the entire Deep South. The election of Abraham Lincoln—who voted for the Wilmot Proviso a number of times while in Congress—directly caused the secession crisis. Led by South Carolina, the states with the highest slave population density proclaimed themselves to be independent. The Union fell apart.[89]

Despite some persistent concerns about the morality and economic progress of slavery, the roots of the proslavery reaction to Abraham Lincoln's victory stretched back to the 1790s and the nervousness slaveholders felt when they contemplated the Haitian Revolution. South Carolinians claimed the fear of enslaved rebellion to be a major reason for their separation from the Union. The secessionists announced, "We affirm that these ends for which this Government was instituted have been defeated, and the Government itself has been made destructive of them by the nonslaveholding states. . . . They have encouraged and assisted thousands of our slaves to leave their homes; and those who remain, have been incited by emissaries, books, and pictures to servile insurrection."[90]

With a Republican in the White House—and, therefore, directing the United States military—proslavery advocates thought that they no longer had federal protection from the "fanatics." A secessionist commissioner to Kentucky argued that, "like an unchained demon," radical abolitionism had seized power in the North. Insurrectionists were "celebrated with public honors," and John Brown was "canonized as a martyr to liberty." They predicted more Browns coming to the South to incite rebellion, but this time, planters believed, the Marines would not arrive to help them. An abolitionist president would allow black Americans to gain freedom through violence, many secessionists warned. For over a century, slaveholders had worried about military conflict upsetting their control over the enslaved. By 1860, those fears became subsumed by concerns about slavery imploding from within while abolitionists in Washington gladly fanned the flames by restricting the expansion of slavery.[91]

Radical South Carolinians asserted that their entire society might collapse into violent racial warfare without the full support of the federal government behind the perpetuation and expansion of slavery. In the minds of the proslavery elite, the nightmares shared by plantation-owning prophets since the turn of the century seemed to be coming true. They charged that the Republicans declared "that the South shall be excluded from the common Territory; that Judicial Tribunals shall be made sectional, and that a war must be waged against slavery until it shall cease throughout the United States." The plantation class lost faith in the Constitution's ability to guard southerners from an uprising by the millions of people they held in chains. Without domination of the federal government, they no longer saw any purpose for the Union.[92]

For decades proslavery politicians held to the notion that the diffusion of slaveholding—and of the enslaved—forestalled societal instability and the bloodshed of race war. Without the commitment of northerners to safeguard white southerners from a growing enslaved population hemmed in by free soil, "the slaveholding States will no longer have the power of self-government, or self-protection, and the Federal Government will have become their enemy," the secessionists in the Palmetto State proclaimed.[93] Planters believed that with Lincoln in the White House, the South would slowly become more and more like Jamaica or Saint-Domingue, a mere colony to the North, dependent on an abolitionist president to defend them from the resistance of those they enslaved. Like a rusted sword, the planter elite discarded the Union once they believed it to be incapable of attacking their ideological opponents.[94]

Many white southerners cared very little that Abraham Lincoln called himself a moderate or that he gave assurances that he would defer to local interests regarding slavery in the South. What mattered was their expectation that the new president would not prosecute abolitionists who threatened to provoke slave revolts while also encouraging black rebellion by refusing to allow the expansion of slaveholding territory. Isham W. Garrott and Robert H. Smith, two Alabamans charged by their governor to preach the message of secession in other slave states, claimed the Republican intentions "to impair the value of slave property in the States by unfriendly legislation" would "render the institution itself dangerous to us, as slaves increase, to abandon it, or be doomed to servile war."[95]

In a letter to the governor and legislature of North Carolina, the two secessionist commissioners explicitly argued that surrounding slave territory with free soil would lead to racial warfare. The natural population growth of enslaved black Americans could not be contained in the South alone, they averred. The result would be "the utter ruin and degradation of most, if not all of the Gulf States." The pro-secession evangelists also deemed the charge by northerners that proslavery advocates supported the reopening of the African slave trade to be "slander." "There may be, here and there, found an advocate for the measure, as there may in every community be found individual advocates of any heresy," they insisted, "but our people, with almost entire unanimity, would reject the proposition as offensive to their sense of propriety and averse to their interests. They feel no desire to depreciate the value of their own property, nor to demoralize their slaves by throwing among them savages and cannibals."[96] Reopening the international trade in human flesh and increasing the enslaved black populace even further would only hasten the South's doom.

Southern theorists had long predicted that any attempt to regulate slavery's expansion in Washington would result in the abolition of the institution and the collapse of white supremacy. The ramifications, they feared, would be the violent end of the racial status quo. Planters had always been aware of the dangers that came from holding millions of human beings in bondage. In the minds of proslavery leaders, having a commander in chief who might not assist them during an insurrection—along with being surrounded by free soil, which they insisted would cause racial unrest—became too risky. The possibility of a civil war seemed safer to slaveholders than staying within the Union. By insisting the new party at the helm of the federal government threatened their homes by promoting instability and revolt, the planter elite gained enough popular approval to create the Confederate States of America: a thoroughly proslavery, modern, centralized state with the military capability to quell massive resistance by the enslaved, expand its territorial borders, and war against the forces of the Atlantic antislavery movement.[97]

During the heated deliberations about secession in Virginia, for example, one delegate claimed, "It is no longer safe for a slave State to remain under that government. Take the history of the abolitionized Governments and it is a history of abolitionized people. Look at England, France, Denmark, and at their magnificent Colonies; the pearls of the Antilles, sacrificed without remorse."[98] A large number of secessionists throughout the slave states referenced Jamaica and Haiti as they frantically tried to convince their neighbors to abandon the authority of the Union. They mostly succeeded. From the late eighteenth century onward, the Haitian Revolution had never left the consciousness of the South and many leaders of the proslavery movement routinely compared their standing under the American system of government to their counterparts in the West Indies decades before.

Confederates declared the Constitution to be a failure and abandoned the notion that it made the United States exceptional. They weighed the likelihood of victory in a civil war with the North against the uncertainty of staying in a Union where an antislavery political party commanded the national government. Once deemed the instrument that made their slaveholding unique and different from their Caribbean counterparts, the planter elite dispatched with the government framework created by their forefathers and replaced it with one of their own. Rather than claiming the rights of revolution, slaveholding leaders argued that secession acted as a way to preserve their proslavery understanding of American exceptionalism. They challenged Lincoln's reading of the American Revolution with their own understanding of the Spirit of 1776. Jefferson Davis, the president of the newly formed Confederacy, eventually claimed the actions taken by the slaveholding class served to "save ourselves from revolution which in its silent but rapid progress, was about to place us under the despotism of numbers, and to preserve in spirit, as well as in form, a system of government we believe to be peculiarly fitted to our condition." The South, he professed, acted out of self-preservation in order to protect whites from those they held in chains.[99]

Secessionists offered a choice to the white South: risk a battle with northerners and their escalating commitment to abolitionism by leaving the Union or prepare to face black rebellion without the backing of a national military. Fire-eaters described disunion as the source of slavery's salvation and southern stability. A significant following of white yeomen farmers believed them. Planters promised that the South would never become like the Caribbean as long as the plantation owners remained in total control of society. Secession meant that slaveholders—and slaveholders alone—shaped the future of slavery. It also functioned as an acknowledgment by proslavery intellectuals that, despite their belief in the superiority of their labor system, slavery needed the full cooperation of government to survive. To stifle black rebellion, the power of the state and the military always had to linger in the background as a backstop against an uprising. A laissez-faire approach by the federal government to the enslavement of millions of Americans could never maintain a secure institution of human enslavement. States' rights did not suffice for the planter elite. White southerners opted to establish a new nation and believed they were changing—or at least preserving—their destiny to be a progressive vehicle for mankind and civilization.[100]

With the election of Abraham Lincoln on a purely sectional electoral vote, slaveholders held that the Union had become a golem that required destruction. Originally thought of as a way to protect them, the Constitution came to be viewed by the plantation class as transformed into the provenance of their ruination. Planters in the South anticipated an increase in slave revolts at the precise moment that antislavery politicians—whom they thought would not assist the slave states in putting down uprisings—occupied the office of the commander in chief. With those expectations in place, white southerners risked civil war and chose secession, initiating a contest over the definition of American exceptionalism, the burden of democracy, and the way that the idealism of the Founding Fathers would be projected to the rest of the world for generations to come.

In the spring of 1861, Edmund Ruffin traveled to South Carolina. In the immediate aftermath of secession, Major Robert Anderson moved his troops to Fort Sumter as Confederate forces seized federal property on the shoreline. Tensions had become strained when southerners had fired upon *The Star of the West,* a civilian merchant ship, as it tried to resupply the garrison. On April 6, President Lincoln received word that the fort's rations ran perilously low. He ordered another attempt to furnish Sumter with supplies and notified the governor of South Carolina of his intentions. Many awaited a battle.

Tempers finally boiled over early in the morning on April 12. A loud boom shook the city. Jefferson Davis, the Confederate president, had given the order to attack and seize Fort Sumter. Knowing the ramifications of the sound, residents hurried to the shoreline. Ruffin, the man who had prophesied a brutal brawl if a Republican won the presidency, rushed to the scene. He went to the Iron Battery in Charleston Harbor and approached a cannon with a smile on his face. After watching a soldier load a sixty-four-pound shell into the gun, aim squarely at his target, and light the fuse, the radical slaveholder cheered gleefully as the metal ball flew toward Major Anderson and his troops. In taking credit for firing the first shot of the Civil War, the Virginian became a self-fulfilling prophet. The long-predicted war over slavery finally came to the United States of America. The bloody struggle to define American exceptionalism began.

EPILOGUE

FIGHTING OVER EXCEPTIONALISM

The caged bird sings with a fearful trill / of things unknown but longed for still / and his tune is heard on the distant hill / for the caged bird sings of freedom.

—Maya Angelou, "I Know Why the Caged Bird Sings"

When the architects of our republic wrote the magnificent words of the Constitution and the Declaration of Independence, they were signing a promissory note to which every American was to fall heir. This note was a promise that all men, yes, black men as well as white men, would be guaranteed the "unalienable Rights" of "Life, Liberty and the pursuit of Happiness."

—Martin Luther King, Jr., "I Have a Dream,"
August 28, 1963, at the Lincoln Memorial, Washington, DC

From fears of insurrection during the colonial period to white flight and legal segregation during the twentieth century to racially motivated church shootings in Charleston in modern times, white fears and stereotypes about black Americans have played a significant role in the history of the United States.[1] While questions over the purpose of the Union were determined with Confederate surrender at Appomattox, the concerns and paranoia that contributed to southern secession in 1860 continued to shape America during Reconstruction and beyond. Stemming from their own anticipations for what emancipation might bring to the South, many whites living in the former slave states made assumptions about black Americans that led them to panic in the aftermath of the Civil War. In the autumn of 1865, only a few short months after Appomattox, a correspondent for the *Nation* exploring the defeated South wrote that whites universally feared a rebellion by the freed population. From Virginia to Louisiana, whites living in the southern states expected chaos and racial warfare to follow Confederate defeat.[2]

As Christmas approached, and news of an uprising in the Caribbean hit the presses of the United States, white southerners worried that, spurred on by a "negroe Jubilee," and following the "horrors of Jamaica and St. Domingo," the formerly enslaved would use the Christmas holiday to carry out vengeance against those who once claimed ownership over their lives and future. In response to the rumors, southern governors asked authorities from the victorious Union Army for protection, demanding weapons and ammunition along with the permission to raise a militia "under officers of our own selection." Although their request was denied, the leaders of the white South contacted military commanders, the Freedmen's Bureau, and the White House all in an effort to gain official support to squelch the possibility of race war in the South.[3]

Invoking concerns about racial violence, Mississippi and South Carolina legislators enacted severely restrictive laws concerning black residents near the end of 1865. The Magnolia State required all black residents to carry written evidence of employment for the coming year while barring them from renting land in urban areas. Any laborer who left a contract early would forfeit money already earned and would be subject to arrest by any white citizen. The state government also passed vagrancy laws that limited everything from making "insulting" gestures to preaching the Bible without a license; even the word of the Lord needed white supervision. As they had for decades, and against Radical Republicans who worked to provide civil rights for African Americans, powerful white southerners used fear of insurrection and a loyalty to a reconstructed vision for the Union to fortify their control over government power. They understood that much of the war-weary North cared more about restoring the Union than ensuring equality for the black population and that many abolitionists, such as Wendell Phillips, still hoped that federalism could resume as "the corner-stone of individual liberty" once peace became settled.[4]

In South Carolina, white leaders used the power to tax as a way to implement a de facto form of enslavement. They barred most black residents from any occupation other than farmer or servant—only paying a tax that ranged from ten to one hundred dollars could lift the ban. Other laws forced black workers to sign contracts that regulated relationships between "masters" and "servants." Fear about racial violence drove more southern states, such as Texas, Louisiana, Florida, and Alabama to promptly follow suit and, after the passage of the 1866 Civil Rights Act, white legislators simply offered no reference to race in order to avoid the appearance of discrimination and remain in concurrence with federal regulations. Despite their defeat, the white supremacists in control of former slave states, including those that never joined the Confederacy, continued to exert authority over black Americans long after the Emancipation Proclamation and the ratification of the Thirteenth, Fourteenth, and Fifteenth amendments.[5]

Ironically, having faltered in their quest to forge a centralized government wholly devoted to planter power and the promotion of slavery, the political elite of the white South turned to a strategy that had once protected abolitionists from proslavery assaults in the 1830s—federalism and local control. While freedom may have been won, the relationship between the black community and government authority, almost entirely still controlled by their former oppressors, changed in no real way. By 1877, the decade-long attempt at reconquering of statehouses across the former slave states became complete, beginning a phase that C. Vann Woodward described as "the abandonment of the Negro as a ward of the nation, the giving up of the attempt to guarantee the freedman his civil and political equality, and the acquiescence of the rest of the country in the South's demand that the whole problem be left to the disposition of the dominant Southern white people."[6] Soon thereafter, legislators enacted Jim Crow laws that came to define the old Confederacy well into the twentieth century.

The Civil Rights Movement continued to apply the antislavery definition of American exceptionalism to United States politics long after the conclusion of the Civil War and the end of southern slavery. Throughout the former Confederacy, the black population held conventions for the purpose of demanding equality. The freed black community pointed to the promises of the Declaration of Independence to bolster their arguments for universal equality. As historian Eric Foner noted, "Like Northern blacks steeped in the Great Tradition or prewar protest, the freedmen and Southern free blacks saw emancipation as enabling the nation to live up to the full implications of its republican creed—a goal that could be achieved only by abandoning racial proscription and absorbing blacks fully into the civil and political order."[7]

The conflict of visions over the meaning of the United States became a major aspect of the long Civil Rights Movement. From the end of the Civil War to the middle of the twentieth century, black Americans and their allies fought for justice, often, like the antislavery movement, relying on the values of the ideals of America's founding to validate their claims. On August 28, 1963, a minister named after a religious reformer walked up the marble steps of the memorial honoring Abraham Lincoln. Martin Luther King, Jr., had been imprisoned only a few months before. He had broken a law with roots to white anxiety about insurrection in the wake of the Haitian Revolution. From his jail cell, the civil rights leader wrote to opponents, "We are caught in an inescapable network of mutuality, tied in a single garment of destiny." To fulfill the promise of 1776, all Americans, of every race, needed to go into the future as equals. The minister predicted, "We will win our freedom because the sacred heritage of our nation and the eternal will of God are embodied in our echoing demands."[8] He thus made those claims not as a prophet, but because he continued the antislavery fight for American exceptionalism.

After making his trek up toward the statue of the first Republican president, King turned and stood before an ocean of people. Behind him, chiseled into stone, were Lincoln's words for characterizing the purpose of the Union and the exceptional nature of the United States: "Four score and seven years ago our fathers brought forth on this continent a new nation, conceived in liberty, and dedicated to the proposition that all men are created equal." His speech acted as the denouement for the freedom movement. America's preeminent civil rights leader wanted to add to the sentiments of the Great Emancipator, asking Americans to choose hope over fear, dreams over injustice. A contract with posterity had been promised in front of a candid world in 1776, he said, and Americans believed that it had resulted in their nation being a unique creation for the rest of humanity. The Civil Rights leader argued that universal liberty and equality offered the only path for continued national uniqueness and leadership in the free world.

Martin Luther King, Jr., insisted that his freedom movement participated in a contest with segregationists over the meaning of American exceptionalism and the way that the idealism of the founding would be projected to the rest of the world. He understood that the battle he fought did not derive from a new idea, but, rather, an old one that a multitude of Americans had grappled with for centuries. Similar to those who came before him, he anticipated that the cause for justice in the United States and the belief in American exceptionalism would be inextricably linked. Like the antislavery movement and Abraham Lincoln, King expected the debate over the nature of the government and the purpose of their nation's founding to compel Americans to continue striving for a more perfect Union long into the future.

NOTES

Abbreviations

CG	*Congressional Globe*
RD	*Register of the Debates*
RichEnq	*Richmond Enquirer*
CharMerc	*Charleston Mercury*
SouPat	*Charleston Southern Patriot*
JSH	*Journal of Southern History*
CWS	*Civil War History*

Introduction: Expectations and Exceptionalism

1. Eric H. Walther, "The Fire-Eaters and ~~Seward~~ Lincoln," *Journal of the Abraham Lincoln Association* 32 (2011): 18–19; Jason Phillips, "The Prophecy of Edmund Ruffin: Anticipating the Future of Civil War History," in *Apocalypse and the Millennium in the American Civil War Era,* ed. Benjamin Wright and Zachary W. Dresser (Baton Rouge: Louisiana State University Press, 2013): 13–30; Drew Gilpin Faust, *A Sacred Circle: The Dilemma of the Intellectual in the Old South, 1840–1860* (Philadelphia: University of Pennsylvania Press, 1977): 77.

2. Edmund Ruffin, *Anticipations of the Future to Serve as Lessons for the Present Time: In the Form of Extracts from an English Resident in the United States, to the London Times, from 1864–1870, with an Appendix, on the Causes and Consequences or Independence of the South* (Richmond: J. W. Randolph, 1860): vi; Walther, "The Fire-Eaters and ~~Seward~~ Lincoln," 13, 19–20.

3. Ruffin, *Anticipations of the Future,* 46, 70.

4. Ibid., 234. See also Steven Hahn, *A Nation under Our Feet: Black Political Struggles in the Rural South from Slavery to the Great Migration* (Cambridge, MA: Harvard University Press, 2003): 13–61; Patrick H. Breen, "In Terror of Their Slaves: White Southern Women's Responses to Slave Insurrections and Scares," in *Warm Ashes: Issues in Southern History at the Dawn of the Twenty-First Century,* ed. Winfred B Moore Jr., Kyle S. Sinsi, and David H. White, Jr. (Columbia: University of South Carolina Press, 2003): 69–84; Wim Klooster, "Slave Revolts, Royal Justice, and a Ubiquitous Rumor in the Age of Revolutions," *William and Mary Quarterly* 71 (July 2014): 401–24; Christopher Leslie Brown, *Moral Capital: Foundations of British Abolitionism* (Chapel Hill: University of North Carolina Press, 2006).

5. Steven Pinker, *The Better Angels of Our Nature: Why Violence Has Declined* (New York: Penguin Books, 2011): 323–25.

6. Steven A. Channing, *Crisis of Fear: Secession in South Carolina* (New York: Simon & Schuster, 1970): 58–93; John Craig Hammond, "Slavery, Sovereignty, and Empires: North American Borderlands and the American Civil War, 1660–1860," *Journal of the Civil War Era* 4 (June 2014): 264–98; George William Van Cleve, *A Slaveholders' Union: Slavery, Politics, and the Constitution in the Early American Republic* (Chicago: University of Chicago Press, 2010): 178–83; Ta-Nehisi Coates, "The Case For Reparations," *Atlantic* (June 2014): 54–71.

7. James McPherson, *Battle Cry of Freedom: The Civil War Era* (New York: Oxford University Press, 1993): 78; David M. Potter, *The Impending Crisis, 1848–1861,* ed. Don. E. Fehrenbacher (New York: Harper & Row, 1976): 33. See also: Eva Sheppard Wolf, *Race and Liberty in the New Nation: Emancipation in Virginia from the Revolution to Nat Turner's Rebellion* (Baton Rouge: Louisiana State University Press, 2006): 172; Elizabeth R. Varon, *Disunion! The Coming of the American Civil War, 1789–1859* (Chapel Hill: University of North Carolina Press, 2008): 45; David Goldfield, *Still Fighting the Civil War: The American South and Southern History* (Baton Rouge: Louisiana State University Press, 2013): 229; William W. Freehling, "Reviving State Rights," in *A Political Nation: New Directions in Mid-Nineteenth-Century American Political History,* ed. Gary W. Gallagher and Rachel A. Shelden (Charlottesville: University of Virginia Press, 2012): 112–25.

8. Gary W. Gallagher, *The Union War* (Cambridge, MA: Harvard University Press, 2012).

9. Gordon Wood, *Empire of Liberty: A History of the Early American Republic 1789–1815* (New York: Oxford University Press, 2009): 44–50, 544.

10. David Brion Davis, *Revolutions: Reflections on American Equality and Foreign Liberations* (Cambridge, MA: Harvard University Press, 1990): 55–122.

11. Eric Foner, *Free Soil, Free Labor, Free Men: The Ideology of the Republican Party before the Civil War: The Ideology of the Republican Party before the Civil War* (New York: Oxford University Press, 1995).

12. John Ashworth, *The Republic in Crisis, 1848–1861* (New York: Cambridge University Press, 2012): 1; Stanley Harrold, *Border Wars: Fighting over Slavery before the Civil War* (Chapel Hill: University of North Carolina Press, 2010); John Ashworth, *Slavery, Capitalism, and Politics in the Antebellum Republic,* vol. 1 and 2 (New York: Cambridge University Press, 1995, 2007); Michael F. Holt, *The Political Crisis of the 1850s* (New York: W. W. Norton, 1978); Edward L. Ayers, *In The Presence of Mine Enemies: War In the Heart of America, 1859–1863* (New York: W. W. Norton, 2003); Nelson Lankford, *Cry Havoc The Crooked Road to the Civil War* (New York: Penguin Books, 2007); Gallagher and Shelden, *A Political Nation.* See also Michael A. Morrison, *Slavery and the American West: The Eclipse of Manifest Destiny* (Chapel Hill: University of North Carolina Press, 1997); J. Mills Thornton, *Politics and Power in a Slave Society: Alabama, 1800–1860* (Baton Rouge: Louisiana State University Press, 1978); Lacy K. Ford Jr., *Origins of Southern Radicalism: The South Carolina Upcountry, 1800–1860* (New York: Oxford University Press, 1991); Leonard L. Richards, *The California Gold Rush and the Coming of the Civil War* (New York: Vintage, 2008); Shearer Davis Bowman, *At the Precipice: North and South during the Secession Crisis* (Chapel Hill: University of North Carolina Press, 2010).

13. Thomas R. Heitala, *Manifest Design: American Exceptionalism and Empire, Revised Edition* (Ithaca, NY: Cornell University Press, 2003); Christopher Childers, *The Failure of Popular Sovereignty: Slavery, Manifest Destiny, and the Radicalization of Southern Politics* (Lawrence: University of Kansas Press, 2012); John Craig Hammond, *Slavery, Freedom, and Expansion in the Early American West* (Charlottesville: University of Virginia Press, 2007); Matthew Mason, *Slavery and Politics in the Early American Republic* (Chapel Hill: University of North Carolina Press, 2006); Joel H. Silbey, *Storm over Texas: The Annexation Controversy and the Road to the Civil War* (New York: Oxford University Press, 2005).

14. Eric Foner, *The Fiery Trial: Abraham Lincoln and American Slavery* (New York: W. W. Norton, 2010): 66; Morrison, *Slavery and the American West*, 6–7. See also William W. Freehling, *The Road to Disunion: Secessionists at Bay, 1776–1854* (New York: Oxford University Press, 1990); Tyler Anbinder, *Nativism and Slavery: The Northern Know Nothings and the Politics of the 1850s* (New York: Oxford University Press, 1992); Robert Pierce Forbes, *The Missouri Compromise and Its Aftermath: Slavery and the Meaning of America* (Chapel Hill: University of North Carolina Press, 2007); Leonard L. Richards, *The Slave Power: The Free North and Southern Domination, 1780–1860* (Baton Rouge: Louisiana State University Press, 2000); Timothy M. Roberts, "'Revolutions Have Become the Bloody Toy of the Multitude': European Revolutions, the South, and the Crisis of 1850s," *Journal of the Early Republic* 25 (Summer 2005): 259–83.

15. Brian Schoen, *The Fragile Fabric of Union: Cotton, Federal Politics, and the Global Origins of the Civil War* (Baltimore: Johns Hopkins University Press, 2009); Seth Rockman, "The Future of Civil War Era Studies: Slavery and Capitalism," *Journal of the Civil War Era* 2 (March 2012): online supplement; Walter Johnson, *River of Dark Dreams: Slavery and Empire in the Cotton Kingdom* (Cambridge, MA: Harvard University Press, 2012); Channing, *Crisis of Fear*, 58–62; William Harper, "Memoir on Slavery," *Southern Literary Messenger* 4 (Oct. 1838): 609–36; Edward E. Baptist, *The Half Has Never Been Told: Slavery and the Making of American Capitalism* (New York: Basic Books, 2014).

16. T. R. Clayton, "Sophistry, Security, and Socio Political Structures in the American Revolution," *Historical Journal* 29 (June 1986): 319–344. See also Andrew Jackson O'Shaughnessy, *An Empire Divided: The American Revolution and the British Caribbean* (Philadelphia: University of Pennsylvania Press, 2000).

17. Matthew J. Clavin, *Toussaint Louverture and the American Civil War: The Promise and Peril of a Second Haitian Revolution* (Philadelphia: University of Pennsylvania Press, 2010).

18. Michael F. Holt, *The Fate of Their Country: Politicians, Slavery Extension, and the Coming of the Civil War* (New York: Hill & Wang, 2004): 29.

19. David Brion Davis, *The Slave Power Conspiracy and the Paranoid Style* (Baton Rouge: Louisiana State University Press, 1969): 32–61.

1. The Haitian Revolution and Slaveholding Anxiety

1. John Holcombe's speech appears in William W. Freehling and Craig M. Simpson, eds., *Showdown in Virginia: The 1861 Convention and the Fate of the Union* (Charlottesville: University of Virginia Press, 2010): 65.

2. Louis Moreau Gottschalk, *Notes of A Pianist: The Chronicles of a New Orleans Music Legend*, ed. Jeanne Behrend (Princeton, NJ: Princeton University Press, 2006): 10.

3. Ibid, 9.

4. Ibid; Laurent Dubois, *Avengers of the New World: The Story of the Haitian Revolution* (Cambridge, MA: Harvard University Press, 2004).

5. Gottschalk, *Notes of a Pianist*, 10–12.

6. Peter H. Wood, *Black Majority: Negroes In Colonial South Carolina from 1670 through the Stono Rebellion* (New York: W. W. Norton, 1975): 13–34; Edward Bartlett Rugemer, *The Problem of Emancipation: The Caribbean Roots of the American Civil War* (Baton Rouge: Louisiana State University Press, 2008): 33–41; Matthew Pratt Guterl, *American Mediterranean: Southern Slaveholders in the Age of Emancipation* (Cambridge, MA: Harvard University Press, 2008): 1–78.

7. Tim Matthewson, *A Proslavery Foreign Policy: Haitian-American Relations during the Early Re-*

public (Westport, CT: Praeger, 2003): 3–4; Robert K. Lacerte, "The Evolution of Land and Labor in the Haitian Revolution, 1791–1820," *The Americas* 34 (April 1978): 449; Michael O. West and William G. Martin, "Haiti, I'm Sorry: The Haitian Revolution and the Forging of the Black International," in *From Toussaint to Tupac: The Black International since the Age of Revolution,* ed. Michael O. West, William G. Martin, and Fanon Che Wilkins (Chapel Hill: University of North Carolina Press, 2009): 73–78; Susan B. Carter, "Black population, by state and slave/free status: 1790–1860," in *Historical Statistics of the United States: Millennial Edition* (New York: Cambridge University Press, 2010).

8. Robert G. Parkinson, "'Manifest Signs of Passion': The First Federal Congress, Antislavery, and the Legacies of the Revolutionary War," in *Contesting Slavery: The Politics of Bondage and Freedom in the New American Nation, ed. John Craig Hammond and Matthew Mason* (Charlottesville: University of Virginia Press, 2011): 49–68. For more on the Quakers and the nascent antislavery movement in the United States, see David Brion Davis, *The Problem of Slavery in the Age of Revolution, 1770–1823* (New York: Oxford University Press, 1999): 213–54. For more on Franklin, see Gordon S. Wood, *The Americanization of Benjamin Franklin* (New York: Penguin Books, 2004): 226–229.

9. Rugemer, *Problem of Emancipation,* 43–44; Winthrop D. Jordan, *White over Black: American Attitudes toward the Negro, 1550–1812* (New York: W. W. Norton, 1968): 378–80; Theodore Dwight, *An Oration, Spoken before "The Connecticut Society, for the Promotion of Freedom and the Relief of Persons Unlawfully Held in Bondage"* (Hartford, CT, 1794): 10–12; M. Garran Coulon, *An inquiry into the causes of the insurrection of the negroes in the island of St. Domingo* (London: J. Johnson, 1792); Brown, *Moral Capital,* 391–450. For West Indians claiming the French Revolution, see also Laurent Dubois, *A Colony of Citizens: Revolution and Slave Emancipation in the French Caribbean 1787–1804* (Chapel Hill: University of North Carolina Press, 2004); David Brion Davis, *Inhuman Bondage: The Rise and Fall of Slavery in the New World* (New York: Oxford University Press, 2006): 158–74.

10. Davis, *Inhuman Bondage,* 147; George Washington to Jean Baptiste Ternant, September 24, 1791, in *The Writings of George Washington,* ed. John C. Fitzpatrick (Washington, DC: Government Printing Office, 1931–44): 31:375. Most support for the Haitian revolutionaries came from the willingness of American merchants to trade.

11. Simon P. Newman, "American Political Culture and the French and Haitian Revolutions: Nathaniel Cutting and the Jeffersonian Republicans," in *The Impact of the Haitian Revolution in the Atlantic World,* ed. David P. Geggus (Columbia: University of South Carolina Press, 2001): 72–85, quoted on 79; Alfred N. Hunt, *Haiti's Influence on Antebellum America: Slumbering Volcano in the Caribbean* (Baton Rouge: Louisiana State University Press, 1988), 111; West and Martin, "Haiti, I'm Sorry," 83–87; Matthewson, *Proslavery Foreign Policy,* 66–71; Gordon S. Brown, *Toussaint's Clause: The Founding Fathers and the Haitian Revolution* (Jackson: University Press of Mississippi, 2005): 139–43.

12. Ralph Izard to Mathias Hutchison, November 20, 1794; Mary Pinckney to Mrs. Manigault, February 5, 1798, both in Ralph Izard Papers, South Caroliniana Library, University of South Carolina Library; Hunt, *Haiti's Influence,* 110–11; Bernard E. Powers Jr., "'The Worst of All Barbarism': Racial Anxiety and the Approach of Secession in the Palmetto State," *South Carolina Historical Magazine* 112 (July-Oct. 2011): 143–44.

13. Donald R. Hickey, "America's Response to the Slave Revolt in Haiti, 1791–1806," *Journal of the Early Republic* 2 (Winter 1982): 364–65; George Washington to John Vaughan, December 27, 1791, in *The Writings of George Washington,* 31:453; Matthewson, *Proslavery Foreign Policy,* 24–26.

14. George C. Rogers, *Evolution of a Federalist: William Loughton Smith of Charleston, 1758–1812* (Columbia: University of South Carolina Press, 1962): 246–50, quoted 249.

15. Governor Charles Pinckney to the South Carolina House and Senate, December 4, 1791, Gov-

ernors' Messages 1783–1870, South Carolina Department of Archives and History, hereafter SCDAH, http://www.archivesindex.sc.gov/onlinearchives/Thumbnails.aspx?recordId=284337; Marty D. Matthews, *Forgotten Founder: The Life and Times of Charles Pinckney* (Columbia: University of South Carolina Press, 2004): 77–78; Timothy Mathewson, "George Washington's Policy toward the Haitian Revolution," *Diplomatic History* 3 (Summer 1979): 324–25; Edward L. Cox, "The British Caribbean in the Age of Revolution," in *Empire and Nation: The American Revolution in the Atlantic World,* ed. Eliga H. Gould and Peter S. Onuf (Baltimore: Johns Hopkins University Press, 2005): 277–94.

16. July 20, 1793, *Charleston City Gazette and Daily Advertiser*; Thomas Jefferson to James Monroe, July 14, 1793, in *The Papers of Thomas Jefferson,* ed. John Catanzarti (Princeton, NJ: Princeton University Press, 1995): 26:501–3; Matthewson, *Proslavery Foreign Policy,* 59–60.

17. Thomas Jefferson to James Monroe, July 14, 1793, in *Papers of Thomas Jefferson,* 26:501–3. See also Joret de Longchamps to Thomas Jefferson, September 23, 1793, in *Papers of Thomas Jefferson,* 27:146; Edward Rutledge to Thomas Jefferson, November 9, 1793, in *Papers of Thomas Jefferson,* 27:336.

18. Adhemar de Brethoux to George Washington, December, 1793, in *The Papers of George Washington,* ed. Theodore J. Crackel (Charlottesville: University of Virginia Press, 2008): 14:654; George Washington to Madames Laurent de Saxji and Laurent de Verneuil, December 26, 1793, in *The Writings of George Washington* 33:217–18; George Washington to Alexander Hamilton, March 21, 1794, in *The Writings of George Washington* 33:299; John E. Baur, "International Repercussions of the Haitian Revolution," *The Americas* 26 (April 1970): 395–98.

19. Susan Branson and Leslie Patrick, "Étrangers dans un Pays Étrange: Saint-Dominguan Refugees of Color in Philadelphia," in *The Impact of the Haitian Revolution in the Atlantic World,* 193–208.

20. Hunt, *Haiti's Influence,* 63, 66–71; Baur, "International Repercussions of the Haitian Revolution," 398–400; A Creole of St. Domingue, *My Odyssey: Experiences of a Young Refugee from Two Revolutions,* trans. Alethea de Peuch Parham (Baton Rouge: Louisiana State University Press, 1959): 98–100; Davis, *Revolutions,* 49–53; *South Carolina Historical and Genealogical Magazine,* ed. Mabel Louise Webber, 23 (1922): 27, 152–53; William Winter, *Life and Art of Joseph Jefferson: Together with Some Account of His Ancestry and the Jefferson Family of Actors* (New York: Macmillan & Co., 1894): 153–55.

21. Jack D. L. Holmes, "The Abortive Slave Revolt at Pointe Coupée, Louisiana, 1795," *Louisiana History: The Journal of the Louisiana Historical Association* 11 (Autumn 1970): 341–62.

22. John D. Cushing, ed., *The First Laws of the State of Georgia, Part 2* (Wilmington, DE: Michael Glazier, 1981): 530; Bill no. 1544, *The State Records of South Carolina: Journals of the House of Representatives, 1792–1794,* ed. Michael E. Stevens (Columbia: University of South Carolina Press, 1988): 614; W. E. B. Dubois, *The Suppression of the African Slave-Trade to The United States of America, 1638–1870* (New York: Longmans, Green, & Co, 1904): 70–74; Lacy K. Ford, *Deliver Us from Evil: The Slavery Question in the Old South* (New York: Oxford University Press, 2009): 82–86; Ira Berlin, *Slaves without Masters: The Free Negro in the Antebellum South* (New York: New Press, 1974): 35–36; Hunt, *Haiti's Influence,* 108–9; Jeffrey J. Crow, "Slave Rebelliousness and Social Conflict in North Carolina, 1775 to 1802," *William and Mary Quarterly* 37 (Jan., 1980): 94; *Annals of Congress,* 7 Cong, 2 sess., pages 1564–1565.

23. South Carolina Department of Archives and History, Petition to the General Assembly, Roll 1331, Item 87, frames 282–90, Dec 11, 1797. Gardener quoted in Powers, "'The Worst of All Barbarism,'" 144.

24. James Sidbury, "Saint-Domingue in Virginia Ideology, Local Meanings, and Resistance to Slavery 1790–1800," *JSH* 63 (Aug. 1997): 539–40; Merton Dillon, *Slavery Attacked: Southern Slaves*

and Their Allies 1619–1865 (Baton Rouge: Louisiana State University Press, 1990): 52; Crow," Slave Rebelliousness and Social Conflict," 72–93. Many slaveholders alive during the Haitian Revolution experienced fear over large-scale slave unrest during the American Revolution when the colonial governor of Virginia, Lord Dunmore, offered freedom to all male slaves who left patriot plantations. See Woody Holton, "'Rebel against Rebel': Enslaved Virginians and the Coming of the American Revolution," *Virginia Magazine of History and Biography* 105 (Spring 1997): 157–92.

25. Disposition of John Randolph, July 21, 1793, in *Calendar of Virginia State Papers and Other Manuscripts from August 11, 1792 to December 31, 1793,* vol. 6, ed. Sherwin McRae (Richmond, 1886): 452–53.

26. Ibid.; Aptheker, *American Negro Slave Revolts: Nat Turner, Denmark Vesey, Gabriel, and others* (New York: International Publishers, 1943): 213–15. See also Alan Taylor, *The Internal Enemy: Slavery and War in Virginia, 1772–1832* (New York: W. W. Norton, 2013): 1–10.

27. Thomas Newton to James Wood, August 8, 1793, SCDAH, http://www.archivesindex.sc.gov/onlinearchives/Thumbnails.aspx?recordId=284391. For more on this rumor, see Robert Alderson, "Charleston's Rumored Revolt of 1793," in *The Impact of the Haitian Revolution in the Atlantic World,* 93–106. Alderson discusses whether the "Secret Keeper" plot was real along with who may have benefitted from the panic caused by the rumor of an impending slave insurrection stemming from the Haitian Revolution. The Secret Keeper letter was enclosed in William Nelson to James Wood, August 8, 1793, enclosed in SCDAH, Governors' Messages, letter number 577–25, http://www.archivesindex.sc.gov/onlinearchives/ViewImage.aspx?imageNumber=S165009057700000000u.jpg&recordId=284391.

28. Thomas Newton to James Wood, August 8, 1793, SCDAH.

29. A Black to William Moultrie, undated, SCADH, Governors' Messages, letter number 577–15, http://www.archivesindex.sc.gov/onlinearchives/ViewImage.aspx?imageNumber=S165009057700000000m.jpg&recordId=284391; A Black to William Moultrie, undated, SCADH, Governors' Messages, letter number 577–13, http://www.archivesindex.sc.gov/onlinearchives/ViewImage.aspx?imageNumber=S165009057700000000k.jpg&recordId=284391; William Moultrie to the South Carolina Senate, November 30, 1793, http://www.archivesindex.sc.gov/onlinearchives/ViewImage.aspx?imageNumber=S165009057700000000e.jpg&recordId=284391.

30. Alderson, "Charleston's Rumored Slave Revolt," 94–101; *Columbian Herald* and the *Charleston Southern Star,* October 19, 1793; *The State Records of South Carolina: Journals of the House of Representatives,* xvi.

31. Thomas Newton to James Wood, undated, SCDAH, Governors' Messages, letter number 577–19, http://www.archivesindex.sc.gov/onlinearchives/ViewImage.aspx?imageNumber=S165009057700000000o.jpg&recordId=284391; Gordon Wood, *Empire of Liberty,* 44–50.

32. Thomas Jefferson to William Moultrie, December 23, 1793, in *Papers of Thomas Jefferson,* 27:614; Peter S. Onuf, "'To Declare Them a Free and Independent People': Race, Slavery, and National Identity in Jefferson's Thought," *Journal of the Early Republic* 18 (Spring 1998): 1–7, and *The Mind of Thomas Jefferson* (Charlottesville: University of Virginia Press, 2007): 209–10; Mathewson, *A Proslavery Foreign Policy,* 45–46.

33. Dillon, *Slavery Attacked,* 52–53; Aptheker, *American Negro Slave Revolts,* 97; Hunt, *Haiti's Influence,* 109.

34. Robert Goodloe Harper to his constituents, March 20, 1799, in *Papers of James A. Bayard, 1796–1815,* ed. Elizabeth Donnan (Washington DC: Eleventh Report of the Historical Manuscripts Commission, 1913): 90; Eric Robert Papenfuse, *The Evils of Necessity: Robert Goodloe Harper and the*

Moral Dilemma of Slavery (Philadelphia: American Philosophical Society, 1997): 27–31. For a list of Federalists who echoed Harper, see Aptheker, *American Negro Slave Revolts,* 44.

35. *Abridgement of the Debates of Congress,* 5th Cong., 3rd sess., 339; Brown, *Toussaint's Clause,* 139–42.

36. Hammond, *Slavery, Freedom, and Expansion,* 22–27.

37. Bert M. Mutersbaugh, "The Background of Gabriel's Insurrection," *Journal of Negro History* 68 (Spring 1983): 209–11; James Sidbury, *Ploughshares into Swords: Race, Rebellion, and Identity in Gabriel's Virginia, 1730–1810* (New York: Cambridge University Press, 1997): 55–57; Taylor, *Internal Enemy,* 69. For more on slavery as a way to climb the economic ladder, see Walter Johnson, *Soul by Soul: Life inside the Antebellum Slave Market* (Cambridge, MA: Harvard University Press, 1999).

38. Mutersbaugh, "The Background of Gabriel's Insurrection," 209–11; Sidbury, *Ploughshares into Swords,* 55–56.

39. Douglas R. Egerton, *Gabriel's Rebellion: The Virginia Slave Conspiracies of 1800 and 1802* (Chapel Hill: University of North Carolina Press, 1993): 20–22.

40. Philip J. Schwarz, "Gabriel's Challenge: Slaves and Crime in Late Eighteenth-Century Virginia," *Virginia Magazine of History and Biography* 90 (July 1982): 283–309.

41. Taylor, *Internal Enemy,* 94–97; Egerton, *Gabriel's Rebellion,* 50–68, details the planning of the insurrection. See also Ford, *Deliver Us from Evil,* 49–54; *Calendar of the Virginia State Papers and Other Manuscripts from January 1, 1799, to December 31, 1807,* xi, ed. H. W. Flournoy (Richmond, 1890): 140–74; *Journal of the Senate of the Commonwealth of Virginia, 1800* (Richmond: Thomas Nicholson, 1800): 26–33; Douglas R. Egerton, "Gabriel's Conspiracy and the Election of 1800," *JSH* 56 (May 1990): 191–214.

42. Egerton, *Gabriel's Rebellion,* 58–60; Taylor, *Internal Enemy,* 95; *Calendar of Virginia State Papers,* 9:141–42.

43. Egerton, *Gabriel's Rebellion,* 58–60.

44. Ibid.; *Calendar of Virginia State Papers,* 9:147. The Haitian Declaration of Independence can be found at the National Archives of the United Kingdom. The success of the Haitian Revolution inspired resistance in the United States; see Davis, *Revolutions,* 51–54.

45. Egerton, *Gabriel's Rebellion,* 69; *Calendar of Virginia State Papers,* 9:164–65.

46. Egerton, *Gabriel's Rebellion,* 70–72.

47. Ibid.; Sidbury, *Ploughshares into Swords,* 105–11.

48. Egerton, *Gabriel's Rebellion,* 78–94; Sidbury, *Ploughshares into Swords,* 120–28; Taylor, *Internal Enemy,* 97. In a letter to Monroe, Jefferson wrote, "There is a strong sentiment that there has been hanging enough. The other states and the world at large will forever condemn us if we indulge a principle of revenge." Thomas Jefferson to James Monroe, September 20, 1800, quoted in Egerton, *Gabriel's Rebellion,* 92–93.

49. Sidbury, *Ploughshares into Swords,* 112–13.

50. Egerton, *Gabriel's Rebellion,* 110–11; Sidbury, *Ploughshares into Swords,* 125–28.

51. Klooster, "Slave Revolts," 405–11; John K. Thornton, "'I Am Subject of the King of Congo': African Political Ideology and the Haitian Revolution," *Journal of World History* 4 (Fall 1993): 181–214; Manuel Barcia, *Seeds of Insurrection: Domination and Resistance on Western Cuban Plantations, 1808–1848* (Baton Rouge: Louisiana State University Press, 2008): 43–44.

52. *Calendar of State Papers of Virginia,* 146–47, 164–65; Sidbury, "Saint-Domingue in Virginia, 531–52.

53. *New London (Conn.) Bee* September 12, 1800; *Philadelphia Gazette* September 18, 1800; *Co-*

lumbian Mirror and Alexandria Gazette, October 4, 1800; Charles Harris to Robert Harris, September 18, 1800, in "The Harris Letters" in *The James Sprunt Historical Publications,* ed. H. M. Wagstaff (Chapel Hill: University of North Carolina Press, 1916): 83–84; Documenting the American South. University Library, University of North Carolina at Chapel Hill; Brian Gabrial, "From Haiti to Nat Turner: Racial Panic Discourse during the Nineteenth-Century Partisan Press Era," *American Journalism* 30 (2013): 336–64; Salley E. Hadden, *Slave Patrols: Law and Violence in Virginia and the Carolinas* (Cambridge, MA: Harvard University Press, 2001): 57.

54. *Calendar of State Papers of Virginia, IX,* 147, 150–152, 164; Taylor, *Internal Enemy,* 110; Sidbury, *Ploughshares into Swords,* 261; Egerton, *Gabriel's Rebellion,* 182–85. Haitians and Frenchmen became a topic in other insurrection scares as well, especially in Louisiana after the Louisiana Purchase. See John Watkins to John Graham, September 6, 1805, in *The Territorial Papers of the United States, vol. 9,* ed. Clarence E. Carter (Washington: Government Printing Office, 1940). See also Junius Rodriguez, "Rebellion on the Rivier Road: The Ideology and Influence of Louisiana's German Coast Slave Insurrection of 1811," in *Antislavery Violence: Sectional, Racial, and Cultural Conflict in Antebellum America,* ed. John R. McKivigan and Stanley Harrold (Knoxville: University of Tennessee Press, 1999): 65–88; Gabrial, "From Haiti to Nat Turner," 343.

55. Douglas R. Egerton, "Gabriel's Conspiracy and the Election of 1800," *JSH* 56 (May 1990): 191–214; Mason, *Slavery and Politics in the Early American Republic,* 9–86; Rachel Hope Cleves, *The Reign of Terror in America: Visions of Violence from Anti-Jacobinism to Antislavery* (New York: Cambridge University Press, 2009): 20–103.

56. *Boston Gazette,* October 23, 1800; Rachel Hope Cleves, "'Hurtful to the State": The Political Morality of Federalist Antislavery," in Hammond and Mason, *Contesting Slavery,* 207–26.

57. *Aurora General Advertiser,* September 24, 1800.

58. Thomas Wentworth Higginson, *Travelers and Outlaws: Episodes in American History* (Boston: Lee & Shepard, 1889): 185; Hunt, *Haiti's Influence,* 118.

59. Taylor, *Internal Enemy,* 87–89, 97–102. George Tucker is often confused with his cousin St. George Tucker, a former merchant, lawyer, and professor at the College of William and Mary who, in the late 1790s, developed a plan for gradual emancipation.

60. Ford, *Deliver Us from Evil,* 54–61; St. George Tucker, *Letter to a Member of the General Assembly of Virginia on the Subject of the Late Conspiracy of the Slaves with a Proposal for Their Colonization* (Baltimore: Bonsal & Niles, 1801): quotes from 10, 18. See also Taylor, *Internal Enemy,* 97–102.

61. Thomas Jefferson to James Monroe, November 24, 1801, quoted in Philip Slaughter; *The Virginian History of African Colonization* (Macfarlane & Fergusson, 1855): 4; Onuf, *The Mind of Thomas Jefferson,* 217; Taylor, *Internal Enemy,* 78.

62. *American State Papers: Documents, Legislative and Executive of the Congress of the United States, From the First Session of the First to the Section Session of the Twenty-Second Congress,* Class VII, ed. Walter Lowrie and Walter S. Franklin (Washington, DC: Gales & Seaton, 1834): 27.

63. Ibid.

64. Matthewson, *Proslavery Foreign Policy,* 97–115; Tench Coxe to James Madison, November 28, 1801, *The Papers of James Madison,* Secretary of State Series vol. 2, ed. Mary Hackett, J. C. Staff, Jeanne Kerr Cross, and Susan Holbrook Purdue (Charlottesville: University of Virginia Press, 1986): 281–82; Robin Blackburn, *The American Crucible: Slavery, Emancipation and Human Rights* (New York: Verso, 2011): 244–46.

65. West and Martin, "Haiti, I'm Sorry," 77–86.

66. Sean Wilentz, *The Rise of American Democracy: Jefferson to Lincoln* (New York: W. W. Norton, 2005): 108–14; Adam Rothman, *American Expansion and the Origins of the Deep South* (Cambridge,

MA: Harvard University Press, 2005): 1–117. Fearing disloyalty and disunion from the residents in the newly acquired territory, leaders in Washington hardly objected to slavery's expansion into the southern half of the Louisiana Purchase. See John Craig Hammond, "'Uncontrollable Necessity': The Local Politics, Geopolitics, and Sectional Politics of Slavery Expansion," in *Contesting Slavery,* 138–60; Hammond, *Slavery, Freedom, and Expansion*; Johnson, *River of Dark Dreams,* 31–45; James Eyre Wainwright, "Both Native South and Deep South: The Native Transformation of the Gulf South Borderlands, 1770–1835" (PhD diss., Rice University, 2013).

67. Tim Matthewson, "Jefferson and the Nonrecognition of Haiti," *Proceedings of the American Philosophical Society* 140 (March 1996): 22–23; Ludwell Lee Montague, *Haiti and the United States, 1714–1938* (Durham, NC: Duke University Press, 1940): 81–90.

68. *Richmond Virginia Argus,* October 3, 1800; Taylor, *Internal Enemy,* 37; Louis B. Wright and Marion Tinling, eds., *The Secret Diary of William Byrd of Westover, 1709–1712* (Richmond, VA: Dietz Press, 1941): 194.

69. William Leckie to Alexander Ban[e], August 15, 1802, Leckie Family Papers, William Clements Library University of Michigan.

70. David Hugh Connolly Jr, "A Question of Honor: State Character and the Lower South's Defense of the African Slave Trade in Congress, 1789–1807," (PhD diss., Rice University, 2008): 25–35.

71. *A collection of the laws of the United States relating to revenue, navigation and commerce, and light-houses, etc: up to March 4, 1843, including the treaties with foreign powers* (Philadelphia: Isaac Ashmead & Company, 1844): 158; Paul Finkelman, "Regulating the African Slave Trade," *CWS* 54 (Dec. 2008): 398–99. For a discussion of the debate over the slave trade at the Constitutional Convention, see Van Cleve, *A Slaveholders' Union,* 144–53.

72. *Annals of Congress,* 8 Cong., 1 sess., 995–96.

73. Connolly, "A Question of Honor," 219–74; Don E. Fehrenbacher, *The Slaveholding Republic: An Account of the United States Government's Relations to Slavery* (New York: Oxford University Press, 2001): 201; *A Compilation of the Messages and Papers of the Presidents,* vol. 1, ed. James D. Richardson (Washington DC: Government Printing Office, 1896): 408; Taylor, *Internal Enemy,* 115.

74. Taylor, *Internal Enemy,* 120–21; Brown, *Moral Capital,* 200–201.

75. Taylor, *Internal Enemy,* 121–25; Donald R. Hickey, *The War of 1812: A Forgotten Conflict* (Urbana: University of Illinois Press, 2012): 11–12; Gene Allen Smith, *Slaves' Gamble: Choosing Sides in the War of 1812* (New York: Palgrave Macmillan, 2013), 51.

76. Spencer Tucker and Frank T. Reuter, *Injured Honor: The "Chesapeake-Leopard" Affair, June 22, 1807* (Annapolis: Naval Institute Press, 1996); Taylor, *Internal Enemy,* 125–29.

77. Robert E. Cray, "Remembering the USS *Chesapeake*: The Politics of Maritime Death and Impressment," *Journal of the Early Republic* 25 (Fall 2005): 445–74; Smith, *Slaves' Gamble,* 1–4; Taylor, *Internal Enemy,* 120–21.

78. Taylor, *Internal Enemy,* 129–31; Reginald Horsman, *The Causes of the War of 1812* (New York: A. S. Barnes & Company, 1962): 101–22; Bradford Perkins, *Prologue to War: England and the United States, 1805–1812* (Berkeley: University of California Press, 1961): 140–83.

79. Horsman, *Causes of the War of 1812,* 123–43.

80. J. A. C. Stagg, *Mr. Madison's War: Politics, Diplomacy, and Warfare in the Early American Republic* (Princeton, NJ: Princeton University Press, 1983): 71–79, 110–14; Taylor, *Internal Enemy,* 129–32; Horsman, *Causes of the War of 1812*; Frank Lawrence Owsley Jr. and Gene A. Smith, *Filibusters and Expansionists: Jeffersonian Manifest Destiny, 1800–1821* (Tuscaloosa: University of Alabama Press, 1997).

81. Taylor, *Internal Enemy,* 5–7, 129, 138, 246–52, 390; Smith, *Slaves' Gamble,* 16–22; John Fa-

bian Witt, *Lincoln's Code: The Laws of War in American History* (New York: Free Press, 2012): 29–35.

82. Smith, *Slaves' Gamble,* 87–88.

83. *National Intelligencer,* May 19, 1814; "A British Appeal to the American Slaves: Bermuda, April 1814," in *The War of 1812: Writings from America's Second War of Independence,* ed. Donald R. Hickey (New York: Library of America, 2013): 424–25; Smith, *Slaves' Gamble,* 87–98, 100.

84. Taylor, *Internal Enemy,* 298–306; Smith, *Slaves' Gamble,* 118–26.

85. Andrew Jackson to William Claiborne, June 22, 1814, in *The Papers of Andrew Jackson, Vol. III, 1814–1815,* ed. Harold D. Moser (Knoxville: University of Tennessee Press, 1991): 91; Rothman, *Slave Country,* 139–54; Smith, *Slaves' Gamble,* 154–71.

86. Quoted in Gabrial, "From Haiti to Nat Turner," 352–55; Daniel Rasmussen, *American Uprising: The Untold Story of America's Largest Slave Revolt* (New York: Harper Perennial, 2012); Matthew Mason, "German Coast Uprising (1811)," in *Encyclopedia of Slave Resistance and Rebellion Volume 1: A-N,* ed. Junius P. Rodriguez (Westport, CT: Greenwood Press, 2007): 213–16.

87. Smith, *Slaves' Gamble,* 154–71.

88. Smith, *Slaves' Gamble,* 117–18, 131–41, 170–71, 211–16; Taylor, *Internal Enemy,* 429–35.

89. Taylor, *Internal Enemy,* 345–49, 396–99; 406; *Carolina Federal Republican,* December 17, 1813.

90. There is much debate over the reality of Vesey's insurrection. See Michael P. Johnson, "Denmark Vesey and His Co-Conspirators," *William and Mary Quarterly* 58, 4 (Oct. 2001): 915–76. In the issue that followed his provocative article, Edward Pearson, Douglas Egerton, David Robertson, Philip Morgan, Thomas J, Davis, Winthrop Jordan, and Robert Paquette responded to Johnson. Johnson built his argument on Richard C. Wade, "The Vesey Plot: A Reconsideration," *JSH* 30 (May 1964): 143–61. See Robert Goss, ed., "Forum: The Making of a Slave Conspiracy II," *William and Mary Quarterly* 59 (January 2002): 135–202. See also Douglas R. Egerton, " 'Why Did They not Preach Up This Thing': Denmark Vesey and Revolutionary Theology," *South Carolina Historical Magazine* 100 (Oct. 1999): 298–318; Robert L. Paquette and Douglas R. Egerton, "Of Facts and Fables: New Light on the Denmark Vesey Affair," *South Carolina Historical Magazine* 105 (January 2004): 8–35; Robert L. Paquette, "From Rebellion to Revisionism: The Continuing Debate about the Denmark Vesey Affair," *Journal of the Historical Society* (Fall 2004): 291–334; and William W. Freehling, "Denmark Vesey's Peculiar Reality," in *New Perspectives on Race and Slavery in America: Essays in Honor of Kenneth Stampp,* ed. Robert H. Abzug and Stephen E. Maizlish (Lexington: University Press of Kentucky, 1986): 25–50.

91. James Hamilton, *An Account of the Late Intended Insurrection among a Portion of the Blacks of the City* (Charleston, SC: Joseph W. Ingraham, 1822): 5, Documenting the American South. University Library, University of North Carolina at Chapel Hill, 1999. http://docsouth.unc.edu/church/hamilton/hamilton.html. Two other important primary sources that discuss the Vesey scare are Lionel H. Kennedy and Thomas Parker, *An Official Report of the Trials of Sundry Negroes Charged with an Attempt to Raise an Insurrection in the State of South Carolina; Preceded by an Introduction and Narrative; and in an Appendix, a Report on the Trials of Four Whites Persons, on Indictments for Attempting to Excite the Slaves to Insurrection* (Charleston, SC: James R. Schenk, 1822); and Document B: Evidence, Governor's Messages, no. 1328, series no, S165009, Records of the General Assembly, SCDAH.

92. Hamilton, *An Account of the Late Intended Insurrection,* 47–50.

93. Ibid.

94. Kennedy and Parker, *An Official Report of the Trials of Sundry Negroes,* 62–68; Douglas R. Egerton, *He Shall Go Out Free: The Lives of Denmark Vesey, Revised and Updated Version* (New York: Rowan & Littlefield, 2004): 3–26.

95. Egerton, *He Shall Go Out Free,* 136–38; Examination and Confession of Monday Gell, July 23, 1822, in *Designs against Charleston,* 244–46; Michael P. Johnson, "Denmark Vesey and His Co-Conspirators," 919.

96. *Augusta Chronicle and Georgia Advertiser,* September 9, 1822; *Alexandria Herald* July 19, 1822.

97. Edward Bartlett Rugemer, "Caribbean Slave Revolts and the Origins of the Gag Rule," in *Contesting Slavery,* 102–6.

98. Ibid.; Philip M. Hamer, "Great Britain, the United States, and the Negro Seamen Acts, 1822–1848," *JSH* 1 (Feb. 1935): 3–28; *The argument of Benj. Faneuil Hunt, in the case of the arrest of the person claiming to be a British seaman, under the 3d section of the State Act of Dec. 1822, in relation to Negroes, &c. before the Hon. Judge Johnson, Circuit Judge of the United States, for 6th Circuit: ex parte Henry Elkison, claiming to be a subject of His Britannic Majesty, vs. Francis G. Deliesseline, sheriff of Charleston District* (Charleston: A. E. Miller, 1823): 7; Michael Alan Schoeppner, "Navigating the Dangerous Atlantic: Racial Quarantines, Black Sailors and United States Constitutionalism (PhD diss., University of Florida, 2010).

99. Forbes, *Missouri Compromise and Its Aftermath,* 141–78; Richard Furman, *Rev. Dr. Richard Furman's Exposition of the Views of the Baptists, Relative to the Coloured Population in the United States In A Communication to the Governor of South-Carolina 2nd edition* (Charleston, 1838): 4–5. Furman attacked abolitionism's interpretation of slavery in the Bible, stating, "In some parts of our Union there are Citizens, who favor the idea of general emancipation; yet, were they to see slaves in our Country, in arms, wading through blood and carnage to effect their purpose, they would do what both their duty and interest would require."

100. Montague, *Haiti and the United States,* 52–53; Ralph Sanders, "Congressional Reaction in the United States to the Panama Congress of 1826," *The Americas* 11 (Oct. 1954): 141–43; Charles Wilson Hackett, "The Development of John Quincy Adams's Policy with Respect to an American Confederation and the Panama Congress, 1822–1825," *American Historical Review* 8 (Nov. 1928): 496–526.

101. Montague, *Haiti and the United States,* 52–53.

102. Register of Debates in Congress, 19 Cong. 1 sess., 330; Jon Meachum, *American Lion: Andrew Jackson in the White House* (New York: Random House, 2009): 29–30.

103. Register of Debates in Congress, 19 Cong. 1 sess., 330; Montague, *Haiti and the United States,* 51–52.

104. *Register of Debates in Congress,* 19 Cong. 1 sess., 330.

105. *The Debates in the Several State Conventions on the Adoption of the Federal Constitution, as Recommended by the General Convention at Philadelphia, in 1787, Together with the Journal of the Federal Convention, Luther Martin's Letters, Yates's Minutes, Congressional Opinions, Virginia and Kentucky Resolutions of '08–09, and other Illustrations of the Constitution 4 volumes,* ed. Jonathan Elliot (Washington, DC: 1836): 485.

2. "Fanaticism" and Southern Fears of Black Rebellion

1. Jeremiah Morton's speech is to be found in Freehling and Simpson, eds., *Showdown in Virginia,* 3.

2. *Milledgeville (Ga.) Southern Recorder,* January 16, 1830.

3. Noah Webster, "Dissertations on the English Language: with Notes, Historical and Critical," in *Creating An American Culture, 1775–1800: A Brief History with Documents,* ed. Evan Kornfeld (New York: Bedford Publishing, 2001): 106; V. P. Bynack, "Noah Webster's Linguistic Thought and the Idea

of an American National Culture," *Journal of the History of Ideas* 45 (Jan.–March 1984): 99–114; Harlow Giles Unger, *Noah Webster: The Life and Times of an American Patriot* (New York: John Wiley & Sons, 1998): 265–303.

4. *Newport Mercury* January 3, 1829; *Jamestown (NY) Journal,* January 14, 1829; *Portsmouth Journal and Rockingham Gazette,* April 11, 1829; *Connecticut Herald,* February 3, 1829.

5. Noah Webster, *The American Dictionary of the English Language* (New York: Johnson Reprint Corp., 1970).

6. [William Drayton], *The South Vindicated from the Treason and Fanaticism of the Northern Abolitionists* (Philadelphia: H. Manly, 1836): xvi; Channing, *Crisis of Fear,* 58–62.

7. *Milledgeville Southern Recorder,* January 16, 1830.

8. Richard R. John, *Spreading The News: The American Postal System from Franklin to Morse* (Cambridge, MA: Harvard University Press, 1995): 3–6; Beth Barton Schweiger, "The Literate South: Reading before Emancipation," *Journal of the Civil War Era* 3 (Sept. 2013): 331–59; Jonathan Daniel Wells, *Women Writers and Journalists in the Nineteenth-Century South* (New York: Cambridge University Press, 2011).

9. *Salem Gazette,* March 9, 1830; Peter P. Hinks, *To Awaken My Afflicted Brethren: David Walker and the Problem of Antebellum Slave Resistance* (University Park: The Pennsylvania State University Press, 1997): 22–62; Herbert Aptheker, *One Continual Cry: David Walker's "Appeal to the Coloured Citizens of the World," 1829–1830* (New York: Humanities Press, 1965); Ford, *Deliver us from Evil,* 230–38.

10. David Walker to Thomas Lewis, December 8, 1829, in *David Walker's "Appeal to the Coloured Citizens of the World,"* ed. Peter P. Hinks (University Park: Pennsylvania State University Press, 2000); "Document IV: Walker's *Appeal* Arrives in Georgia," published in Hinks, *David Walker's Appeal;* Hasan Crockett, "The Incendiary Pamphlet: David Walker's *Appeal* in Georgia," *Journal of Negro History* 86 (Summer 2001): 305–18.

11. Hinks, *David Walker's "Appeal,"* xxvi–xxix, 17–18; West and Martin, "Haiti, I'm Sorry," 95–97; Onuf, " 'To Declare Them a Free and Independent People,' 1–7; Hinks, *To Awaken My Afflicted Brethren,* 237–58; Manisha Sinha, "To 'Cast Just Obliquy' on Oppressors: Black Radicalism in the Age of Revolution," *William and Mary Quarterly* 64 (Jan. 2007): 158. Located in modern-day Guyana, Demerara was a British colony in the West Indies that experienced a massive insurrection in 1823. See Emila Vieotti da Costa, *Crowns of Glory, Tears of Blood: The Demerara Slave Rebellion of 1823* (New York: Oxford University Press, 1994).

12. Hinks, *David Walker's "Appeal,"* 2–8, quoted on 14; Hinks, *To Awaken My Afflicted Brethren,* 30–31; Dubois, *Avengers of the New World,* 99–101.

13. Hinks, *David Walker's "Appeal,"* 22. Toussaint also was compared to Hannibal. See John Relly Beard, *The Life of Toussaint L'Ouverture, the Negro Patriot of Hayti* (London, 1853): 274.

14. Hinks, *David Walker's "Appeal,"* 22.

15. Ibid., 43; Rugemer, *Problem of Emancipation,* 96–108.

16. Samuel Eliot Morison, *The Life and Letters of Harrison Gray Otis: Federalist, 1765–1848,* vol. 2 (Boston: Houghton Mifflin, 1913): 257; Clement Eaton, "A Dangerous Pamphlet in the Old South," *JSH* 2 (Aug. 1936): 327.

17. Morison, *Life and Letter of Harrison Gray Otis,* 219–30, 274; Forbes, *Missouri Compromise and Its Aftermath,* 144–55.

18. Harrison B. Otis to William B. Giles, February 16, 1830, printed in *RichEnq,* February 18. 1830; *Boston Courier,* March 1, 1830.

19. Harrison Gray Otis to William T. Williams, February 10, 1830, published in *RichEnq,* February 18, 1830.

20. Ibid.; *Newburyport Herald,* March 9, 1830.

21. *Essex Gazette,* March 6, 1830.

22. *Boston Courier,* March 22, 1830.

23. Ibid.; *Greenville Mountaineer,* April 30, 1830.

24. H. W. Flournoy, ed., *Calendar of Virginia State Papers and Other Manuscripts from January 1, 1808, to December 31, 1835,* vol. 10 (Richmond, 1892): 567–69.

25. R. H. Taylor, "Slave Conspiracies in North Carolina," *North Carolina Historical Review* V (Raleigh: North Carolina Historical Commission, 1928): 24; Joseph Holloway, "Slave Insurrections in the United States: An Overview," http://slaverebellion.org

26. Taylor, *Internal Enemy,* 69–76; Hadden, *Slave Patrols,* 172.

27. James Stuart, *Three Years in North America, vol. II* (Edinburgh: Robert Cadell & Whittaker and Co, 1831): 123; Eaton, "A Dangerous Pamphlet," 323–34; Crockett, "The Incendiary Pamphlet," 309.

28. *Milledgeville Southern Recorder,* January 16, 1830; Rugemer, "Caribbean Slave Revolts and the Origins of the Gag Rule," in *Contesting Slavery,* 94–109.

29. *Milledgeville Southern Recorder,* January 16, 1830; Crockett, "The Incendiary Pamphlet," 312–13.

30. Stuart, *Three Years in North America,* 1:230, 2:129–30.

31. *Columbian Centinel,* January 16, 1830.

32. Crockett, "The Incendiary Pamphlet," 313–16; Glenn M. McNair, "The Elijah Burritt Affair: David Walker's *Appeal* and Partisan Journalism in Antebellum Milledgeville," *Georgia Historical Quarterly* 83 (Fall 1999): 448–78.

33. *Charleston City Gazette and Commercial Daily Advertiser,* March 3, 1830.

34. William H. Pease and Jane H. Pease, "Walker's Appeal Comes to Charleston: A Note and Documents," *Journal of Negro History* 59, no. 3 (July 1974): 287–92; Hinks, *To Awaken My Afflicted Brethren,* 145–47.

35. Both Pease and Pease, "Walker's Appeal Comes to Charleston" and Hinks, *To Awaken My Afflicted Brethren.* For other examples of abolitionists being caught in the South, see Stanley Harrold, *The Abolitionists and the South: 1831–1861* (Lexington: University Press of Kentucky, 1995): 64–83.

36. *Charleston City Gazette and Commercial Daily Advertiser,* October 2, 1830.

37. "Document VIII: Walker's *Appeal* Alarms North Carolina, 1830," in Hinks, *David Walker's "Appeal,"* 104–6; James McKee to the Police of Mobile, November 3, 1831, in Alabama Department of History and Archives; Eaton, "A Dangerous Pamphlet in the Old South, 331–34.

38. "Document VIII: Walker's *Appeal";* and Eaton, "A Dangerous Pamphlet."

39. *New York Morning Herald,* September 10, 1830; *Boston Courier,* September 16, 1830; Caryn Cossé Bell, *Revolution, Romanticism, and the Afro-Creole Protest Tradition in Louisiana, 1718–1868* (Baton Rouge: Louisiana State University Press, 2004): 91–95.

40. *Boston Weekly Messenger,* April 8, 1830; *Pittsfield Sun,* May 27, 1830; *A Digest of the Ordinances, Resolutions, By-Laws, and Regulations of the Corporation of New Orleans, and a collection of the laws of the Legislature Relative to the said City* (New Orleans: Gaston Brusle, 1836): 559; Benjamin Lundy and Thomas Earl, *The Life, Travels, and Opinions of Benjamin Lundy, Including His Journeys to Texas and Mexico, with a Sketch of Contemporary Events, and a Notice of the Revolution of Hayti* (Philadelphia: William D. Parrish, 1847): 241; Ford, *Deliver Us from Evil,* 334–35.

41. Leon Litwack, *North of Slavery: The Negro in the Free States, 1790–1860* (Chicago: University of Chicago Press, 1961): 64–112.

42. *Milledgeville Southern Recorder,* June 12, 1830.

43. Eaton, "A Dangerous Pamphlet in the Old South," 329–31.

44. The *Richmond Whig* was quoted in the *Baltimore Patriot* January 13, 1830, and *Norwich Courier* January 27, 1830.

45. David F. Allmendinger, Jr., *Nat Turner and the Rising in Southampton County* (Baltimore: Johns Hopkins University Press, 2014): 11–24; Anthony Santoro, "The Prophet in His Own Words: Nat Turner's Biblical Construction," *Virginia Magazine of History and Biography* 116 (2008): 114–49; Thomas R. Gray, *The Confessions of Nat Turner, the Leader of the Late Insurrection in Southampton, VA* (Baltimore: Luca & Deaver, 1831), in *The Southampton Slave Revolt of 1831: A Compilation of Source Material,* ed. Henry Irving Tragle (Amherst: University of Massachusetts Press, 1971): 308–11; Bryan Rommel-Ruiz, "Vindictive Ferocity: Virginia's Response to the Nat Turner Rebellion," in *Enemies of Humanity: The Nineteenth-Century War on Terrorism,* ed. Isaac Land (New York: Palgrave Macmillan, 2008): 67–68.

46. Allmendinger, *Nat Turner and the Rising in Southampton County,* 3; *Verbatim Record of the Trials in the Court of Oyer and Terminer of Southampton County* in Tragle, *Southampton Slave Revolt,* 202–3; See also Stephen B. Oates, *The Fires of Jubilee: Nat Turner's Fierce Rebellion* (New York: Perennial, 1975): 35–57; Walter Rucker, "Magic, and Power: The Influence of Afro-Atlantic Religious Practices of Slave Resistance and Rebellion," *Journal of Black Studies* 32 (Sept. 2001): 84–103.

47. Gray, *The Confessions of Nat Turner* in Tragle, *Southampton Slave Revolt,* 311; Allmendinger, *Nat Turner,* 87–101.

48. Gray, *The Confessions of Nat Turner,"* 311.

49. Ibid., 312; Allmendinger, *Nat Turner and the Rising in Southampton County,* 25–86, 102–35.

50. Gray, *The Confessions of Nat Turner,* 313–14.

51. Ibid., 315–16; *Norfolk Herald,* August 26, 1831, reprinted in *RichEnq,* August 30, 1831; , *American Beacon* September 3, 1831; Allmendinger, *Nat Turner and the Rising in Southampton County,* 136–65.

52. *Richmond Compiler,* August 27, 1831. reprinted in Tragle, *Southampton Slave Revolt,* 47; N. E. Sutton to John Floyd, September 21, 1831, Executive Papers of John Floyd, Library of Virginia.

53. *Norfolk American Beacon,* August 26, 1831; *Richmond Compiler,* August 24, 1831; *Petersburg Intelligencer,* August 26, 1831, all republished in Tragle, *Southampton Slave Revolt,* 36–40.

54. The *Richmond Constitutional Whig,* August 29, September 3, 1831, in Tragle, *Southampton Slave Revolt,* 50–52, 66–72.

55. Linda Brent [Harriet Ann Jacobs], *Incidents in the Life of a Slave Girl,* ed. L. Maria Child (Boston, 1861): 97–98; Johnson, *Soul by Soul;* and Stephanie McCurry, *Masters of Small Worlds: Yeoman Households and the Political Culture of the Antebellum South Carolina Low Country* (New York: Oxford University Press, 1995).

56. Brent, *Incidents in the Life of a Slave Girl,* 102–3.

57. Ibid.

58. *Richmond Compiler,* August 29, 1831, reprinted in *RichEnq,* August 30, 1831, September 9, 1831; *Constitutional Whig,* August 29, 1831, in Tragle, *Southampton Slave Revolt,* 50–53; Rommel-Ruiz, "Vindictive Ferocity," 66–67.

59. George and Eliza Reid to William Moultree Reid, Charleston, SC, October 5, 1831. William Clements Library, University of Michigan-Ann Arbor; Charles Edward Morris, "Panic and Reprisal: Reaction in North Carolina to the Nat Turner Insurrection of 1831," *North Carolina Historical Review 62 (Jan. 1985):*29–52, 30–33; Governor John Floyd Diary, November 21, 28, 1831, in Tragle, *Southampton Slave Revolt,* 262; Hahn, *A Nation under Our Feet,* 116–62; Baptist, *The Half Has Never Been Told,* 207–11.

60. William Lloyd Imes, "The Legal Status of Free Negroes and Slaves in Tennessee," *Journal of Negro History* 4 (July 1919): 260; John Hope Franklin, *The Free Negro in North Carolina, 1790–1860* (Chapel Hill: University of North Carolina Press, 1943): 70–120.

61. Draft of a Bill Concerning "Slaves, Free Negroes and Mulattoes," in Tragle, *Southampton Slave Revolt*, 455–62.

62. Benjamin Cabell to John Floyd, September 20, 1831, Executive Papers of John Floyd, Library of Virginia.

63. *The Liberator*, October 22, 1831; Diary of John Floyd, in Tragle, *Southampton Slave Revolt*, 251–52.

64. "After Nat Turner: A Letter from the North," *Journal of Negro History* 55 (April 1970): 144–51.

65. Ibid., 149.

66. Ibid., 146–47.

67. Ibid., 147.

68. Ibid., 148.

69. Alison Goodyear Freehling, *Drift toward Dissolution: The Virginia Slavery Debate of 1831–1832* (Baton Rouge: Louisiana State University Press, 1982); Legislative Petition, Culpepper County, December 9, 1831, in Eric Foner, *Nat Turner* (Englewood Cliffs, NJ: Prentice Hall, 1971): 96–97; David Hackett Fischer and James C. Kelly, *Virginia and the Westward Movement* (Charlottesville: University of Virginia Press, 2000): 135–228; Sarah Bischoff Paulus, "Abraham Lincoln's Northwestern Approach to the Secession Crisis," (PhD diss., Rice University, 2013): 17–54.

70. *RichEnq*, November 15, 1831; James Madison to R. R. Gurley, December 29, 1831, in *The Writings of James Madison*, ed. Gaillard Hunt (New York: G. P. Putnam & Sons, 1910): 9:468–70.

71. Ford, *Deliver Us from Evil*, 389.

72. Many southerners lamented that *Review of the Debate in Virginia* gained little traction in the North. See William Harper, "Memoir on Slavery," *Southern Literary Messenger* 4 (Oct. 1838): 609–36; Michael O'Brien, *Conjectures of Order: Intellectual Life and the American South, 1810–1860*, 2:946–52.

73. Drew Gilpin Faust, ed., *The Ideology of Slavery: Proslavery Thought in the Antebellum South, 1830–1860* (Baton Rouge: Louisiana State University Press, 1981): 21–23; Peter Wallenstein, "Thomas Roderick Dew (1802–1846)," in *Slavery in the United States: A Social Political, and Historical Encyclopedia, Volume One*, ed. Junius P. Rodriguez (Santa Barbara: ABC-Clio, 2007): 254–55.

74. Thomas R. Dew, *Review of the Debate in the Virginia Legislature of 1831 and 1832* (Richmond: T. W. White, 1832): 11, 32, 44–45; Hinks, *David Walker's "Appeal,"* 9. For more on slaveholders pointing to slavery as a progressive movement, see William Harper, "Memoir on Slavery," in *The Proslavery Argument; as maintained by the most distinguished Writers of the Southern States, containing the several Essays on the subject, of Chancellor Harper, Governor Hammond, Dr. Simms, and Professor Dew* (Philadelphia: Lippincott, Grambo, & Company, 1853).

75. Dew, *Review of the Debate*, 106–8; John Patrick Daly, *When Slavery Was Called Freedom: Evangelicalism, Proslavery, and the Causes of the Civil War* (Lexington: University Press of Kentucky, 2002): 68–70.

76. Dew, *Review of the Debate*, 5–6.

77. Ibid.

78. Ibid., 113–14, 119–30. Dew also wrote a detailed argument about the productivity of slave labor and westward immigration in which he opposed the nascent free-soil ideology being developed in the North.

79. Ibid., 105, 113–14.

80. Ibid., 101–2.

81. Ibid., 67, 101.

82. Ibid., 102.

83. Ibid. 114–15; Robert Brent Toplin, "The Specter of Crisis: Slaveholder Reaction to Abolitionism in the United States and Brazil," *CWS* 18 (June 1972): 129–38.

84. G. Millan to John Floyd, September 9, 1833, Floyd Executive Papers, Library of Virginia.

85. Ibid.

3. Atlantic Abolitionism and American Exceptionalism

1. *Charleston SouPat,* March 22, 1833; *RichEnq,* March 26, 1833. See also *Macon Weekly Telegraph,* April 10, 1833; *Athens (Ga.) Southern Banner,* June 29, 1833. See also *Charleston SouPat* May 8, 16, June 11, 18, 1833; *RichEnq,* May 10, June 21, 25, July 26, 1833, and July 10, 16, 22, 23, 27, 30, 1833.

2. *Charleston SouPat,* March 22, 1833; *RichEnq,* March 26, 1833.

3. *RichEnq,* June 25, 1833; Joe Bassette Wilkins, "Window on Freedom: The South's Response to the Emancipation of the Slaves in the British West Indies, 1833–1861" (PhD diss., University of South Carolina, 1977): 50–52, 68–70.

4. Edward Rugemer, "The Southern Response to British Abolitionism: The Maturation of Proslavery Apologetics," *JSH* 70 (May 2004): 221–48; Larry E. Tise, *Proslavery: A History of the Defense of Slavery in America, 1701–1840* (Athens: University of Georgia Press, 1987): 94–96; Gelien Matthews, *Caribbean Slave Revolts and the British Abolitionist Movement* (Baton Rouge: Louisiana State University Press, 2006); Brian Schoen, *Fragile Fabric of Union,* 161–74.

5. The series appeared in the *CharMerc,* August 9, 10, 12, 13, 14. 15; Rugemer, "The Southern Response to British Abolitionism," 224–47; Sinha, "Revolution or Counterrevolution? The Political Ideology of Secession in Antebellum South Carolina," *CWS* 46 (Sept. 2000): 205–26; and Peter Kolchin, *American Slavery: 1619–1877* (New York: Hill & Wang, 1993): 194–97.

6. *CharMerc,* August 10, 1833; Richard Alston, "The Good Master: Pliny, Hobbes, and the Nature of Freedom," in *Ancient Slavery and Abolition: From Hobbes to Hollywood,* ed. Edith Hall, Richard Alson, and Justine McConnell (New York: Oxford University Press, 2011): 41–64.

7. *CharMerc,* August 15, 1833.

8. Ibid. See also Steven R. Haynes, *Noah's Curse: The Biblical Justification of American Slavery* (New York: Oxford University Press, 2002). See David M. Whitford, *The Curse of Ham in the Early Modern Era: The Bible and the Justifications for Slavery* (Burlington, VT: Ashgate Publishing, 2009).

9. *The Writings of Hugh Swinton Legaré,* 292–93.

10. Ibid., 17, 215; *Washington (DC) United States Telegraph,* May 22, 1834; Wilkins, "Window on Freedom," 42–43, 64–65; O'Brien, *A Character of Hugh Legaré,* 165–66. On nullification see William W. Freehling, *Prelude to the Civil War: The Nullification Controversy in South Carolina, 1816–1836* (New York: Oxford University Press, 1992).

11. *Columbus (Ga.) Enquirer,* August 10, 1833.

12. Charles Drayton II to his son, August 13, 1833, in Drayton Letterbook, Drayton Hall, Charleston, SC, quoted in both Wilkins, "Window on Freedom," 60, and Rugemer, *Problem of Emancipation,* vii.

13. Brutus [Robert Turnbull], *The Crisis: or, Essays on the Usurpations of the Federal Government* (Charleston, SC: A. E. Miller, 1827): 128; Wilkins, "Window on Freedom," 61–62; William W. Freehling, ed., *The Nullification Era: A Documentary Record* (New York: Harper Torchbooks, 1967): 26–27; James Oakes, *The Scorpion's Sting: Antislavery and the Coming of the Civil War* (New York: W.W. Norton, 2014): 22–50.

14. Brutus [Turnbull], "The Crisis," 64, 132.

15. Henry Clay to James Madison, May 28, 1833, in *Papers of Henry Clay,* ed. Robert Seager and Melba Porter Hay (Lexington: University Press of Kentucky, 1984): 8, 643; Manisha Sinha, *The Counterrevolution of Slavery* (Chapel Hill: University of North Carolina Press, 2000).

16. Thomas Jefferson to William Short, September 8, 1823, Manuscript Division, Library of Congress. Charles Henry Ambler, *Thomas Ritchie: A Study in Virginia Politics* (Richmond: Bell Book and Stationary, 1913): 18–20; Jeffrey L. Pasley, *"The Tyranny of Printers": Newspaper Politics in the Early American Republic* (Charlottesville: University Press of Virginia, 2001): 260–64.

17. *RichEnq,* March 20, 1820; Childers, *Failure of Popular Sovereignty,* 56–59, 76–80.

18. *RichEnq,* June 18, 1833.

19. Ibid.

20. Ibid., October 15, 1833; Ambler, *Thomas Ritchie,* 176.

21. *RichEnq,* October 15, 1833.

22. *CharMerc,* July 6, 1833.

23. Ibid.

24. Ibid.

25. Charles H. Ambler, *The Life and Diary of John Floyd: Governor of Virginia, An Apostle of Secession, and the Father of Oregon Country* (Richmond: Richmond Press, 1918): 161–62.

26. *CharMerc,* July 23, 1833. See also May 31, 1833.

27. *CharMerc,* July 10, 1833.

28. Ibid.

29. *Charleston SouPat,* July 29, 1835.

30. Ibid.; Donna Lee Dickerson, *Course of Tolerance: Freedom of the Press in Nineteenth-Century America* (New York: Greenwood Press, 1990): 85–86; John, *Spreading the News,* 260–61; James Brewer Stewart, *Holy Warriors: The Abolitionists and American Slavery, revised edition* (New York: Hill and Wang, 1997); Ronald G. Walters, *American Reformers, 1815–1860, revised edition* (New York: Hill and Wang, 1997): 77–102.

31. Freehling, *Prelude to the Civil War,* 340–346; Donna Lee Dickerson, *Course of Tolerance,* 81–113; John, *Spreading the News,* 257–80; W. Sherman Savage, "Abolitionist Literature in the Mails, 1835–1836," *Journal of Negro History* 13 (April 1928): 150–84; Bertram Wyatt-Brown, "The Abolitionists' Postal Campaign of 1835," *Journal of Negro History* 50, no. 4 (Oct. 1965): 227–38; Susan Wyly-Jones, "The 1835 Anti-Abolition Meetings in the South: A New Look at the Controversy over the Abolition Postal Campaign," *CWS* 47 (2001): 289–309; Jennifer Rose Mercieca, "The Culture of Honor: How Slaveholders Responded to the Abolitionist Mail Crisis of 1835," *Rhetoric and Public Affairs* 10 (2007): 51–76.

32. Alfred Huger to Amos Kendall, July 30, 1835, published in *RichEnq,* August 25, 1835.

33. Ibid.; *Charleston SouPat,* July 30, 1835; Wyly-Jones, "A New Look at the Controversy over the Abolition Postal Campaign," 289. Southern military schools, such as the Citadel, provided the bulk of officers for the Confederate military: see Bruce Allardice, "West Points of the Confederacy: Southern Military Schools and the Confederate Army," *CWS* 43 (Dec. 1997): 310–31.

34. *CharMerc,* July 31, 1835.

35. *Virginia Resolutions on the Subject of Domestic Slavery,* 1836; *Mississippi Resolutions on the Subject of Domestic Slavery,* 1836; *Alabama Resolutions on the Subject of Domestic Slavery,* 1836.

36. *National Banner and Nashville Whig,* August 5, 1835; *CharMerc,* July 30, 1835; *Niles' Weekly Register,* 48:402–3.

37. *RichEnq,* August 4, 1835.

38. Ibid.

39. *Ibid.*, August 7, 1835; *National Banner and Nashville Whig,* August 12, 1835.

40. Wyly-Jones, "The 1835 Anti-Abolition Meetings in the South," 299–304.

41. *RichEnq,* September 29, 1835; David Grimsted, *American Mobbing, 1828–1861: Toward the Civil War* (New York: Oxford University Press, 1995): 154–56.

42. *Niles' Weekly Register,* 49:10–12. See also Harrison Gray Otis, "Abolitionism Is Equal to Revolution" in *The Fear of Conspiracy: Images of Un-American Subversion from the Revolution to the Present,* ed. David Brion Davis (Ithaca, NY: Cornell University Press, 1971): 138–39.

43. Otis, "Abolitionism Is Equal to Revolution."

44. *Niles' Weekly Register,* 48:448, 49:73; *Hazard's Register of Pennsylvania* 16:139–40; Mercieca, "The Culture of Honor," 59–61.

45. *Niles' Weekly Register,* 48:455–56. Dickerson, *Course of Tolerance,* 91–92.

46. *Ohio State Journal and Columbus Gazette,* August 7, 1835.

47. Grimsted. *American Mobbing,* 35–38, 293; Theodore M. Hammett, "Two Mobs of Jacksonian Boston: Ideology and Interest," *Journal of American History* 62 (March 1976): 845–68; Leonard L. Richards, *"Gentlemen of Property and Standing": Anti-Abolition Mobs in Jacksonian America* (New York: Oxford University Press, 1970): 51–74.

48. *Memoirs of John Quincy Adams Comprising Portions of His Diary from 1795 to 1848,* ed. Charles Francis Adams (Philadelphia: J. B. Lippincott & Co, 1876): 10:366. For a biography of Amos Kendall, see Donald B. Cole, *A Jackson Man: Amos Kendall and the Rise of American Democracy* (Baton Rouge: Louisiana State University Press, 2004).

49. *Niles' Weekly Register.* 48:448.

50. Ibid.

51. Ibid.; Oakes, *Scorpion's Sting,* 51–76.

52. *Niles' Weekly Register,* 48:448; Theodore Sedgwick, ed., *A Collection of Political Writings of William Leggett, volume II* (New York: Taylor and Dodd, 1840): 18–20; Dickerson, *Course of Tolerance,* 89–90.

53. *Natchez (La.) Courier,* quoted in *The Anti-Slavery Record,* vol. 2 (New York: R. G. Williams, 1836): 164; *Athens (Ga.) Southern Banner,* September 24, 1835; Dickerson, *Course of Tolerance,* 90–91.

54. Amos Kendall to Andrew Jackson, August 7, 1835, in *Correspondence of Andrew Jackson V,* ed. John Spencer Bassett (Washington, DC: Carnegie Institution of Washington, 1931: 359–61.

55. Andrew Jackson to Amos Kendall, August 9, 1835, in ibid.

56. Andrew Jackson to Amos Kendall, August 9, 1835.

57. *Niles' Weekly Register,* 48:457.

58. Ibid.

59. James D. Richardson, ed., *A Compilation of the Messages and Papers of the Presidents* (New York: Bureau of National Literature, 1897): 4:1394–95; Savage, "Abolitionist Literature in the Mails, 1835–1836," 169–84.

60. Richardson, *A Compilation,* 4:1394–95; and Savage, "Abolitionist Literature," 169–84.

61. *RD,* 24 Cong. 1 sess., 26–34; Savage, "Abolitionist Literature in the Mails," 171–72.

62. *Niles' Weekly Register,* 49:408.

63. *CG,* 24 Cong. 1 sess., 164–65.

64. John C. Calhoun, bitter about losing his chance at the presidency, understood that a major motivation for Jackson's attack on abolitionists came from wanting to help Van Buren win in 1836. When it became apparent the bill would not pass, Calhoun manufactured a tie on a test vote regarding the engrossment of the bill, forcing Van Buren to vote against the bill and against the South, or in

favor of the proposal, and therefore possibly undermining northern support. The vice president voted in favor of the South and eventually the presidency and still won the northern vote. Calhoun underestimated the northern loyalty to slavery. See Savage, "Abolitionist Literature in the Mails," 180–81.

65. *Appendix to the CG,* 24 Cong. 1 sess., 454.

66. *Appendix to the CG,* 24 Cong. 1 sess., 455; Savage, "Abolitionist Literature in the Mails," 179–80.

67. *CG,* 24 Cong. 1 sess., 539.

68. Savage, "Abolitionist Literature in the Mails," 170.

69. *List of Post Offices in the United States, with the Names of Postmasters on the 1st of April 1859; Also the Laws and Regulations of the Post Office Department* (Washington, DC: John C. Rives, 1859): 32; Savage, "Abolitionist Literature in the Mails," 183.

70. Brian Schoen, "Positive Goods and Necessary Evils: Commerce, Security, and Slavery in the Lower South, 1787–1837," in *Contesting Slavery,* 161–82.

4. Proslavery Fear and the Rise of the Abolitionist Power

1. Epigraph source: Jefferson Davis, "Remarks on the Special Message on Affairs in South Carolina. Jan. 10, 1861," in *Southern Pamphlets on Secession, November 1860–April 1861,* ed. Jon L. Wakelyn (Chapel Hill: University of North Carolina Press, 1996): 139.

2. Charles Sumner to Francis Lieber, January 9, 1836, in *Memoirs and Letters of Charles Sumner,* ed. Edward L. Piece (Boston: Roberts Brothers, 1877): 1:173; Anne-Marie Taylor, *Young Charles Sumner and the Legacy of the American Enlightenment, 1811–1851* (Amherst: University of Massachusetts Press, 2001): 48–87.

3. Frank Freidel, "Francis Lieber, Charles Sumner, and Slavery," *JSH* 9 (Feb. 1943): 75–93; Peter W. Becker, "Prologue: Lieber's Place in History," in *Francis Lieber and the Culture of the Mind* (Columbia: University of South Carolina Press, 2005): 1–9.

4. "Governor McDuffie's Message on the Slavery Question, 1835," in *American History Leaflets Colonial and Constitutional*, ed. Albert Bushnell Hart and Edward Channing (New York: A. Lovell & Company, 1893); *Farmer's Register* III (1836): 571–74; *The Liberator,* December 12, 1835; *Niles' Weekly Register,* September 21, 1835; Ben Perley Moore, *Perley's Reminiscences of the Sixty Years in the National Metropolis* (Tecumseh, MI: A. W. Mills, 1886): 81.

5. "Governor McDuffie's Message on the Slavery Question, 1835," 2.

6. Ibid., 2–3; Daniel P. Resnick, "The Societe des Amis des Noirs and the Abolition of Slavery," *French Historical Studies* 7 (Autumn 1972): 558–69.

7. "Governor McDuffie's Message on the Slavery Question, 1835," 2–3.

8. Ibid., 3.

9. Ibid.

10. Ibid., 3–4.

11. Ibid., 6.

12. Ibid.

13. Ibid., 11–13.

14. James Henry Hammond to M. M. Noah, August 19, 1835, in the Papers of James Henry Hammond (Library of Congress); Drew Gilpin Faust, *James Henry Hammond and the Old South: A Design for Mastery* (Baton Rouge: Louisiana State University Press, 1982).

15. James Henry Hammond to I. W. Hayne, September 21, 1835; James Henry Hammond to Dear

Sir, September 4, 1835, both in the Papers of James Henry Hammond (Library of Congress); Faust, *James Henry Hammond,* 157–64.

16. Stephen A. Higginson, "A Short History of the Right to Petition Government for the Redress of Grievances," *Yale Law Journal* 96 (Nov. 1986): 142–66; Faust, *James Henry Hammond,* 156–64. For the debate over the "gag rule," see William Lee Miller, *Arguing about Slavery: The Great Battle in the United States Congress* (New York: Alfred A. Knopf, 1996): 197–214; Freehling, *Road to Disunion,* 1:308–36; Susan Wyly-Jones, "The Antiabolitionist Panic: Slavery, Abolition, and Politics in the U.S. South, 1835–1844" (PhD diss., Harvard University, 2000): 209–88.

17. *CG,* 24 Cong., 1 sess., 24.

18. Ibid., 24–25.

19. Ibid.

20. Ibid., 27.

21. Ibid., 27.

22. Ibid., 27–35.

23. Ibid., 31–33; Kenneth S. Greenberg, *Honor and Slavery: Lies, Duels, Noses, Masks, Dressing as a Woman, Gifts, Strangers, Humanitarianism, Death, Slave Rebellions, the Proslavery Argument, Baseball, Hunting, and Gambling in the Old South* (Princeton, NJ: Princeton University Press, 1996): 51–86; Bertram Wyatt-Brown, *Southern Honor: Ethics and Behavior in the Old South* (New York: Oxford University Press, 1982): 43.

24. Faust, *James Henry Hammond,* 176.

25. *RD,* 24th Cong., 1 sess., 2450; Clyde N. Wilson, ed., *Selections from the Letters and Speeches of the Hon. James Henry Hammond of South Carolina* (Spartanburg, SC: Reprint Company, 1978).

26. *RD.* 24th Cong., 1 sess., 2450.

27. Ibid., 2453–2454.

28. Ibid.

29. Ibid.

30. Ibid., 2454–2455; Furman, *Rev. Dr. Richard Furman's Exposition,* 7, 13–19; Mitchell Snay, *Gospel of Disunion.* (Cambridge: Cambridge University Press, 1993): 28–49.

31. *RD,* 24 Cong. 1 sess., 2455; *Historical Statistics of the United States: Colonial Times to 1970, Bicentennial Edition, Part 2* (Washington DC: U.S. Bureau of the Census, 1975): 1104.

32. *RD,* 24 Cong. 1 sess., 2455; Oakes, *Scorpion's Sting,* 104–65.

33. *RD,* 24 Cong. 1 sess., 2455.

34. Ibid., 2457.

35. Ibid.

36. Ibid., 2456; Charlton W. Yingling, "No One Who Reads the History of Hayti Can Doubt the Capacity of Colored Men: Racial Formation and the Atlantic Rehabilitation in New York City's Early Black Press, 1827–1841," *Early American Studies: An Interdisciplinary Journal* 11 (Spring 2013): 314–48.

37. *RD,* 24 Cong. 1 sess., 2458.

38. Ibid.

39. For more on moderation and compromise before the Civil War, see Sarah Bischoff Paulus, "America's Long Eulogy for Compromise: Henry Clay and American Politics, 1854–1858." *Journal of the Civil War Era* 4 (March 2014): 28–52; and Peter B. Knupfer, *The Union As It Is: Constitutional Unionism and Sectional Compromise, 1787–1861* (Chapel Hill: University of North Carolina Press, 1991).

40. *RD,* 24 Cong. 1 sess., 2006.

41. Ibid., 2059.

42. Ibid., 2066–2067.

43. Ibid.

44. Ibid., 1978, 2066–2067; Wyly-Jones, "The Antiabolitionist Panic," 234–36.

45. *RD,* 24 Cong. 1 sess, 2006. See also Freehling, *Road to Disunion,* 1:287–352.

46. Wyly-Jones, "The Antiabolitionist Panic," 234.

47. Ford, *Origins of Southern Radicalism,* 156–58; J. R. Poinsett to James B. Campbell, October 20, 1836, in "Poinsett-Campbell Correspondence (Continued)," ed. Samuel Gaillard Stoney, *South Carolina Historical and Genealogical Magazine* 42 (Oct. 1941): 149–68; Freehling, *Road to Disunion,* 1:345–49; Miller, *Arguing about Slavery,* 366–72. For an examination of the Senate's gag rule, which caused less public outrage, see Daniel Wirls, "'The Only Mode of Avoiding Everlasting Debate': The Overlooked Senate Gag Rule for Antislavery Petitions," *Journal of the Early Republic* 27 (Spring 2007): 115–38.

48. Resolutions of the Legislature of Kentucky, S.doc 249, 24th Cong, 1 sess. See also Resolutions of the Legislature of Virginia, Adverse to the movements made for the abolition of slavery, &c,, Senate document 233; Memorial of the Legislature of Alabama, Against the measures of the abolitionists, and against interfering with the subject of slavery in the District of Columbia, Senate document 124.

49. James K. Polk to William R. Rucker, February 22, 1836, in *Correspondence of James K. Polk,* ed. Herbert Weaver (Nashville: Vanderbilt University Press, 1975): 3:511–13; Wyly-Jones, "The Abolitionist Panic," 232–63.

50. *RichEnq,* January 14, 1836.

51. James Kirke Paulding, *Slavery in the United States* (New York: Harper & Brothers, 1836): 134–35, 284. See also James Kirke Paulding, "Abolitionism Is the Product of a Foreign Plot" in Davis, *The Fear of Conspiracy,* 135–37; W. Caleb McDaniel, *The Problem of Democracy in the Age of Slavery: Garrisonian Abolitionists and Transatlantic Reform* (Baton Rouge: Louisiana State University Press, 2013): 45–47.

52. *Appendix to the CG,* 24 Cong. 1 sess., 142–44.

53. Ibid.

54. *RD,* 24 Cong. 1 sess., 2005–2006.

55. Edward Bartlett Rugemer, "Robert Monroe Harrison, British Abolition, Southern Anglophobia and Texas Annexation," *Slavery and Abolition* 28 (Aug. 2007): 172–73; Rugemer, *Problem of Emancipation,* 180–221.

56. Rugemer, "Robert Monroe Harrison," 172–73; *Public Statutes at Large of the United States of America,* 5:47; *Baltimore Gazette and Daily Advertiser,* June 9, 1836; *CG,* 24 Cong. 1 sess., 588–89.

57. *Niles' National Register* (Washington, DC: WM. Ogden Niles, 1838): 53:356–58.

58. *Writings of Hugh Swinton Legaré,* 322.

59. Ibid., 326–27; *Columbus Ohio Statesman,* March 3, 1840.

60. *Writings of Hugh Swinton Legaré,* 326–27; Matthew J. Karp, "Slavery and American Sea Power: The Navalist Impulse in the Antebellum South," *JSH* 87 (May 2011): 284–324.

61. *CG,* 25 Cong. 3 sess., 35–44.

62. Karp, "Slavery and American Sea Power," 296; *Writings of Hugh Swinton Legaré,* 334.

63. *Charleston SouPat,* January 27, 1840.

64. *Army and Navy Chronicle,* February 4, 1837.

65. Matthew Karp, "Arsenal of Empire: Southern Slaveholders and the U.S. Military in the 1850s," *Common Place* 12 (July 2012), http://www.common-place-archives.org/vol-12/no-04/karp/

66. Fehrenbacher, *Slaveholding Republic,* 108–11, 161–72.

67. "Report of the Secretary of the Navy," *Senate Documents,* 27th Cong. 2 sess., nos. 1/6, serial 395 (Washington, DC, 1841).

68. Ibid.; Karp, "Slavery and American Sea Power," 295–301.

69. *House Reports,* 27 Cong. 1 sess., No. 3: Recommending Appropriations for Home Squadron, serial 393 (Washington, DC, 1841): 2.

70. Karp, "Slavery and American Sea Power," 320–24.

71. *Army and Navy Chronicle,* March 5, 1840; Sam W. Haynes, "Anglophobia and the Annexation of Texas: The Quest for National Security," in *Manifest Destiny and Empire: American Antebellum Expansionism,* ed. Sam W. Haynes and Christopher Morris (College Station: Texas A&M University Press, 1997): 115–45.

5. Texas Annexation and the Proslavery Promise

1. Epigraph source: David Franklin Houston, ed., *American History Leaflets, Colonial and Constitutional, November 1893: Ordinances of Secession and Other Documents, 1860–1861* (New York: A. Lovell & Company, 1893): 15–16.

2. Pekka Hämäläinen, *The Comanche Empire* (New Haven, CT: Yale University Press, 2008): 150–56, 182–94.

3. Stephen F. Austin to Samuel May Williams, April 16, 1831, in *The Papers of Stephen F. Austin,* ed. Eugene C. Barker (Washington, DC, 1924–28): 2:645; Randolph B. Campbell, *An Empire for Slavery: The Peculiar Institution in Texas, 1821–1865* (Baton Rouge: Louisiana State University Press, 1989): 1–34; Randolph B. Campbell, *Gone to Texas: A History of the Lone Star State* (New York: Oxford University Press, 2003): 110–14.

4. Campbell, *Empire for Slavery,* 40–41.

5. "Curtius" [William H. Wharton], February, 1836, in *The Papers of the Texas Revolution,* ed. John H. Jenkins (Austin: Presidial Press, 1973): 9:240; Campbell, *Empire for Slavery,* 42–47; *Journal of the Proceedings of the General Council of the Republic of Texas Held at San Felipe de Austin, November 14th, 1835* (Houston, 1839): 173.

6. *National Banner and Nashville Whig,* May 25, 1836; *Baltimore Gazette and Daily Advertiser,* May 10, 1836; *RichEnq,* May 17, 1836; *St. Louis Daily Commercial Bulletin,* June 3, 1836.

7. *National Banner and Nashville Whig,* May 25, 1836, *Baltimore Gazette and Daily Advertiser,* May 10, 1836, and *RichEnq,* May 17, 1836; Hämäläinen, *The Comanche Nation,* 214–19.

8. *National Banner and Nashville Whig,* May 25, 1836, *Baltimore Gazette and Daily Advertiser,* May 10, 1836, and *RichEnq,* May 17, 1836; *St. Louis Daily Commercial Bulletin,* June 3, 1836.

9. Campbell, *Gone to Texas,* 160–65; Sam Houston to Andrew Jackson, November 22, 1836, republished in *Washington (TX) Texas National Register,* December 17, 1845.

10. *RD,* 24 Cong., 2 sess., 1137–1140; John M. Belohlavek, *"Let the Eagle Soar!" The Foreign Policy of Andrew Jackson* (Lincoln: University of Nebraska Press, 1985): 117–18, 233–34.

11. Arthur W. Brown, *William Ellery Channing* (New York: Twayne Publishers, 1962): 45–48; Rugemer, *Problem of Emancipation,* 145–79.

12. William E. Channing, *A Letter on the Annexation of Texas to the United States* (London, 1837): 2; *Boston Liberator,* June 30, 1837; *Portsmouth Journal of Literature and Politics,* August 12, 1837;, *Philadelphia National Gazette,* August 12, 1837; *Baltimore Sun,* August 12, 1837; *Cincinnati Weekly Herald and the Philanthropist,* August 18, 1837; *Boston Courier,* August 28, 1837.

13. Channing, *A Letter on the Annexation of Texas to the United States,* 2.

14. Ibid., 8.

15. Ibid., 12–14.

16. Ibid., 17–18.

17. Ibid., 26.

18. Ibid., 30–31.

19. *Speech of John Quincy Adams of Massachusetts, Upon the Right of the People, Men and Women, to Petition; on the Freedom of Speech and of Debate in the House of Representatives of the United States; on the Resolutions of Seven State Legislatures and the Petitions of More Than One Hundred Thousand Petitioners, Relating to the Annexation of Texas to This Union* (Washington, DC: Gales & Seaton, 1938): 8–9, 30–38; *Portsmouth (NH) Journal of Literature and Politics,* February 4, 1837; *Hartford Times,* February 4, 1837; *Saratoga Sentinel,* February 7, 1837; *Hallowell (ME) Cultivator and Hallowell Gazette,* June 6, 1840.

20. *Speech of John Quincy Adams,* 82.

21. Ibid.

22. Michael F. Holt, *The Rise and Fall of the American Whig Party: Jacksonian Politics and the Onset of the Civil War* (New York: Oxford University Press, 1999): 89–121; Wilentz, *Rise of American Democracy,* 501–2.

23. Harry L. Watson, *Liberty and Power: The Politics of Jacksonian America* (New York: Hill & Wang, 1990): 215–28; Holt, *Rise and Fall of the American Whig Party,* 89–121; Quoted in Wilentz, *Rise of American Democracy,* 504.

24. "Inaugural Address [William Henry Harrison], Tuesday, March 4, 1841," in *Inaugural Addresses of the Presidents of the United States from George Washington, 1789, to George Bush, 1989* (Washington, DC: Government Printing Office, 1989): 79–97; A. B. Norton, *Reminiscences of the Log Cabin and Hard Cider Campaign* (Dallas: A. B. Norton, 1888).

25. Norma Lois Peterson, *The Presidencies of William Henry Harrison and John Tyler* (Lawrence: University Press of Kansas, 1989): 31–44; Holt, *Rise and Fall of the American Whig Party,* 127.

26. Holt, *Rise and Fall of the American Whig Party,* 127; *Memoirs of John Quincy Adams Comprising Portions of His Diary from 1795 to 1848,* ed. Charles Francis Adams (Philadelphia: J. B. Lippincott & Co., 1876): 10:455–57; *CG,* 27 Cong., 1 sess., 3–4; Lyon Gardiner Tyler, *The Letters and Times of the Tylers in Two Volumes* (Richmond, VA: Whittett & Shepperson, 1884): 1:572–82.

27. *Memoirs of John Quincy Adams,* 456–57; John Tyler, "From the Sinks of Europe a Plotter Has Come," in Davis, *Fear of Conspiracy,* 140–44.

28. Edward P. Crapol, *John Tyler: The Accidental President* (Chapel Hill: University of North Carolina Press, 2006): 16–20; Freehling, *Road to Disunion,* Vol. 1, *1776–1854,* 362–64.

29. John Tyler to Littleton W. Tazewell, May 28, 1830, in Tyler, *Letters and Times of the Tylers,* 1:412; *Message from The President of the United States Transmitting with his Objections, the bill entitled, "An Act to incorporate the Subscribers to the Fiscal Bank of the United States,"* Senate Document 93, 27 Cong., 1 sess., 5.

30. Freehling, *Road to Disunion,* 1:363–64; Claude H. Hall, *Abel P. Upshur: Conservative Virginian* (Madison: State Historical Society of Wisconsin, 1964).

31. [Abel P. Upshur], *A brief enquiry into the true nature and character of our Federal Government: being a review of Judge Story's Commentaries on the Constitution of the United States* (Petersburg, VA: Edmund and Julian C. Ruffin, 1840); Hall, *Abel P. Upshur,* 69–105.

32. Abel Upshur, "Domestic Slavery," *Southern Literary Messenger* 5 (Oct. 1839): 677.

33. Ibid., 684–87; Elizabeth Fox-Genovese and Eugene Genovese. *Mind of the Master Class: History and Faith in the Southern Slaveholders' Worldview* (New York: Cambridge University Press, 2005), 152–55.

34. Upshur, "Domestic Slavery," 684–87.

35. Ibid., 682.

36. Karp, "Slavery and American Sea Power," 284–324; Claude H. Hall, "Abel P. Upshur and the Navy as an Instrument of Foreign Policy," *Virginia Magazine of History and Biography* 69 (July 1961): 290–99; *Columbus Ohio State Journal,* September 29, 1841.

37. Frederick Merk, *Slavery and the Annexation of Texas* (New York: Alfred A. Knopf, 1972); Hietala, *Manifest Design,* 10–54; Freehling, *Road to Disunion,* 1:353–440; Silbey, *Storm over Texas*; Roger G. Kennedy, *Cotton and Conquest: How the Plantation System Acquired Texas* (Norman: University of Oklahoma Press, 2013): 3–74.

38. *Washington (DC) Daily Madisonian,* January 23, 1843; *Houston Telegraph,* February 15, 1843. Gilmer's letter was initially published in the *Baltimore Republican and Argus,* on January 19.

39. *Daily Madisonian,* January 3, 1843; *Houston Telegraph,* February 15, 1843; *Baltimore Republican and Argus,* January 19, 1843.

40. Ibid.

41. Ibid.

42. Ibid.

43. Haynes, "Anglophobia and the Annexation of Texas," 115–45.

44. W. Stephen Belko, *The Invincible Duff Green: Whig of the West* (Columbia: University of Missouri Press, 2006): 210–25, 332–33; Fehrenbacher, *Slaveholding Republic,* 108–11.

45. Belko, *Invincible Duff Green,* 210–25, 332–33; and Fehrenbacher, *Slaveholding Republic,* 108–11.

46. Duff Green to John C. Calhoun, January 24, 1842, in *The Papers of John C. Calhoun* (Columbia: University of South Carolina Press, 1953–2003): 14:83–87; Belko, *The Invincible Duff Green,* 336–41; Varon, *Disunion!* 67–171.

47. Abel Upshur to John C. Calhoun, August 14, 1843, in *Papers of John C. Calhoun,* 17:354–57.

48. Ashbel Smith to John C. Calhoun, June 19, 1843, in *Papers of John C. Calhoun,* 17:252–53.

49. Abel P. Upshur to Edward Everett, September 28, 1843, in *Diplomatic Correspondence of the United States: Inter-American Series, 1831–1860* ed. William R. Manning (Washington, DC: Carnegie Endowment for International Peace, 1936): 6–11.

50. Ibid.

51. Ibid.

52. Abel Upshur to John C. Calhoun, August 14, 1843, in *Papers of John C. Calhoun,* 17:354–57.

53. Hall, *Abel Parker Upshur,* 209–13.

54. James P. Shenton, *Robert John Walker: A Politician from Jackson to Lincoln* (New York: Columbia University Press, 1961): 1–21; Frederick Merk, *Fruits of Propaganda in the Tyler Administration* (Cambridge, MA: Harvard University Press, 1971).

55. Robert J. Walker, *Letter of Mr. Walker, of Mississippi, Relative to the Annexation of Texas: In Reply to the Call of the People of Carroll County, Kentucky, to Communicate His Views on that Subject* (Washington, DC: Globe Office, 1844); Merk, *Slavery and the Annexation,* 9–10; Thomas B. Alexander, *Sectional Stress and Party Strength: A Study of Roll-Call Voting Patterns in the United States House of Representatives, 1836–1860* (Nashville: Vanderbilt University Press, 1967): 51.

56. Merk, *Slavery and the Annexation,* 7–8.

57. Ibid.

58. Merk, *Slavery and the Annexation,* 127–28; House Documents, 28th Cong., 1. sess., serial 446, no. 404, 125–44; McDaniel, *Problem of Democracy in the Age of Slavery,* 178–79.

59. Walker, *Letter of Mr. Walker,* 13-14.

60. *CG,* 28 Cong., 1 sess., 722.

61. Walker, *Letter of Mr. Walker,* 13; Baptist, *The Half Has Never Been Told,* 297–305.

62. Walker, *Letter of Mr. Walker,* 5, 13; David R. Roediger, *The Wages of Whiteness: Race and the Making of the American Working Class, Revised Edition* (New York: Verso, 2007): 43–64; Alexander Saxton, *The Rise and Fall of the White Republic: Class Politics and Mass Culture in Nineteenth-Century America* (New York: Verso, 2003): 95–182; Sean Wilentz, *Chants Democratic: New York City and the Rise of the American Working Class* (New York: Oxford University Press, 2004): 263–64; James Stewart Brewer, *Abolitionist Politics and the Coming of the Civil War* (Amherst: University of Massachusetts Press, 2008): 176–78. See also Linda K. Kerber, "Abolitionists and Amalgamators: The New York City Riots of 1834," *New York City History* 48 (January 1967): 34.

63. Walker, *Letter of Mr. Walker,* 12–13.

64. Ibid., 12.

65. *Ibid.,* 13; *CG,* 28 Cong., 1 sess., 108–110.

66. Walker, *Letter of Mr. Walker,* 13.

67. Ibid., 13–14.

68. *CG,* 28 Cong. 1 sess., 722.

69. John C. Calhoun to Richard Pakenham, April 18, 1844, in Manning, *Diplomatic Correspondence of the United States,* 18–25.

70. *Charleston* SouPat, March 25, 1844; *New Orleans Times-Picayune,* March 29, 1844. Support for Texas in the South, however, was not close to unanimous. For instance, the *Macon Weekly Telegraph* championed Clay because of fears that Texas debt, which the United States would assume, might cause disunion, leaving slave states unprotected. See *Macon Daily Telegraph,* July 23, 1844.

71. *Bridgeport (Conn.) Republican Farmer,* July 7, 1844.

72. Robert J. Walker, *The South in danger: read before you vote: address of the Democratic Association of Washington, D.C.* (Washington, DC: Gales & Seaton, 1844): 1, 4.

73. Michael Morrison, "Martin Van Buren, the Democracy, and the Partisan Politics of Texas Annexation," *JSH* 61 (Nov. 1995): 697–707; Morrison, *Slavery and the American West,* 19–33.

74. Rachel A. Shelden, "Not So Strange Bedfellows: Northern and Southern Whigs and the Texas Annexation Controversy, 1844–1845," in Gallagher and Shelden, *A Political Nation,* 11–35.

75. Merk, *Slavery and the Annexation,* 157–59.

76. Paul Finkelman, *Millard Fillmore* (New York: Times Books, 2011): 21–26. A Clay victory most likely would have altered the course of the nation dramatically, causing Americans to focus on internal improvements. See Gary J. Kornblith, "Rethinking the Coming of the Civil War: A Counterfactual Exercise," *Journal of American History* 90 (June 2003): 76–105.

6. Wilmot's Proviso and the Slaveholding Crisis

1. Epigraph source: Freehling and Simpson, eds., *Showdown in Virginia,* 69.

2. *Joint Congressional Committee on Inaugural Ceremonies, President James Knox Polk, 1845,* http://inaugural.senate.gov/history/chronology/jkpolk1845.cfm.

3. Thomas Hart Benton, *Abridgment of the Debates of Congress from 1789 to 1856: Dec. 4, 1843–June 18, 1846,* vol. 15 (New York: D. Appleton & Company, 1861): 237–38.

4. Ibid., 239.

5. Ibid., 239–40.

6. Edwin A. Miles, "'Fifty-four Forty or Fight'—An American Political Legend," *Mississippi Valley Historical Review* 44 (Sept., 1957): 291–309.

7. Kirk H. Porter and Donald Bruce Johnson, eds., *National Party Platforms, 1840–1964* (Urbana: University of Illinois Press, 1966): 3–4; Frederick Merk, *The Oregon Question: Essays in Anglo-American Diplomacy and Politics* (Cambridge, MA: Belknap Press of Harvard University Press, 1967): 364–417.

8. David A. Clary, *Eagles and Empire: The United States, Mexico, and the Struggle for a Continent* (New York: Bantam Books, 2009): 62–103; Hietala, *Manifest Destiny,* 153–56; Robert W. Merry, *A Country of Vast Designs: James K Polk, the Mexican War, and the Conquest of the American Continent* (New York: Simon & Schuster, 2009): 194–95; John C. Pinheiro, *Manifest Ambition: James K. Polk and the Civil-Military Relations during the Mexican War* (Westport, CT: Praeger Security International, 2007).

9. Merry, *A Country of Vast Designs,* 238–45.

10. Ulysses S. Grant, *Personal Memoirs of U.S. Grant, Two Volumes In One* (Old Saybrook, CT: Konecky & Konecky, 1999): 45; *A Compilation of the Messages and Papers of the Presidents,* Vol. 3, *1877*: 2287–2293; Clary, *Eagles and Empire,* 95–99.

11. John C. Calhoun to Thomas Clemson, May 12, 1846, in *Papers of John C. Calhoun,* 95–96; *CG,* 29 Cong., 1 sess., 783–87; Merry, *A Country of Vast Designs,* 245–52.

12. Merry, *A Country of Vast Designs,* 278–91.

13. Potter, *Impending Crisis,* 18–24, 64–75; Chaplain W. Morrison, *Democratic Politics and Sectionalism: The Wilmot Proviso Controversy* (Chapel Hill: University of North Carolina Press, 1967).

14. Scot Schraunagel, *Historical Dictionary of the U.S. Congress* (Lanham, MD: Scarecrow Press, 2011): 64.

15. *CG,* 29 Cong. 1 sess., 1211–1213.

16. Ibid., 1214; Charles Buxton Going, *David Wilmot: Free-Soiler* (New York: D. Appleton & Company, 1924): 47–93; Office of the Clerk, U.S. House of Representatives, http://artandhistory.house.gov/highlights.aspx?action=view&intID=100

17. *CG,* 29 Cong. 1 sess., 1214.

18. Ibid., 1217; Campbell, *Gone to Texas,* 110–11.

19. Morrison, *Democratic Politics and Sectionalism,* 3–20; Eric Foner, "The Wilmot Proviso Revisited," *Journal of American History* 56, no. 2 (Sept. 1969): 262–79.

20. *CG. 29 Cong., 1 sess.,* 1217–1221; Potter, *Impending Crisis,* 21–23; Going, *David Wilmot,* 94–105.

21. *CG,* 29 Cong., 1 sess., 1217.

22. Michael F. Holt, "The Slavery Issue," in *The American Congress: The Building of Democracy,* ed. Julian E. Zelizer (New York: Houghton Mifflin, 2004): 191; Miller, *Arguing about Slavery,* 476–87; Richards, *Slave Power,* 145–46, 153.

23. *CG, 29 Cong., 1 sess.* , 1220; Potter, *Impending Crisis,* 22; Going, *David Wilmot,* 101–2.

24. Milo Milton Quaife, ed., *The Diary of James K. Polk: During His Presidency, 1845 to 1849,* vol. 2 (Chicago: A. C. McClurg & Co., 1910): 75.

25. Ibid., 288–89, 299.

26. *CG,* 29 Cong., 2 sess., 105; Potter, *Impending Crisis,* 64–65; Morrison, *Democratic Politics and Sectionalism,* 30–32.

27. Wilentz, *Rise of American Democracy,* 596–601; Holt, *Rise and Fall of the American Whig*

Party, 250–55; Richards, *Slave Power,* 150–54; Joseph G. Rayback, *Free Soil: The Election of 1848* (Lexington: University Press of Kentucky, 1970): 23–33.

28. *New Orleans Times Picayune,* August 26, 1847; "The Wilmot Proviso speech of Hon. J.C. Dobbin, of N. Carolina, delivered in the House of Representatives, February 11, 1847, on the Wilmot Proviso prohibiting slavery in any territories whatever that may hereafter be acquired by the United States" (Washington, DC: Blair & Rives, 1847): 1; William Dusinberre, *Slavemaster President: The Double Career of James K. Polk* (New York: Oxford University Press, 2003): 144. For doughfaces see Richards, *Slave Power,* 83–189.

29. *Appendix to the CG,* 29 Cong., 2 sess., 1847, 149–54.

30. *RichEnq,* February 19, 1847; *Charleston SouPat,* February 26, 1847; Varon, *Disunion!* 189–90. After supporting Polk for the nomination, Thomas Ritchie moved away from the *Enquirer* to launch a pro-administration newspaper, *The Union,* in Washington, DC; Ambler, *Thomas Ritchie,* 253–54, 273–75.

31. Rachel A. Shelden, *Washington Brotherhood: Politics, Social Life, and the Coming of the Civil War* (Chapel Hill: University of North Carolina Press, 2013): 14–40.

32. *CG,* 29 Cong., 2 sess., 111, 134; Childers, *Failure of Popular Sovereignty,* 115–17.

33. Morrison, *Slavery and the American West,* 1–13, 39–65; Paulus, "America's Long Eulogy for Compromise," 28–32.

34. *Charleston SouPat,* November 9, 1847; J. C. Dobbin, *The Wilmot Proviso Speech of Hon. J. C. Dobbin, of North Carolina, Delivered in the House of Representatives, February 11, 1847,* 3.

35. *Charleston SouPat,* November 18, 1847.

36. Roberts, "'Revolutions Have Become the Bloody Toy of the Multitude,'" 264–68.

37. Peter V. Daniel to Martin Van Buren, November 1, 1847, Van Buren Papers, Library of Congress; Holt, *Fate of Their Country,* 33.

38. Fehrenbacher, *Slaveholding Republic,* 49–88.

39. *CG,* 29 Cong., 2 sess., 453–55; *Macon Daily Telegraph,* March 2, 1847.

40. *CG,* 29 Cong., 2 sess., 453–55.

41. Ibid; Holt, *Fate of Their Country,* 33; Varon, *Disunion!* 191.

42. *CharMerc,* August 10, 11, 17, 1847.

43. Ibid.

44. *Ibid.,* August 11, 21, 1847.

45. *Macon Weekly Telegraph,* July 25, 1848; McDaniel, *Problem of Democracy in the Age of Slavery.*

46. *CG,* 29 Cong., 2 sess., 112.

47. Ibid., 352–55.

48. Ibid., 353.

49. Ibid.

50. Ibid.

51. *Appendix to the CG,* 29 Cong., 2 sess., 317; Saxton, *The Rise and Fall of the White Republic,* 154.

52. Fox-Genovese and Genovese, *Mind of the Master Class,* 7–8, 170–200; Michael O'Brien, *Conjectures of Order: Intellectual Life and the American South, 1810–1860, Volume II.* (New York: Cambridge University Press, 2005): 591–671.

53. Fox-Genovese and Genovese, *Mind of the Master Class,* 38–39.

54. *Appendix to the CG,* 28 Cong., 2 sess., 1845, 108; Freehling, *Road to Disunion,* 1:418–23.

55. James L. Huston, "Theory's Failure: Malthusian Population Theory and the Projected Demise of Slavery," *CWS* 55 (Sept. 2009): 354–81.

56. *CharMerc,* August 25, 1847. According to the U.S. Census, the total population of the slave states grew to roughly 50 million by 1950.

57. *CharMerc,* August 25, 1847; Ford, *Origins of Southern Radicalism,* 184–88.

58. *CharMerc,* August 25, 1847.

59. *Montgomery Advertiser,* November 21, 1849; February 12, 1851, quoted in Thornton, *Politics and Power,* 207–8.

60. *CG,* 29 Cong., 2 sess., 134.

61. *CharMerc,* August 14, 16, 1847.

62. Ibid., August 14, 16, 17, 1847.

63. *Tallahassee Floridian,* August 8, 1840; Faust, *James Henry Hammond,* 284.

64. Frances Anne Kemble, *Journal of a Residence on a Georgian Plantation in 1838–1839,* ed. John A. Scott (New York: Alfred A. Knopf, 1961): 39, 221.

65. Quoted in William Barney, *The Road to Secession: A New Perspective on the Old South* (New York: Praeger, 1972): 104–5.

66. *Greenville Mountaineer,* October 15, 1847.

67. *CG,* 29 Cong., 2 sess., 1847, 348.

68. Ibid.

69. Yingling, "No One Who Reads the History of Hayti Can Doubt the Capacity of Colored Men," 328–34; John Stauffer, *The Black Hearts of Men: Radical Abolitionists and the Transformation of Race* (Cambridge, MA: Harvard University Press, 2002): 123–27.

70. *Pendleton (SC) Messenger,* December 17, 1847; Patricia McNeely, "Dueling Editors: The Nullification Plot of 1832," in *Words at War: The Civil War and American Journalism* ed. David B. Sachsman, S. Kittrel Rushing, and Roy Morris Jr. (West Lafayette, IN: Purdue University Press, 2008): 25–36.

71. *Papers of John C. Calhoun,* 24:190.

72. Ibid., 25:347.

73. Ibid.

74. Ibid.; *CharMerc,* August 11, 1847.

75. *Papers of John C. Calhoun,* 25:347, and *CharMerc,* August 11, 1847.

76. Childers, *Failure of Popular Sovereignty,* 119–21.

77. "Address of the Southern Delegates in Congress," *Works of John C. Calhoun,* 6:290–93.

7. The Proslavery Turn against American Exceptionalism

1. *Journal of the Convention of the People of South Carolina, Held in 1860, 1861, and 1862* (Columbia, SC: R. W. Gibbes, 1862): 473; H. L. Mencken, *On Politics: A Carnival of Buncombe,* ed. Malcom Moos (Baltimore: Johns Hopkins University Press, 1956): 83.

2. Knupfer, *Union As It Is,* 200–211.

3. O. C. Gardiner, *The Great Crisis; or, Three Presidential Candidates, Being A Brief Historical Sketch of the Free Soil Question in the United States, From The Congresses 1774 and '87 to the Present Time* (New York: WM. C. Bryant & Company, 1848): 138–39; Joel H. Silbey, *Party over Section: The Rough and Ready Presidential Election of 1848* (Lawrence: University Press of Kansas, 2009): 76–85, 164–66; Joseph G. Rayback, *Free Soil,* 201–30; Richards, *Slave Power,* 154–55; Jonathan H. Earle, *Jacksonian Antislavery and Politics of Free Soil, 1824–1854* (Chapel Hill: University of North Caro-

lina, 2004): 49–77, 161–69; Wilentz, *Rise of American Democracy,* 602–28; Holt, *Rise and Fall of the American Whig Party,* 343–44.

4. Silbey, *Party over Section,* 76–78; Rayback, *Free Soil,* 228–29; Earle, *Jacksonian Antislavery,* 163–68; Richards, *Slave Power,* 154–55.

5. Silbey, *Party over Section,* 62–65. Robert E. May, *John A. Quitman: Old South Crusader* (Baton Rouge: Louisiana State University Press, 1985): 212–15.

6. Porter and Johnson, *National Party Platforms,* 10–12; Silbey, *Party over Section,* 65–67.

7. Gardiner, *The Great Crisis,* 43; Morrison, *Slavery and the American West,* 84–86; Potter, *Impending Crisis,* 56–64.

8. Childers, *Failure of Popular Sovereignty,* 136–48; Christopher Childers, "Interpreting Popular Sovereignty: A Historiographical Essay," *CWS* 57 (March 2011): 48–70.

9. Eric H. Walther, *William Lowndes Yancey: The Coming of the Civil War* (Chapel Hill: University of North Carolina Press, 2006): 101–4; Thornton, *Politics and Power,* 172–75; *Macon Weekly Telegraph,* January 7, 1851.

10. Walther, *William Lowndes Yancey,* 101–4, Thornton, *Politics and Power,* 172–75, and *Macon Weekly Telegraph,* January 7, 1851; Childers, *Failure of Popular Sovereignty,* 150–54; Silbey, *Party over Section,* 67.

11. Holt, *Rise and Fall of the American Whig Party,* 259–330.

12. Ibid.; Quoted in John C. Waugh, *On The Brink of Civil War: The Compromise of 1850 and How It Changed the Course of American History* (Wilmington, DE: Scholarly Resources, 2003): 34–35; Mary Tyler Peabody Mann, *Life of Horace Mann* (Boston: Lee & Shepard, 1904): 292.

13. Silbey, *Party over Section,* 68–71; Finkelman, *Millard Fillmore,* 26–50.

14.Silbey, *Party over Section,* 108–10.

15. *A Sketch of The Life and Public Services of General Zachary Taylor, the People's Candidate for the Presidency, with Considerations in Favor of his Election* (Washington, DC: J. T. Towers, 1848): 1:24–25. Democrats countered with stories of their own about Cass; see *A Sketch of the Life and Public Services of General Lewis Cass,* YA Pamphlet Collection, Library of Congress.

16. Holt, *Rise and Fall of the American Whig Party,* 339–45.

17. Carol Bleser, ed., *Secret and Sacred: The Diaries of James Henry Hammond, a Southern Slaveholder* (Columbia: University of South Carolina Press, 1988): 189–91; *Address adopted by the Whig State Convention, at Worcester, September 13, 1848. Together with the Resolutions and Proceedings,* 9–12.

18. *Address Of The Democratic State Convention to the People of Virginia,* in *RichEnq,* September 26, 1848; *Facts for those who will understand them: Gen. Cass's Position on the Slavery Question Defined By Himself and His Friends* (Washington, DC: J. & G. S. Gideon 1848). See also Zachary Taylor to Jefferson Davis, April 20, 1848, in *The Papers of Jefferson Davis* ed. James T. McIntosh (Baton Rouge: Louisiana State University Press, 1981): 3:304–11. Southern Democrats tried to tie Wilmot to Zachary Taylor; see *Milledgeville Federal Union,* July 4, 1848.

19. Silbey, *Party over Section,* 129–46. Although Woodrow Wilson was born in Virginia and grew up in Georgia, he came to prominence as the president of Princeton University and governor of New Jersey.

20. Malcolm J. Rohrbough, "The California Gold Rush as a National Experience," *California History* 77 (Spring 1998): 16–29.

21. Morrison, *Slavery and the American West,* 96–100.

22. Ibid., 100–101; Potter, *Impending Crisis,* 76.

23. Elbert B. Smith, *The Presidencies of Zachary Taylor and Millard Fillmore* (Lawrence: University of Kansas, 1988): 1–158. It is a curious phenomenon that the contention that the enslaved could not work in a similar capacity to the low-paid Asian and Irish immigrants who filled many jobs in the West still persists. See Charles B. Dew, *Bond of Iron: Master and Slave at Buffalo Forge* (New York: W. W. Norton, 195): 107; W. David Lewis, *Sloss Furnaces and the Rise of the Birmingham District: An Industrial Epic* (Tuscaloosa: University of Alabama Press, 1994): 33–34; Richard J. Follett, "The Sugar Masters: Slavery, Economic Development, and Modernization on Louisiana Plantations, 1820–1860," PhD diss., Louisiana State University, 1997, 377–39; Larry E. Hudson Jr., Steven Deyle, James L. Huston, Frank Towers, William G. Thomas, and Diane L. Barnes, in *The Old South's Modern Worlds: Slavery, Region, and Nation in the Age of Progress*, ed. Diana L. Barnes, Brian Schoen, and Frank Towers (New York: Oxford University Press, 2011): 87–208. See also Joseph A. Schumpeter, "The Creative Response in Economic History," *Journal of Economic History* 7 (November 1947): 149–59.

24. Fehrenbacher, *Slaveholding Republic*, 269–71; quoted in Smith, *Presidencies of Zachary Taylor and Millard Fillmore*, 94; James D. Richardson, ed., *A Compilation of the Messages and Papers of the Presidents, 1789–1908*, vol. 5 (Washington, DC: Bureau of National Literature and Art, 1908): 7–8.

25. *Niles' National Register*, 75: 84–88.

26. *Appendix to the CG*, 31 Cong., 1 sess., 224; Potter, *Impending Crisis*, 93–94; Fehrenbacher, *Slaveholding Republic*, 52; Roberts, "'Revolutions Have Become the Bloody Toy of the Multitude,'" 274–76.

27. Remini, *At The Edge of the Precipice*, 37–62; Merrill D. Peterson, *The Great Triumvirate: Webster, Clay, and Calhoun* (New York: Oxford University Press, 1987): 431–75; Knupfer, *Union As It Is*, 158–200.

28. *CG*, 31 Cong., 1 sess., 451–52.

29. Ibid., 452.

30. Ibid., 453; Charles M. Wiltse, *John C. Calhoun: Sectionalist, 1840–1850* (Indianapolis: Bobbs-Merrill, 1951): 423–27.

31. Potter, *Impending Crisis*, 104–6; Walther, *William Lowndes Yancey*, 119–23; Thelma Jennings, *The Nashville Convention Southern Movement for Unity, 1848–1851* (Memphis, TN: Memphis State University Press, 1980): 105–34. Rhett quoted in Walther, *The Fire-Eaters*, 137; *CharMerc*, September 29, 1848.

32. Nathaniel Beverley Tucker, *Prescience: Speech Delivered By Hon. Beverly Tucker, of Virginia, in the Southern Convention, Held At Nashville, Tenn.*, (Richmond, VA: West & Johnson, 1862) 31–32; Walther, *The Fire-Eaters*, 44–46; Freehling, *Road to Disunion*, 2:485.

33. Jennings, *The Nashville Convention Southern Movement for Unity*, 135–66.

34. Richards, *Slave Power*, 96–99; Potter, *Impending Crisis*, 90–99, 106–7; Forbes, *Missouri Compromise and Its Aftermath*, 63–71, 89–95; Fehrenbacher, *Slaveholding Republic*, 271–72; Remini, *At The Edge of the Precipice*, 37–90. Michael F. Holt, "Politics, Patronage, and Public Policy: The Compromise of 1850," and Paul Finkelman, "The Appeasement of 1850," both in *Congress and the Crisis of the 1850s*, ed. Paul Finkelman and Donald R. Kennon (Athens: Ohio University Press, 2012): 36–79. Clay's compromise consisted of eight measures: California would be admitted as a free state; New Mexico would be allowed to vote on the issue of slavery without congressional interference; Texas would relinquish its claim on New Mexico territory; the federal government would assume all of Texas's revolutionary debt; Congress would declare it "inexpedient" to prohibit slavery in Washington, DC, while Maryland remained a slave state; the slave trade would be banned in the nation's capital; the fugitive slave law would be strengthened; and, finally, Congress would have no power under the Commerce Clause to prohibit the interstate slave trade.

35. Smith, *Presidencies of Zachary Taylor and Millard Fillmore,* 100–104.

36. K. Jack Bauer, *Zachary Taylor: Soldier, Planter, Statesman of the Old Southwest* (Baton Rouge: Louisiana State University Press, 1985): 314–16; *Washington (DC) Daily Union,* January 6, 1850.

37. Potter, *Impending Crisis,* 110; Waugh, *On The Brink of Civil War,* 180; Holt, *Rise and Fall of the American Whig Party,* 598–634; *Washington (DC) Daily Union,* July 17, 1850. See also Mark J. Stegmaier, *Texas, New Mexico, and the Compromise of 1850: Boundary Dispute and Sectional Crisis (Lubbock: Texas Tech University Press, 2012).*

38. Potter, *Impending Crisis,* 109–10.

39. Ibid., 108–14.

40. Thomas Hart Benton, ed., *Abridgement of the Debates of Congress, from 1789 to 1856, vol. XVI* (New York: D. Appleton & Company, 1861): 601; *Appendix to the CG,* 31 Cong., 1 sess., 65; Potter, *Impending Crisis,* 114–20.

41. *Milwaukee (Wisc.) Free Democrat,* September 24, 1850. Fillmore took more antislavery action during his short presidency. Most notably, he pardoned abolitionists connected to the Pearl Incident, the second-largest slave escape attempt in American history. See Josephine F. Pacheco, *The Pearl: A Failed Slave Escape on the Potomac* (Chapel Hill: University of North Carolina Press, 2005): 229–32.

42. Karp, "Arsenal of Empire," 2.

43. Yonatan Eyal, *The Young America Movement and the Transformation of the Democratic Party, 1828–1861* (New York: Cambridge University Press, 2007): 135–39; Charles H. Brown, *Agents of Manifest Destiny: The Lives and Times of the Filibusters* (Chapel Hill: University of North Carolina Press, 1980): 26, 109–23.

44. *House Miscellaneous Documents,* 33 Cong., 1 sess,, no. 79; C. Stanley Urban, "The Africanization of Cuba Scare, 1853–1855," *Hispanic American Historical Review* 37 (Feb. 1957): 29–45.

45. Brown, *Agents of Manifest Destiny,* 89–123; Karp, "Arsenal of Empire," 2–3.

46. Document XVI, The Ostend Manifesto, in Willis Fletcher Johnson, *America's Foreign Relations* (New York: Century Co,. 1921): 2:439–41; Brown, *Agents of Manifest Destiny,* 140–41.

47. Document XVI, The Ostend Manifesto, in Willis Fletcher Johnson, *America's Foreign Relations* (New York: Century Co,. 1921): 2:439–41.

48. Richards, *Slave Power,* 190–95; Potter, *Impending Crisis,* 192. While the battle, both with words and swords, raged over the Kansas-Nebraska Act and the Ostend Manifesto, the Pierce administration added nearly thirty thousand square miles of land on the southern border in what became known as the Gadsden Purchase without much dispute. See also Amy S. Greenberg, "Manifest Destiny's Hangover: Congress Confronts Territorial Expansion and Martial Masculinity in the 1850s," in Finkelman and Kennon, *Congress and the Crisis of the 1850s,* 97–119.

49. Anbinder, *Nativism and Slavery,* 75–102; Freehling, *Road to Disunion,* 2:85–108. The best works on the rise of the Republican Party remain Eric Foner, *Free Soil, Free Labor, Free Men,* and William E. Gienapp, *The Origins of the Republican Party, 1852–1856* (New York: Oxford University Press, 1988). See also Heather Cox Richardson, *To Make Men Free: A History of the Republican Party* (New York: Basic Books, 2014): 1–54.

50. Potter, *Impending Crisis,* 225–66; Freehling, *Road to Disunion,* 2:109–22.

51. *Appendix to the CG,* 34 Cong., 3 sess., 271–72.

52. Austin Allen, *Origins of the Dred Scott Case: Jacksonian Jurisprudence and the Supreme Court, 1837–1857* (Athens: University of Georgia Press, 2006); Potter, *Impending Crisis,* 267–98; Childers, *Failure of Popular Sovereignty,* 250–58.

53. Potter, *Impending Crisis,* 281–96; Frank Towers, "Another Looks at Inevitability: Compromise in the Secession Crisis," *Tennessee Historical Quarterly* 70 (Summer 2011): 108–25.

54. *Inaugural Address of R. J. Walker, Governor of Kansas Territory, delivered in Lecompton, K., May 27, 1857* (Lecompton, KS: 1857): 5; *CharMerc*, June 9, 1857; Freehling, *Road to Disunion*, 2:129.

55. Freehling, *Road to Disunion*, 2:125–30.

56. Etcheson, *Bleeding Kansas*, 139–67.

57. Freehling, *Road to Disunion*, 2:134–40; Etcheson, *Bleeding Kansas*, 168–89.

58. Freehling, *Road to Disunion*, 2:140–41; Etcheson, *Bleeding Kansas*, 159–62.

59. *CharMerc*, April 5, 1858; Oakes, *Scorpion's Sting*, 22–50.

60. Matthew Clavin, *Toussaint Louverture and the American Civil War*, 33–54; *New York Times*, August 8, 1860.

61. Matthew Clavin, "A Second Haitian Revolution: John Brown, Toussaint Louverture, and the Making of the American Civil War." *CWS* 54 (June 2008): 117–45; Catherine Clinton, *Harriet Tubman: The Road to Freedom* (New York: Little, Brown & Company, 2004): chap. 9.

62. *Governor's Messages and Reports of the Public Officers of the State, of the Board of Directors, and of the Visitors, Superintendents, and Other Agents of Public Institutions or Interests of Virginia*, Document No. 1 (Richmond: William F. Ritchie, 1859): 92–95.

63. *Senate Report*, 36 Cong., 1 sess., no. 278, 22. Tony Horwitz, *Midnight Rising: John Brown and the Raid That Sparked the Civil War* (New York: Henry Holt, 2011): 1–3.

64. Horwitz, *Midnight Rising*, 127–83.

65. Ibid., 201–15; Brian McGinty, *John Brown's Trial* (Cambridge, MA: Harvard University Press, 2009).

66. *New Haven (Conn) Columbian Register*, November 5, 1859.

67. *New York Herald*, November 7, 1859; Horwitz, *Midnight Rising*, 76–79, 208–211; Stauffer, *Black Hearts of Men*, 236–81; Edward J. Renehan Jr., *The Secret Six: The True Tale of the Men Who Conspired with John Brown* (Columbia: University of South Carolina Press, 1997).

68. Channing, *Crisis of Fear*, 18–57.

69. *CharMerc*, November 4, 1859.

70. *Washington (DC) Constitution*, November 4, 1859. See also April 14, May 6, June 18, July 21, September 6, 17, October 4, 15, 1859.

71. Lorman A. Ratner and Dwight L. Teeter Jr., *Fanatics and Fire-eaters: Newspapers and the Coming of the Civil War* (Urbana: University of Illinois Press, 2003): 75–77. *New Orleans Crescent* quoted on 76.

72. *Governor's Message and Reports of the Public Officers of the State*, 54.

73. Horwitz, *Midnight Rising*, 243–44.

74. Ibid., 225–30, 258–61.

75. *Boston Liberator*, December 2, 1859; *New York Herald*, December 2, 1859; *Philadelphia Public Ledger*; December 2, 1859; *Madison (Wisc.) Weekly Patriot*; December 3, 1859; *Columbus Daily Ohio Statesman*, December 3, 1859; Joe Lockard, "'Earth Feels the Time of Prophet-Song': John Brown and Public Poetry," in *The Afterlife of John Brown*, ed. Andrew Taylor and Eldrid Herrington (New York: Palgrave Macmillan, 2005): 69–87. Northern reaction to Brown mirrored reaction to other slave rescuers; see Harrold, *Abolitionists and the South*, 64–83.

76. Peter Wallenstein, "Incendiaries All: Southern Politics and the Harpers Ferry Raid," in *His Soul Goes Marching on: Responses to John Brown and the Harpers Ferry Raid*, ed. Paul Finkelman (Charlottesville: University of Virginia Press, 1995): 149–73.

77. "Transforming the 'Madman into a Saint': The Cultural Memory Site of John Brown's Raid on Harper's Ferry in Antislavery Literature and History," in Taylor and Herrington, *The Afterlife of John Brown*, 107–20; R. Blakeslee Gilpin, *John Brown Still Lives! America's Long Reckoning with Violence,*

Equality, and Change (Chapel Hill: University of North Carolina Press, 2011): 55–78; Potter, *Impending Crisis,* 403–4.

78. Potter, *Impending Crisis,* 407–13.

79. Frederick Douglass, "What to the Slave Is the Fourth of July?" July 5, 1852.

80. Ibid.; Peter Onuf, Edward Ayers, and Brian Balogh, *Independence Daze: A History of July Fourth,* Podcast audio, Backstory with the American History Guys, June 29, 2012, http://backstoryradio.org/shows/independence-daze-a-history-of-july-fourth-2/. See also David W. Blight, *Frederick Douglass' Civil War: Keeping Faith in Jubilee* (Baton Rouge: Louisiana State University Press, 1991).

81. Walther, *The Fire-Eaters,* 260–61; Veron, *Disunion!* 331–35; Jonathan Earle, "The Political Origins of the Civil War," *OAH Magazine of History* 25: 8–13; Harold Holzer, *Lincoln at Cooper Union: The Speech That Made Abraham Lincoln President* (New York: Simon & Schuster, 2004): 128–29.

82. Earle, "The Political Origins of the Civil War," 11.

83. James Oakes, *Freedom National: The Destruction of Slavery in the United States, 1861–1865* (New York: W. W. Norton, 2012): ix–xv.

84. Oakes, *Scorpion's Sting,* 13–50.

85. David C. Keehn, *Knights of the Golden Circle: Secret Empire, Southern Secession, Civil War* (Baton Rouge: Louisiana State University Press, 2013): 59; Donald E. Reynolds, *Texas Terror: The Slave Insurrection Panic of the 1860 and the Secession of the Lower South* (Baton Rouge: Louisiana State University Press, 2007); Ollinger Crenshaw, *The Slave States in the Presidential Election of 1860* (Gloucester, MA: Peter Smith Press, 1969): 286–87.

86. Quoted in Walther, *The Fire-Eaters,* 185; Keehn, *Knights of the Golden Circle,* 60–61.

87. *Address of the National Executive Committee of the Constitutional Union Party to the People of the United States* (Washington, DC: W. H. Moore, 1860); Daniel W. Crofts, "The Southern Opposition and the Crisis of the Union," in Gallagher and Shelden, *A Political Nation,* 85–111.

88. *Address of the National Executive Committee of the Constitutional Union Party to the People of the United States* (Washington, DC: W. H. Moore, 1860); Towers, "Another Looks at Inevitability," 111–15.

89. Douglas R. Egerton, *Year of Meteors: Stephen Douglas, Abraham Lincoln, and the Election That Brought on the Civil War* (New York: Bloomsbury Press, 2010); Abraham Lincoln to Joshua Speed, August 24, 1855, in *The Collected Works of Lincoln, Volume 2,* ed. Roy P. Basler (Ann Arbor: University of Michigan Digital Library Production Services, 2001), http://name.umdl.umich.edu/lincoln2.

90. *Declaration of the Immediate Causes Which Induce and Justify the Secession of South Carolina from the Federal Union and the Ordinance of Secession* (Charleston, SC: Evans & Cogswell, 1860): 8–9.

91. William E. Barney, "Rush to Disaster: Secession and the Slaves' Revenge," in *Secession Winter: When the Union Fell Apart,* ed. Robert J. Cook, William L. Barney, and Elizabeth R. Varon (Baltimore: Johns Hopkins University Press, 2013): 10–33; Charles B. Dew, *Apostles of Disunion: Southern Secession Commissioners and the Causes of the Civil War* (Charlottesville: University Press of Virginia, 2001): 95; Hadden, *Slave Patrols,* 137–166.

92. Ibid.

93. Ibid., 10.

94. Montgomery *Daily Confederation* March 24, 1860.

95. Dew, *Apostles of Disunion,* 34–35.

96. "To His Excellency the Governor, and to the Honorable the members of the General Assembly of the State of North Carolina" in Walter R. Smith, ed., *The History and Debates of the Convention of the People of Alabama, Begun and held in the City of Montgomery, on the seventh day of January, 1861* (Montgomery, Al: White, Pfister & Co, 1861): 432–436.

97. Henry Cleveland, *Alexander H. Stephens, in Public and Private: With Letters and Speeches, Before, During, and Since the War* (Philadelphia: National Publishing Company, 1886): 717–729; Robert H. Smith, *An address to the citizens of Alabama, on the constitution and laws of the Confederate States of America* (Mobile: Mobile Daily Register Print, 1861): 19; George C. Rable, *The Confederate Republic: A Revolution Against Politics* (Chapel Hill: University of North Carolina Press, 1994).

98. Ibid., 29. See also Jon, L. Wakelyn, ed., *Southern Pamphlets on Secession: November 1860–April 1861,* 186.

99. Dunbar Rowland, ed., *Jefferson Davis, Constitutionalist* vol. 5 (Mississippi Department of Archives and History, 1923): 198–203; Bowman, *At the Precipice,* 39–40, 49; Robery J. Cook, "The Shadow of the Past: Collective Memory and the Coming of the American Civil War," in Cook, Barney, and Varon, *Secession Winter,* 58–85.

100. Peter S. Onuf, "Antebellum Southerners and the National Idea," in Barnes, Shoen, and Towers, *The Old South's Modern Worlds,* 25–46.

Epilogue: Fighting over Exceptionalism

1. Coates, "The Case For Reparations," 54–71; Channing; *Crisis of Fear,* 58–93; Thomas J. Sugrue, *The Origins of the Urban Crisis: Race and Inequality in Postwar Detroit* (Princeton, NJ: Princeton University Press, 1996).

2. Dan T. Carter, "The Anatomy of Fear: The Christmas Day Insurrection Scare of 1865," *JSH* 42 (Aug. 1976): 345–64.

3. Ibid.; Steven Hahn, "'Extravagant Expectations' of Freedom: Rumour, Political Struggle, and the Christmas Insurrection Scare of 1865 in the American South," *Past and Present* 157 (Nov. 1997): 122–58, quoted on 123; Chad L. Williams, "Symbols of Defeat: African American Soldiers, White Southerners, and the Christmas Insurrection Scare of 1865," in *Black Flag over Dixie: Racial Atrocities and Reprisals in the Civil War,* ed. Gregory J. W. Urwin (Carbondale: Southern Illinois University Press, 2004): 210–30; Steven Hahn, *A Nation under Our Feet,* 146–54, quoted on 149.

4. Eric Foner, *Reconstruction: America's Unfinished Revolution, 1863–1877* (New York: Perennial Classics, 2002): 199–202; Leon F. 1–35Knopf, 1979): 366–71; Mark Wahlgren Summers, *The Ordeal of the Reunion: A New History of Reconstruction* (Chapel Hill: University of North Carolina Press, 2014): 1–35, quoted on page 13.

5. Foner, *Reconstruction,* 199–202, Litwack, *Been in the Storm So Long,* 366–71, and Summers, *Ordeal of the Reunion,* 1–35; Luke E. Harlow, *Religion, Race, and the Making of Confederate Kentucky, 1830–1880* (New York: Cambridge University Press, 2014): 157–218.

6. C. Vann Woodward, *The Strange Career of Jim Crow: A Commemorative Edition* (New York: Oxford University Press, 2002): 6, and *Origins of the New South, 1877–1913* (Baton Rouge: Louisiana State University Press, 1971); Edward L Ayers, *The Promise of the New South: Life after Reconstruction* (New York: Oxford University Press, 1992).

7. Foner, *Reconstruction,* 110–18, quoted on 114.

8. Martin Luther King, Jr., "The Negro Is Your Brother" *Atlantic Monthly* (Aug. 1963): 278–88.

BIBLIOGRAPHY

Archival Sources

African American History Collection. William Clements Library, University of Michigan, Ann Arbor.

Documenting the South. University Library, University of North Carolina, Chapel Hill.

Executive Papers of John Floyd. Library of Virginia, Richmond.

Governors' Messages 1783–1870. South Carolina Department of Archives and History, Columbia.

Leckie Family Papers. William Clements Library, University of Michigan, Ann Arbor.

Papers of James Henry Hammond. Library of Congress, Washington, DC.

Ralph Izard Papers, South Caroliniana Library, University of South Carolina Library, Columbia.

Tazewell Family Papers. Library of Virginia, Richmond.

YA Pamphlet Collection, Library of Congress, Washington, DC.

Government Documents

A collection of the laws of the United States relating to revenue, navigation and commerce, and light-houses, etc: up to March 4, 1843, including the treaties with foreign powers. Philadelphia: Isaac Ashmead & Company, 1844.

Acts Passed at a General Assembly of the Commonwealth of Virginia. Richmond, 1831.

An Appendix, a Report on the Trials of Four White Persons, on Indictments for Attempting to Excite the Slaves to Insurrection. Charleston, SC: James R. Schenk, 1822.

An Official Report of the Trials of Sundry Negroes Charged with an Attempt to Raise an Insurrection in the State of South Carolina; Preceded by an Introduction and Narrative; and in an Appendix, a Report on the Trials of Four White Persons, on Indictments for Attempting to Excite the Slaves to Insurrection. Charleston, SC: James R. Schenk, 1822.

Basler, Roy P., ed. *The Collected Works of Lincoln, volume 2.* Ann Arbor: University of Michigan Digital Library Production Services, 2001.

Benton, Thomas Hart. *Abridgement of the Debates of Congress from 1789 to 1856: Dec. 4, 1843–June 18, 1846, vol. XV* (New York: D. Appleton & Company, 1861.

Carter, Clarence, ed. *The Territorial Papers of the United States, vol. 9.* Washington, DC: Government Printing Office, 1940.

Cushing, John D., ed. *The First Laws of the State of Georgia, Part 2.* Wilmington, DE: Michael Glazier, Inc., 1981.

Declaration of the Immediate Causes Which Induce and Justify the Secession of South Carolina from the Federal Union and the Ordinance of Secession. Charleston, SC: Evans & Cogswell, 1860.

Elliot, Jonathan. ed. *The Debates in the Several State Conventions on the Adoption of the Federal Constitution, as Recommended by the General Convention at Philadelphia, in 1787, Together with the Journal of the Federal Convention, Luther Martin's Letters, Yates's Minutes, Congressional Opinions, Virginia and Kentucky Resolutions of '08–09, and other Illustrations of the Constitution. 4 volumes.* Washington, DC, 1836.

Flournoy, H. W. *Calendar of the Virginia State Papers and Other Manuscripts from January 1, 1799 to December 31, 1807,* vol. XI. Richmond, 1890.

Governor's Messages and Reports of the Public Officers of the State, of the Board of Directors, and of the Visitors, Superintendents, and Other Agents of Public Institutions or Interests of Virginia. Document No. 1. Richmond: William F. Ritchie, 1859.

Historical Statistics of the United States: Colonial Times to 1970, Bicentennial Edition, Part 2. Washington, DC: U.S. Bureau of the Census, 1975.

Inaugural Addresses of the Presidents of the United States from George Washington, 1789, to George Bush, 1989. Washington, DC: Government Printing Office, 1989.

Jackson, Maurice, and Jacqueline Bacon, eds. *African Americans and the Haitian Revolution: Selected Essays and Historical Documents.* New York: Routledge, 2010.

Joint Congressional Committee on Inaugural Ceremonies. *President James Knox Polk, 1845,* http://inaugural.senate.gov/history/chronology/jkpolk1845.cfm.

Johnson, Willis Fletcher, ed. Document XVI, The Ostend Manifesto. In *America's Foreign Relations,* volume II. New York: The Century Co., 1921.

Journal of the Convention of the People of South Carolina, Held in 1860, 1861, and 1862. Columbia, SC: R. W. Gibbes, 1862.

Journal of the Proceedings of the General Council of the Republic of Texas Held at San Felipe de Austin, November 14th, 1835. Houston, 1839.

Journal of the Senate of the Commonwealth of Virginia, 1800. Richmond: Thomas Nicholson, 1800.

Lowrie, Walter, and Walter S. Franklin, eds. *American State Papers: Documents, Legislative and Executive of the Congress of the United States, From the First Session of the First to the Second Session of the Twenty-Second Congress.* Class VII. Washington DC: Gales & Seaton, 1834.

Manning, William R. ed. *Diplomatic Correspondence of the United States: Inter-American Series, 1831–1860.* Washington, DC: Carnegie Endowment for International Peace, 1936.

McRae, Sherwin, ed. *Calendar of Virginia State Papers and Other Manuscripts from August 11, 1792 to December 31, 1793, vol. VI.* Richmond, 1886.

Moser, Harold D., ed. *The Papers of Andrew Jackson.* Vol. 3, *1814–1815.* Knoxville: University of Tennessee Press, 1991.

Resolutions of the Legislature of Georgia in Relation to the American Colonization Society.

Richardson, James D. *A Compilation of the Messages and Papers of the Presidents, vol. 1.* Washington, DC: Government Printing Office, 1896.

Rowland, Dunbar, ed., *Jefferson Davis, Constitutionalist.* Vol. 5. Mississippi Department of Archives and History, 1923.

Smith, Robert H. *An address to the citizens of Alabama, on the constitution and laws of the Confederate States of America.* Mobile: Mobile Daily Register Print, 1861.

Stevens, Michael E. *The State Records of South Carolina: Journals of the House of Representatives, 1792–1794.* Columbia, SC: University of South Carolina Press, 1988.

The argument of Benj. Faneuil Hunt, in the case of the arrest of the person claiming to be a British seaman, under the 3d section of the State Act of Dec. 1822, in relation to Negroes, &c. before the Hon. Judge Johnson, Circuit Judge of the United States, for 6th Circuit: ex parte Henry Elkison, claiming to be a subject of His Britannic Majesty, vs. Francis G. Deliesseline, sheriff of Charleston District. Charleston, SC: A. E. Miller, 1823.

U.S. Congress. *Annals of Congress of the United States, 1789–1824.* 42 vols. Washington, DC, 1834–56.

U.S. Congress. *Appendix of the Congressional Globe of the United States.* 46 vols. Washington, D.C. 1834–73.

U.S. Congress. *Congressional Globe.* 46 vols. 1834–73.

U.S. Congress. House of Representatives. *Miscellaneous Documents,* 33 Cong., 1 sess., no. 79.

U.S. Congress. House of Representatives. *Reports,* 27 Cong., 1 sess., no. 3: Recommending Appropriations for Home Squadron Serial 393 Washington, 1841.

U.S. Congress. House of Representatives. *Documents,* 28 Cong., 1 sess. (serial 446), no 404, 125–44.

U.S. Congress. *Public Statutes at Large of the United States of America.* Vol. 5.

U.S. Congress. *Register of the Debates of Congress of the United States.*

U.S. Congress. Senate. "Report of the Secretary of the Navy," 27 Cong., 2 sess. no 1/6 (serial 395). Washington, 1841.

U.S. Congress. Senate. *Report.* 36 Cong., 1 sess., no. 278, 22

U.S. Congress. Senate. *Message from The President of the United States Transmitting with his Objections, the bill entitled, "An Act to incorporate the Subscribers to the Fiscal Bank of the United States."* S. doc. 93. 27 Cong., 1 sess., 5.

U.S. Congress. Senate. Memorial of the Legislature of Alabama, against the measures of the abolitionists, and against interfering with the subject of slavery in the District of Columbia. S. doc. 124.

U.S. Congress. Senate. Resolutions of the Legislature of Kentucky. S. doc. 249. 24 Cong, 1 sess.

U.S. Congress. Senate. Resolutions of the Legislature of Virginia, Adverse to the movements made for the abolition of slavery, &c, S. doc. 233.

Newspapers

Alexandria Herald
American Beacon (Norfolk, VA)
Army and Navy Chronicle
Augusta Chronicle and Georgia Advertiser
Aurora General Advertiser (Philadelphia)
Baltimore Patriot
Bee (New London, CT)
Boston Weekly Messenger
Carolina Federal Republican (New Bern, NC)
City Gazette and Daily Advertiser (Charleston, SC)
Columbian Centinel (Boston)
Columbian Herald
Columbian Mirror and Alexandria Gazette
Columbian Register (New Haven, CT)
Columbus Daily Ohio Statesman
Connecticut Herald
Constitution (Washington, DC)
Constitutional Whig (Richmond)
Courier (Boston)
Cultivator (Hallowell, ME)
Daily Commercial Bulletin (St. Louis)
Daily Confederation (Montgomery)
Daily Madisonian (Washington, DC)
Daily Union (Washington, DC)
Enquirer (Columbus, GA)
Farmer's Register
Federal Union (Milledgeville, GA)
Floridian (Tallahassee)
The Friend (New Orleans)
Gazette (Boston)
Gazette (Hallowell, ME)
Gazette (Haverhill, MA)
Gazette (Philadelphia)
Greenville Mountaineer
Hazard's Register of Pennsylvania
Journal (Jamestown, NY)
Journal of Literature and Politic (Portsmouth, NH)
The Liberator (Boston)
Mercury (Charleston, SC)
Mississippian (Jackson)
Natchez Courier (Natchez, LA)

National Banner and Nashville Whig
National Intelligencer (Washington, DC)
Newburyport Herald
New Orleans Times-Picayune
Newport Mercury
Niles' Weekly Register
North Carolina Standard (Raleigh, NC)
Norwich Courier
Ohio State Journal and Columbus Gazette
Pendleton Messenger (Pendleton, SC)
Pittsfield Sun
Portsmouth Journal and Rockingham Gazette
Public Ledger (Philadelphia)
Republican and Argus (Baltimore)
Republican and State Gazette (Nashville)
Republican Farmer
Richmond Enquirer
Salem Gazette
Saratoga Sentinel
Southern Banner (Athens, GA)
*S*outhern Patriot (Charleston, SC)
Southern Recorder (Milledgeville, GA)
Southern Star (Charleston)
Times (Hartford)
United States Telegraph (Washington, DC)
Virginia Argus (Richmond)
Weekly Herald and the Philanthropist (Cincinnati)
Wisconsin Free Democrat (Milwaukee)
Wisconsin Weekly Patriot (Madison)

Published Primary Correspondence, Diaries, Manuscripts, Speeches, Writings

Adams, Charles Francis, ed. *Memoirs of John Quincy Adams Comprising Portions of His Diary from 1795 to 1848*. Philadelphia: J. B. Lippincott & Co, 1876.

Adams, John Quincy. *Speech of John Quincy Adams of Massachusetts, Upon the Right of the People, Men and Women, to Petition; on the Freedom of Speech and of Debate in the House of Representatives of the United States; on the Resolutions of Seven State Legislatures and the Petitions of More Than One Hundred Thousand Petitioners, Relating to the Annexation of Texas to This Union.* Washington, DC: Gales & Seaton, 1938.

Address of the National Executive Committee of the Constitutional Union Party to the People of the United States. Washington, DC: W. H. Moore, 1860.

Address adopted by the Whig State Convention, at Worcester, September 13, 1848. Together with the Resolutions and Proceedings.

"After Nat Turner: A Letter from the North." *Journal of Negro History* 55 (April 1970): 144–51.

Bailey, Rufus William. *The Issue Presented in a Series of Letters on Slavery.* New York: John S. Taylor, 1837.

Barker, Eugene C., ed. *The Papers of Stephen F. Austin.* Washington & Austin, 1924–1928.

Barker, Joseph, ed. *The Works of William Ellery Channing in Six Volumes.* London: Chapman, 1845.

Bassett, John Spencer, ed. *Correspondence of Andrew Jackson.* 7 vols. Washington, DC: Carnegie Institution of Washington, 1931.

Bellinger, Edmund. *A Speech on the Subject of Slavery: Delivered 7 September 1835 at a Public Meeting of the Citizens of Barnwell District, South Carolina.* Charleston: Dan J. Dowling, 1835.

Benton, Thomas H. *Thirty Years in the Senate; or, A History of the Working of the American Government for Thirty Years From 1820 to 1850.* 2 vols. New York: D. Appleton & Company, 1856.

Bleser, Carol, ed. *Secret and Sacred: The Diaries of James Henry Hammond, a Southern Slaveholder.* Columbia: University of South Carolina Press, 1988.

Brown, Edward. *Notes on the Origins and Necessity of Slavery.* Charleston, SC: A. E. Miller, 1826.

Brent, Linda [Harriet Ann Jacobs]. *Incidents in the Life of a Slave Girl,* ed. L. Maria Child. Boston, 1861.

Brutus [Robert Turnbull]. *The Crisis: or, Essays on the Usurpations of the Federal Government.* Charleston, SC: A. E. Miller, 1827.

Bushnell, Albert, and Hart and Edward Channing, eds. *American History Leaflets Colonial and Constitutiona*l. New York: A. Lovell & Company, 1893.

Catanzarti, John, ed. *The Papers of Thomas Jefferson: Second Series.* Princeton, NJ: Princeton University Press, 1995.

Channing, William E. *A Letter on the Annexation of Texas to the United States.* London, 1837.

Cleveland, Henry. *Alexander H. Stephens, in Public and Private: With Letters and Speeches, Before, During, and Since the War.* Philadelphia: National Publishing Company, 1886.

Coulon, Garran. *An inquiry into the causes of the insurrection of the negroes in the island of St. Domingo.* London: J. Johnson, 1792.

Crackel, Theodore J. *The Papers of George Washington.* Vol. 14. Charlottesville: University of Virginia Press, 2008.

De Tocqueville, Alexis. *Democracy in America.* Ed. Bruce Frohnen. Washington, DC: Regnery Publishing, 2002.

Dew, Thomas R. *Review of the Debate in the Virginia Legislature of 1831 and 1832.* Richmond: T. W. White, 1832.

A Digest of the Ordinances, Resolutions, By-Laws, and Regulations of the Corporation of New Orleans, and a collection of the laws of the Legislature Relative to the said City (New Orleans: Gaston Brusle, 1836).

Dobbin, J. C. *The Wilmot Proviso speech of Hon. J.C. Dobbin, of N. Carolina, delivered in the House of Representatives, February 11, 1847, on the Wilmot Proviso prohibiting slavery in any territories whatever that may hereafter be acquired by the United States.* Washington, DC: Blair & Rives, 1847.

Donnan, Elizabeth, ed. *Papers of James A. Bayard, 1796–1815.* Washington, DC: Eleventh Report of the Historical Manuscripts Commission, 1913.

[Drayton, William.] *The South Vindicated from the Treason and Fanaticism of the Northern Abolitionists.* Philadelphia: H. Manly, 1836.

Dwight, Theodore. *An Oration, Spoken before "The Connecticut Society, for the Promotion of Freedom and the Relief of Persons Unlawfully Held in Bondage."* Hartford, CT, 1794.

Faulkner, James, *The Speech of Charles James Faulkner (of Berkeley) in the House of Delegates of Virginia, On the Policy of the State with Respect to Her Colored Population.* Richmond: Thomas W. White, 1832.

Freehling, William W., ed. *The Nullification Era: A Documentary Record.* New York: Harper Torchbooks, 1967.

——, and Craig M. Simpson, eds. *Showdown in Virginia: The 1861 Convention and the Fate of the Union.* Charlottesville: University of Virginia Press, 2010.

Freidel, Frank, "Francis Lieber, Charles Sumner, and Slavery," *Journal of Southern History* 9 (Feb. 1943): 75–93.

Furman, Richard. *Rev. Dr. Richard Furnan's Exposition of the Views of the Baptists, Relative to the Coloured Population in the United States In A Communication to the Governor of South-Carolina.* 2nd ed. Charleston, 1838.

Gardiner, O. C. *The Great Crisis; or, Three Presidential Candidates, Being a Brief Historical Sketch of the Free Soil Question in the United States, From The Congresses 1774 and '87 to the Present Time.* New York: WM. C. Bryant & Company, 1848.

Gottschalk, Louis Moreau. *Notes of a Pianist: The Chronicles of a New Orleans Music Legend.* Ed. Jeanne Behrend. Princeton, NJ: Princeton University Press, 2006.

Grant, Ulysses S. *Personal Memoirs of U. S. Grant.* Two Volumes in One. Old Saybrook, CT: Konecky & Konecky, 1999.

Hackett, Mary, J. C. Staff, Jeanne Kerr Cross, and Susan Holbrook Purdue, eds. *The Papers of James Madison.* Secretary of State Series, vol. 2. Charlottesville: University of Virginia Press, 1986.

Hamilton, James. *An Account of the Late Intended Insurrection Among a Portion of the Blacks of the City.* Charleston, SC: A. E. Miller: 1822.

Harper, William. "Memoir on Slavery," *Southern Literary Messenger* 4 (Oct. 1838): 609–36.

Houston, David Franklin, ed. *American History Leaflets, Colonial and Constitutional, November 1893: Ordinances of Secession and Other Documents, 1860–1861.* New York: A. Lovell & Company, 1893.

Kemble, Frances Anne. *Journal of a Residence on a Georgian Plantation in 1838–1839.* Ed. John A. Scott. New York: Alfred A. Knopf, 1961.

King, Martin Luther, Jr. "The Negro Is Your Brother." *Atlantic Monthly* (Aug. 1963): 278–88.

Legaré, Hugh Swinton. *The Writings of Hugh Swinton Legaré*. Vol. 2. New York: Da Capo Press, 1970.

Leigh, Benjamin Watkins. *The Letter of Appomattox to the People of Virginia: Exhibiting a Connected View of the Recent Proceedings in the House of Delegates on the Subject of the Abolition of Slavery.* Richmond: Thomas W. White, 1832.

Lundy, Benjamin, and Thomas Earl. *The Life, Travels, and Opinions of Benjamin Lundy Including His Journeys to Texas and Mexico, with a Sketch of Contemporary Events, and a Notice of the Revolution of Hayti.* Philadelphia: William D. Parrish, 1847.

McIntosh, James T., ed. *The Papers of Jefferson Davis.* Vol. 3. Baton Rouge: Louisiana State University Press, 1981.

Moore, Ben Perley. *Perley's Reminiscences of the Sixty Years In The National Metropolis.* Tecumseh, MI: A. W. Mills, 1886.

Parham, Alethea de Peuch, trans. *My Odyssey: Experiences of a Young Refugee from Two Revolutions, by a Creole of St. Domingue.* Baton Rouge: Louisiana State University Press, 1959.

Paulding, James Kirke. *Slavery in the United States.* New York: Harper & Brothers, 1836.

Perkins, Bradford. *Prologue to War: England and the United States, 1805–1812.* Berkeley: University of California Press, 1961.

Pierce, Edward L, ed. *Memoirs and Letters of Charles Sumner.* Boston: Roberts Brothers, 1877.

Polk, Milo Milton Quaife, ed. *The diary of James K. Polk during his Presidency, 1845–1849.* 2 vols. New York: A. C. McClurg & Co., 1910.

The Proslavery Argument; as maintained by the most distinguished Writers of the Southern States, containing the several Essays on the subject, of Chancellor Harper, Governor Hammond, Dr. Simms, and Professor Dew. Philadelphia: Lippincott, Grambo, & Company, 1853.

Seabrook, Whitemarsh. *A Concise View of the Critical Situation and Future Prospects of the Slaveholding States.* Charleston. SC: A. E. Miller, 1825.

Seager, Robert, and Melba Porter Hay, eds. *The Papers of Henry Clay.* Lexington: University Press of Kentucky, 1984.

Sedgwick, Theodore, ed. *A Collection of Political Writings of William Leggett, volume II.* New York: Taylor & Dodd, 1840.

A Sketch of the Life and Public Services of General Zachary Taylor, the People's Candidate for the Presidency, with Considerations in Favor of his Election. Washington, DC: J. T. Towers, 1848.

Smith, Walter R., ed. *The History and Debates of the Convention of the People of Alabama, Begun and held in the City of Montgomery, on the seventh day of January, 1861.* Montgomery: White, Pfister & Co., 1861.

Stoney, Samuel Gaillard, ed. "Poinsett-Campbell Correspondence (Continued)," *South Carolina Historical and Genealogical Magazine* 42 (Oct., 1941): 31–52.

Stuart, James. *Three Years in North America, vol. II.* Edinburgh: Robert Cadell and Whittaker & Co., 1831.

Tragle, Henry Irving, *The Southampton Slave Revolt of 1831: A Compilation of Source Material.* Amherst: University of Massachusetts Press, 1971.

Tucker, Nathaniel Beverley. *Prescience: Speech Delivered By Hon. Beverly Tucker, of Virginia, in the Southern Convention, Held At Nashville, Tenn.* Richmond, VA: West & Johnson, 1862.

Tucker, St. George. *Letter to a Member of the General Assembly of Virginia on the Subject of the Late Conspiracy of the Slaves with a Proposal for Their Colonization.* Baltimore: Bonsal & Niles, 1801.

Tyler, Lyon Gardiner, ed. *The Letters and Times of the Tylers in Two Volumes.* Richmond: Whittett & Shepperson, 1884.

Upshur, Abel P. *A brief enquiry into the true nature and character of our Federal Government: being a review of Judge Story's Commentaries on the Constitution of the United States.* Petersburg: Edmund and Julian C. Ruffin, 1840.

——. "Domestic Slavery." *Southern Literary Messenger* 5 (Oct. 1839): 677–87.

U.S. Post Office. *List of Post Offices in the United States, with the Names of Postmasters on the 1st of April 1859; Also the Laws and Regulations of the Post Office Department.* Washington: John C. Rives, 1859.

U.S. Printing Office. *The writings of George Washington from the original manuscript sources, 1745–1799; prepared under the direction of the United States George Washington Bicentennial Commission and published by authority of Congress.* Vol. 33. Washington, DC, 1931.

Wagstaff, H. M., ed. *The James Sprunt Historical Publications.* Chapel Hill: University of North Carolina Press, 1916.

Wakelyn, Jon L. ed. *Southern Pamphlets on Secession, November 1860–April 1861.* Chapel Hill: University of North Carolina Press, 1996.

Walker, Robert J. *Inaugural Address of R. J. Walker, Governor of Kansas Territory, delivered in Lecompton, K. May 27, 1857.* Lecompton, 1857.

——. Letter of Mr. Walker, of Mississippi, Relative to the Annexation of Texas: In Reply to the Call of the People of Carroll County, Kentucky, to Communicate His Views on that Subject. Washington, DC: Globe Office, 1844.

——. *The South in danger: read before you vote: address of the Democratic Association of Washington, D.C.* Washington, DC: Gales & Seaton, 1844.

Weaver, Herbert, ed. *Correspondence of James K. Polk.* Nashville: Vanderbilt University Press, 1975.

Webster, Noah. *The American Dictionary of the English Language.* New York: Johnson Reprint Corp., 1970.

——. "Dissertations on the English Language: with Notes, Historical and Critical." In *Creating an American Culture, 1775–1800: A Brief History with Documents, ed. Evan Kornfeld.* New York: Bedford Publishing, 2001.

Wilson. Clyde N., ed. *The Papers of John C. Calhoun.* 28 vols. Columbia: University of South Carolina Press, 1953–2003.

Wright Louis B., and Marion Tinling, eds., *The Secret Diary of William Byrd of Westover, 1709–1712.* Richmond, VA: Dietz Press, 1941.

Secondary Sources

Alexander, Thomas B. *Sectional Stress and Party Strength: A Study of Roll-Call Voting Patterns in the United States House of Representatives, 1836–1860.* Nashville: Vanderbilt University Press, 1967.

BIBLIOGRAPHY

Allardice, Bruce. "West Points of the Confederacy: Southern Military Schools and the Confederate Army." *Civil War History* 43 (December 1997): 310–31.

Allen, Austin. *Origins of the Dred Scott Case: Jacksonian Jurisprudence and the Supreme Court, 1837–1857.* Athens: University of Georgia Press, 2006.

Allmendinger Jr., David F. *Nat Turner and the Rising in Southampton County.* Baltimore: Johns Hopkins University Press, 2014.

Alston, Richard. "The Good Master: Pliny, Hobbes, and the Nature of Freedom." In *Ancient Slavery and Abolition: From Hobbes to Hollywood,* ed. Edith Hall, Richard Alston, and Justine McConnell. New York: Oxford University Press, 2011: 41–64.

Altschuler, Glenn C., and Stuart M. Blumin. *Rude Republic: Americans and Their Politics in the Nineteenth Century.* Princeton, NJ: Princeton University Press, 2000.

Ambler, Charles Henry. *Thomas Ritchie: A Study in Virginia Politics.* Richmond: Bell Book and Stationary, 1913.

——. *The Life and Diary of John Floyd: Governor of Virginia, An Apostle of Secession, and the Father of Oregon Country.* Richmond, VA: Richmond Press, 1918.

Anbinder, Tyler. *Nativism and Slavery: The Know Nothings and the Politics of the 1850s.* New York: Oxford University Press, 1992.

Angelou, Maya. *Poems.* New York: Bantam Books, 1993.

Appleby, Joyce. *Inheriting the Revolution: The First Generations of Americans.* Cambridge, MA: Belknap Press of Harvard University, 2000.

Aptheker, Herbert. *American Negro Slate Revolts.* New York: Columbia University Press, 1943.

——. *One Continual Cry, David Walker's Appeal to the Coloured Citizens of the World, 1829–1830.* New York: Humanities Press, 1965.

——. *Abolitionism: A Revolutionary Movement.* Boston: Twayne Publishers, 1989.

Ashworth, John. *Slavery, Capitalism, and Politics in the Antebellum Republic.* Vols. 1 and 2. New York: Cambridge University Press, 1995, 2007.

——. *The Republic in Crisis, 1848–1861.* New York: Cambridge University Press, 2012.

Atkins, Jonathan M. *Parties, Politics and the Sectional Conflict of Tennessee, 1832–1861.* Knoxville: University of Tennessee Press, 1997.

Ayers, Edward L. *Vengeance and Justice: Crime and Punishment in the Nineteenth-Century American South.* New York: Oxford University Press, 1984.

——. *The Promise of the New South: Life after Reconstruction.* New York: Oxford University Press, 1992.

——. *In The Presence of Mine Enemies: War In the Heart of America, 1859–1863.* New York: W. W. Norton, 2003.

Baptist, Edward E. *The Half Has Never Been Told: Slavery and the Making of American Capitalism.* New York: Basic Books, 2014.

Barcia, Manuel. *Seeds of Insurrection: Domination and Resistance on Western Cuban Plantations, 1808–1848.* Baton Rouge: Louisiana State University Press, 2008.

Barnes, Diane L., Brian Schoen, and Frank Towers, eds. *The Old South's Modern Worlds: Slavery, Region, and Nation in the Age of Progress.* New York: Oxford University Press, 2011.

BIBLIOGRAPHY

Barney, William. *The Road to Secession: A New Perspective on the Old South.* New York: Praeger Publishers, 1972.

Bauer, K. Jack. *Zachary Taylor: Soldier, Planter, Statesman of the Old Southwest.* Baton Rouge: Louisiana State University Press, 1985.

Baur, John E. "International Repercussions of the Haitian Revolution." *The Americas* 26 (April 1970): 394–418.

Belko, W. Stephen. *The Invincible Duff Green: Whig of the West.* Columbia: University of Missouri Press, 2006.

Bell, Caryn Cossé. *Revolution, Romanticism, and the Afro-Creole Protest Tradition in Louisiana, 1718–1868.* Baton Rouge: Louisiana State University Press, 2004.

Belohlavek, John M. *"Let the Eagle Soar!" The Foreign Policy of Andrew Jackson.* Lincoln: University of Nebraska Press, 1985.

Bergeron, Paul H. *Antebellum Politics in Tennessee.* Lexington: University Press of Kentucky, 1989.

Berlin, Ira. *Slaves without Masters: The Free Negro in the Antebellum South.* New York: New Press, 1974.

———. *Many Thousands Gone: The First Two Centuries of Slavery in North America.* Cambridge, MA: Harvard University Press, 1998.

Berwanger, Eugene H. *The Frontier against Slavery: Western Anti-Negro Prejudice and the Slavery Extension Controversy.* Chicago: University of Illinois Press, 1967.

Bishop, Abraham. "'The Rights of Black Men,' and the American Reaction to the Haitian Revolution," *Journal of Negro History* 67 (Summer 1982): 148–54.

Blackburn, Robin. *The American Crucible: Slavery, Emancipation and Human Rights.* New York: Verso, 2011.

Blight, David W. *Frederick Douglass' Civil War: Keeping Faith in Jubilee.* Baton Rouge: Louisiana State University Press, 1991.

Bonner, Robert. *Mastering America: Southern Slaveholders and the Crisis of American Nationhood.* New York: Cambridge University Press, 2009.

Bowman, Shearer Davis. *At the Precipice: North and South during the Secession Crisis.* Chapel Hill: University of North Carolina Press, 2010.

Branson, Susan, and Leslie Patrick. "Étrangers dans un Pays Étrange: Saint-Dominguan Refugees of Color in Philadelphia." In *The Impact of the Haitian Revolution in the Atlantic World,* 193–208.

Breen, Patrick H. "In Terror of Their Slaves: White Southern Women's Responses to Slave Insurrections and Scares." In *Warm Ashes: Issues in Southern History at the Dawn of the Twenty-First Century,* ed. Winfred B. Moore, Jr., Kyle S. Sinsi, and David H. White, Jr. Columbia: University of South Carolina Press, 2003: 69–84.

Brown, Arthur W. *William Ellery Channing.* New York: Twayne Publishers, 1962.

Brown, Charles H. *Agents of Manifest Destiny: The Lives and Times of the Filibusters.* Chapel Hill: University of North Carolina Press, 1980.

Brown, Christopher Leslie. *Moral Capital: Foundations of British Abolitionism.* Chapel Hill: University of North Carolina Press, 2006.

Brown, Gordon S. *Toussaint's Clause: The Founding Fathers and the Haitian Revolution.* Jackson: University Press of Mississippi, 2005.

Buchanan, Thomas C., *Black Life on the Mississippi: Slaves, Free Blacks and the Western Steamboat World.* Chapel Hill: University of North Carolina Press, 2004.

Bynack, V. P. "Noah Webster's Linguistic Thought and the Idea of an American National Culture," *Journal of the History of Ideas* 45 (Jan.-March 1984): 99–114.

Campbell, Randolph B. *An Empire for Slavery: The Peculiar Institution in Texas, 1821–1865.* Baton Rouge: Louisiana State University Press, 1989.

———. *Gone to Texas: A History of the Lone Star State.* New York: Oxford University Press, 2003.

Carter, Susan B. "Black population, by state and slave/free status: 1790–1860." In *Historical Statistics of the United States: Millennial Edition.* New York: Cambridge University Press, 2010.

Channing, Steven A. *Crisis of Fear: Secession in South Carolina.* New York: Simon & Schuster, 1970.

Cheng, Eileen Ka-may. "American Historical Writers and the Loyalists, 1788–1856: Dissent, Consensus, and American Nationality." *Journal of the Early Republic* 23 (Winter 2003): 491–519.

Childers, Christopher. *The Failure of Popular Sovereignty: Slavery, Manifest Destiny, and the Radicalization of Southern Politics.* Lawrence: University of Kansas Press, 2012.

———. "Interpreting Popular Sovereignty: A Historiographical Essay." *Civil War History* 57 (March 2011): 48–70.

———. "Civil War Sesquicentennial: The Political Crisis of the 1850s and the Irrepressible Historians." *Civil War Book Review* (Summer 2014).

Clary, David A. *Eagles and Empire: The United States, Mexico, and the Struggle for A Continent.* New York: Bantam Books, 2009.

Clavin, Matthew. "A Second Haitian Revolution: John Brown, Toussaint Louverture, and the Making of the American Civil War." *Civil War History* 54 (June 2008): 117–45.

———. *Toussaint Louverture and the American Civil War: The Promise and Peril of a Second Haitian Revolution.* Philadelphia: University of Pennsylvania Press, 2010.

Cleves, Rachel Hope. *The Reign of Terror in America: Visions of Violence from Anti-Jacobinism to Antislavery.* New York: Cambridge University Press, 2009.

Clinton, Catherine. *Harriet Tubman: The Road to Freedom.* New York: Little, Brown & Company, 2004.

Coates, Ta-Nehisi. "The Case for Reparations." *Atlantic* (June 2014): 54–71.

Cole, Donald B. *A Jackson Man: Amos Kendall and the Rise of American Democracy.* Baton Rouge: Louisiana State University Press, 2004.

Connolly Jr., David Hugh. "A Question of Honor: State Character and the Lower South's Defense of the African Slave Trade in Congress, 1789–1807." PhD diss., Rice University, 2008.

Cook, Robert J., William L. Barney, and Elizabeth R. Varon. *Secession Winter: When the Union Fell Apart.* Baltimore: Johns Hopkins University Press, 2013.

Cooper, William J. *The South and the Politics of Slavery. 1828–1856.* Baton Rouge: Louisiana State University Press, 1978.

——. *Liberty and Slavery: Southern Politics to 1860.* New York: McGraw-Hill, 1983.

Cox, Edward L. "The British Caribbean in the Age of Revolution." In *Empire and Nation: The American Revolution in the Atlantic World,* ed. Eliga H Gould and Peter S. Onuf. Baltimore: Johns Hopkins University Press, 2005: 277–94.

Crapol, Edward P. *John Tyler: The Accidental President.* Chapel Hill: University of North Carolina Press, 2006.

Craven, Avery O. *The Growth of Southern Nationalism, 1848–1861.* Baton Rouge: Louisiana State University Press, 1953.

Cray, Robert E. "Remembering the USS *Chesapeake*: The Politics of Maritime Death and Impressment." *Journal of the Early Republic* 25 (Fall 2005): 445–74.

Crenshaw, Ollinger. *The Slave States in the Presidential Election of 1860.* Gloucester, MA: Peter Smith Press, 1969.

Crockett Hasan. "The Incendiary Pamphlet: David Walker's Appeal in Georgia." *Journal of Negro History* 86 (Summer 2001): 305–18.

Crofts, Daniel W. *Old Southampton: Politics and Society in a Virginia County, 1834–1869.* Charlottesville: University of Virginia Press, 1992.

Crow, Jeffrey J. "Slave Rebelliousness and Social Conflict in North Carolina, 1775 to 1802," *William and Mary Quarterly* 37 (Jan. 1980): 79–102.

Da Costa, Emilia Viotti. *Crowns of Glory, Tears of Blood: The Demerara Slave Rebellion of 1823.* New York: Oxford University Press, 1994.

Daly, John Patrick. *When Slavery Was Called Freedom: Evangelicalism, Proslavery, and the Causes of the Civil War.* Lexington: University Press of Kentucky, 2002.

David, Mary Kemp. *Nat Turner before the Bar of Judgment: Fictional Treatments of the Southampton Slave Insurrection.* Baton Rouge: Louisiana State University Press, 1999.

Davis, David Brion. *The Slave Power Conspiracy and the Paranoid Style.* Baton Rouge: Louisiana State University Press, 1969.

——, ed. *The Fear of Conspiracy: Images of Un-American Subversion from the Revolution to the Present.* Ithaca, NY: Cornell University Press, 1971.

——. *The Problem of Slavery in the Age of Revolution, 1770–1823.* New York: Oxford University Press, 1999.

——. *Inhuman Bondage: The Rise and Fall of Slavery in the New World.* New York: Oxford University Press, 2006.

——. *Revolutions: Reflections on American Equality and Foreign Liberations.* Cambridge, MA: Harvard University Press.

Deburg, William L. *Slavery and Race in American Popular Culture.* Madison: University of Wisconsin Press, 1984.

Dew, Charles B. *Bond of Iron: Master and Slave at Buffalo Forge.* New York: W. W. Norton, 1995.

——. *Apostles of Disunion: Southern Secession Commissioners and the Causes of the Civil War.* Charlottesville: University of Virginia Press, 2001.

Dickerson, Donna Lee. *The Course of Tolerance: Freedom of the Press in Nineteenth-Century America.* New York: Greenwood Press, 1990.

Dillon, Merton. *Slavery Attacked: Southern Slaves and Their Allies 1619–1865.* Baton Rouge: Louisiana State University Press, 1990.

Dubois, Laurent. *Avengers of the New World: The Story of the Haitian Revolution.* Cambridge, MA: Harvard University Press, 2004.

——. *A Colony of Citizens: Revolution and Slave Emancipation in the French Caribbean 1787–1804.* Chapel Hill: University of North Carolina Press, 2004.

Dubois, W. E. B. *The Suppression of the African Slave-Trade to the United States of America, 1638–1870.* New York: Longmans, Green, & Co., 1904.

Dusinberre, William. *Slavemaster President: The Double Career of James Polk.* New York: Oxford University Press, 2003.

Earle, Jonathan H. *Jacksonian Antislavery and Politics of Free Soil, 1824–1854.* Chapel Hill: University of North Carolina, 2004.

——. "The Political Origins of the Civil War." *OAH Magazine of History* 25: 8–13.

Eaton, Clement. "A Dangerous Pamphlet in the Old South." *Journal of Southern History* 2 (Aug. 1936): 512–34.

Egerton, Douglas R. "'Its Origin Is Not a Little Curious': A New Look at the American Colonization Society." *Journal of the Early Republic* 5 (Winter 1985): 463–80.

——. *Gabriel's Rebellion: The Virginia Slave Conspiracies of 1800 and 1802.* Chapel Hill: University of North Carolina Press, 1993.

——. "'Why Did They Not Preach Up This Thing': Denmark Vesey and Revolutionary Theology." *South Carolina Historical Magazine* 100 (Oct. 1999): 298–318.

——. *He Shall Go Out Free: The Lives of Denmark Vesey, Revised and Updated Version.* New York: Rowan & Littlefield, 2004.

——. *Year of Meteors: Stephen Douglas, Abraham Lincoln, and the Election That Brought on the Civil War.* New York: Bloomsbury Press, 2010.

Etcheson, Nicole. *Bleeding Kansas: Contested Liberty in the Civil War Era.* Lawrence: University Press of Kansas, 2004.

Eyal, Yonatan. *The Young America Movement and the Transformation of the Democratic Party, 1828–1861.* New York: Cambridge University Press, 2007.

Faust, Drew Gilpin. *A Sacred Circle: The Dilemma of the Intellectual in the Old South. 1840–1860.* Philadelphia: University of Pennsylvania Press, 1977.

——. ed. *The Ideology of Slavery: Proslavery Thought in the Antebellum South, 1830–1860.* Baton Rouge: Louisiana State University Press, 1981.

——. *James Henry Hammond and the Old South: A Design for Mastery* (Baton Rouge: Louisiana State University Press, 1982.

Fehrenbacher, Don E. *The Slaveholding Republic: An Account of the United States Government's Relation to Slavery.* Ed. Ward M. McAfee. New York: Oxford University Press, 2001.

Finkelman, Paul. *Slavery and the Founders: Race and Liberty in the Age of Jefferson.* New York: M. E. Sharpe, 2001.

——. "Regulating the African Slave Trade." *Civil War History* 54 (Dec. 2008): 379–405.

——. *Millard Fillmore.* New York: Times Books, 2011.

——, and Donald R. Kennon, eds., *Congress and the Crisis of the 1850s.* Athens: Ohio University Press, 2012.

Fischer, David Hackett, and James C. Kelly. *Virginia and the Westward Movement.* Charlottesville: University of Virginia Press, 2000.

Follett, Richard J. "The Sugar Masters: Slavery, Economic Development, and Modernization on Louisiana Plantations, 1820–1860." PhD diss., Louisiana State University, 1997.

Foner, Eric. "The Wilmot Proviso Revisited." *Journal of American History* 16, no. 2 (Sept. 1969): 262–79.

——. *Free Soil, Free Labor, Free Men: The ideology of the Republican Party before the Civil War.* New York: Oxford University Press, 1970.

——. *Reconstruction: America's Unfinished Revolution, 1863–1877.* New York: Perennial Classics, 2002.

——. *The Fiery Trial: Abraham Lincoln and American Slavery.* New York: W. W. Norton, 2010.

Forbes, Robert Pierce. *The Missouri Compromise and Its Aftermath: Slavery and the Meaning of America* Chapel Hill: University of North Carolina Press, 2007.

Ford, Lacy. *Deliver Us from Evil: The Slavery Question in the Old South.* New York: Oxford University Press, 2009.

——. *Origins of Southern Radicalism: The South Carolina Upcountry, 1800–1860.* New York: Oxford University Press, 1988.

Fox-Genovese, Elizabeth, and Eugene Genovese. *Mind of the Master Class: History and Faith in the Southern Slaveholders' Worldview.* New York: Cambridge University Press, 2005.

Franklin, John Hope, *The Free Negro in North Carolina, 1790–1860.* Chapel Hill: University of North Carolina Press, 1943.

Freehling, Alison Goodyear, *Drift toward Dissolution: The Virginia Slavery Debate of 1831–1832.* Baton Rouge: Louisiana State University Press, 1982.

Freehling, William. *Prelude to the Civil War: The Nullification Controversy in South Carolina 1816–1836.* New York: Oxford University Press, 1965.

——. "Denmark Vesey's Peculiar Reality." In *New Perspectives on Race and Slavery in America: Essays in Honor of Kenneth Stampp.* Ed. by Robert H. Abzug and Stephen E. Maizlish. Lexington: University Press of Kentucky, 1986.

——. *The Road to Disunion: Secessionists at Bay, 1776–1854.* Vol. 1. New York: Oxford University Press, 1990.

——. *The Road to Disunion: Secessionists Triumphant, 1854–1861.* Vol. 2. New York: Oxford University Press, 2007.

Gabrial, Brian. "From Haiti to Nat Turner: Racial Panic Discourse during the Nineteenth Century Partisan Press Era," *American Journalism* 30 (2013): 336–64.

Gallagher, Gary W. *The Union War.* Cambridge, MA: Harvard University Press, 2012.

——, and Rachel A. Shelden, eds. *A Political Nation: New Directions in Mid-Nineteenth-Century American History.* Charlottesville: University of Virginia Press, 2012.

Gatell, Frank Otto, ed. "Postmaster Huger and the Incendiary Publications." *South Carolina Historical Magazine* 64 (Oct. 1963): 93–201.

Geggus, David P., ed. *The Impact of the Haitian Revolution in the Atlantic World.* Columbia: University of South Carolina Press, 2001.

Genovese, Eugene D. *Roll, Jordan, Roll: The World Slaves Made.* New York: Vintage Books, 1976.

——. *The Slaveholders' Dilemma: Freedom and Progress in Southern Conservative Thought, 1820–1860.* Columbia: University of South Carolina Press, 1991.

Gienapp, William E. *The Origins of the Republican Party, 1852–1856.* New York: Oxford University Press, 1988.

Gilpin, R. Blakeslee. *John Brown Still Lives! America's Long Reckoning with Violence, Equality, and Change.* Chapel Hill: University of North Carolina Press, 2011.

Going, Charles Buxton. *David Wilmot: Free-Soiler.* New York: D. Appleton & Co., 1924.

Goldfield, David. *Still Fighting the Civil War: The American South and Southern History.* Baton Rouge: Louisiana State University Press, 2013.

Grant, Susan-Mary. *North over South: Northern Nationalism and American Identity in the Antebellum Era.* Lawrence: University Press of Kansas, 2000.

Green, Michael S. *Politics and America in Crisis: The Coming of the Civil War.* Santa Barbara: Praeger, 2010.

Greenberg, Kenneth S. *Honor and Slavery: Lies, Duels, Noses, Masks, Dressing as A Woman, Gifts, Strangers, Humanitarianism, Death, Slave Rebellions, the Proslavery Argument, Baseball, Hunting, and Gambling in the Old South.* Princeton, NJ: Princeton University Press, 1996.

Grimsted, David. *American Mobbing: 1828–1861.* New York: Oxford University Press, 1998.

Guterl, Matthew Pratt. *American Mediterranean: Southern Slaveholders in the Age of Emancipation.* Cambridge, MA: Harvard University Press, 2008.

Hadden, Salley E. *Slave Patrols: Law and Violence in Virginia and the Carolinas.* Cambridge, MA: Harvard University Press, 2001.

Hahn, Steven. *The Roots of Southern Populism: Yeomen Farmers and the Transformation of the Georgia Upcountry, 1850–1890.* New York: Oxford University Press, 1983.

——. "'Extravagant Expectations' of Freedom: Rumour, Political Struggle, and the Christmas Insurrection Scare of 1865 in the American South," *Past and Present* 157 (Nov. 1997): 122–58.

——. *A Nation under Our Feet: Black Political Struggles in the Rural South from Slavery to the Great Migration.* Cambridge, MA: Harvard University Press, 2003.

Hall, Claude H. "Abel P. Upshur and the Navy as an Instrument of Foreign Policy." *Virginia Magazine of History and Biography* 69 (July 1961): 290–99.

——. *Abel P. Upshur: Conservative Virginian.* Madison: State Historical Society of Wisconsin, 1964.

Hämäläinen, Pekka. *The Comanche Empire.* New Haven, CT: Yale University Press, 2008.

Hamer, Philip. "Great Britain, the United States, and the Negro Seamen Acts, 1822–1848." *Journal of Southern History* 1 (Feb. 1935): 3–28.

Hammett, Theodore M. "Two Mobs of Jacksonian Boston: Ideology and Interest." *Journal of American History* 62 (March 1976): 845–68.

Hammond, John Craig. *Slavery, Freedom, and Expansion in the Early American West.* Charlottesville: University of Virginia Press, 2007.

——. "Slavery, Sovereignty, and Empires: North American Borderlands and the American Civil War, 1660–1860." *Journal of the Civil War Era* 4 (June 2014): 264–98.

Hammond, John Craig, and Matthew Mason, eds. *Contesting Slavery: The Politics of Bondage and Freedom in the New American Nation.* Charlottesville: University of Virginia Press, 2011.

Harding, Vincent. "Symptoms of Liberty and Blackhead Signposts: David Walker and Nat Turner." In *Nat Turner: A Slave Rebellion in History and Memory,* ed. Kenneth Greenberg. New York: Oxford University Press, 2004.

Harlow, Luke E. *Religion, Race, and the Making of Confederate Kentucky, 1830–1880.* New York: Cambridge University Press, 2014.

Harrold, Stanley. *The Abolitionists and the South: 1831–1861.* Lexington: University Press of Kentucky, 1995.

———. *Border Wars: Fighting over Slavery before the Civil War.* Chapel Hill: University of North Carolina Press, 2010.

Hartnett, Stephen John, *Democratic Dissent and the Cultural Fictions of Antebellum America,* Chicago: University of Illinois Press, 2002.

Haynes, Sam W. "Anglophobia and the Annexation of Texas: The Quest for National Security," In *Manifest Destiny and Empire: American Antebellum Expansionism,* ed. Sam W. Hayner and Christopher Morris. College Station: Texas A&M University Press, 1997: 115–45.

Haynes, Steven R. *Noah's Curse: The Biblical Justification of American Slavery.* New York: Oxford University Press, 2002.

Henkin, David M. *The Postal Age: The Emergence of Modern Communication in Nineteenth-Century America.* Chicago: University of Chicago Press, 2006.

Hickey, Donald R. "America's Response to the Slave Revolt in Haiti, 1791–1806." *Journal of the Early Republic* 2 (Winter 1982): 361–79.

———. *The War of 1812: A Forgotten Conflict.* Urbana: University of Illinois Press, 2012.

———, ed. *The War of 1812: Writings from America's Second War of Independence.* New York: Library of America, 2013.

Hietala, Thomas R. *Manifest Design: American Exceptionalism and Empire, Revised Edition.* Ithaca, NY: Cornell University Press, 1985.

Higginson, Stephen A. "A Short History of the Right to Petition Government for the Redress of Grievances." *Yale Law Journal* 96 (Nov. 1986): 142–66.

Higginson, Thomas Wentworth. *Travelers and Outlaws, Episodes in American History.* Boston: Lee & Shepard Publishers, 1889.

Hinks, Peter P. *To Awaken My Afflicted Brethren: David Walker and the Problem of Slave Resistance.* University Park: Pennsylvania State University Press, 1997.

Holloway, Joseph. "Slave Insurrections in the United States: An Overview." http://slaverebellion.org.

Holmes, Jack D. L. "The Abortive Slave Revolt of Pointe Coupée, Louisiana, 1795." *Louisiana History: The Journal of the Louisiana Historical Association* 11 (Autumn 1970): 341–62.

Holt, Michael F. *The Political Crisis of the 1850s.* New York: W. W. Norton, 1978.

———. *The Rise and Fall of the American Whig Party: Jacksonian Politics and the Outset of the Civil War.* New York: Oxford University Press, 1999.

———. "The Slavery Issue." In *The American Congress: The Building of Democracy,* ed. Julian E. Zelizer. New York: Houghton Mifflin, 2004: 189–206.

———. *The Fate of Their Country: Politicians, Slavery Extension, and the Coming of the Civil War.* New York: Hill & Wang, 2004.

Holton, Woody. "'Rebel against Rebel': Enslaved Virginians and the Coming of the American Revolution." *Virginia Magazine of History and Biography* 105 (Spring 1997): 157–92.

Holzer, Harold. *Lincoln at Cooper Union: The Speech That Made Abraham Lincoln President.* New York: Simon & Schuster, 2004.

Horsman, Reginald. *The Causes of the War of 1812.* New York: A. S. Barnes, 1962.

Horwitz, Tony. *Midnight Rising: John Brown and the Raid That Sparked the Civil War.* New York: Henry Holt, 2011.

Howe, Daniel Walker. *The Political Culture of the American Whigs.* Chicago: University of Chicago Press, 1979.

———. *What Hath God Wrought: The Transformation of America, 1815–1848.* New York: Oxford University Press, 2007.

Hunt, Alfred N. *Haiti's Influence on Antebellum America: Slumbering Volcano in the Caribbean.* Baton Rouge: Louisiana State University Press, 1988.

Huston, James L. "Theory's Failure: Malthusian Population Theory and the Projected Demise of Slavery," *Civil War History* 55 (Sept. 2009): 354–81.

January, Allen F. "The South Carolina Association: An Agency for Race Control in Antebellum Charleston." *South Carolina Historical Magazine* 78 (July 1977): 191–201.

Jennings, Thelma. *The Nashville Convention Southern Movement for Unity, 1848–1851.* Memphis, TN: Memphis State University Press, 1980.

John, Richard R. *Spreading the News: The American Postal System from Franklin to Morse.* Cambridge, MA: Harvard University Press, 1995.

Johnson, Michael P. "Denmark Vesey and His Co-Conspirators." *William and Mary Quarterly* 58, no. 4 (Oct. 2001): 915–76.

Johnson, Roy. *The Nat Turner Slave Insurrection.* Murfeesburo, NC: Johnson Publishing Company, 1966.

Johnson, Walter. *Soul by Soul: Life Inside the Antebellum Slave Market.* Cambridge, MA: Harvard University Press, 1999.

———. *River of Dark Dreams: Slavery and Empire in the Cotton Kingdom.* Cambridge, MA: Belknap Press of Harvard University Press, 2013.

Jordan, Winthrop D. *White over Black: American Attitudes toward the Negro, 1550–1812.* New York: W. W. Norton, 1968.

Karp, Matthew J. "Slavery and American Sea Power: The Navalist Impulse in the Antebellum South." *Journal of Southern History* 87 (May 2011): 284–324.

———. "'This Vast Southern Empire': The South and the Foreign Policy of Slavery, 1833–1861." PhD diss., University of Pennsylvania, 2011.

———. "Arsenal of Empire: Southern Slaveholders and the U.S. Military in the 1850s." *Common Place* 12 (July 2012).

Keehn, David C. *Knights of the Golden Circle: Secret Empire, Southern Secession, Civil War.* Baton Rouge: Louisiana State University Press, 2013.

Kennedy, Roger G. *Cotton and Conquest: How the Plantation System Acquired Texas.* Norman: University of Oklahoma Press, 2013.

Kerber, Linda K. "Abolitionists and Amalgamators: The New York City Riots of 1834." *New York City History* 48 (Jan. 1967): 28–39.

Killens, John Oliver. *Introduction to the Trial Records of Denmark Vesey.* Boston: Beacon Press, 1970.

Klooster, Wim. "Slave Revolts, Royal Justice, and a Ubiquitous Rumor in the Age of Revolutions." *William and Mary Quarterly* 71 (July 2014): 401–24.

Knupfer, Peter B. *The Union As It Is: Constitutional Unionism and Sectional Compromise, 1787–1861.* Chapel Hill: University of North Carolina Press, 1991.

Kolchin, Peter. *American Slavery: 1619–1877.* New York: Hill & Wang, 1993.

Kornblith, Gary J. "Rethinking the Coming of the Civil War: A Counterfactual Exercise." *Journal of American History* 90 (June 2003): 76–105.

Lacerte, Robert K. "The Evolution of Land and Labor in the Haitian Revolution, 1791–1820." *The Americas* 34 (April 1978): 449–59.

Lachance, Paul F. "The Politics of Fear: French Louisianans and the Slave Trade, 1786–1809." *Plantation Society in the Americas* 1 (June 1972): 162–97.

Lankford, Nelson. *Cry Havoc: The Crooked Road to the Civil War.* New York: Penguin Books, 2007.

Lewis, W. David. *Sloss Furnaces and the Rise of the Birmingham District: An Industrial Epic.* Tuscaloosa: University of Alabama Press, 1994.

Link, William. *Roots of Secession: Slavery and Politics in Antebellum Virginia.* Chapel Hill: University of North Carolina Press, 2003.

Litwack, Leon F. *North of Slavery: The Negro in the Free States, 1790–1860.* Chicago: University of Chicago Press, 1961.

———. *Been in the Storm So Long: The Aftermath of Slavery.* New York: Alfred A. Knopf, 1979.

Mason, Mathew. *Slavery and Politics in the Early American Republic.* Chapel Hill: University of North Carolina, 2006.

Matthews, Gelien. *Caribbean Slave Revolts and the British Abolitionist Movement.* Baton Rouge: Louisiana State University Press, 2006.

Matthewson, Tim. "George Washington's Policy toward the Haitian Revolution." *Diplomatic History* 3 (Summer 1979): 321–36.

———. "Jefferson and the Nonrecognition of Haiti," *Proceedings of the American Philosophical Society,* 140 (March 1996).

———. *A Proslavery Foreign Policy: Haitian-American Relations during the Early Republic.* Westport, CT: Praeger, 2003.

McCurry, Stephanie. *Masters of Small Worlds: Yeoman Households, Gender Relations, and the Political Culture of the Antebellum South Carolina Low Country.* New York: Oxford University Press, 1995.

McDaniel, W. Caleb. *The Problem of Democracy in the Age of Slavery: Garrisonian Abolitionists and Transatlantic Reform.* Baton Rouge: Louisiana State University Press, 2013.

McGinty, Brian. *John Brown's Trial.* Cambridge, MA: Harvard University Press, 2009.

McNair, Glenn M. "The Elijah Burritt Affair: David Walker's *Appeal* and Partisan Journalism in Antebellum Milledgeville." *Georgia Historical Quarterly* 83 (Fall 1999): 448–78.

McNeely, Patricia. "Dueling Editors: The Nullification Plot of 1832." In *Words at War: The Civil War and American Journalism,* ed. David B. Sachsman, S. Kittrell Rushing, and Roy Morris, Jr. West Lafayette, IN: Purdue University Press, 2008.

McPherson, James. *Battle Cry of Freedom: The Civil War Era.* New York: Oxford University Press, 1988.

Mann, Mary Tyler Peabody. *Life of Horace Mann.* Boston: Lee & Shepard, 1904.

May, Robert E. "Epilogue to the Missouri Compromise: The South, the Balance of Power, and the Tropics in the 1850s," *Plantation Society in the Americas* 1. no. 2 (June 1972): 201–25.

——. *The Southern Dream of Caribbean Empire, 1854–1861.* Baton Rouge: Louisiana State University Press, 1973.

——. *John A. Quitman: Old South Crusader* (Baton Rouge: Louisiana State University Press, 1985.

Meachum, Jon. *American Lion: Andrew Jackson in the White House.* New York: Random House, 2009.

Mencken, H. L. *On Politics: A Carnival of Buncombe.* Ed. Malcolm Moos. Baltimore: Johns Hopkins University Press, 1956.

Merchant, Holt. *South Carolina Fire-Eater: The Life of Laurence Massillon Keitt, 1824–1864.* Columbia: University of South Carolina Press, 2014.

Mercieca, Jennifer Rose. "The Culture of Honor: How Slaveholders Responded to the Abolitionist Mail Crisis of 1835." *Rhetoric and Public Affairs* 10 (2007): 51–76.

Merk, Frederick. *The Oregon Question: Essays in Anglo-American Diplomacy and Politics.* Cambridge, MA: Belknap Press of Harvard University Press, 1967.

——. *Fruits of Propaganda in the Tyler Administration.* Cambridge, MA: Harvard University Press, 1971.

——. *Slavery and the Annexation of Texas.* New York: Alfred A. Knopf, 1972.

Merry, Robert W. *A Country of Vast Designs: James K Polk, the Mexican War, and the Conquest of the American Continent.* New York: Simon & Schuster, 2009.

Miles, Edwin A. "'Fifty-four Forty or Fight'—An American Political Legend," *Mississippi Valley Historical Review* 44 (Sept. 1957): 291–309.

——. "The Mississippi Slave Insurrection Scare of 1835." *Journal of Negro History* 42 (Jan., 1957): 48–60.

Miller, William Lee. *Arguing about Slavery: The Great Battle in the United States Congress.* New York: Alfred A. Knopf, 1996.

Montague, Ludell Lee. *Haiti and the United States, 1714–1938.* Durham, NC: Duke University Press, 1940.

Morgan, Edmund S. *American Slavery, American Freedom.* New York: W. W. Norton, 1975.

Morison, Samuel Eliot. *The Life and Letters of Harrison Gray Otis: Federalist, 1765–1848.* Vol. 2. Boston: Houghton Mifflin, 1913.

Morris, Charles Edward. "Panic and Reprisal: Reaction in North Carolina to the Nat Turner Insurrection of 1831." *North Carolina Historical Review* 62 (Jan. 1985): 29–52.

Morrison, Chaplain W. *Democratic Politics and Sectionalism: The Wilmot Proviso Controversy.* Chapel Hill: University of North Carolina Press, 1967.

Morrison, Michael A. "Martin Van Buren, the Democracy, and the Partisan Politics of Texas Annexation," *Journal of Southern History* 61 (November 1995): 697–707.

——. *Slavery and the American West: The Eclipse of Manifest Destiny and the Coming of the Civil War.* Chapel Hill: University of North Carolina Press, 1997.

Munro, Martin, and Elizabeth Walcott-Hackshaw, eds. *Echoes of the Haitian Revolution, 1804–2004.* Jamaica: University of the West Indies, 2008.

Mutersbaugh, Burt M. "The Background of Gabriel's Insurrection." *Journal of Negro History* 68 (Spring 1983): 209–11.

Norton, A. B. *Reminiscences of the Log Cabin and Hard Cider Campaign.* Dallas: A. B. Norton, 1888.

Oakes, James. *Freedom National: The Destruction of Slavery in the United States, 1861–1865.* New York: W. W. Norton, 2012.

——. *The Scorpions Sting: Antislavery and the Coming of Civil War.* New York: W. W. Norton, 2014.

Oates, Stephen B. *The Fires of Jubilee: Nat Turner's Fierce Rebellion.* New York: Harper & Row, 1975.

O'Brien, Michael. *A Character of Hugh Legaré.* Knoxville: University of Tennessee Press, 1985.

——. *Conjectures of Order: Intellectual Life and the American South, 1810–1860.* New York: Cambridge University Press, 2005.

Onuf, Peter. "To Declare Them Free and Independent People: Race, Slavery, and National Identity in Jefferson's Thought." *Journal of the Early Republic* 18 (Spring 1998): 1–46.

——. *The Mind of Thomas Jefferson.* Charlottesville: University of Virginia Press, 2007.

Onuf, Peter, Edward Ayers, and Brian Balogh. *Independence Daze: A History of July Fourth.* Podcast audio. Backstory with the American History Guys. June 29, 2012. http://backstoryradio.org/shows/independence-daze-a-history-of-july-fourth-2/.

O'Shaughnessy, Andrew Jackson. *An Empire Divided: The American Revolution and the British Caribbean.* Philadelphia: University of Pennsylvania Press, 2000.

Owsley Jr., Frank Lawrence, and Gene A. Smith, *Filibusters and Expansionists: Jeffersonian Manifest Destiny, 1800–1821.* Tuscaloosa: University of Alabama Press, 1997.

Pacheco, Josephine F. *The Pearl: A Failed Slave Escape on the Potomac.* Chapel Hill: University of North Carolina Press, 2005.

Papenfuse, Eric Robert. *The Evils of Necessity: Robert Goodloe Harper and the Moral Dilemma of Slavery.* Philadelphia: American Philosophical Society, 1997.

Paquette, Robert L. "Revolutionary Saint-Domingue in the Making of Territorial Louisiana." In *A Turbulent Time: The French Revolution and the Greater Caribbean,* ed. David Barry Gaspar and David Patrick Geggus. Bloomington: Indiana University Press, 1997.

Paquette, Robert L., and Douglas R. Egerton. "Of Facts and Fables: New Light on the Denmark Vesey Affair." *South Carolina Historical Magazine* 105 (Jan. 2004): 8–35.

Pasley, Jeffrey L. *"The Tyranny of Printers": Newspaper Politics in the Early American Republic.* Charlottesville: University Press of Virginia, 2001.

Paulus, Sarah Bischoff. "Abraham Lincoln's Northwestern Approach to the Secession Crisis." PhD diss., Rice University, 2013.

——. "America's Long Eulogy for Compromise: Henry Clay and American Politics, 1854–1858." *Journal of the Civil War Era* 4 (March 2014): 28–52.

Pease, William H, and Jane H. Pease. "Walker's Appeal Comes to Charleston: A Note and Documents." *Journal of Negro History* 59 (July 1974): 287–92.

Peterson, Merrill D. *The Great Triumvirate: Webster, Clay, and Calhoun.* New York: Oxford University Press, 1987.

Peterson, Norma Lois. *The Presidencies of William Henry Harrison and John Tyler.* Lawrence: University Press of Kansas, 1989.

Phillips, Christopher N. "Epic, Anti-Eloquence, and Abolitionism: Thomas Branagan's 'Avenia' and 'The Penitential Tyrant.'" *Early American Literature* 44 (2009): 606–37.

Phillips, Jason. "The Prophecy of Edmund Ruffin: Anticipating the Future of Civil War History." In *Apocalypse and the Millennium in the American Civil War Era,* ed. Benjamin Wright and Zachary W. Dresser. Baton Rouge: Louisiana State University Press, 2013.

Pinheiro, John C. *Manifest Ambition: James K. Polk and the Civil-Military Relations during the Mexican War.* Westport, CT: Praeger Security International, 2007.

Pinker, Steven. *The Better Angels of Our Nature: Why Violence Has Declined.* New York: Penguin Books, 2011.

Porter, Kirk H., and Donald Bruce Johnson, eds. *National Party Platforms, 1840–1964.* Urbana: University of Illinois Press, 1966.

Potter, David M. "The Historians' Use of Nationalism and Vice Versa." *American Historical Review* 67 (July 1962): 924–50.

——. *The Impending Crisis: 1841–1861.* Completed and edited by Don. E. Fehrenbacher. New York: Harper & Row, 1976.

Powers Jr., Bernard E. "'The Worst of All Barbarism': Racial Anxiety and the Approach of Secession in the Palmetto State." *South Carolina Historical Magazine* 112 (July-Oct. 2011): 139–56.

Rable, George C. *The Confederate Republic: A Revolution against Politics.* Chapel Hill: University of North Carolina Press, 1994.

Rasmussen, Daniel. *American Uprising: The Untold Story of America's Largest Slave Revolt.* New York: Harper Perennial, 2012.

Ratner, Lorman A., and Dwight L. Teeter Jr. *Fanatics and Fire-eaters: Newspapers and the Coming of the Civil War.* Urbana: University of Illinois Press, 2003.

Rayback, Joseph G. *Free Soil: The Election of 1848.* Lexington: University Press of Kentucky, 1970.

Remini, Robert V. *At the Edge of the Precipice: Henry Clay and the Compromise That Saved the Union.* New York: Basic Books, 2010.

Renehan Jr., Edward J. *The Secret Six: The True Tale of the Men Who Conspired with John Brown.* Columbia: University of South Carolina Press, 1997.

Resnick, Daniel P. "The Societe des Amis des Noirs and the Abolition of Slavery." *French Historical Studies* (Autumn 1972): 558–69.

Reynolds, Donald E. *Texas Terror: The Slave Insurrection Panic of 1860 and the Secession of the Lower South.* Baton Rouge: Louisiana State University Press, 2007.

Richards, Leonard L. *"Gentlemen of Property and Standing": Anti-Abolition Mobs in Jacksonian America.* New York: Oxford University Press, 1970.

——. *The Slave Power: The Free North and Southern Domination 1780–1860.* Baton Rouge: Louisiana State University Press, 2000.

Richardson, Heather Cox. *To Make Men Free: A History of the Republican Party.* New York: Basic Books, 2014.

Roberts, Timothy M. "'Revolutions Have Become the Bloody Toy of the Multitude': European Revolutions, the South, and the Crisis of 1850s." *Journal of the Early Republic* 25 (Summer 2005): 259–83.

Rockman, Seth. "The Future of Civil War Era Studies: Slavery and Capitalism." *Journal of the Civil War Era* 2 (March 2012): online supplement.

Rodriguez, Junius. "Rebellion on the Rivier Road: The Ideology and Influence of Louisiana's German Coast Slave Insurrection of 1811." In *Antislavery Violence: Sectional, Racial, and Cultural Conflict in Antebellum America,* ed. John R. McKivigan and Stanley Harrold. Knoxville: University of Tennessee Press, 1999.

——, ed. *Encyclopedia of Slave Resistance and Rebellion Volume 1 and 2.* Westport, CT: Greenwood Press, 2007.

Roediger, David R. *The Wages of Whiteness: Race and the Making of the American Working Class.* New York: Verso, 1991.

——. *How Race Survived U.S. History: From Settlement to the Obama Phenomenon.* New York: Verso, 2008.

Rogers, George C. *Evolution of a Federalist: William Loughton Smith of Charleston, 1758–1812.* Columbia: University of South Carolina Press, 1962.

Rohrbough, Malcolm J. "The California Gold Rush as a National Experience." *California History* 77 (Spring 1998): 16–29.

Rommel-Ruiz, Bryan. "Vindictive Ferocity: Virginia's Response to the Nat Turner Rebellion." In *Enemies of Humanity: The Nineteenth-Century War on Terrorism,* ed. Isaac Land. New York: Palgrave Macmillan: 2008.

Rothman, Adam, *Slave Country: American Expansion and the Origins of the Deep South.* Cambridge, MA: Harvard University Press, 2005.

Rucker, Walter. "Magic and Power: The Influence of Afro-Atlantic Religious Practices of Slave Resistance and Rebellion." *Journal of Black Studies* 32 (Sept. 2001): 84–103.

Rugemer, Edward Bartlett. "The Southern Response to British Abolitionism: The Maturation of Proslavery Apologetics." *Journal of Southern History* 70 (May 2004): 221–48.

——. "Robert Monroe Harrison, British Abolition, Southern Anglophobia and Texas Annexation." *Slavery and Abolition* 28 (Aug. 2007): 169–91.

——. *The Problem of Emancipation: The Caribbean Roots of the American Civil War.* Baton Rouge: Louisiana State University Press, 2008.

Santoro, Anthony. "The Prophet in His Own Words: Nat Turner's Biblical Construction." *Virginia Magazine of History and Biography* 116 (2008): 114–49.

Savage, W. Sherman. "Abolitionist Literature in the Mails, 1835–1836." *Journal of Negro History* 13 (April 1928): 150–84.

Saxton, Alexander. *The Rise and Fall of the White Republic: Class Politics and Mass Culture in Nineteenth-Century America.* New York: Verso, 1990.

Schoen, Brian. *The Fragile Fabric of Union: Cotton, Federal Politics, and the Global Origins of the Civil War.* Baltimore: Johns Hopkins University Press, 2009.

Schoeppner, Michael Alan. "Navigating the Dangerous Atlantic: Racial Quarantines, Black Sailors and United States Constitutionalism." PhD diss., University of Florida, 2010.

Schraunagel, Scot. *Historical Dictionary of the U.S. Congress.* Lanham, MD: Scarecrow Press, 2011.

Schumpeter, Joseph A. "The Creative Response in Economic History." *Journal of Economic History* 7 (November 1947): 149–59.

Schwarz, Philip J. "Gabriel's Challenge: Slaves and Crime in Late Eighteenth-Century Virginia." *Virginia Magazine of History and Biography* 90 (July 1982): 283–309.

Schweiger, Beth Barton. "The Literate South: Reading before Emancipation." *Journal of the Civil War Era* 3 (Sept. 2013): 331–59.

Shelden, Rachel A. *Washington Brotherhood: Politics, Social Life, and the Coming of the Civil War.* Chapel Hill: University of North Carolina Press, 2013.

Shenton, James P. *Robert John Walker: A Politician from Jackson to Lincoln.* New York: Columbia University Press, 1961.

Sidbury, James. *Ploughshares into Swords: Race, Rebellion, and Identity in Gabriel's Virginia, 1730–1810.* New York: Cambridge University Press, 1997.

——. "Saint-Domingue in Virginia": Ideology, Local Meanings, and Resistance to Slavery 1790–1800." *Journal of Southern History* 63 (Aug. 1997): 531–52.

Silbey, Joel H. *Storm over Texas: The Annexation Controversy and the Road to the Civil War.* New York: Oxford University Press, 2005.

——. *Party over Section: The Rough and Ready Presidential Election of 1848.* Lawrence: University of Kansas Press, 2009.

Sinha, Manisha. *The Counterrevolution of Slavery.* Chapel Hill: University of North Carolina Press, 2000.

——. "Revolution or Counterrevolution? The Political Ideology of Secession in Antebellum South Carolina." *Civil War History* 46 (Sept. 2000): 205–26.

——. "To 'Cast Just Obliquy' on Oppressors: Black Radicalism in the Age of Revolution." *William and Mary Quarterly* 64 (Jan. 2007): 149–60.

Skelton, William B. *An American Profession of Arms: The Army Officer Corps, 1784–1861.* Lawrence: University of Kansas Press, 1992.

Slaughter; Philip. *The Virginian History of African Colonization.* Macfarlane & Fergusson, 1855.

Smith, Elbert B. *The Presidencies of Zachary Taylor and Millard Fillmore.* Lawrence: University of Kansas Press, 1988.

Smith, Gene Allen. *The Slaves' Gamble: Choosing Sides in the War of 1812.* New York: Palgrave Macmillan, 2013.

Snay, Mitchell. *Gospel of Disunion.* New York: Cambridge University Press, 1993.

Stagg, J. A. C. *Mr. Madison's War: Politics, Diplomacy, and Warfare in the Early American Republic.* Princeton, NJ: Princeton University Press, 1983.

Stauffer, John. *The Black Hearts of Men: Radical Abolitionists and the Transformation of Race.* Cambridge, MA: Harvard University Press, 2002.

Stegmaier, Mark J. *Texas, New Mexico, and the Compromise of 1850: Boundary Dispute and Sectional Crisis. Lubbock: Texas Tech University Press, 2012.*

Sterkx, Herman. *The Free Negro in Antebellum Louisiana.* Rutherford, NJ: Farleigh Dickinson University Press, 1972.

Stewart, James Brewer. *Holy Warriors: The Abolitionists and American Slavery, Revised Edition.* New York: Hill & Wang, 1997.

——. *Abolitionist Politics and the Coming of the Civil War.* Amherst: University of Massachusetts Press, 2008.

Sugrue, Thomas J. *Origins of the Urban Crisis: Race and Inequality in Postwar Detroit.* Princeton, NJ: Princeton University Press, 1996.

Summers, Mark Wahlgren. *The Ordeal of the Reunion: A New History of Reconstruction.* Chapel Hill: University of North Carolina Press, 2014.

Taylor, Alan. *The Internal Enemy: Slavery and War in Virginia, 1772–1832.* New York: W. W. Norton, 2013.

Taylor, Anne-Marie. *Young Charles Sumner and the Legacy of the American Enlightenment, 1811–1851.* Amherst: University of Massachusetts Press, 2001.

Taylor, R. H. "Slave Conspiracies in North Carolina." *North Carolina Historical Review,* vol. 5. Raleigh: North Carolina Historical Commission, 1928.

Thornton, J. Mills. *Politics and Power in a Slave Society: Alabama, 1800–1860.* Baton Rouge: Louisiana State University Press, 1978.

Thornton, John K. "'I Am Subject of the King of Congo': African Political Ideology and the Haitian Revolution." *Journal of World History* 4 (Fall 1993): 181–214.

Tise, Larry E. *Proslavery: A History of the Defense of Slavery in America, 1701–1840.* Athens: University of Georgia Press, 1987.

Toplin, Robert Brent. "The Specter of Crisis: Slaveholder Reaction to Abolitionism in the United States and Brazil." *Civil War History* 18 (June 1972): 129–38.

Towers, Frank. "Another Looks at Inevitability: Compromise in the Secession Crisis." *Tennessee Historical Quarterly* 70 (Summer 2011): 108–25.

——. "Partisans, New History, and Modernization: The Historiography of the Civil War's Causes, 1861–2011." *Journal of the Civil War Era* 1 (June 2011): 237–64.

Tucker, Spencer, and Frank T. Reuter. *Injured Honor: The* Chesapeake-Leopard *Affair, June 22, 1807.* Annapolis: Naval Institute Press, 1996.

Unger, Harlow Giles. *Noah Webster: The Life and Times of an American Patriot.* New York: John Wiley & Sons, 1998.

Urban, C. Stanley. "The Africanization of Cuba Scare, 1853–1855." *Hispanic American Historical Review* 37 (Feb. 1957): 89–123.

Van Cleve, George William. *A Slaveholders' Union: Slavery, Politics, and the Constitution in the Early American Republic.* Chicago: University of Chicago Press, 2010.

C. Vann Woodward, *Origins of the New South, 1877–1913.* Baton Rouge: Louisiana State University Press, 1971.

——. *The Strange Career of Jim Crow: A Commemorative Edition.* New York: Oxford University Press, 2002.

Varon, Elizabeth. *Disunion! The Coming of the American Civil War, 1789–1859.* Chapel Hill: University of North Carolina Press, 2008.

Wainwright, James Eyre. "Both Native South and Deep South: The Native Transformation of the Gulf South Borderlands, 1770–1835." PhD diss., Rice University, 2013.

Wallenstein, Peter. "Incendiaries All: Southern Politics and the Harpers Ferry Raid." In *His Soul Goes Marching On: Responses to John Brown and the Harpers Ferry Raid,* ed. Paul Finkelman. Charlottesville: University of Virginia Press, 1995.

——. "Thomas Roderick Dew (1802–1846)." In *Slavery in the United States: A Social Political, and Historical Encyclopedia, Volume One,* ed. Junius P. Rodriguez. Santa Barbara: ABC-Clio, 2007. Pages 254–55.

Walters, Ronald G. *American Reformers, 1815–1860, revised edition.* New York: Hill & Wang, 1997.

Walther, Eric H. *The Fire-Eaters.* Baton Rouge: Louisiana State University Press, 1992.

——. *The Shattering of the Union: America in the 1850s.* New York: SR Books, 2004.

——. *William Lowndes Yancey: The Coming of the Civil War.* Chapel Hill: University of North Carolina Press, 2006.

——. "The Fire-Eaters and ~~Seward~~ Lincoln." *Journal of the Abraham Lincoln Association* 32 (2011): 18–19.

Watson, Harry L. *Liberty and Power: The Politics of Jacksonian America.* New York: Hill & Wang, 1990.

Waugh, John C. *On The Brink of Civil War: The Compromise of 1850 and How It Changed the Course of American History.* Wilmington, DE: Scholarly Resources, 2003.

Wells, Jonathan Daniel. *The Origins of the Southern Middle Class: 1800–1861.* Chapel Hill: University of North Carolina Press, 2004.

——. *Women Writers and Journalists in the Nineteenth-Century South.* New York: Cambridge University Press, 2011.

West, Michael O. William G. Martin, and Fanon Che Wilkins, eds. *From Toussaint to Tupac: The Black International since the Age of Revolution.* Chapel Hill: University of North Carolina Press, 2009.

Whitford, David M. *The Curse of Ham in the Early Modern Era: The Bible and the Justifications for Slavery* (Burlington, VT: Ashgate, 2009).

Wilentz, Sean. *Chants Democratic: New York City and the Rise of the American Working Class, 1788–1850.* New York: Oxford University Press, 1984.

——. *The Rise of American Democracy: Jefferson to Lincoln.* New York: W. W. Norton, 2005.

Wilkins, Joe Bassette. "Window on Freedom: The South's Response to the Emancipation of the Slaves in the British West Indies, 1833–1861." PhD diss., University of South Carolina, 1977.

Williams, Chad L. "Symbols of Defeat: African American Soldiers, White Southerners, and the Christmas Insurrection Scare of 1865." In *Black Flag over Dixie: Racial Atrocities and Reprisals in the Civil War,* ed. Gregory J. W. Urwin. Carbondale: Southern Illinois University Press, 2004: 210–30.

Wiltse, Charles M. *John C. Calhoun: Sectionalist, 1840–1850.* Indianapolis: Bobbs-Merrill Company, 1951.

Winter, William. *Life and Art of Joseph Jefferson: Together with Some Account of His Ancestry and the Jefferson Family of Actors.* New York: Macmillan & Co,, 1894.

Wirls, Daniel. "'The Only Mode of Avoiding Everlasting Debate': The Overlooked Senate Gag Rule for Antislavery Petitions," *Journal of the Early Republic* 27 (Spring 2007): 115–38.

Witt, John Fabian. *Lincoln's Code: The Laws of War in American History.* New York: Free Press, 2012.

Wolf, Eva Sheppard. *Race and Liberty in the New Nation: Emancipation in Virginia from the Revolution to Nat Turner's Rebellion.* Baton Rouge: Louisiana State University Press, 2006.

Wood, Gordon. *The Americanization of Benjamin Franklin.* New York: Penguin Books, 2004.

——. *Empire of Liberty: A History of the Early American Republic 1789–1815.* New York: Oxford University Press, 2009.

Wood, Peter H. "The Abolition Postal Campaign of 1835." *Journal of Negro History* 50 (Oct. 1965): 227–38.

——. *Black Majority: Negroes in Colonial South Carolina from 1670 through the Stono Rebellion.* New York: W. W. Norton, 1975.

Woods, Michael E. "What Twenty-first Century Historians Have Said about the Causes of Disunion: A Civil War Sesquicentennial Review of the Recent Literature." *Journal of American History* 99 (Sept. 2012): 415–39.

Wyatt-Brown, Bertram. *Southern Honor: Ethics and Behavior in the Old South.* New York: Oxford University Press, 1982.

Wyly-Jones, Susan. "The Antiabolitionist Panic: Slavery, Abolition, and Politics in the U.S. South, 1835–1844." PhD diss., Harvard University, 2000.

——. "The 1835 Anti-Abolition Meetings in the South: A New Look at the Controversy over the Abolition Postal Campaign." *Civil War History* 47 (2001): 289–309.

Yingling, Charlton W. "No One Who Reads the History of Hayti Can Doubt the Capacity of Colored Men: Racial Formation and the Atlantic Rehabilitation in New York City's Early Black Press, 1827–1841." *Early American Studies: An Interdisciplinary Journal* 11 (Spring 2013): 314–48.

INDEX

Note: page numbers in *italics* refer to illustrations; those followed by "n" indicate endnotes.